Praise for *Quantitative Methods for ESG Finance*

"It is a great book for people trying to learn quickly about the state of the art of ESG modelling, evaluation, regulations, forecasting, and other relevant issues. It covers difficult topics in a simple, clear format. I strongly recommend this book for researchers interested in ESG as well as a textbook in a course covering ESG topics from a financial perspective."

—**Stan Uryasev,** Professor and Frey Family Endowed Chair,
Stony Brook University

"Indexes are more and more crucial in finance and asset management and properly understanding their constituents is the base for any effective benchmarking. The authors show how to compute ESG indexes and present the related theory in a very clear and useful manner for sophisticated as well more naïve investors. Starting with traditional indexes (equal-weighted, market cap-weighted, etc.) to most recent computation approaches (smart beta, optimization driven indexes, etc.) wide-ranging explanations are given both from a theoretical point of view to as well as how to structure them: not an easy task, but successfully performed."

—**Carlo Maria Pinardi,** Professor, International Corporate Finance,
Bocconi University of Milan

Quantitative Methods for ESG Finance

CYRIL SHMATOV
CINO ROBIN CASTELLI

Published by John Wiley & Sons, Inc., Hoboken, New Jersey.
Published simultaneously in Canada.

For general information on our other products and services or for technical support, please contact our Customer Care Department within the United States at (800) 762-2974, outside the United States at (317) 572-3993 or fax (317) 572-4002.

Wiley also publishes its books in a variety of electronic formats. Some content that appears in print may not be available in electronic formats. For more information about Wiley products, visit our web site at www.wiley.com.

Library of Congress Cataloging-in-Publication Data is Available:

ISBN 9781119903802 (Hardback)

ISBN 9781119903826 (ePDF)

ISBN 9781119903819 (ePub)

Cover Design: Wiley
Cover Images: © d.ee_angelo/Shutterstock; Jackyenjoyphotography/Getty Images
Author photo credit: Cyril Shmatov - Courtesy of author; Robin Castelli - © Rob Tannenbaum Photography

SKY10036596_101222

Contents

Foreword   **vii**

Introduction and Book Overview   **1**

1. Overview 1
2. Why ESG Finance? 2
3. Why Quantitative Methods? 2
4. Target Audience and Timing of This Book 2
5. Book Outline 3

1   Introduction to ESG Finance   **5**

    1.1   Preface: ESG Is Not a Niche Strategy Anymore 5
    1.2   Introduction and Definitions 7
    1.3   ESG Investment Performance 21
    1.4   Sustainability and Sustainable Finance 25

2   Factor Investing and Smart Beta   **39**

    2.1   Index Construction Basics 39
    2.2   Smart Beta Indexes 40
    2.3   Risk Factor Investing 48
    2.4   Fama-MacBeth Regressions 50
    2.5   Expanding the Risk Factor Universe 53

3   ESG Ratings   **55**

    3.1   Introduction 55
    3.2   Overview of ESG Rating Methodologies 57
    3.3   Regression Trees as an Alternative Scoring Technique 61
    3.4   Random Forest 69

4   Alternative Data   75

4.1   What Are Alternative Data and Their ESG Applications? 75
4.2   How to Validate an ESG Data Provider 81
4.3   Processing Satellite Data 83

5   Alternative Text Data   105

5.1   Alternative Text Data on ESG 105
5.2   Corporate ESG Reports 108
5.3   Topic Modeling 114
5.4   Latent Dirichlet Allocation 118
5.5   Outlier Topics 126

6   Introduction to Agent-Based Modeling for ESG Finance   129

6.1   Preface 129
6.2   Use of Agent-Based Models in Other Fields and Their Applicability to ESG Finance 131
6.3   Use of ABMs in the ESG Field 132
6.4   General Overview of ABMs 133
6.5   General Operating Principles of ABMs 136
6.6   Example of the PARTE Framework Applied to an ESG Scenario 136
6.7   Why We Should Look Closely at ABMs 138
6.8   Challenges in the Use of ABMs 139
6.9   Example: Buildup of a Population Model ABM 140
6.10   In-Depth Review: ABMs in Academic and Regulatory Publications 154

7   Climate Risk: Macro Perspective   165

7.1   Climate Change: Background Information and Definitions 165
7.2   Regulatory Response to Climate Change 185
7.3   Climate Change Modeling 191
7.4   Carbon Risk and Carbon Pricing 199
7.5   Climate Risk in Investment Practice 202

8   Stress Testing for Banks   207

8.1   Stress Testing as a Risk Management Tool 207
8.2   Macroeconomic Stress Scenarios for Climate Risk 213
8.3   Climate Loss Modeling 220
8.4   Climate Stress Testing Exercise 223
8.5   Concluding Notes 224

Index   227

Foreword

I am delighted and honored to introduce *Quantitative Methods for ESG Finance*, a must-have reference for the student of finance, the investment practitioner, and the banker who wants to understand the intricacies of environmental, social, and governance (ESG) finance.

Cyril Shmatov and C. Robin Castelli bring to the table many years of first hand experience across diverse areas of finance and are currently at the forefront, tackling ESG-related questions the banks face in their management and operations. This extensive practical experience is what allows them to turn a fragmented topic such as ESG into a logical and easy-to-understand book that provides insight to audiences from graduate students to seasoned investors. Cyril and Robin have succeeded in demystifying the topic with well-documented data and sources, as well as practical examples of how to implement and use the relevant techniques in the real world.

ESG has taken the world of finance by storm. Due to the novelty of this field and its obvious differences from the more traditional areas of finance, the study of ESG finance requires an entirely different skillset. Fortunately, this emergence of ESG finance as a major new area of finance coincides with more affordable data storage. Unstructured "alternative" data are finally becoming widely available to the investor community at large. These developments result in tremendous opportunities for the world of finance at large but also require that we reassess and refresh the techniques we commonly use when dealing with data and financial analysis in general.

There is an obvious need for a defining document, not available on the market until this moment, to be a comprehensive exposition of ESG finance and the quantitative methodologies that are needed in its new environment, a fundamental starting point for anyone wanting to learn about the field, from the theoretical to the practical.

The book you are holding is that document. This work is a significant contribution to the understanding of ESG finance. It is a fundamental starting point for anyone wanting to learn about the field, from the theoretical to the practical. It provides all the necessary building blocks that the reader will need to embark on their journey in this exciting and uncharted field. Finally, it provides both the expert and the beginner with a 360-degree review of what is needed to gain understanding of ESG finance, from the basics of climate risk to the very important and popular topics such as alternative data and factor investing, all the way to up-and-coming methodologies such as agent-based modeling for ESG applications. This book has it all! If you are thinking of ESG finance, either as a field of study or as an area of practice, you should start your journey by reading this book.

Soulaymane Kachani
Professor of Industrial Engineering and Operations Research and
Senior Vice Provost, Columbia University

Introduction and Book Overview

1. OVERVIEW

ESG (environmental, social, and corporate governance) finance is a rapidly growing area of investment management – and finance more broadly – that has received a lot of attention in the past several years from the investor community, financial regulatory agencies, and the general public alike. This book introduces ESG finance from a quantitative analyst's perspective.

The authors are not aware of any existing publication that focuses specifically on the quantitative side of ESG finance, while – due to increasing reliance of ESG analyses on alternative data and the need to process it efficiently – there is an undeniable interest and need for such materials.

The ESG acronym refers to key risk factors that reflect the sustainability and societal impact of an investment, and socially responsible investing (SRI) seeks to combine financial returns with the achievement of social and environmental goals and progress. Within the last three years, responsibly managed assets under professional management in the US almost doubled, and a vast majority of investors now identify ESG risk factors as an area of interest.

This book combines the theoretical and quantitative basis underlying risk factor investing and risk management with an in-depth discussion of ESG applications. Both investment management (buy-side) and investment banking (sell-side) applications are discussed. For an investment manager, areas of particular interest are an exposition of risk factor investing, portfolio and index construction, as well as ESG scoring. From a banker's perspective, areas of focus are a newly emerging class of ESG-driven financial products, as well as financial risk management applications, some of which are driven by new financial regulation. These focus topics constitute the core of the book's contents.

Common to both perspectives is the paramount importance of both "traditional" and "alternative" data now available to financial professionals. This book discusses proliferation of newly available data sources and the associated quantitative techniques necessary to process them.

Importantly, a major component of this book is a discussion of climate risk, an area of increasing focus. The book includes an overview of recent advances and the evolving regulatory landscape in the climate risk space. An in-depth discussion of financial impact assessment of various climate risk-driven scenarios (climate risk stress testing) concludes the book.

Both theoretical and practical views on the same topics are presented in the book. To facilitate this, in each chapter, theoretical discussion is supplemented with code snippets and a walkthrough of a Python Jupyter notebook that makes use of publicly available data to demonstrate on a practical example the techniques introduced in the chapter. These Jupyter notebook exercises allow the reader to immediately attempt to apply learned techniques to data.

2. WHY ESG FINANCE?

ESG is not a niche strategy anymore. According to recent Bloomberg analysis,[1] ESG assets may reach $53 trillion by 2025, a third of total projected assets under management. This assumes that the growth continues at a 15% pace, half of the average growth rate of the last two years.

Currently, the EMEA (Europe, the Middle East and Africa) region is the global leader in ESG adoption and accounts for approximately half of global ESG assets, while US ESG has experienced the fastest growth in 2020–2021, a trend that is expected to continue, followed by an expansion of the ESG space in Asia, a region currently lagging in ESG adoption.

Further development of the ESG market in EMEA provides hints for what to expect globally: Explosive expansion in new product development is expected to continue, with climate change as the dominant theme, accounting for approximately a quarter of new ESG funds launched last year.

Beyond ESG equity investments, ESG debt markets are also poised for explosive growth. Green, social, and sustainability bonds may already have exceeded $2 trillion in cumulative issuance in 2021. The growth in ESG debt is also partially driven by the post-pandemic recovery across continents.

This is but a single illustration of a persistent trend where ESG investment and ESG finance are rapidly rising in prominence. The percentage of requests for proposals to asset managers that require at least some variant of ESG tracking/screening is growing exponentially across regions (again, led by EMEA at this time).

3. WHY QUANTITATIVE METHODS?

As the amount of overall data available to investors grows rapidly, the proportional share of "unstructured" data also increases. ESG finance has an even stronger reliance on unstructured or "alternative" data, because the traditional structured sources for ESG data are – at the moment – still very inconsistent. ESG data are largely self-reported by companies, and even reporting by companies within the same industry is voluntary and far from standardized. (The book discusses in detail the lack of standardization in ESG reporting and, therefore, in the resulting ESG ratings.) Due to the lack of reporting standards, investors are largely left to rely on alternative data sources. Fintech startups have taken the lead in offering both ESG rating services and the underlying data used in ratings' generation and bespoke ESG analyses.

New data sources require entirely new methods of processing them and a completely novel set of skills for a quantitative professional interested in analyzing the ESG space. Prominent examples include techniques for natural language processing and processing of satellite imagery – both topics discussed in detail in this book.

The book assumes that readers are familiar with basic finance concepts such as Markowitz portfolio theory; it also assumes the audience possesses working knowledge of Python and its package ecosystem, including pandas (or another appropriate scripting language such as R). This is a standard requirement for any modern quantitative professional, as Python (and, to a lesser degree, R) has become a lingua franca of modern data science and quantitative finance.

4. TARGET AUDIENCE AND TIMING OF THIS BOOK

There are two primary categories of readers that would be interested in this book:

- Graduate students of quantitative finance who are interested in this large and rapidly emerging topic but are currently facing a severe lack of appropriate and relevant textbooks, largely because the field of ESG finance is still evolving.

---

[1]"ESG Assets May Hit $53 Trillion by 2025, a Third of Global AUM," Bloomberg Intelligence, February 23, 2023, https://www.bloomberg.com/professional/blog/esg-assets-may-hit-53-trillion-by-2025-a-third-of-global-aum/

- Finance professionals who have experience applying traditional quantitative and statistical techniques to more traditional areas of finance (e.g., derivative pricing or high-frequency trading of securities) and now face the growing need to analyze ESG markets and financial risks and opportunities in the ESG space but realize that traditional quantitative techniques are insufficient or downright inadequate.

As mentioned earlier, ESG finance has rapidly emerged as a significant area of finance broadly, while even the core definitions within the ESG space continue to evolve. This creates an already significant – and growing – need for new quantitative techniques, which has flourished recently with the growing availability of alternative data, as well as the need for a text available to a wide array of practitioners and students of finance alike that can describe these new techniques in a consistent and accessible form.

5. BOOK OUTLINE

The book follows (and expands upon) a course one of the authors has recently taught to students of the Financial Engineering Master's program at Columbia University as an adjunct professor.

Chapter 1. Introduction to ESG Finance. This chapter introduces readers to the current landscape of ESG finance both from a buy-side and sell-side perspective and describes recent evolution of this area of finance, its recent challenges, and future opportunities.

Such topics as the general definition of ESG finance, ESG funds and indexes, green bonds, basics of climate risk, carbon trading and pricing, and relevant banking regulation and risk management are introduced.

This chapter also includes Jupyter notebook code that demonstrates techniques for retrieving ESG data freely available online, such as web scraping.

Chapter 2. Factor Investing and Smart Beta. This chapter lays a theoretical groundwork for most of the rest of the material. It starts by discussing the basic principles of systematic portfolio construction and performance evaluation and provides an exposition of factor investing and the concepts of risk factor beta and "smart beta." Modern approaches to risk factor indexes' construction are discussed.

In the same chapter, readers also observe the process of a simple beta-tracking index creation through a series of step-by-step code examples. Similarly, the chapter includes a detailed discussion of code used to estimate risk premia series.

Chapter 3. ESG Ratings. Multiple index and analytics providers have recently emerged, offering differing (and sometimes conflicting) takes on ESG risk factors' quantification. This chapter discusses different concepts of rating score construction, along with a methodology for inference of main drivers of ratings.

Hands-on examples from Chapter 3 are extended to adopt specific scoring methodologies common in the ESG space.

Chapter 4. Alternative Data. This chapter starts out by introducing characteristic uses of different types of Big Data in ESG scoring and different analytical methods relevant to the processing of different data types.

The discussion then focuses specifically on techniques for processing one of the increasingly important types of unstructured data, whose applications are becoming increasingly common: satellite imagery. The text introduces basic concepts behind geographical data processing and the handling of maps. Discussion includes hands-on exercises demonstrating how satellite data from various available data sources is accessed and processed.

Chapter 5. Alternative Text Data. The vast majority of ESG data are "alternative" (i.e., they do not come in standard tabular/numerical form). Within the alternative category, the most commonly used (at least as of today) is text data, sourced from corporate reports as well as external media publications. The amount of available text data is massive, which makes it very impractical or even impossible to process manually.

One of the most important and commonly used methodologies for the analysis of alternative data in ESG finance (and other areas of finance, of course) is, therefore, natural language processing (NLP). This chapter includes a brief overview of relevant NLP techniques with examples of their application. We particularly focus on topic modeling techniques, an important area of NLP with wide-ranging applications to analysis of financial reports, financial research publications, and other relevant documents.

Chapter 6. Introduction to Agent-Based Modeling for ESG Finance. ESG finance requires novel approaches and modeling methodologies, as it is characterized by complex interconnections between environmental variables, networks, and second- and third-order consequences of policy and climate changes. The traditional models used in the macroeconomic and financial space do not allow the ESG practitioner to model these complexities in a workable fashion, and new methodologies need to be brought into the fray to stand up to the challenge. In this chapter, we review how agent-based models (ABMs), which are commonly used in other fields such as climatology, ecology, evolutionary biology, epidemiology, medicine, social sciences, engineering, and computer science, are uniquely suited to the purpose at hand. We review the basic components of ABMs, how they operate, and how to design and implement them, as well as provide a cursory review of examples of ABMs usage in the financial and ESG space by major regulators worldwide. The second part of the chapter covers a coding example, where the user will be shown how to implement a simple epidemiologic spread model, based on the recent COVID epidemic.

Chapter 7. Climate Risk: Macro Perspective. Climate risk is a special environmental topic in ESG finance that is now a major focus for the financial industry and its regulatory agencies. Chapters 7 and 8 focus on the evolving regulatory landscape and current practices of financial climate risk management.

This chapter starts by providing a general overview of climate risk and its special place in the ESG taxonomy, followed by a discussion of carbon pricing and observed risk premium in relevant securities.

Chapter 8. Stress Testing for Banks. The second chapter devoted to climate risk focuses on climate risk management by financial institutions and relevant requirements from regulatory agencies.

Physical risks (including stranded assets), legal liability risks, and transition risk categories are defined and described. The chapter then focuses on large banks' practical responses to these types of risks, including examples of risk management methodologies that make heavy use of alternative data.

The chapter concludes with an in-depth discussion of bank stress testing mandated by European regulators and the approaches employed by large banks in quantifying climate risk in their holdings. Following this chapter, readers will have an opportunity to complete their own quantitative assessment of potential losses to a hypothetical large bank as a hands-on exercise.

CHAPTER 1

Introduction to ESG Finance

1.1 PREFACE: ESG IS NOT A NICHE STRATEGY ANYMORE

Environmental, social, and corporate governance (ESG), as a wide-arching strategy adopted initially through the United States' financial industry and later globally, has grown from a small, relatively obscure topic to a mainstream concern that affects every financial institution and major corporation.

This transition has occurred over less than 20 years, beginning in the early 2000s, starting as a small initiative spearheaded by the United Nations and ballooning into a global phenomenon with, according to Bloomberg research, over $30 trillion in assets under management (AUMs) in 2018 and projections surpassing $50 trillion by 2025. This implies a conservative growth of 15% year over year, which is half of what it has been on average for the last two years. If these projections hold true, ESG will represent a third of total global projected AUMs by that date.

The interest and adoption of ESG strategies is not uniform across continents and markets, with Europe, Middle East, and Africa (EMEA) leading the pack (half of the global ESG assets), closely followed by the USA, which experienced the fastest growth rate in the asset class in 2020–2021, with analysts predicting this trend to continue. Asia-Pacific countries (APAC), on the other hand, lag in ESG adoption, providing a robust area for potential expansion in coming years.

The more advanced stage of the ESG market in EMEA allows us to gain some useful insight and hints on what the global framework could reasonably look like. If the rest of the world follows a similar pathway, we can expect an explosive growth in new product development and implementation, mostly focused in the area of equities, followed by credit (covering approximately 20% of new ESG funds). In the equities space, we have witnessed a diversification into thematic products. Climate change, as the predominant theme, has represented just over a quarter of the new ESG funds launched in 2020.

If we turn our focus on ESG from equities to debt, it becomes very clear that ESG credit markets are poised for a phase of exponential growth in the coming years. Green, social, and sustainability bonds could well have exceeded $2 trillion in cumulative issuance in 2021 (final data has not yet been published at the time of writing), driven in part by the post-pandemic recovery across various continents and markets.

This trend is one of many indicators that show how both ESG investment and ESG finance are rapidly and steadily rising in prominence on the global stage. This is further exemplified by the

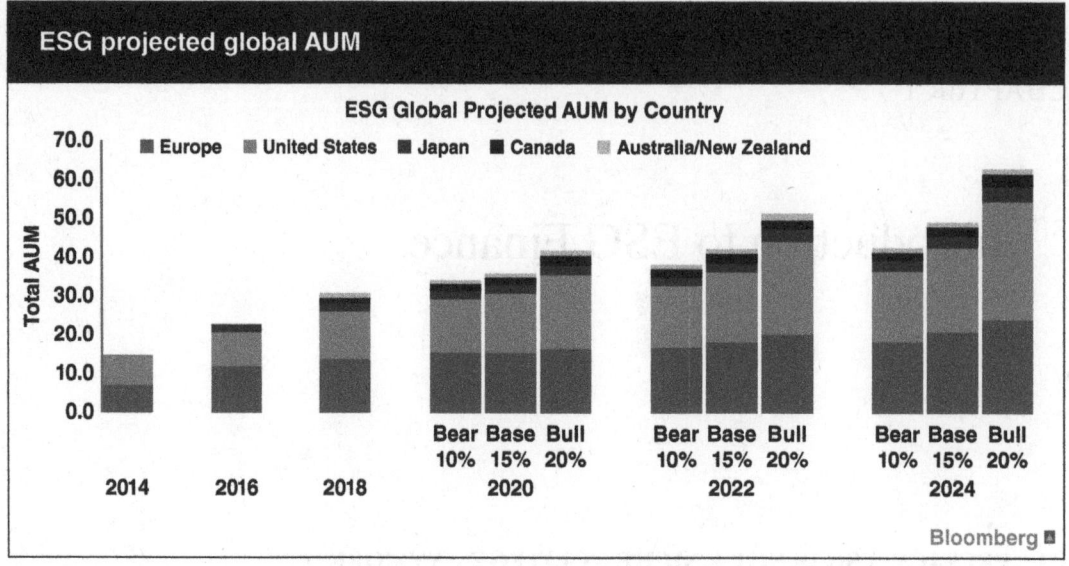

FIGURE 1.1   Projection of global ESG AUMs.
Source: Bloomberg.

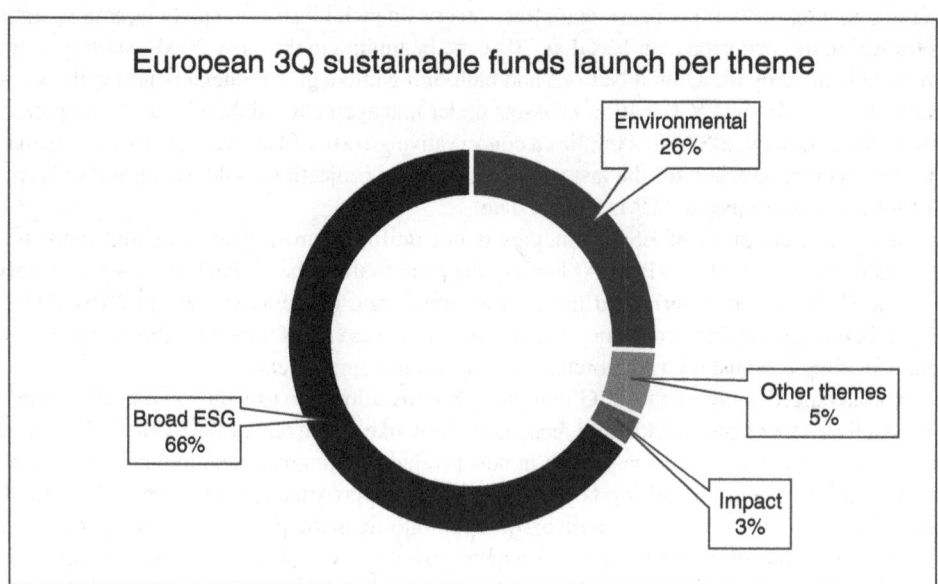

FIGURE 1.2   European 3Q sustainable funds launch per theme.
Source: Adapted from Bloomberg, Morningstar Research.

ever-increasing growth in requests for proposals to asset managers that require at least some variant/component of ESG tracking and/or screening of the investments (once again, led by EMEA and followed across the other regions with slightly delayed timelines).

In the following paragraphs, we introduce in more detail some of the concepts that we have mentioned above, as well as others, which we will review in the remaining chapters.

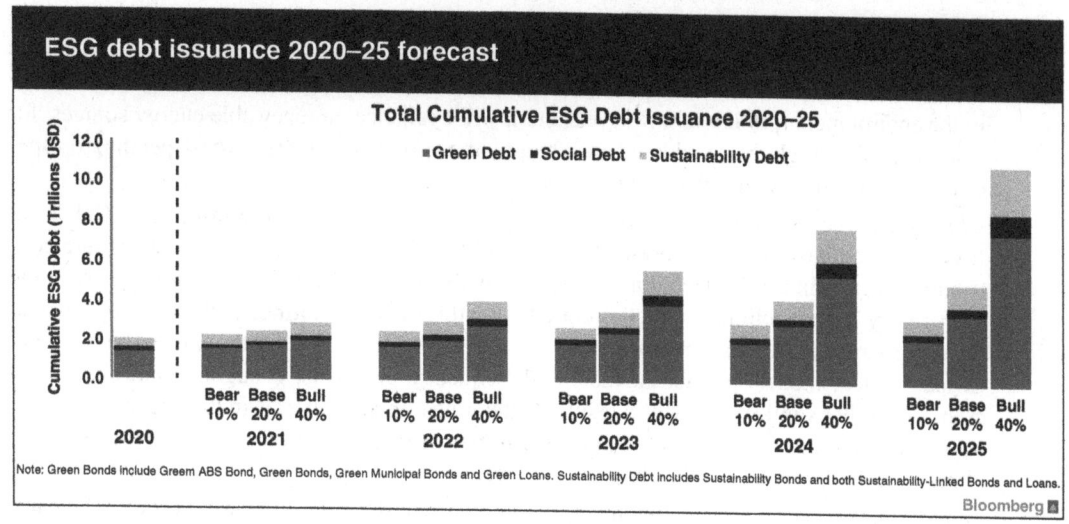

FIGURE 1.3   ESG debt issuance forecast 2020–2025.
Source: Bloomberg.

1.2   INTRODUCTION AND DEFINITIONS

Before we start looking at definitions of specific topics, it is important that we preface them with a key *caveat*. As briefly mentioned, the field of ESG finance is a new and rapidly developing area of finance, and, as such, many concepts and ideas are in a state of flux, often lacking universally accepted and established definitions. The field is dominated by common thinking, which is in a state of perpetual evolution, and concepts and ideas are constantly being challenged and refined.

Wherever possible, we try to leverage accepted and established definitions created by global expert organizations such as the Network for Greening the Financial System (NGFS; see below for details). Whenever such definitions are not available, we describe "common practice" definitions as we see them currently being utilized, with the understanding that these are merely a reflection of the current state of affairs in the field of ESG finance and reflect a common thinking and nomenclature that may continue to evolve, sometimes very rapidly.

ESG Definition – Socially Responsible Investing (SRI). We define socially responsible investing (SRI) as any investment strategy which, in addition to the traditional objective of maximizing financial return, also seeks to at least "do no harm" or, potentially even proactively, contribute to positive environmental, social, or corporate governance change (this last subset being known as "impact investing").

To address and evaluate the "do no harm" mandate for investment purposes, there is an accepted set of three relevant dimensions to measure, collectively referred to as ESG. The following paragraphs will provide an admittedly brief and high-level attempt to classify a wide range of concerns related to one or more of the E, S, or G dimensions:

Environmental concerns. The objective for this dimension is the minimizing of harm to the environment and the promotion of environmentally conscious and sustainable technologies. The concerns typically fall into one or more of the following major categories:

○ *Sustainability.* Sustainability is traditionally defined as the capacity of a system to endure in a metastable way across various domains of life. For ESG purposes, it normally is meant as the faculty for Earth's biosphere and human civilization to coexist. SRI has a mandate to invest, and therefore promote, production that is demonstrably sustainable. The definition of "sustainable" is that it does not deplete finite natural resources and does not result in permanent damage to the environment, in a broader sense. An example of this is reliance of fossil fuel energy, which fails the sustainability criteria, as it depletes finite natural resources and results in permanent damage to the environment (pollution, CO_2 levels, etc.), while reliance on renewable energy sources, for example, solar, might be considered an example of a sustainable alternative (depending on specific choices and ways of measuring impact).

○ *Climate change.* Anthropogenically released greenhouse gases in the atmosphere (CO_2 from fossil fuel combustion and deforestation and methane from livestock and agriculture) are contributing factors in accelerated climate change trends that have been observed globally over the last century. Current climate models are predicting this trend to continue in the near future, with resulting larger-scale climate changes and consequent disruptions to the current status quo. Climatological models predict an increased frequency of floods, droughts, wildfires, failed crops, and other similar events, as a result of changing climate patterns, in the decades ahead of us. Climate risk, and the way to quantify the impact it might have on credit and markets, is a major portion of this text in the chapters to come.

○ *Animal welfare.* This specific dimension can be either in the environmental or the social category, depending on the lens under which it is viewed. Animal welfare is formally defined as the well-being of non human animals. The concerns in the ESG space focus mostly on the commercial aspects of animals used for agriculture, for food production, or for research purposes, as well as the impact of human activities on wild animal populations. These concerns typically cover how animals are slaughtered for food, which conditions they are kept under in agricultural setups, which protocols are followed covering animal use for scientific research, and how our activities might impact wild species' survival and well-being.

Social concerns. The objective for this dimension is ensuring that the activities that are undertaken, in the pursuit of profit, are not detrimental to the interest of consumers, social issues of interest to the community, human rights, and general social and ethical aspects worthy of consideration. The areas of concern can loosely be grouped in the following four overlapping categories:

1. *Consumer protection.* Since SRI holds corporate entities accountable for their treatment of consumers, it is necessary to have a way of measuring performance of companies in this dimension. The rationale behind this accountability is to ensure that profitability is sought without sacrificing long-term sustainability of demand. An example of this is predatory lending, which can be more profitable in the short term but is harmful to the consumer body in the longer run and therefore is not a sustainable practice that SRI approves of.

2. *Talent diversity.* SRI follows the assumption that, in the long run, having diversity of perspectives within a corporation is beneficial to the business in general and to capability for resilience and innovation. Consequently, talent diversity in hiring, and in a broader sense in human capital, becomes one of the metrics that are measured and sought after in the ESG space.

3. *Human rights.* Considerations that are reviewed under this pillar of the social part of ESG SRI are typically related to health and welfare of employees and potential negative impacts on local communities of the activities undertaken by the companies. Besides the legal and moral aspects, there are many financial incentives for corporations to respect human rights, including reputational considerations, operational considerations, as well as regulatory and reporting commitments.

4. *"Sin stocks."* This is a topic closely related to the social dimension, as certain corporations are involved in activities and fields that some consider immoral (thus, their stocks are described as sin stocks). The businesses that are included in this category vary, depending on who is creating the list, and are subject to interpretation. Typical examples can include corporations involved in tobacco, alcohol, gambling, and manufacture and trade of firearms.

Corporate governance concerns. The objective for this dimension is focusing on corporate management structures and management practices. The goal is to ensure that generally accepted best practices and principles for corporate governance are in place, in companies in which SRI investors are invested, to minimize conflicts of interest between management and common shareholders as well as other stakeholders. Most governance concerns fall into one or more of the following categories:

- ○ *Management structure.* This area covers independence of the board of directors from company management as a central tenet for strong governance practices. It also includes provisions to ensure that the CEO and president roles are separate, to avoid centralization of executive power into a single individual (checks and balances).
- ○ *Executive compensation.* This area, albeit formally separate, can be seen as a subset of management structure, and is concerned with ensuring that executive compensation norms are closely linked to performance and best practices. It includes asking companies to list the percentage levels of bonus payments and the levels of remuneration of the highest-paid executives, to allow equity investors and stockholders to review and opine.
- ○ *Employee relations.* This is a category that pertains to considerations related to employee work conditions and communications/relationship with management. It also includes the topic of representation of workers in the process of decision-making within companies, as well as whether workers have the option to participate in a union.

A very early and prominent example of the idea of SRI, *ante litteram*, can be seen in the famous "Use of Money" sermon by John Wesley (1703–1791), founder of the Methodist Church, where he summarized the rules pertaining to money as ". . . , *gain(..) all you can, and, secondly save(..) all you can, then 'give all you can.*"

In more recent years, the Sullivan Code of Conduct, drafted by Rev. Leon Sullivan, board member of General Motors, is a leading example of what would morph into the more widespread and far-reaching ESG movements that followed in the later decades. It was promulgated to regulate practicing business with South Africa during the regime of apartheid (racial segregation) and was an instrumental factor in coalescing pressure on the South African regime that would eventually lead to the abandonment of apartheid.

In his 1970 essay for the *New York Times* titled "A Friedman Doctrine: The Social Responsibility of Business Is to Increase Its Profits,"[1] Milton Friedman presented a viewpoint that became mainstream until recent years, stating that social responsibility adversely affects a firm's financial performance. The Friedman doctrine focused exclusively on the pure bottom line, and considered the costs incurred by social responsibility as nonessential to the corporate mission and mandate.

In recent years, however, different lines of academic thought, such as the stakeholder theory, as proposed by Edward Freedman, have gained more widespread acceptance, and are more closely linked to the principles that drive ESG finance and SRI. This theory argues that the responsibility of a corporation is not limited exclusively to its shareholders, as in the Friedman doctrine, but it also extends more broadly to other categories that are affected by the corporation in a broader sense.

The constituencies that business entities are responsible toward now include employees, suppliers, local communities, creditors, and others. This doctrine, therefore, adds the dimensions of addressing morals and values in managing an organization, such as those related to corporate social responsibility, market economy, and social contract theory. To implement the doctrine in practical terms, Freeman proposes corporate social responsibility (CSR) as an alternative method to ensure private self-regulation accounts for the utilities of societal goals beyond pure profit maximization.

ESG Finance. We define *ESG finance* as a general term that captures multiple different subjects under it, including SRI in different forms (buy-side finance), as well as ESG-conscious financing (sell-side finance). There are no specific differences in taxonomy between ESG finance and traditional

---

[1] The Social Responsibility of Business Is to Increase Its Profits," Springer Books, in: Walther Ch Zimmerli & Markus Holzinger & Klaus Richter (ed.), Corporate Ethics and Corporate Governance, pages 173–178, Springer.

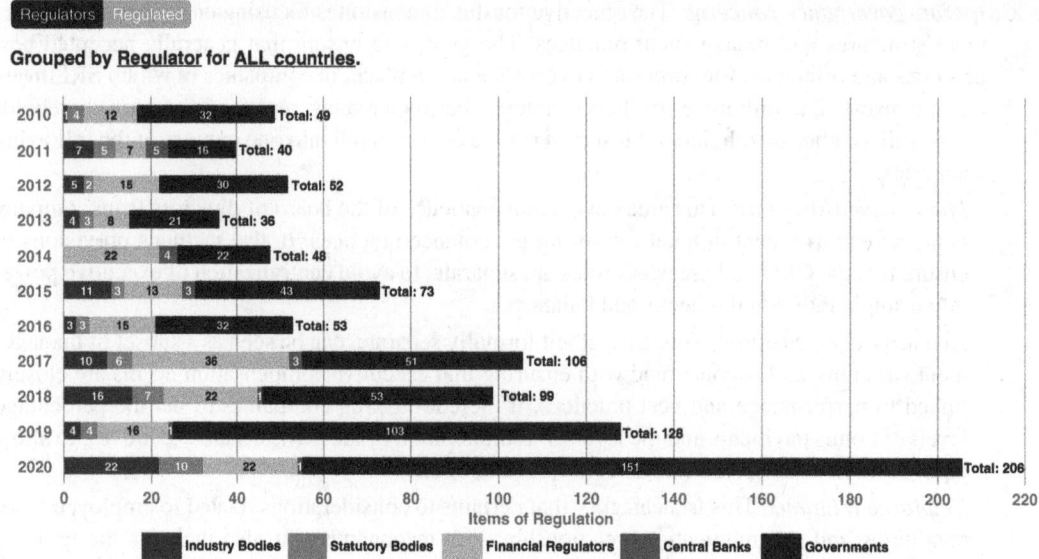

FIGURE 1.4   MSCI: Who will regulate ESG?

finance as such, and the types of participants that make up the ESG finance ecosystem closely mirror the financial markets as a whole. Ultimately, in every category of general financial market participants, there are ones that can be defined as being part of ESG finance, by their focus on ESG to a certain degree. The broad categories in which the ESG finance market participants fall under are the following:

- Institutional investors: pension funds, sovereign wealth funds, insurance companies, endowments, mutual funds, family offices, etc.
- Retail investors: Investees (issuers of securities), Investment and corporate banks
- Market utilities: ESG rating agencies and data providers, ESG index sponsors Government regulatory agencies and other regulatory bodies (non-government governance entities, industry associations, etc.)

The "government agencies and regulatory bodies" category is one of significant importance, which we have briefly mentioned in earlier paragraphs, with multiple regulatory bodies focusing in part or entirely on ESG concerns. The number of regulatory agencies that have a say in ESG matters has steadily grown in the last decade globally, from less than 50 in 2020 to over 200 today, and includes industry bodies, statutory bodies, financial regulators, central banks, and governments. Figure 1.4 provides a view of the growth in the number of regulators involved in this space.

Several international/multinational organizations and associations have been established to allow collective development of best practices and guidelines for ESG-related matters, as can be seen in Table 1.1.

As an example of how these international and multinational organizations operate and exert influence in the ESG space, we can look at the Principles for Responsible Investment (PRI), which has established the following six principles that investors that are signatories to the group agree to abide by:

1. Will incorporate ESG issues into investment analysis and decision-making processes.
2. Will be active owners and incorporate ESG issues into our ownership policies and practices.
3. Will seek appropriate disclosure on ESG issues by the entities in which we invest.
4. Will promote acceptance and implementation of the principles within the investment industry.

TABLE 1.1   Key international organizations and associations in the ESG context.

Network for Greening the Financial System (NGFS) https://www.ngfs.net/en 	The Network of Central Banks and Supervisors for Greening the Financial System, launched at the first One Planet Summit in 2017, is a group of central banks and supervisors willing, on a voluntary basis, to share best practices and contribute to the development of environment and climate risk management in the financial sector and to mobilize mainstream finance to support the transition toward a sustainable economy. It publishes NGFS climate scenarios.
Global Sustainable Investment Alliance (GSIA) http://www.gsi-alliance.org/ 	A global association of membership-based sustainable investment organizations. The GSIA's mission is to deepen the impact and visibility of sustainable investment organizations at the global level. Members include European sustainable investment forum (EUROSIF), UKSIF, US SIF, JSIF, etc.
Principles for Responsible Investment (PRI) https://www.unpri.org/ 	An international group of large institutional investors (signatories) who have joined a process to develop Principles for Responsible Investment, facilitated by the UN. The PRI encourages investors globally to adhere to responsible investment principles.

5. Will work together to enhance our effectiveness in implementing the principles.

6. Will each report on our activities and progress towards implementing the principles.

ESG Strategies. We define "ESG strategy" as an approach to sustainable investing. If we take the approaches that are recognized by the Global Sustainable Investment Alliance, we can highlight seven core approaches to sustainable investing (Table 1.2). Typically, one or more of these will be combined into any given ESG investment strategy chosen by investors in the ESG space.

Given the fact that the ESG investment ecosystem is undergoing rapid growth, which extends also across most of the approaches listed above, it is very likely that these strategies will be in a state of flux for the foreseeable future. In order to be fully up to date, we recommend referring to the most recent GSIA report on a regular basis.

Greenwashing. The term *greenwashing* is used to describe a form of marketing spin that many corporations use, where green PR (green values) and green marketing are deceptively used to try to persuade the general public, consumers, and investors that a corporation's products, activities, aims, policies, and practices are environmentally friendly when, in reality, they are not.

There are several ways greenwashing can occur, such as, but not limited to:

- *Hidden trade-offs.* Claiming "green" credentials for a product or practice based on a single attribute or a very narrowly focused set of attributes, while entirely ignoring and obfuscating other areas where the product or practice is demonstrably harmful to the environment.

TABLE 1.2   Core approaches to sustainable investing.

Core Approach	Description
ESG integration	The systematic and explicit inclusion by investment managers of ESG factors into financial analysis.
Corporate engagement and shareholder action	Employing shareholder power to influence corporate behavior, including through direct corporate engagement (i.e., communicating with senior management and/or boards of companies), filing or co-filing shareholder proposals, and proxy voting that is guided by comprehensive ESG guidelines.
Norms-based screening	Screening of investments against minimum standards of business or issuer practice based on international norms such as those issued by the UN, ILO, OECD, and NGOs (e.g., Transparency International).
Negative/exclusionary screening	The exclusion from a fund or portfolio of certain sectors, companies, countries, or other issuers based on activities considered not investable. Exclusion criteria (based on norms and values) can refer, for example, to product categories (e.g., weapons, tobacco), company practices (e.g., animal testing, violation of human rights, corruption), or controversies.
Best-in-class/positive screening	Investment in sectors, companies, or projects selected for positive ESG performance relative to industry peers and that achieve a rating above a defined threshold.
Sustainability themed/ thematic investing	Investing in themes or assets specifically contributing to sustainable solutions – environmental and social (e.g., sustainable agriculture, green buildings, lower carbon tilted portfolio, gender equity, diversity).
Impact investing and community investing	**Impact investing** – Investing to achieve positive, social, and environmental impacts – requires measuring and reporting against these impacts, demonstrating the intentionality of investor and underlying asset/investee, and demonstrating the investor contribution. **Community investing** – Where capital is specifically directed to traditionally underserved individuals or communities, as well as financing that is provided to businesses with a clear social or environmental purpose. Some community investing is impact investing, but community investing is broader and considers other forms of investing and targeted lending activities.

Source: http://www.gsi-alliance.org/wp-content/uploads/2021/08/GSIR-20201.pdf

- *Lack of substance/third-party review.* Claiming "green" credentials by using data that cannot be substantiated easily and accessibly by reliable third parties.
- *Vagueness/misleading claims.* Claiming "green" credentials by using fuzzy and vague terms meant to confuse and obfuscate consumers and trick them into misunderstanding the meaning of what the company states.
- *False labeling/endorsement.* Claiming "green" credentials by creating misleading associations, in writing or imagery, that seem to imply endorsements/credentials by legitimate and credible third parties while, in reality, no such endorsement is present.
- *Irrelevance.* Claiming "green" credentials by focusing on aspects of no relevance or importance to customers and to the environment, in the effort to mislead them into believing that a certain product is environmentally superior to competing products (e.g., "this product does not contain any XYZ while our competitor does" with item XYZ being completely irrelevant for environmental purposes).
- *Lesser of two evils.* Claiming "green" credentials by distracting consumer attention from the overall environmental impact of the product or practice and focusing the attention on claims/aspects that are specific within the category of the product itself (e.g., "this pesticide only pollutes 80% as much as our competitor").
- *Outright lying.* Claiming "green" credentials by making false claims.

Greenwashing can take even more extreme forms, known as *greenscamming*, which involve the creation of deceptively named organizations. A few examples include the National Wetlands Coalition, which is backed by oil-drilling companies and real estate developers, the Friends of Eagle Mountain, backed by a mining company that wants to convert open-cast mines into landfills, and the Global Climate Coalition, backed by commercial enterprises that fought against government-imposed climate protection measures.

Investors in the ESG space must be very aware of greenwashing, as well as focused on ways to avoid it in their portfolios and in their own practices alike.

One of the major drivers for greenwashing is, in a nutshell, that it is effectively allowed by the lack of clear and common definitions of what constitutes "green" activities and defined consequences for deceptive practices and claims related to it. It is expected, however, that this situation will change rapidly, with a consensus that uniform standard requirements for corporate disclosures, standards for ESG scoring, and "sustainable" designations will emerge soon to address this problem.

As an example of an ongoing initiative that aims to tackle this issue, the European Green Deal, which is a set of policy initiatives by the European Commission with the overarching aim of making the European Union climate neutral by 2050, states that "Companies making 'green claims' should substantiate these against a standard methodology to assess their impact on the environment."

Additionally, the 2020 EU Circular Economy action plan commits that:

the Commission will also propose that companies substantiate their environmental claims using Product and Organization Environmental Footprint methods.

[. . .] It is important that claims on the environmental performance of companies and products are reliable, comparable and verifiable across the EU. Reliable environmental information would allow market actors – consumers, companies, investors – to take greener decisions.[2]

While these specific initiatives are happening in the European Union, it is expected that similar initiatives will soon follow in North America and, with some delay due to the current state of the ESG field, in Asia-Pacific.

EXERCISE 1.A   Retrieving ESG Data Freely Available Online

While at a later stage we will discuss more production-quality data extraction techniques and data available from dedicated commercial/paid sources, we start with a simple "toy" exercise of accessing and using data from the Yahoo Finance service.

Using *yfinance* package

Yahoo Finance web page publishes (current) ESG ratings and a range of other ESG-related data supplied by Sustainalytics, a dedicated ESG rating agency/data provider, for US equities. The most straightforward way of accessing those data programmatically is by leveraging the *yfinance* Python package.

We start by loading the relevant packages:

```
In [1]:   import yfinance as yf
          import pandas as pd
```

We will assume that the audience has working knowledge of Python and its ecosystem, including *pandas*. There are innumerable excellent textbooks on the topic; one (of many) we would

(Continued)

---

[2] "Initiative on Substantiating Green Claims," European Commission, https://ec.europa.eu/environment/eussd/smgp/initiative_on_green_claims.htm

recommend as background reading is *Python for Data Analysis* (2nd ed.) by Wes McKinney, the author of *pandas*, https://wesmckinney.com/.

As a reminder, to install a new package using Conda, we may use the following command line:

conda install -c conda-forge package_name

Using *yfinance*, all that is needed to retrieve the table of ESG data is to access the sustainability property of the Ticker class:

```
In [17]:  obj = yf.Ticker("C")
          dfSustainabilityTable = obj.sustainability.T
```

Let us add the ticker that we used to reference the equity to the same table and review the result:

```
In [18]:  dfSustainabilityTable["ticker"] = obj.ticker
          dfSustainabilityTable
```

Out[18]:

	2021-9	palmOil	controversialWeapons	gambling	socialScore	nuclear	furLeather	alcoholic	gmo	catholic	socialPercentile	...	coal	pesticides	adult	pe
Value	False		False	False	10.83	False	False	False	False	False	None	...	False		False	False

1 rows × 28 columns

The data in the sustainability table is collected from the Yahoo Finance service; we can view the same ratings on the Yahoo Finance webpage, but the *sustainability* table also contains further details, such as specific binary flags indicating whether the company is involved in alcohol production, uses palm oil, etc., that do not show up on the webpage.

In a similar fashion, we can extract these data for a list of tickers in a loop. Let us start by assembling a list of tickers of interest.

It is also possible to collect the list of S&P 500 tickers from Wikipedia: *read_html* function in *pandas* allows us to easily extract all the tables from a particular webpage; the first table on the page contains the needed list of tickers.

Prior to reading the table, we download the relevant Wikipedia page by executing the GET method implemented in the *requests* package:

```
In [8]:  import requests
```

```
In [9]:  wikiPg = requests.get("https://en.wikipedia.org/wiki/List_of_S%26P_500_companies").text
         dfSpx = pd.read_html(wikiPg)[0]
```

The *Symbol* column – when converted to a list – represents a list of tickers in the S&P 500 index. For our exercise, let us restrict our attention to a particular sector, for instance, Energy:

```
In [29]:  lstTickers = dfSpx[dfSpx["GICS Sector"] == "Energy"]["Symbol"].tolist()
          lstTickers
```

```
Out[29]:  ['APA',
           'BKR',
           'CVX',
           'COP',
           'CTRA',
           'DVN',
           'FANG',
           'EOG',
           'XOM',
           'HAL',
           'HES',
           'KMI',
           'MRO',
           'MPC',
           'OXY',
           'OKE',
           'PSX',
           'PXD',
           'SLB',
           'VLO',
           'WMB']
```

For each ticker on the list, we repeat the *yfinance* query discussed earlier to collect the current sustainability data. We just need to catch exceptions for tickers that do not have the relevant data available:

```
In [34]:    dfSustainabilityTable = pd.DataFrame()
            for ii in lstTickers:
                obj = yf.Ticker(ii)
                if obj.sustainability is not None:
                    v = obj.sustainability.T
                    v["ticker"] = obj.ticker
                    dfSustainabilityTable = dfSustainabilityTable.append(v)
                    print(" : ".join([ii, "done"]))
                else:
                    print(" : ".join([ii, "NA"]))

APA : done
BKR : NA
CVX : done
COP : done
CTRA : done
DVN : done
FANG : NA
EOG : done
XOM : done
HAL : done
HES : done
KMI : done
MRO : done
MPC : done
OXY : done
OKE : done
PSX : done
PXD : done
SLB : done
VLO : done
WMB : done
```

We review the output once we make the *ticker* column the new index:

```
In [35]:    dfSustainabilityTable.set_index("ticker", inplace=True)
            dfSustainabilityTable.T
```

Out[35]:

ticker	APA	CVX	COP	CTRA	DVN	EOG	XOM	HAL	HES	KMI	MRO
2021-9											
palmOil	False	False	False	False	False	False	False	False	False	False	False
controversialWeapons	False	False	False	False	False	False	False	False	False	False	False
gambling	False	False	False	False	False	False	False	False	False	False	False
socialScore	8.88	10.67	9.83	14.01	8.32	11.06	10.57	9.62	6.36	6.09	10.27
nuclear	False	False	False	False	False	False	False	False	False	False	False
furLeather	False	False	False	False	False	False	False	False	False	False	False
alcoholic	False	False	False	False	False	False	False	False	False	False	False
gmo	False	False	False	False	False	False	False	False	False	False	False
catholic	False	False	False	False	False	False	False	False	False	False	False
socialPercentile	0	0	0	0	0	0	0	0	0	0	0

Of course, the *yfinance* package makes use of free Yahoo data and is hardly fit for production-quality investment analysis. However, APIs offered by commercial (paid) data providers are similar in nature; therefore, our toy example still has some value as an introduction to a wide class of data APIs.

How does *yfinance* populate the sustainability table internally?

It is instructive to review the open-source code of the *yfinance* package; it is easily accessible by invoking the double-question mark:

```
In [36]:    ??yf
```

(Continued)

The package first uses the *requests* package to download the webpage's HTML:

```
In [37]:  ▶  import requests
             import json
```

```
In [40]:  ▶  html = requests.get(url="https://finance.yahoo.com/quote/C", headers=user_agent_headers).text
             html
```

```
Out[40]:  '<!DOCTYPE html><html id="atomic" class="NoJs chrome desktop" lang="en-US"><head prefix="og: http://ogp.me/ns#">
          <script>window.performance && window.performance.mark && window.performance.mark(\'PageStart\');</script><meta ch
          arset="utf-8"/><title>Citigroup Inc. (C) Stock Price, News, Quote &amp; History - Yahoo Finance</title><meta name
          ="keywords" content="C, Citigroup Inc., C stock chart, Citigroup Inc. stock chart, stock chart, stocks, quotes, f
          inance"/><meta http-equiv="x-dns-prefetch-control" content="on"/><meta property="twitter:dnt" content="on"/><meta
          property="fb:app_id" content="458584288257241"/><meta name="theme-color" content="#400090"/><meta name="viewport"
          content="width=device-width, initial-scale=1"/><meta name="description" lang="en-US" content="Find the latest Cit
          igroup Inc. (C) stock quote, history, news and other vital information to help you with your stock trading and in
          vesting."/><meta name="oath:guce:consent-host" content="guce.yahoo.com"/><meta name="msvalidate.01" content="A986
          2C0E6E1BE95BCE0BF3D0298FD58B"/><link rel="manifest" href="/manifest.json"/><link rel="dns-prefetch" href="//l.yim
          g.com"/><link rel="dns-prefetch" href="//s.yimg.com"/><link rel="dns-prefetch" href="//geo.query.yahoo.com"/><lin
          k rel="dns-prefetch" href="//b.scorecardresearch.com"/><link rel="dns-prefetch" href="//iquery.finance.yahoo.co
          m"/><link rel="dns-prefetch" href="//fc.yahoo.com"/><link rel="dns-prefetch" href="//video-api.yql.yahoo.com"/><l
          ink rel="dns-prefetch" href="//consent.cmp.oath.com"/><link rel="dns-prefetch" href="//geo.yahoo.com"/><link rel
          ="preconnect" href="//l.yimg.com" crossorigin="anonymous"/><link rel="preconnect" href="//s.yimg.com" crossorigin
          ="anonymous"/><link rel="preconnect" href="//geo.query.yahoo.com"/><link rel="preconnect" href="//b.scorecardrese
          arch.com"/><link rel="preconnect" href="//iquery.finance.yahoo.com"/><link rel="preconnect" href="//fc.yahoo.co
          m"/><link rel="preconnect" href="//video-api.yql.yahoo.com"/><link rel="preconnect" href="//consent.cmp.oath.co
          m"/><link rel="preconnect" href="//geo.yahoo.com"/><link rel="preconnect" href="//ads.yahoo.com"/><link rel="prel
```

The GET method with the default value for headers also sometimes works but has shown itself to be considerably less stable. Here the headers argument is as shown below; you can copy the full value from the package code:

```
In [39]:  ▶  user_agent_headers = {"User-Agent": "Mozilla/5.0 (Macintosh; Intel Mac OS X 10_10_1) AppleWebKit/537.36 (KHTML, like
```

The *yfinance* package then uses the *json* package to extract and manipulate a data JSON from the webpage HTML source. The resulting large *data* dictionary contains the sustainability table as a component (if it is available from Yahoo for the ticker of interest):

```
In [41]:  ▶  json_str = html.split("root.App.main =")[1].split("(this)")[0].split(";\n}")[0].strip()
             data = json.loads(json_str)["context"]["dispatcher"]["stores"]["QuoteSummaryStore"]
             data
```

```
Out[41]:  {'defaultKeyStatistics': {'annualHoldingsTurnover': {},
             'enterpriseToRevenue': {'raw': -3.794, 'fmt': '-3.79'},
             'beta3Year': {},
             'profitMargins': {'raw': 0.30629, 'fmt': '30.63%'},
             'enterpriseToEbitda': {},
             '52WeekChange': {'raw': 0.004822135, 'fmt': '0.48%'},
             'morningStarRiskRating': {},
             'forwardEps': {'raw': 7.86, 'fmt': '7.86'},
             'revenueQuarterlyGrowth': {},
             'sharesOutstanding': {'raw': 1984269952,
              'fmt': '1.98B',
              'longFmt': '1,984,269,952'},
             'fundInceptionDate': {},
             'annualReportExpenseRatio': {},
             'totalAssets': {},
             'bookValue': {'raw': 92.165, 'fmt': '92.17'},
             'sharesShort': {'raw': 41248863, 'fmt': '41.25M', 'longFmt': '41,248,863'},
             'sharesPercentSharesOut': {'raw': 0.0208, 'fmt': '2.08%'},
             'fundFamily': None,
```

Within the extracted JSON dictionary, *yfinance* searches for the "esgScores" portion and uses it to populate the resulting sustainability table. We leave it to the interested reader to further explore the *yfinance* code.

Web Scraping

As an alternative to relying on *yfinance* or similar data-sourcing packages, one can extract the data shown on the webpage directly by parsing raw HTML; this method is commonly referred to as web scraping. This approach has limited value in our context, as we have downloaded the information we need in a richer and more detailed JSON above. As mentioned earlier, most of the aggregated commercial data are delivered in processed form, and accessing it does not require scraping; however, web scraping is a very valuable technique in other contexts, such as natural language processing of news.

The starting point for the scraping process is the same as the first step performed internally by *yfinance*. It downloads the HTML page source:

```
In [43]:  M  html = requests.get("https://finance.yahoo.com/quote/C/sustainability", headers=user_agent_headers).text
```

In the subsequent steps, we leverage the *bs4* package for HTML parsing. You can obviously find abundant info on the package and its use cases just by googling.

```
In [45]:  M  import bs4
```

Web scraping naturally relies on some rudimentary HTML knowledge.

Let us start by extracting the total ESG score from the webpage. If you load the Yahoo Finance webpage in your browser and use the browser's object inspector feature, you can see that the total ESG score resides on the page inside a class tagged "*D(ib) Fz(23px) smartphone_Fz(22px) Fw(600)*." The webpage can, of course, be changed by Yahoo developers without prior notice, which will break your code. This makes web scraping a "hack" solution that is less than perfectly reliable.

The inspector tool is loaded in Firefox by right-clicking the page and selecting "*Inspect (Q)*" (or similarly in other browsers):

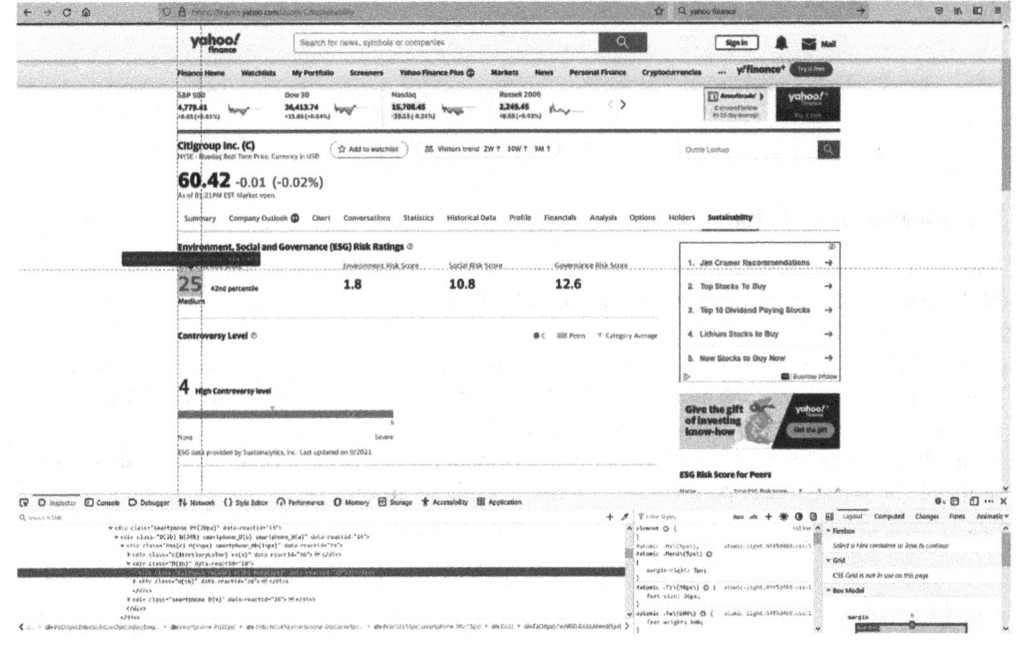

(*Continued*)

Next, we use the *BeautifulSoup* parser to locate the class with the tag we identified via the browser inspector. We can see that the value enclosed within the div brackets is 25, same as in the figure above:

```
In [48]:  ▶  soup = bs4.BeautifulSoup(html, "html.parser")
             totalEsgRiskScore = soup.find("div", class_="Fz(36px) Fw(600) D(ib) Mend(5px)")
             totalEsgRiskScore

   Out[48]:  <div class="Fz(36px) Fw(600) D(ib) Mend(5px)" data-reactid="19">25</div>
```

The controversy score is read following the same approach as the value within the class tagged "*D(ib) Fz(36px) Fw(500)*." Note that printing the class itself reveals the full HTML class definition; we use the *text* property to retrieve the value between the brackets.

```
In [49]:  ▶  controversyLevel = soup.find("div", class_="D(ib) Fz(36px) Fw(500)").text
             controversyLevel

   Out[49]:  '4'
```

Similarly, we extract individual E, S, and G scores located in their respective dedicated *div* classes. This time, we use the *find_all* method that returns an iterator. Note that we need to know the order of E, S, and G to properly differentiate them:

```
In [51]:  ▶  scores = [ii.text for ii in soup.find_all("div", class_="D(ib) Fz(23px) smartphone_Fz(22px) Fw(600)")]
```

Finally, we collect all retrieved scores into a single *DataFrame*:

```
In [54]:  ▶  pd.DataFrame({"Total" : totalEsgRiskScore.text,
                           "E Score" : scores[0], "S Score" : scores[1], "G Score" : scores[2],
                           "Controversy Level" : controversyLevel}, index=[""])

   Out[54]:
```

Total	E Score	S Score	G Score	Controversy Level
25	1.8	10.8	12.6	4

Performance by ESG Rating (First Attempt)

Now that we are able to collect some ESG data, we can attempt to verify some of the earlier performance claims regarding companies with high vs. low ESG score (or any of its single-letter components).

In subsequent chapters, we discuss in much more detail relevant index construction principles and risk factor analysis. For the purpose of this illustration, though, we will ignore these complications. Using the current ESG score retrieved from Yahoo Finance for S&P 500 companies within the Energy sector, we will assemble all companies into groups in terms of score distribution and compare average performance of stocks in these groups.

First, let us sort the tickers for which the ESG score is available in the order of increasing score:

```
In [58]:   dfSustainabilityTable.sort_values("totalEsg", inplace=True)
           dfSustainabilityTable.T
```

Out[58]:

ticker 2021-9	KMI	WMB	SLB	HAL	OKE	MPC	VLO	HES	DVN	PSX	PXD	XOM
palmOil	False	False	False	False	False	False	False	False	False	False	False	False
controversialWeapons	False	False	False	False	False	False	False	False	False	False	False	False
gambling	False	False	False	False	False	False	False	False	False	False	False	False
socialScore	6.09	8.52	9.82	9.62	8.13	6.71	6.87	6.36	8.32	8.08	9.14	10.57
nuclear	False	False	False	False	False	False	False	False	False	False	False	False
furLeather	False	False	False	False	False	False	False	False	False	False	False	False
alcoholic	False	False	False	False	False	False	False	False	False	False	False	False
gmo	False	False	False	False	False	False	False	False	False	False	False	False
catholic	False	False	False	False	False	False	False	False	False	False	False	False
socialPercentile	0	0	0	0	0	0	0	0	0	0	0	0
peerCount	37	37	10	10	37	37	39	64	64	37	71	64
governanceScore	3.72	3.2	6.7	6.85	3.4	5.96	5.41	7.15	7.74	5.54	8.8	8.26
environmentPercentile	0	0	0	0	0	0	0	0	0	0	0	0
animalTesting	False	False	False	False	False	False	False	False	False	False	False	False
tobacco	False	False	False	False	False	False	False	False	False	False	False	False
totalEsg	18.36	20.7	23.82	24.07	25.36	27.72	28.4	29.7	31.67	32.87	33.08	35.77
highestControversy	2	2	1	2	1	3	3	2	2	3	1	3
esgPerformance	LAG_PERF	None	None	None	None	None	None	None	LEAD_PERF	LEAD_PERF	LEAD_PERF	LEAD_PERF
coal	False	False	False	False	False	False	False	False	False	False	False	False
pesticides	False	False	False	False	False	False	False	False	False	False	False	False
adult	False	False	False	False	False	False	False	False	False	False	False	False
percentile	17.95	25.22	36.26	37.3	42.24	51.11	51.79	58.43	65.35	69.39	68.72	77.93
peerGroup	Refiners & Pipelines	Refiners & Pipelines	Energy Services	Energy Services	Refiners & Pipelines	Refiners & Pipelines	Refiners & Pipelines	Oil & Gas Producers	Oil & Gas Producers	Refiners & Pipelines	Oil & Gas Producers	Oil & Gas Producers
smallArms	False	False	False	False	False	False	False	False	False	False	False	False
environmentScore	8.55	8.96	7.31	7.8	13.83	15.06	16.12	16.18	15.61	19.25	15.15	16.94
governancePercentile	0	0	0	0	0	0	0	0	0	0	0	0
militaryContract	False	False	False	False	False	False	False	False	False	False	False	False

To compare performance between portfolios of securities representing different ESG score ranges, we download historical price quotes for the underlying securities (again, using *yfinance*):

```
In [56]:   dfPx = yf.download(" ".join(allTix), start="2015-01-01")["Adj Close"]
           [*********************100%**********************]  19 of 19 completed
```

Here, *allTix* is a list of all tickers present in the sustainability data table (tickers for which ESG scores are available), not the full list of tickers in S&P 500 Energy sector:

```
In [60]:   allTix = dfSustainabilityTable.index.to_list()
           dfSustainabilityTable.shape
   Out[60]:  (19, 27)
```

We fill missing values in the quotes *DataFrame* by carrying over existing values from other dates. Note that – in practice – a much more sophisticated *data enrichment* process is necessary to intelligently choose the replacement for missing values, but for the purposes of this example, a simple approach taken here suffices:

```
In [59]:   dfPx.fillna(method="ffill", inplace=True)
           dfPx.fillna(method="bfill", inplace=True)
```

(Continued)

Next, we group all the securities into three portfolios and compute an index for the *lagging tertile* and *leading tertile* portfolio by averaging prices. Again, this is an overly simplistic technique; we will discuss index construction in much greater detail in the next chapter.

There are 19 tickers in total; therefore, the top six and the bottom six after sorting by ESG score represent the lagging and leading tertile portfolios, respectively:

```
In [64]:  ▶  lstLag = allTix[:6]
             seriesLag = dfPx[lstLag].sum(axis=1)
             seriesLag /= seriesLag[0]

             lstLead = allTix[13:]
             seriesLead = dfPx[lstLead].sum(axis=1)
             seriesLead /= seriesLead[0]
```

Finally, we aggregate the resulting series into a single *DataFrame* and plot the results (which can be done trivially for a *pandas DataFrame*). Interestingly, the performance of the two portfolios is quite similar!

```
In [66]:  ▶  dfRes = pd.concat([seriesLag, seriesLead], axis=1)
             dfRes.columns = ["lead", "lag"]

In [67]:  ▶  dfRes.plot()
```

Out[67]: <AxesSubplot:xlabel='Date'>

What Are the Biggest Weaknesses of Our "Toy" Performance Analysis? As mentioned above, the exercise described in this session is far from production-strength and suffers from a few deficiencies. In subsequent exercises we discuss in more detail how these can be remediated. It is also a good exercise to attempt spotting major deficiencies on your own before reviewing the list below.

The major weaknesses of the solution presented above fall into the following three categories:

1. *Historical data availability*. ESG scores are not available for some of the equities in S&P 500; removing them reduces our sample. Furthermore, historical prices are not available for the full date range (some of the companies in the index were added or removed over the length of available data); our handling of holidays/non-trading days in the sample is also somewhat crude.
2. *Portfolio index weighting*. We apply price-weighting to available securities within each quintile portfolio. Many more sophisticated weighting schemes exist for portfolio indexes; these will be discussed in more detail in the next session.
3. *Look-ahead bias from constant ESG scores*. Perhaps most importantly, we are relying on current/latest ESG scores; the history of scores is not available from Yahoo. However, the scores are not constant over time, especially not over longer periods of time. Some companies may have significantly improved (or worsened) their score and would have migrated between quintile portfolios. The proper way to account for this would be to rearrange portfolios dynamically through time based on the ESG scores at that time. As mentioned, we will discuss weighting schemes in more depth in the next section.

1.3   ESG INVESTMENT PERFORMANCE

If we look at ESG strategies and compare them to the universe of securities available for investment, it is immediately evident that, by simple logical argument, ESG strategies impose a narrowing constraint on what securities the portfolio manager can decide to invest in and, therefore, the ESG strategy, all other things being equal, can be at most as good as an "unconstrained" investment strategy. This stems from the logical assumption that any ESG strategy can be mimicked by a non-ESG investor and improved by adding to the portfolio a single non-ESG stock that happens to have better returns than the overall strategy (the existence of which does not take a large leap of faith to assume). This is valid for any direct investment strategy, and if we assume strategies that include short-selling, the case is even stronger.

On the other hand, pure profitability is not the only factor in generating interest in ESG strategies, as we have seen earlier in this chapter, and growing societal/regulatory interest in ESG as a topic is causing an increase in demand for ESG investments, which, by the nature of the mechanisms that drive stock market prices, can lead to an outperformance of ESG stocks compared to the broader market stocks.

The overall performance of ESG strategies is, however, an uncertain topic, with authoritative voices in academia making the case for outperform, underperform, and perform in line with the broader market. For this reason, we will not try to add our voice to these esteemed colleagues and will not opine on this topic any further.

As we discuss in the next chapter, ESG can be isolated as a specific equity risk factor, with a performance that will vary over time, dependent on the changing market perceptions and evolving attractiveness/popularity of the strategy among the investor population.

In this textbook, we limit our observations and commentary to a few sources regarding recent historical performance that focus on the quantitative techniques relevant to such analyses rather than trying to reach definitive conclusions.

Some of the claims considered are the following:

- Stronger shareholder rights lead to stronger corporate and market performance.[3]
- High corporate social responsibility leads to lower cost of capital.[4] Note that corporate performance and financing costs do not have to be fully aligned with equity market performance (for the primary reason that stock market pricing emphasizes investor perceptions of future expectations rather than current-period financial performance).
- Corporate financial performance is not a monotonic function of corporate social performance; rather, an optimal point exists.[5]
- No evidence of ESG focus leading to stronger financial performance.[6]
- In the presence of information asymmetries, a firm may reduce earnings variability by binding itself to ESG rules, lowering the interest rates, and raising expected profits. If no information asymmetries exist, adherence to ESG lowers returns and increases risk.[7]

---

[3] Paul Gompers, Joy Ishii, and Andrew Metrick, "Corporate Governance and Equity Prices," *Quarterly Journal of Economics* 118(1) (February. 2003): 107–155.

[4] Sadok El Ghoul, Omrane Guedhami, Chuck C.Y. Kwok, and Dev Mishra, "Does Corporate Social Responsibility Affect the Cost of Capital?" *Journal of Banking & Finance* 35 (9) (2011): 2388–2406.

[5] Michael L. Barnett and Robert M. Salomon, "Does It Pay to Be Really Good? Addressing the Shape of the Relationship between Social and Financial Performance," *Strategic Management Journal* 33 (11) (November 2012): 1304–1320.

[6] Andreas Ziegler, Michael Schröder, and Klaus Rennings, "The Effect of Environmental and Social Performance on the Stock Performance of European Corporations," *Environmental & Resource Economics* 40 (2008): 609–609. 10.1007/s10640-007-9082-y

[7] Richard Robb, Vinay Viswanathan, and Martin Sattell, "An Equilibrium Model of Corporate Environmental and Social Governance," *Capitalism & Society* 15 (1), December 14, 2021. Available at SSRN: https://ssrn.com/abstract=3987303

Additionally, we also have considered the following key observations which pertain to historical performance:

- ESG investments underperformed until 2014 but outperformed from 2014 onward in EMEA and North America (NAM).
- Particularly strong performance was observed in environmental investments in NAM and governance investments in EMEA.

Sorted Portfolios Approach. If we were to ask the question, "What are the relative effects of ESG risk factors on investment performance, and how do they vary by region?" there would be several possible ways to approach the issue. For the purposes of this textbook, we have selected to present the sorted portfolios approach, as used by Fama and French, and will formally introduce the details of this approach in the next chapter, once we focus on risk factor investing. The following paragraphs will, therefore, only serve as a preliminary limited introduction to the general topic.

The major steps in the sorted portfolios approach are the following:

- At each rebalancing date (i.e., the scheduled interval for rebalancing the components of the portfolio or their weightings), rank all securities in the portfolio according to their ESG score as of that date.
- Create several portfolios by bucketing the securities into consecutive ranges of ESG scores; for instance, sort all securities into five quintile portfolios: securities from the best ESG score up to but not including the 20% percentile of scores form the first quintile portfolio; securities between 20th and 40th percentiles form the second portfolio; and so on. The fifth portfolio would, therefore, contain securities with the worst scores (between 80th percentile and the worst).
- Portfolios are invested between consecutive rebalancing dates. In this example, we choose to rebalance portfolios quarterly.
- Compare the results of each portfolio for performance.

According to the analysis of empirical performance of portfolios between 2010 and 2017 conducted by Roncalli and others, a peculiar regime switch occurred around 2014.[8] Prior to 2014, it was clear that higher ESG scores were tied to lower performances, while, after 2014, this correlation inverted, with higher ESG scores predicting better returns.

Reviewing the portfolio data in a more granular fashion, and splitting the portfolios along the three E, S, and G categories, we can see that the patterns hold true for all three (i.e., the correlation inversion is not driven by only one category). Additionally, the social risk factor has been an even stronger outperformer in the 2016–2017 time frame.[9]

If a geographic dimension is introduced, the pattern of regime switch holds generally true, with some exceptions (notably Japan and Europe Ex-EMU [European Monetary Union]), which show unusual patterns and decoupled factors from the general global trends).

While it is not possible to definitively pinpoint the exact reason for this regime switch, and it is certainly beyond the scope of this textbook, there are many possible drivers that can have contributed to it. Some of these drivers are likely to be related with changed investor perceptions and the way that future impact of ESG considerations is evaluated in corporate financial projections (cash flows and earnings).

Another, and probably more likely, driver for outperformance, however, is technical in nature and is tied to the increased demand for a limited number of securities with good ESG scores, resulting from ESG becoming a popular topic and consideration. This directly increased demand and, as a result, prices.

---

[8] Angelo Drei, Theo Le Guendedal, Frederic Lepetit, Vincent Mortier, Thierry Roncalli, and Takaya Sekine, "ESG Investing in Recent Years: New Insights from Old Challenges," *SSRN Electronic Journal (November 2019),* http://thierry-roncalli.com/download/Alpha_Beta_ESG_Update_2019.pdf
[9] Drei et al., 2019.

Fixed Income Performance. If we look at price sensitivity to ESG scores in equities and debt, we can certainly notice how equities are generally more volatile and reactive than debt is. This is likely due to the perception that ESG is expected to have a direct and strong impact on long-term business strategies and prospects, and therefore be a direct driver for equities pricing, as stock price generally reflects expectations of long-term financial performance.

Debt pricing, on the other hand, reflects creditworthiness over, typically, shorter horizons and is therefore structurally less sensitive to the effects of ESG factors. As a result, ESG strategies in the fixed income space tend to focus on inclusion/exclusion based on binary criteria. Additionally, there is also a growing and dedicated area of fixed income ESG securities that cater to the ESG investor (green bonds, social bonds, etc.).

If we analyze the linkage between ESG scores and credit ratings, we can easily detect what appears to be a certain level of correlation. Higher-rated obligors (investment grade) tend to have better ESG scores when compared to high-yield issues. Before we jump to the conclusion that high ESG scores cause corporations to have higher credit ratings, we must, however, remember the key tenet of statistics: "Correlation does not imply causation." This linkage is likely to be driven by industry representation, with the average technology obligor having higher credit ratings (and incidentally ESG scores) than the typical obligor in the oil and gas industry (who would also happen to have low ESG scores).

EXERCISE 1.B Historical Performance Analysis of S&P Constituents vs. Their ESG Ratings

This and virtually every other exercise in this text relies on the *pandas* data handling package.

```
In [17]:  ▶  import pandas as pd
```

In this exercise, we will use historical data retrieved ahead of time and saved locally as CSV; the *"esg rating history E.csv"* file contains quarterly *Sustainalytics* environmental ratings for each S&P 500 constituent (the same exercises can then be easily repeated for the social and governance rating categories, or for the composite ESG ratings from the same vendor). *"spx-hist. csv"* is simply a table of daily closing prices for the same tickers since 2016.

```
In [18]:  ▶  dfESG = pd.read_csv("esg rating history E.csv", index_col=0)
              dfPx = pd.read_csv("spx-hist.csv", index_col=0)
```

We will need to manipulate the data based on relevant dates; therefore, we convert the index column containing dates into the appropriate data type.

```
In [19]:  ▶  dfESG.index = pd.to_datetime(dfESG.index)
              dfPx.index = pd.to_datetime(dfPx.index)
```

The historical data, unfortunately, has a few gaps where the rating was not available for a particular name. For purposes of this exercise, we assume that the earliest known rating after the gap also holds for the missing periods. Since there are very few instances of such kind, this assumption does not materially influence our conclusions.

```
In [20]:  ▶  dfESG.fillna(method="bfill", inplace=True)
```

(Continued)

Expanding on the approach taken in the previous exercise, we construct quintile series more accurately, considering the changes in ratings from one quarter to the next.

ESG ratings data are quarterly. For each quarter (represented by a single row in *dfESG*), we compute quintile indexes intraquarter following a sequence of steps:

- Isolate and retrieve a subset of daily price data starting from the last trading day of the previous quarter and ending on the last trading day of the quarter in question; this data subset is saved as *dfQtr*.

- Tickers with not enough price data points in that quarter (more than 20 days missing) are excluded from the analysis; all remaining gaps are filled by carrying over available earlier/ later values.

- Tickers are sorted based on ESG rating values in that quarter. *dfQtr* columns are sorted accordingly, accounting for the fact that tickers with price data gaps have been removed.

- *dfQtr* columns are divided by the price on the first date in the table: this normalizes the time series that all start at a value of 1 now. This is needed to ensure that their weights within each bucket are equal and tickers that happen to have high per share prices do not dominate unduly the rest.

- Next, split all tickers into five buckets – the same way as in the previous exercise – representing subgroups of tickers sorted by ESG rating, from best (first quintile) to worst (fifth quintile), and compute average indexes for all five buckets.

As the last step, indexes for the five quintile buckets are merged with the time series for previous quarters by rescaling them to match the levels at the end of the previous quarter. Note that the list of individual tickers that fall into a particular quintile bucket every quarter changes as the ESG ratings change from one quarter to the next.

```
In [21]:   ▶ lstRes = []
              for ii in range(len(dfESG.index) - 1):
                  dfQtr = dfPx.loc[dfESG.index[ii]:dfESG.index[ii + 1]].copy()

                  dfQtr = dfQtr.loc[:, [dfQtr[jj]].isna().sum().sum() < 20 for jj in dfQtr.columns]]
                  dfQtr.fillna(method="ffill", inplace=True)
                  dfQtr.fillna(method="bfill", inplace=True)

                  dfQtr = dfQtr[[jj for jj in dfESG.iloc[ii].sort_values().index.to_list() if jj in dfQtr.columns]]
                  dfQtr = dfQtr.div(dfQtr.iloc[0,:], axis=1)

                  nBucketSize = round(len(dfQtr.columns) / 5)
                  lstSer = []
                  for jj in range(5):
                      tixList = dfQtr.columns[nBucketSize * jj:nBucketSize * (jj + 1)].to_list()
                      seriesX = dfQtr[tixList].sum(axis=1)
                      seriesX /= seriesX[0]
                      lstSer.append(seriesX)
                  dfRes = pd.DataFrame(lstSer).T
                  dfRes.columns = ["Quintile {:d}".format(5 - jj) for jj in range(5)]

                  if len(lstRes):
                      z = lstRes[-1].iloc[-1, :]
                      dfRes = dfRes.mul(z, axis=1)
                      lstRes.append(dfRes.iloc[1:, :])
                  else:
                      lstRes.append(dfRes)
              lstRes = pd.concat(lstRes)
```

The *lstRes* list of data frames is converted into a single data frame of daily index levels for the quintile buckets. Finally, we construct a data frame of annual returns for the quintile indexes by dividing the ending level by the level at the end of the previous year.

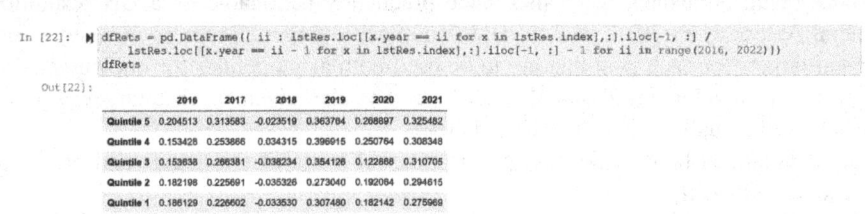

```
In [22]:  M  dfRets = pd.DataFrame({ ii : lstRes.loc[[x.year == ii for x in lstRes.index],:].iloc[-1, :] /
              lstRes.loc[[x.year == ii - 1 for x in lstRes.index],:].iloc[-1, :] - 1 for ii in range(2016, 2022)})
          dfRets
```

Out[22]:

	2016	2017	2018	2019	2020	2021
Quintile 5	0.204513	0.313583	-0.023519	0.363784	0.268897	0.325482
Quintile 4	0.153428	0.253866	0.034315	0.396915	0.250764	0.308348
Quintile 3	0.153838	0.266381	-0.038234	0.354126	0.122868	0.310705
Quintile 2	0.182198	0.225691	-0.035326	0.273040	0.192084	0.294615
Quintile 1	0.186129	0.226602	-0.033530	0.307480	0.182142	0.275969

We can visualize the resulting returns as a single chart. It appears that, while YoY returns for each year since 2016 are markedly different, the impact of ESG rating on the ultimate performance is not conclusive (at least for the large-cap universe of S&P 500). A similarly inconclusive picture emerges when considering composite ESG scores instead of environmental scores alone.

```
In [23]:  M  dfRets.plot(marker='o')
```

Out[23]: <AxesSubplot:>

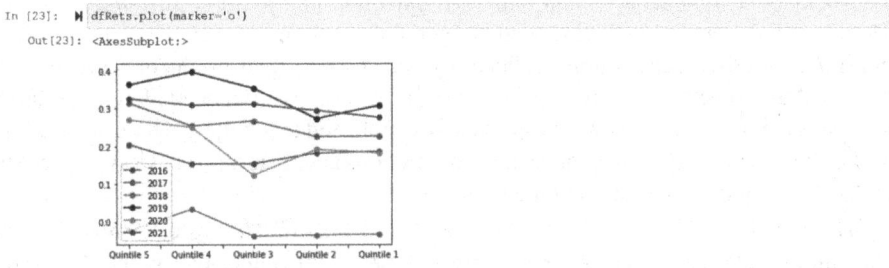

We leave it as (a highly instructive) exercise for the reader to consider repeating this analysis while restricting the universe of stocks to a particular sector within S&P (e.g., to Industrials only).

1.4 SUSTAINABILITY AND SUSTAINABLE FINANCE

Sustainable Development Goals. The Sustainable Development Goals (SDGs) or Global Goals are a collection of 17 interlinked global goals (see Figure 1.5) designed in 2015 by the United Nations General Assembly (UN-GA) to be a "blueprint to achieve a better and more sustainable future for all." The SDGs are included in a UN-GA resolution (Agenda 2030) and are intended to be achieved by the year 2030 by all UN member countries. The SDGs were a follow-up to the previous Millennium Development Goals which ended in 2015.

FIGURE 1.5

The SDGs, besides being published, were also made practically actionable by a UN resolution passed by the General Assembly in 2017, which identified specific targets, progress indicators, and means of achievement targets for each goal that are to be used both as guidelines for implementation and to assess progress toward achieving the goal. Each goal was also given specific target years by which it should be achieved (usually between 2020 and 2030).

The 17 goals are summarized here, with short descriptions of some of the targets and means of achievement (where space allows it):

1. *"End poverty in all its forms everywhere."* The aim of this goal is to end extreme poverty globally by 2030. It is divided in seven targets, including: eradication of extreme poverty; reduction of all poverty by half; implementation of social protection systems; ensuring equal rights to ownership, basic services technology and economic resources; and the building of resilience to environmental, economic, and social disasters.

2. *"End hunger, achieve food security and improved nutrition, and promote sustainable agriculture."* There are eight targets, including: end hunger and improve access to food; end all forms of malnutrition; improve agricultural productivity, sustainable food production systems, and resilient agricultural practices; improve genetic diversity of seeds, cultivated plants, and farmed and domesticated animals; and grow investments, research, and technology. There are also three "means of achievement" targets to address trade restrictions and distortions in world agricultural markets, food commodity markets, and their derivatives.

3. *"Ensure healthy lives and promote well-being for all at all ages."* There are 13 targets, including: reduction of maternal mortality; end all preventable deaths under five years of age; fight communicable diseases; ensure reduction of mortality from non-communicable diseases and promote mental health; prevent and treat substance abuse; reduce road injuries and deaths; grant universal access to sexual and reproductive care, family planning, and education; achieve universal health coverage; and reduce illnesses and deaths from hazardous chemicals and pollution. The "means of achievement" targets are to implement the WHO Framework Convention on Tobacco Control; support research, development, and universal access to affordable vaccines and medicines; increase health financing and support health workforce in developing countries; and improve early warning systems for global health risks.

4. *"Ensure inclusive and equitable quality education and promote lifelong learning opportunities for all."* There are 10 targets, including: free primary and secondary education; equal access to quality pre-primary education; affordable technical, vocational, and higher education; increased number of people with relevant skills for financial success; elimination of all discrimination in education; universal literacy and numeracy; and education for sustainable development and global citizenship. The "means of achievement" targets are to build and upgrade inclusive and safe schools; expand higher education scholarships for developing countries; and increase the supply of qualified teachers in developing countries.

5. *"Achieve gender equality and empower all women and girls."* There are nine targets, including: end all forms of discrimination against all women and girls everywhere; end violence and exploitation of women and girls; eliminate harmful practices such as child, early, and forced marriage, and female genital mutilation; increase value of unpaid care and promoting shared domestic responsibilities; ensure full participation of women in leadership and decision-making; and ensure access to universal reproductive rights and health. The "means of achievement" targets are to foster equal rights to economic resources, property ownership, and financial services for women; promote empowerment of women through technology; and adopt and strengthen policies and enforceable legislation for gender equality.

6. *"Ensure availability and sustainable management of water and sanitation for all."* There are six targets, including: safe and affordable drinking water; end open defecation; and provide access to sanitation and hygiene, improve water quality, wastewater treatment, and safe reuse, increase

water-use efficiency; and ensure freshwater supplies, implement integrated water resource management (IWRM); and protect and restore water-related ecosystems. The "means of achievement" targets are to expand water and sanitation support to developing countries and to support local engagement in water and sanitation management.

7. *"Ensure access to affordable, reliable, sustainable and modern energy for all."* There are five targets, including: universal access to modern energy; increase global percentage of renewable energy; and double the improvement in energy efficiency. The "means of achievement" targets are to promote access to research, technology, and investments in clean energy, and to expand and upgrade energy services for developing countries.

8. *"Promote sustained, inclusive and sustainable economic growth, full and productive employment and decent work for all."* There are 12 targets, including: sustainable economic growth; diversify, innovate, and upgrade for economic productivity; promote policies to support job creation and growing enterprises; improve resource efficiency in consumption and production; full employment and decent work with equal pay; promote youth employment, education, and training; end modern slavery, trafficking, and child labor; protect labor rights and promote safe working environments; promote beneficial and sustainable tourism; universal access to banking, insurance, and financial services. The "means of achievement" targets are to increase aid for trade support and develop a global youth employment strategy.

9. *"Build resilient infrastructure, promote inclusive and sustainable industrialization, and foster innovation."* There are eight targets, including: develop sustainable, resilient, and inclusive infrastructures; promote inclusive and sustainable industrialization; increase access to financial services and markets; upgrade all industries and infrastructures for sustainability; enhance research; and upgrade industrial technologies. The "means of achievement" targets are to facilitate sustainable infrastructure development for developing countries, support domestic technology development and industrial diversification, and provide universal access to information and communications technology.

10. *"Reduce income inequality within and among countries."* There are 10 targets, including: reduce income inequalities; promote universal social, economic, and political inclusion; ensure equal opportunities and end discrimination; adopt fiscal and social policies that promote equality; improve regulation of global financial markets and institutions; enhance representation for developing countries in financial institutions; and promote responsible and well-managed migration policies. The "means of achievement" targets are to provide special and differential treatment for developing countries; encourage development assistance and investment in least-developed countries; and reduce transaction costs for migrant remittances.

11. *"Make cities and human settlements inclusive, safe, resilient, and sustainable."* There are 10 targets, including: provide adequate, safe, and affordable housing and basic services; upgrade slums; provide safe, affordable, accessible, and sustainable transport systems; enhance inclusive and sustainable urbanization and capacity for participatory, integrated, and sustainable human settlement planning and management in all countries; strengthen efforts to protect and safeguard the world's cultural and natural heritage; reduce the number of deaths and the number of people affected by disasters and decrease the direct economic losses relative to global gross domestic product caused by disasters; reduce the adverse per capita environmental impact of cities, including by paying special attention to air quality and municipal and other waste management; provide universal access to safe, inclusive, and accessible green and public spaces; support positive economic, social, and environmental links between urban, peri-urban, and rural areas by strengthening national and regional development planning; increase the number of cities and human settlements adopting and implementing integrated policies and plans toward inclusion, resource efficiency, mitigation, and adaptation to climate change and resilience to disasters; develop and implement, in line with the Sendai Framework for Disaster Risk Reduction 2015–2030, holistic disaster risk managements at all levels; and support least developed countries,

including through financial and technical assistance, in building sustainable and resilient buildings utilizing local materials.

12. *"Ensure sustainable consumption and production patterns."* There are 11 targets, including: implement the 10-Year Framework of Programs on Sustainable Consumption and Production Patterns; achieve sustainable management and efficient use of natural resources; reduce by half the per capita global food waste at the retail and consumer levels and the reduction of food losses along production and supply chains, include post-harvest losses; achieve environmentally sound management of chemicals and all wastes throughout their life cycle; reduce waste generation through prevention, reduction, recycling, and reuse; encourage companies to adopt sustainable practices; promote public procurement practices that are sustainable; and ensure that people everywhere have the relevant information and awareness for sustainable development. The "means of achievement" targets are to support developing countries to strengthen their scientific and technological capacity; develop and implement tools to monitor sustainable development impacts; and remove market distortions, like fossil fuel subsidies, that encourage wasteful consumption.

13. *"Take urgent action to combat climate change and its impacts by regulating emissions and promoting developments in renewable energy."* There are five targets, including: strengthen resilience and adaptive capacity to climate-related disasters; integrate climate change measures into policies and planning; and build knowledge and capacity to meet climate change. The "means of achieving" targets are to implement the UN Framework Convention on Climate Change and to promote mechanisms to raise capacity for planning and management.

14. *"Conserve and sustainably use the oceans, seas, and marine resources for sustainable development."* There are 10 targets, including: reduce marine pollution; protect and restore ecosystems; reduce ocean acidification; develop sustainable fishing; conserve coastal and marine areas; end subsidies contributing to overfishing; and increase the economic benefits from sustainable use of marine resources. The "means of achieving" targets are to increase scientific knowledge, research, and technology for ocean health; support small-scale fishers; and implement and enforce international sea law.

15. *"Protect, restore and promote sustainable use of terrestrial ecosystems, sustainably manage forests, combat desertification, and halt and reverse land degradation, and halt biodiversity loss."* There are nine targets, including: conserve and restore terrestrial and freshwater ecosystems; end deforestation and restore degraded forests; end desertification and restore degraded land; ensure conservation of mountain ecosystems, protect biodiversity and natural habitats; protect access to genetic resources and fair sharing of the benefits; eliminate poaching and trafficking of protected species; prevent invasive alien species on land and in water ecosystems; and integrate ecosystem and biodiversity in governmental planning. The "means of achieving" targets are to increase financial resources to conserve and sustainably use ecosystem and biodiversity; finance and incentivize sustainable forest management; and combat global poaching and trafficking.

16. *"Promote peaceful and inclusive societies for sustainable development, provide access to justice for all, and build effective, accountable and inclusive institutions at all levels."* There are 10 targets, including: reduce violence; protect children from abuse, exploitation, trafficking, and violence; promote the rule of law and ensure equal access to justice; combat organized crime and illicit financial and arms flows; substantially reduce corruption and bribery; develop effective, accountable, and transparent institutions; ensure responsive, inclusive, and representative decision-making; strengthen the participation in global governance; provide universal legal identity; and ensure public access to information and protect fundamental freedoms. The "means of achieving" targets are to strengthen national institutions to prevent violence and combat crime and terrorism and promote and enforce nondiscriminatory laws and policies.

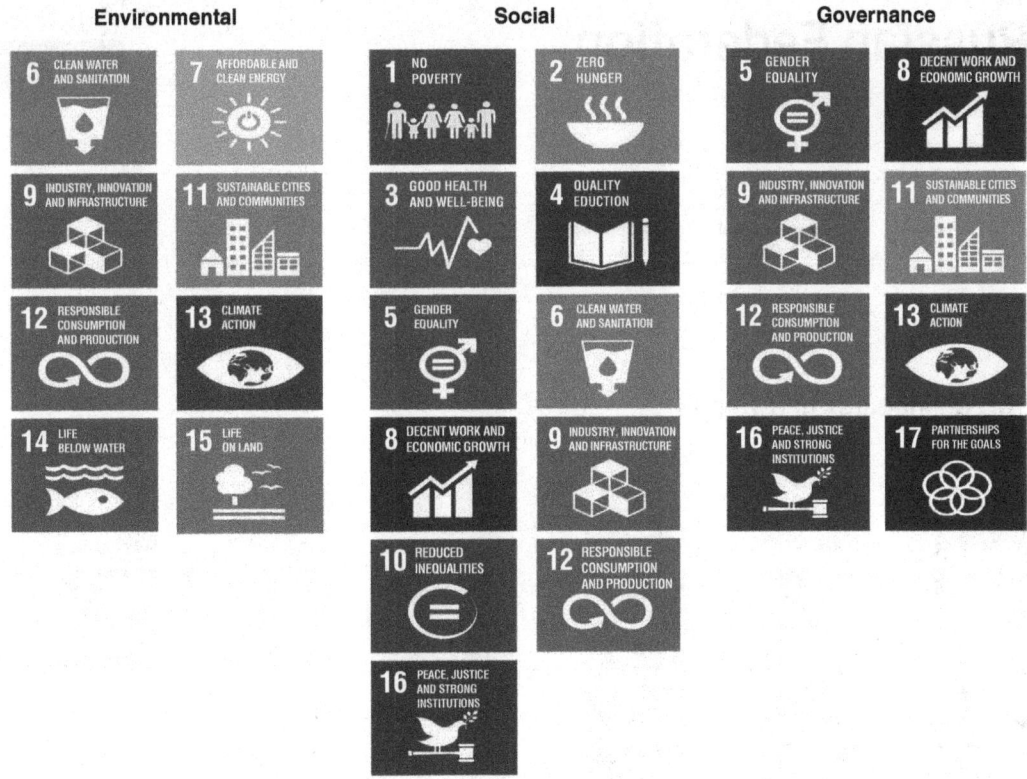

FIGURE 1.6 Sustainable Development Goals grouped by E/S/G category.

17. *"Strengthen the means of implementation and revitalize the global partnership for sustainable development."* There are 19 outcome targets and 24 indicators (not listed here). Sustainable goal 17 targets long-term investments to empower sectors and companies in need, fostering global partnerships and investments. The overarching goal is to improve the following aspects of member countries: energy, infrastructure, transportation systems, IT infrastructure, and communications technologies. This goal also includes long-term investments in developing countries, including foreign direct investment, in critical sectors. These range from sustainable energy, infrastructure, and transport to IT and communications technologies.

Figure 1.6 shows how all 17 goals align to one or more of the ESG dimensions, and thus are extremely relevant for the ESG practitioner and the purposes of this textbook.

The progress that each country is making toward achieving the SDGs can be monitored online by accessing the Sustainable Development Report (SDR).[10] The SDR sets standards not only for emerging and developing countries but also for the industrialized nations. Each country is graded against the 17 sustainable goal dimensions, progress is tracked, and gaps are identified that must be closed in order to achieve the SDGs by 2030.

An example of a high-level dashboard country profile from SDR for the Russian Federation is shown in Figure 1.7 (detailed reports can be downloaded from the website).

---

[10]Sustainable Development Report (June 2, 2022), https://sdgindex.org/

Russian Federation
Eastern Europe and Central Asia

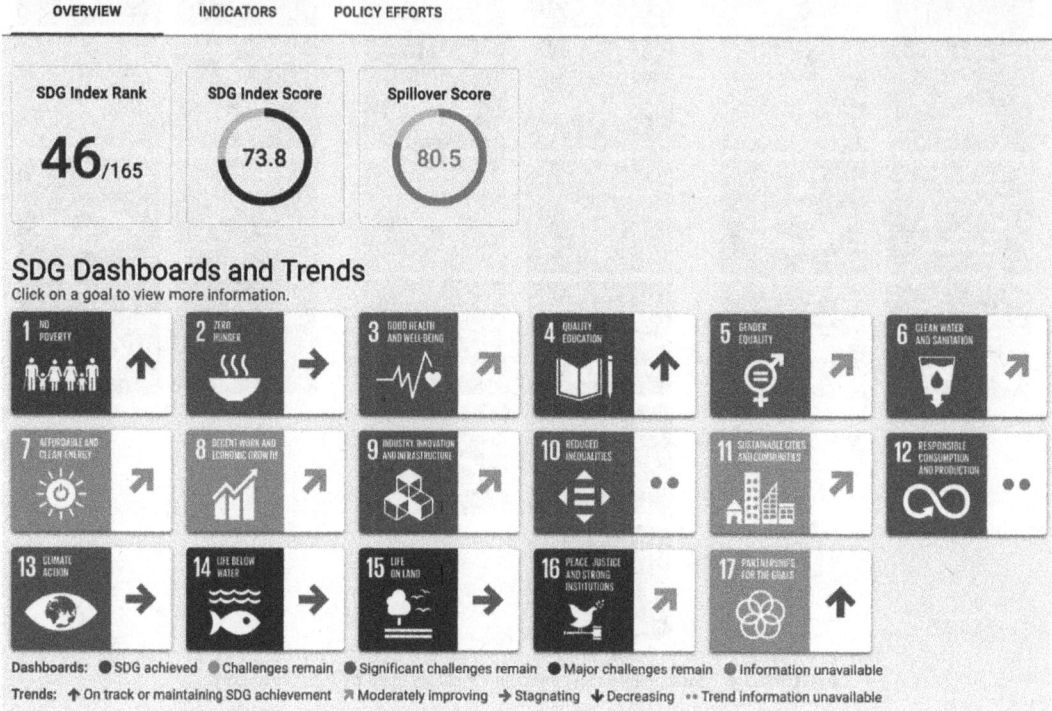

FIGURE 1.7   Sample SDG country profile.

Sustainable Finance and Financing Products. The ecosystem of socially responsible investment funds, including mutual funds, ETFs, and other more specialized investment vehicles, is vast and rapidly expanding, as we mentioned earlier.

These funds display varying ESG strategies, as seen in the previous sections, and may be narrowly focused, thematic funds (e.g., focusing exclusively on investing in climate solutions, water resources, renewable energy, etc.) or wide-spectrum all-encompassing ESG generalists. The performance that they show can either derive from risk factor beta (which we will discuss in detail in the next chapter) or alpha (defined as measure of the active return on an investment, that is, the performance of the investment compared with the relevant market index of reference).

Within the ESG asset management space, independent of the investment strategy pursued, all players face a major concern with issues of greenwashing and false sustainability claims, as we have had a chance to review earlier in this chapter. In order to address these issues and provide assurance to investors that a specific fund does not engage in greenwashing and other similar unethical practices, most funds rely on independent third parties to confirm their SRI credentials and administer sustainable finance labeling, which they can use for marketing and compliance purposes.

An example of one of these third-party labels for sustainable finance is *LuxFLAG*,[11] the Luxembourg Finance Labelling Agency. LuxFLAG is an independent and nonprofit international association that was created by the Luxembourg government, the European Investment Bank, Luxembourg for Finance,

---

[11]https://www.luxflag.org

the Luxembourg Stock Exchange, and other organizations in 2006, with the stated goal to support sustainable finance. The agency's goal is to promote the raising of capital for sustainable investments via the issuing of recognizable labels to eligible investment vehicles. The objective is to ensure investors that all labeled investment vehicles truly invest in the responsible investment sector. The labels are divided by categories, which include microfinance, environment, ESG, climate finance, and green bonds.

In the sustainable finance market, in addition to ESG-focused funds, there is also a specific set of sustainability-linked securities, often in the fixed income space. These include the green bonds and social bonds that we mentioned earlier, as well as other instruments.

Green bonds (also known as climate bonds), for example, are normally used to fund projects that have positive environmental and/or climate benefits. They have to comply with the Green Bond Principles stated by the International Capital Market Association (ICMA), and the capital raised can only be used for prespecified types of projects.

Social bonds are any type of bond instrument where the proceeds will be exclusively applied to finance or refinance in part or in full new and/or existing social projects, aimed at improving the social outcomes for a specific group of citizens.

Sustainability bonds, on the other hand, are bonds where the proceeds will be exclusively used to finance or refinance a combination of green and social projects.

While there is no formal mandatory standardization in the market at the moment, both the regulators and the investors are strongly encouraging adherence to common standards and practices, such as the Green Bond Principles (GBP) in the USA, as issued by ICMA[12] and the social bond principles (see below) as well as other similar frameworks for other sustainable financing products.

Green Bonds. The four core components of ICMA green bonds are:

1. *Use of proceeds.* The cornerstone of a green bond is the utilization of the proceeds of the bond for eligible green projects, which should be appropriately described in the legal documentation of the security. All designated eligible green projects should provide clear environmental benefits, which will be assessed and, where feasible, quantified by the issuer. The issuer is required to identify the set of green and social sustainable categories or list of projects and assets to be financed by the proceeds from the bond issuance. If all or a proportion of the proceeds are or may be used for refinancing, it is recommended that issuers provide an estimate of the share of financing vs. refinancing and, where appropriate, clarify which investments or project portfolios may be refinanced and, to the extent relevant, the expected look-back period for refinanced eligible green projects. The GBP explicitly recognize several broad categories of eligibility for green projects, which contribute to environmental objectives such as climate change mitigation, climate change adaptation, natural resource conservation, biodiversity conservation, and pollution prevention and control.

2. *Process for project evaluation and selection.* The issuer of a green bond should clearly communicate to investors: the environmental sustainability objectives of the eligible green projects; the process by which the issuer determines how the projects fit within the eligible green projects categories; and information on processes by which the issuer identifies and manages perceived social and environmental risks associated with the relevant project(s). Issuers are also encouraged to: position the information communicated above within the context of the issuer's overarching objectives, strategy, policy, and/or processes relating to environmental sustainability; provide information, if relevant, on the alignment of projects with official or market-based taxonomies,

---

[12]"The Green Bond Principles," International Capital Market Association, https://www.icmagroup.org/sustainable-finance/the-principles-guidelines-and-handbooks/green-bond-principles-gbp/

related eligibility criteria, including, if applicable, exclusion criteria; and disclose any green standards or certifications referenced in project selection. The issuer must have a process in place to identify mitigants to known material risks of negative social and/or environmental impacts from the relevant project(s). Such mitigants may include clear and relevant trade-off analysis undertaken and monitoring required where the issuer assesses the potential risks to be meaningful.

3. *Management of proceeds.* The net proceeds of the green bond, or an amount equal to these net proceeds, should be credited to a sub account, moved to a sub portfolio, or otherwise tracked by the issuer in an appropriate manner, and attested to by the issuer in a formal internal process linked to the issuer's lending and investment operations for eligible green projects. So long as the green bond is outstanding, the balance of the tracked net proceeds should be periodically adjusted to match allocations to eligible green projects made during that period. The issuer should make known to investors the intended types of temporary placement for the balance of unallocated net proceeds. The proceeds of green bonds can be managed per bond (bond-by-bond approach) or on an aggregated basis for multiple green bonds (portfolio approach). The GBP encourages a high level of transparency and recommends that an issuer's management of proceeds be supplemented using an external auditor, or other third party, to verify the internal tracking method and the allocation of funds from the green bond proceeds.

4. *Reporting.* Issuers should make, and keep, readily available, up-to-date information on the use of proceeds to be renewed annually until full allocation, and on a timely basis in case of material developments. The annual report should include a list of the projects to which green bond proceeds have been allocated, as well as a brief description of the projects, the amounts allocated, and their expected impact. Where confidentiality agreements, competitive considerations, or many underlying projects limit the amount of detail that can be made available, the GBP recommends that information be presented in generic terms or on an aggregated portfolio basis (e.g., percentage allocated to certain project categories). The GBP recommends the use of qualitative performance indicators and, where feasible, quantitative performance measures and disclosure of the key underlying methodology and/or assumptions used in the quantitative determination. Issuers should refer to and adopt, where possible, the guidance and impact reporting templates provided in the Harmonized Framework for Impact Reporting.[13]

In addition to these four principles, in order for a bond to be considered a sustainability bond, the proceeds of the bond need to be applied in both the green project and social project categories.

Green project categories suggested by the principles include:

- Renewable energy (including production, transmission, appliances, and products)
- Energy efficiency (such as in new and refurbished buildings, energy storage, district heating, smart grids, appliances and products)
- Pollution prevention and control (including reduction of air emissions, greenhouse gas control, soil remediation, waste prevention, waste reduction, waste recycling, and energy/emission-efficient waste to energy)
- Environmentally sustainable management of living natural resources and land use (including environmentally sustainable agriculture; environmentally sustainable animal husbandry; climate-smart farm inputs such as biological crop protection or drip irrigation; environmentally sustainable fishery and aquaculture; environmentally sustainable forestry, including afforestation or reforestation, and preservation or restoration of natural landscapes)
- Terrestrial and aquatic biodiversity conservation (including the protection of coastal, marine, and watershed environments)
- Clean transportation (such as electric, hybrid, public, rail, non motorized, multi modal transportation, infrastructure for clean energy vehicles, and reduction of harmful emissions)

---

[13]"https://www.ifc.org/wps/wcm/connect/3deee5d3-9073-4eff-99fb-b061d7137ff6/Handbook-Harmonized-Framework-for-Impact-Reporting-220420.pdf?MOD=AJPERES&CVID=nx6alip

The Principles

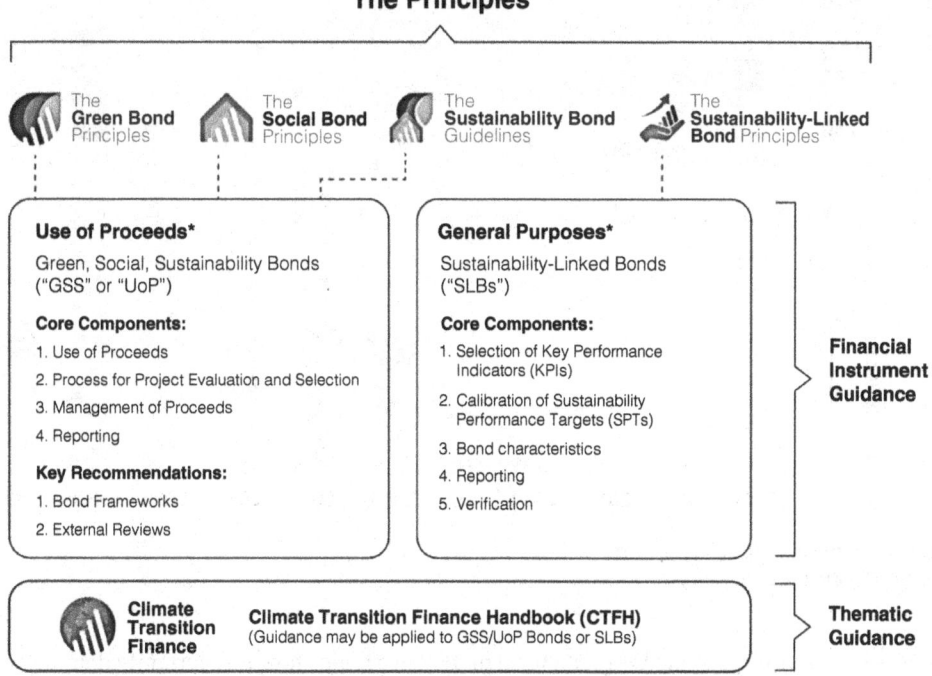

The
Green Bond
Principles

The
Social Bond
Principles

The
Sustainability Bond
Guidelines

The
Sustainability-Linked
Bond Principles

Use of Proceeds*

Green, Social, Sustainability Bonds
("GSS" or "UoP")

Core Components:

1. Use of Proceeds
2. Process for Project Evaluation and Selection
3. Management of Proceeds
4. Reporting

Key Recommendations:

1. Bond Frameworks
2. External Reviews

General Purposes*

Sustainability-Linked Bonds
("SLBs")

Core Components:

1. Selection of Key Performance Indicators (KPIs)
2. Calibration of Sustainability Performance Targets (SPTs)
3. Bond characteristics
4. Reporting
5. Verification

Financial Instrument Guidance

Climate Transition Finance   **Climate Transition Finance Handbook (CTFH)**
(Guidance may be applied to GSS/UoP Bonds or SLBs)

Thematic Guidance

* Under the GBP, SBP, and SBG, an amount equal to the net bond proceeds is dedicated to financing eligible projects (Use of Proceeds Bonds) while under the SLBP, proceeds are primarily for the general purposes of an issuer in pursuit of identified KPIs and SPTs
A bond that combines SLB and Use of Proceeds features should apply guidance for both types of bonds.

FIGURE 1.8   SRI "Principles" framework by ICMA.

- Sustainable water and wastewater management (including sustainable infrastructure for clean and/or drinking water, wastewater treatment, sustainable urban drainage systems, and river training and other forms of flooding mitigation)
- Climate change adaptation (including efforts to make infrastructure more resilient to impacts of climate change, as well as information support systems, such as climate observation and early warning systems)
- Circular economy adapted products, production technologies, and processes (such as the design and introduction of reusable, recyclable, and refurbished materials, components, and products; circular tools and services); and/or certified eco-efficient products
- Green buildings that meet regional, national, or internationally recognized standards or certifications for environmental performance

A very useful online resource for tracking the state of the climate bonds market is represented by the Climate Bonds Initiative, (https://www.climatebonds.net/) an international not-for-profit organization focused on market intelligence (reporting on green bond market evolution, sizing the climate bonds universe, demonstrating green infrastructure pipelines), developing a trusted standard (Climate Bonds Standard and Certification Scheme labeling for bonds), and providing policy models and advice (developing policy proposals). According to the latest published report from 2021, as shown in Figure 1.9, green bonds still are the dominating issuance in the GSS (green, social, and sustainable) space, although the growth of social and sustainable (the latter being a combination of green and social) has been very rapid in the last three years.

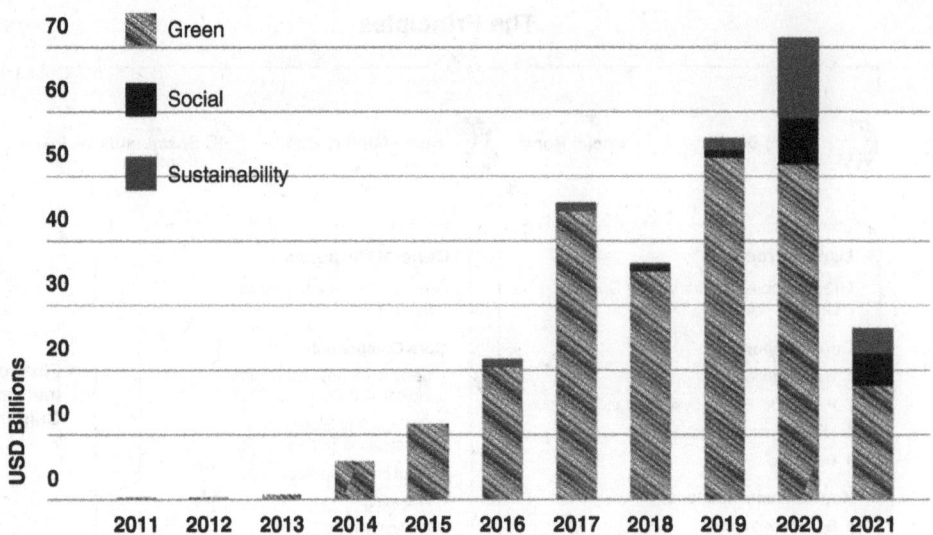

FIGURE 1.9   GSS volumes to Q1, 2021.
Source: Climate Bonds Initiative

If we turn our focus to the US green bond market, we notice how it is currently dominated by agency mortgage-backed securities (MBS, under the ABS, or asset-backed securities, issuer type), and US municipal bonds (aka munis, categorized either as local government or government-backed entities issuer types). The agency MBS bonds are mostly issued by Fannie Mae, with the proceeds used for financing green mortgage loans.

Figure 1.10 shows us how the market has evolved in the last eight years and how the different types of issuances percentages have changed.

Overall, the market for green bonds has been very strong, and is characterized by very high demand from investors, with most new issuance being oversubscribed. This has led to several new funds launching in recent years, with the goal of focusing their investment activities exclusively in green bonds. Some of these funds are specifically designed to track the newly established green bond indices, such as the MSCI Global Green Bond Index or the S&P Green Bond Index, or other similar ones that are being created at more granular levels.

If we analyze the average option-adjusted spreads (OAS) for green bonds and compare it to average OAS of a non-green benchmark, it is evident how the difference has been consistently negative over time, as shown conclusively by the findings of Ben Slimane, Mahtani, and da Fonseca. in 2021.[14] To clarify, this means that green bonds are, on average, priced slightly higher than equivalent non-green bonds, as summarized by Table 1.3.

Social Bonds. This category of bonds, as briefly introduced earlier, includes any type of bond instruments where the proceeds of the issuance will be exclusively applied to social projects that align with the four core components of the social bonds principles (SBP), in a similar way as discussed for the green bonds.

[14] Mohamed Ben Slimane, Vivek Mahtani, and Dany da Fonseca, "Facts and Fantasies about the Green Bond Premium," ResearchGate (November 2020), DOI:10.13140/RG.2.2.19600.84486.

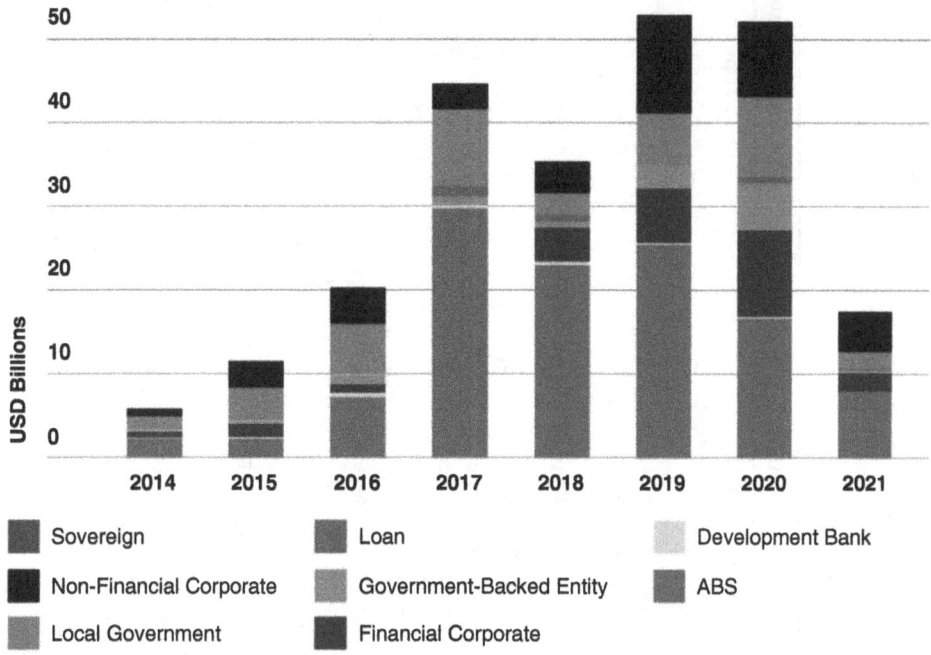

FIGURE 1.10 Evolution of the US green bond market.
Source: Climate Bonds Initiative

The four core components of SBP are:

1. *Use of proceeds.* The cornerstone of a social bond is the utilization of the proceeds of the bond for eligible social projects, which should be appropriately described in the legal documentation of the security. All designated eligible social projects should provide clear social benefits, which will be assessed and, where feasible, quantified by the issuer. In the event that all or a proportion of the proceeds are or may be used for refinancing, it is recommended that issuers provide an estimate of the share of financing vs. refinancing and, where appropriate, also clarify which investments or project portfolios may be refinanced, and, to the extent relevant, the expected look-back period for refinanced eligible social projects. Social projects directly aim to address or mitigate a specific social issue and/or seek to achieve positive social outcomes especially, but not exclusively, for a target population(s). A social issue threatens, hinders, or damages the well-being of society or a specific target population.

2. *Process for project evaluation and selection.* The issuer of a social bond should clearly communicate to investors: the social objectives of the social projects; the process by which the issuer determines how the projects fit within the eligible social project categories; and complementary information on processes by which the issuer identifies and manages perceived social and environmental risks associated with the relevant project(s). Issuers are also encouraged to: position the information communicated above within the context of the issuer's overarching objectives, strategy, policy, and/or processes relating to social sustainability; provide information on the related eligibility criteria, including, if applicable, exclusion criteria, and also disclose any social standards or certifications referenced in project selection; and have a process in place to identify mitigants to known material risks of negative social and/or environmental impacts from the

TABLE 1.3 Overview of GB pricing in the literature

Study	Market	#GBs	Universe	Period	Method	Premium estimate
Bachelet et al. (2019)	Secondary	89	Global	2013–2017	OLS model	2.1 to 5.9 bps
Baker et al. (2018)	Secondary	2,083	US Municipals	2010–2016	OLS model	−7.6 to −5.5 bps
		19	US Corporates	2014–2016		
Bour (2019)	Secondary	95	Global	2014–2018	Fixed effects model	−23.2 bps
Ehlers and Packer (2017)	Primary	21	EUR & USD	2014–2017	Yield compraison	−18 bps
Fatica et al. (2019)	Primary	1,397	Global	2007–2018	OLS model	−18 bps
Gianfrate and Peri (2019)	Primary	121	EUR	2013–2017	Propensity score matching	−11 to −5 bps
	Secondary	70–118		3 dates in 2017		
Hachenberg and Schiereck (2018)	Secondary	63	Global	August 2016	Panel data regression	Not significant
Hyun et al. (2020)	Secondary	60	Global	2010–2017	Fixed effects GLS model	Not significant
Kapraun and Scheins (2019)	Primary	1,513	Global	2009–2018	Fixed effects model	−18 bps
	Secondary	769				+10 bps
Karpf and Mandel (2018)	Secondary	1,880	US Municipals	2010–2016	Oaxaca-Blinder decomposition	+7.8 bps
Larcker and Watts (2019)	Secondary	640	US Municipals	2013–2018	Matching & Yield comparison	Not significant
Lau et. al. (2020)	Secondary	267	Global	2013–2017	Two-way fixed effects method	−1.2 bps
Nanayakkara and Colombage (2019)	Secondary	43	Global	2016–2017	Panel data with hybrid model	−62.7 bps
Ostlund (2015)	Secondary	28	Global	2011–2015	Yield comparaison	Not significant
Partridge and Medda (2018)	Primary	521	US Municipals	2013–2018	Yield curve analysis	−4 bps
	Secondary					small but below 0
Preclaw and Bakshi (2015)	Secondary	Index	Global	2014–2015	OLS model	−16.7 bps
Schmitt (2017)	Secondary	160	Global	2015–2017	Fixed effects model	−3.2 bps
Zerbib (2019)	Secondary	110	Global	2013–2017	Fixed effects model	−1.8 bps

Source: Ben Slimane et al., (2021) / Mohamed Ben Slimane

relevant project(s). Such mitigants may include clear and relevant trade-off analysis undertaken and monitoring required where the issuer assesses the potential risks to be meaningful.

3. *Management of proceeds*. The net proceeds of the social bond, or an amount equal to these net proceeds, should be credited to a sub account, moved to a sub portfolio, or otherwise tracked by the issuer in an appropriate manner, and attested to by the issuer in a formal internal process linked to the issuer's lending and investment operations for social projects. So long as the social bond is outstanding, the balance of the tracked net proceeds should be periodically adjusted to match allocations to eligible social projects made during that period. The issuer should make known to investors the intended types of temporary placement for the balance of unallocated net proceeds. The proceeds of social bonds can be managed per bond (bond-by-bond approach) or on an aggregated basis for multiple social bonds (portfolio approach). The SBP encourages a high level of transparency and recommend that an issuer's management of proceeds be supplemented using an external auditor, or other third party, to verify the internal tracking method and the allocation of funds from the social bond proceeds.

4. *Reporting*. Issuers should make, and keep, readily available, up-to-date information on the use of proceeds to be renewed annually until full allocation, and on a timely basis in the case of material developments. This annual report should include a list of the projects to which social bond proceeds have been allocated, as well as a brief description of the projects, the amounts allocated, and their expected impact. Where confidentiality agreements, competitive considerations, or many underlying projects limit the amount of detail that can be made available, the SBP recommends that information be presented in generic terms or on an aggregated portfolio basis (e.g., percentage allocated to certain project categories). Transparency is of particular value in communicating the expected and/or achieved impact of projects. The SBP recommends the use of qualitative performance indicators and, where feasible, quantitative performance measures (e.g., number of beneficiaries, especially from target populations) and disclosure of the key underlying methodology and/or assumptions used in the quantitative determination. Issuers should refer to and adopt, where possible, the guidance and impact reporting templates provided in the Harmonized Framework for Impact Reporting for Social Bonds. The use of a summary, which reflects the main characteristics of a social bond or a social bond program and illustrates its key features in alignment with the four core components of the SBP, may help inform market participants.

The types of projects that are covered by the principles must fall into one or more of the following categories:

- Affordable basic infrastructure (e.g., clean drinking water, sewers, sanitation, transport, energy)
- Access to essential services (e.g., health, education and vocational training, healthcare, financing, and financial services)
- Affordable housing
- Employment generation, and programs designed to prevent and/or alleviate unemployment stemming from socioeconomic crises, including through the potential effect of SME financing and microfinance
- Food security and sustainable food systems (e.g., physical, social, and economic access to safe, nutritious, and sufficient food that meets dietary needs and requirements; resilient agricultural practices; reduction of food loss and waste; and improved productivity of small-scale producers)

- Socioeconomic advancement and empowerment (e.g., equitable access to and control over assets, services, resources, and opportunities; equitable participation and integration into the market and society, including reduction of income inequality)

Examples of target populations include, but should not be limited to, those that are in one or more of the following conditions:

- Living below the poverty line
- Excluded and/or marginalized populations and/or communities
- People with disabilities
- Migrants and/or displaced persons
- Undereducated
- Underserved, owing to a lack of quality access to essential goods and services
- Unemployed
- Women and/or sexual and gender minorities
- Aging populations and vulnerable youth
- Other vulnerable groups, including as a result of natural disasters.

Concluding this introductory chapter, we reiterate that the ESG concept, as well as its associated universe of financial products, continues to evolve rapidly. Therefore, the overview above should not be viewed as a static and comprehensive picture but a point-in-time snapshot that requires constant updates. Nevertheless, we believe that the exposition provided here correctly portrays the fundamentals of ESG and lays the groundwork for further analysis and observation. Equipped with this overview, interested readers will be capable of updating and refining it on their own, going forward.

CHAPTER 2

Factor Investing and Smart Beta

ESG concepts introduced in the previous chapter lend themselves naturally to systematic investing practices. "ESG" may, in fact, be easily perceived as a family of *risk factors,* that is, quantifiable characteristics that, when defined in a particular manner, help explain the differences in securities' returns and attribute those differences to specific internal characteristics. Before we proceed to discuss ESG-associated risk factors, however, it is useful to set the stage by introducing relevant definitions and basic principles.

2.1 INDEX CONSTRUCTION BASICS

Definition of an Index. Consider a portfolio of (up to) N securities. Every period t (e.g., every day) a w_{it} portion of the portfolio is invested in security $i = 1, \ldots, N$. These portions add up to 100%:

$$\sum_{i=1}^{N} w_{it} = 1$$

During each period, security i earns return r_{it}. Then, at the end of the period (end of the day), the total value of the portfolio is

$$I_t = I_{t-1} \sum_{i=1}^{N} w_{it} \left(1 + r_{it}\right)$$

We define our "index" as the value of this portfolio I_t.

Note that we end up with different indexes if we choose to interpret "return" r_{it} differently: we can differentiate between a "price return" index, where

$$r_{it} = \frac{P_{it}}{P_{i,t-1}} - 1$$

and a "total return" index, where the numerator above includes any distributions, such as cash dividends.

For simplicity, we are omitting here a discussion of index adjustments for stock splits, stock dividends, and the like. These adjustments are reasonably straightforward; commercial indexes' methodology documentation usually explains in detail how such adjustments are handled by any particular index.[1]

Note also the convention we use here: w_{it} is the portfolio weight of security i during period t. It is more common in literature to use w_{it} to denote the weight held in period $i+1$ (but determined on previous day's close, in period i). This is just a matter of convention, of course, but we are pointing this out now so that it does not become a source of confusion/lurking bugs in the future.

Finally, we could, of course, define r_{it} as a logarithmic rather than an arithmetic return; the discussion which follows remains applicable to both.

Numerous choices exist for how w_{it} can be determined; the richness of these choices leads to the richness of the indexes' universe, even for the same underlying portfolio of securities. Let us start by defining the simplest (and most common) traditional choices.

Equal-Weighted Index. In this type of index, all securities have the same weights:

$$w_{it} = 1/N.$$

Many popular equity indexes publish equal-weighted versions.[2]

Market Cap-Weighted Index. Weights are chosen proportional to each stock's market capitalization (in practice, float). This is likely the most popular weighting scheme on offer. Examples of this type include the S&P 500, NASDAQ, EURO STOXX 50, and similar.

Price-Weighted Index. For this type of index, weights are proportional to the individual share price:

$$w_{it} = \frac{P_{i,t-1}}{\sum_{j=1}^{N} P_{j,t-1}}$$

(We must recall that prices at the end of period t P_{it} are not known yet when w_{it} are being determined, which is *before* period i). An example of this kind of index methodology is the Dow-Jones Industrial Average Index (DJIA).

2.2 SMART BETA INDEXES

Traditionally, index construction focused on the selection criteria for the appropriate universe: for example, "N largest (by market capitalization) stocks traded in the US market" or "N most liquid stocks," and so on. (In practice, inclusion/exclusion of specific stocks may not be 100% rule based but rather determined by a committee.) Once the universe of underlying stocks had been determined, one of the simpler weighting schemes discussed above would be applied.

As an alternative to the simple methodologies for index building that we have seen above, many other systematic weighting schemes have been devised over time (of varying complexity). The term *smart beta* is often defined and interpreted loosely in practice to some of these alternative weighting methods. Here we will refer to indexes that rely on systematic weight rebalancing as smart beta indexes.

Background: Definition of Alpha and Beta. The terms *alpha* and *beta* refer to the coefficients in

$$r_{it} = \alpha + \beta r_{Mt} + \varepsilon_t$$

---

[1] For an example of this, please refer to example from S&P Dow Jones Indices, *Equity Indices Policies and Practices Methodology* (August 2021), https://www.spglobal.com/spdji/en/documents/methodologies/methodology-sp-equity-indices-policies-practices.pdf

[2] Example: S&P 500 Equal Weight Index, https://www.spglobal.com/spdji/en/indices/equity/sp-500-equal-weight-index/#overview

where r_{Mt} refers to a broad *market portfolio* return and ε_t to an unbiased idiosyncratic term. This definition expands on (and is inspired by) the Nobel prize-winning Capital Asset Pricing Model (CAPM) theory of Sharpe et al.

Beta represents the contribution of the broad market to the return of a specific security in question, while alpha represents excess return specific to the security. Alternative specifications are also common, where risk-free rate is subtracted from both r_{it} and r_{Mt} before estimating the linear relationship above.

Furthermore, subsequent (Nobel prize-winning) studies, including those of Fama and French, have demonstrated that broad market r_{Mt} is not the only source of returns that is not idiosyncratic to the security. To account for those, beta terms for other identifiable risk factors are added to the r_{it} equation above. Subsequent sections discuss the introduction of these "factors" in more detail.

Low-Volatility Indexes. A common category of systematically rebalanced indexes (that we refer to here as "smart beta") are "low-volatility" indexes. Probably the simplest version of a low-volatility index is an index that assigns weights that are inversely proportional to the constituent stocks' volatilities:

$$w_{it} = 1 / \sigma_{it}.$$

A commercially available index implementing this approach is the S&P Low Volatility Index.[3]

EXERCISE 2.A   Constructing a Low-Volatility Index

This section continues a series of exercises that leverage *Jupyter* notebooks to demonstrate a particular topic. The reader is encouraged to follow along by running relevant cells in the accompanying notebook.

We start by loading the relevant packages:

```
In [9]:    from datetime import datetime
           import pandas as pd
           import pandas_datareader.data as pdr
           import matplotlib.pyplot as plt

           plt.rcParams["figure.dpi"] = 100
```

We make use of the *pandas-datareader* package to load historical stock prices from Yahoo. *pandas-datareader* is a handy utility that supports a number of free-access data sources for historical data.[4]

In this exercise, we will use several pharma stocks (S&P Pharmaceutical sub-industry index members):

```
In [10]:   tickers = ["JNJ", "MRK", "PFE", "BMY", "CTLT", "LLY", "VTRS", "PRGO", "ZTS"]
           dfPx = pdr.DataReader(tickers, "yahoo", start=datetime(2000, 1, 1))["Adj Close"]
```

(Continued)

---

[3] S&P Low Volatility Index, HSBC, https://www.sec.gov/Archives/edgar/data/83246/000114420412056127/v758274-1_fwp.pdf
[4] Please refer to its documentation for details: https://pydata.github.io/pandas-datareader/index.html

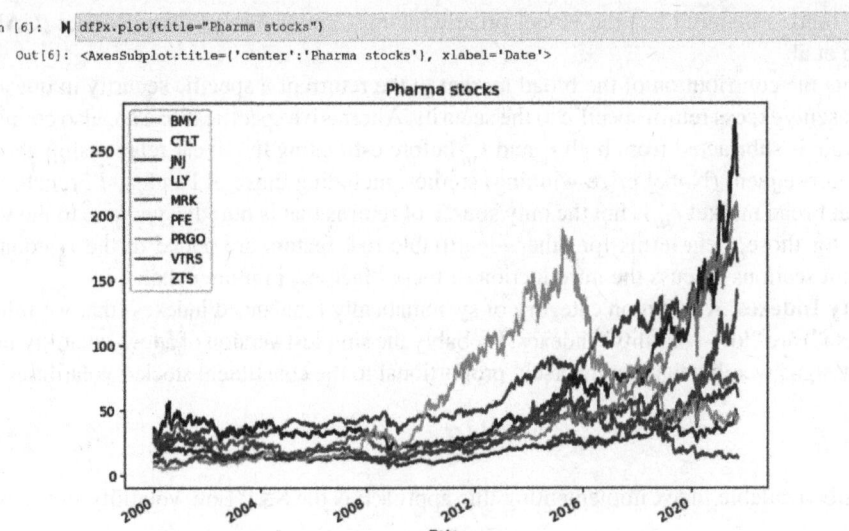

```
In [6]:  ▶  dfPx.plot(title="Pharma stocks")

Out[6]:  <AxesSubplot:title={'center':'Pharma stocks'}, xlabel='Date'>
```

First, we ensure that we keep only stocks with sufficiently long data history, and calculate daily returns:

```
In [11]:  ▶  dfPx = dfPx.loc[:, [dfPx[[ii]].isna().sum().sum() < 100 for ii in dfPx.columns]]
             dfPx.fillna(method="ffill", limit=3, inplace=True)
             dfRets = dfPx.pct_change().dropna()
```

We then compute standard deviations on a rolling window for each stock; note the shift in date index to accommodate our convention: weights w_{it} of securities held during day t are based on market information available at the end of the previous period; realized volatilities are calculated on a rolling 200-day window up to an including the previous day $t - 1$.

Weights are collectively scaled to sum up to 100%:

```
In [12]:  ▶  dfStds = dfRets.rolling(200).std().dropna()
             dfW = 1 / dfStds.shift(1)
             dfW = dfW.div(dfW.sum(axis=1), axis=0)
```

Finally, we construct the index series by cumulating each day's returns (the index starts at a conventionally chosen value of 100 on the first day):

```
In [13]:  ▶  tsIndex = 100 * (1 + (dfW * dfRets).sum(axis=1)).cumprod()[dfW.index.min():]
             tsIndex.plot()

Out[13]:  <AxesSubplot:xlabel='Date'>
```

A simple low-volatility index constructed here may be viewed as a simplified version of an "equal risk contribution" portfolio.[5] Several other volatility-minimizing approaches to index construction are possible; these (and many other indexes that do not minimize volatility, of course) often require that weights be derived by repeatedly solving some optimization problem.

Optimization-Driven Indexes. An example of a portfolio with weights derived via an optimization problem is the Global Minimum Variance index:

$$w = argmin \ \frac{1}{2}\sum_{i,j=1}^{N}\Sigma_{ij}w_iw_j \quad s.t.\sum_{i=1}^{N}w_i = 1$$

It can be shown that the optimal solution to the above is a vector where weights are proportional to the sum of rows of Σ^{-1}: $const * \Sigma^{-1} 1_N$.

It is common to introduce additional constraints on the weights in the optimization: To make the portfolio long-only (weights are required to be nonnegative), we need to require a minimum Herfindahl index level, or minimum representation constraints by sector:

$$\kappa_{j,-} \leq \sum_{i\in K_j}w_i \leq \kappa_{j,+}$$

The Herfindahl (or Herfindahl-Hirschman) index is a popular measure of concentration defined as:

$$HHI = \sum_{i=1}^{N}w_i^2$$

Its inverse may be interpreted as the "effective number of members" in the index.

Another noteworthy systematic allocation approach produces the *most diversified portfolio*:

$$w = argmax \ln D(\circ) \quad s.t.\sum_{i=1}^{N}w_i = 1, \ 0 \leq w_i \leq 1,$$

$$D(w) = \frac{\sum_{i=1}^{N}w_i\sigma_i}{\sqrt{\sum_{i,j=1}^{N}\Sigma_{ij}w_iw_j}}$$

This portfolio maximizes the "diversification ratio" $D(w)$, defined as the ratio between the *weighted average volatility* (numerator) and the *total portfolio volatility* (denominator). The *most diversified portfolio* concept was introduced by Choueifaty and Coignard (2008).

Sharpe Ratio Maximization. Perhaps the most common and popular class of smart beta indexes is the Sharpe ratio maximization, which determines weights by maximizing the portfolio's Sharpe ratio under a variety of constraints. These approaches differ greatly in the assumptions being made about the future expected return and future volatility (particularly the former). It is common to leverage the factor investing framework (discussed further in later sections) to arrive at the Sharpe ratio numerator estimates.[6]

---

[5] See, for instance, "Risk Parity," https://en.wikipedia.org/wiki/Risk_parity
[6] See Noël Amenc, Felix Goltz, and Ashish Lodh, "Choose Your Betas: Benchmarking Alternative Equity Index Strategies," *Journal of Portfolio Management* 39 (1) (2012): 88–111.

EXERCISE 2.B   Brute-Force Sharpe Ratio Optimization

Here, we will make a *rather strong and inaccurate assumption* that future expected returns of individual index member securities are well predicted by observed average returns over a rolling past window. Under this simplified assumption, we can use brute-force optimization to derive index weights every day.

We will use an off-the-shelf optimization routine from *scipy*:

```
In [14]:  ▶ from scipy import optimize
            import numpy as np
```

The objective function defines the Sharpe ratio as a function of weights w (parameter C is the historical sample covariance matrix and M is a vector of average historical returns):

```
In [33]:  ▶ def fnObj(w, C, M, Rf=.0):
                return float((Rf - w.dot(M)) / np.sqrt(w.dot(C).dot(w.T)))
```

We now create an empty *dataframe* to house member weights for each day and then run the optimization for each day, based on a rolling historical window:

```
In [98]:  ▶ dfW0 = pd.DataFrame(index=dfRets.index, columns=dfRets.columns)
            cons = [{"type": "eq", "fun": lambda x: np.sum(x) - 1},
                    {"type": "ineq", "fun": lambda x: np.min(x)}]
            for ii in range(200, dfRets.shape[0]):
                df = dfRets[(ii - 200):ii]
                res = optimize.minimize(fnObj, np.ones(df.shape[1]) / df.shape[1],
                                        args=(df.cov().values, df.mean().values), constraints=cons)
                dfW0.iloc[ii, :] = res.x if res.success else None
```

An explicit loop over row numbers is rather inelegant, but we failed to come up with a functional style code alternative.

We now can calculate the index series using weights, very much in the same way as in the previous exercise:

```
In [99]:  ▶ dfW0.dropna(inplace=True)
            tsIndex0 = 100 * (1 + (dfW0 * dfRets).sum(axis=1)).cumprod()[dfW0.index.min():]
```

Finally, we plot both indexes side by side:

```
In [26]:  ▶ pd.merge(tsIndex.rename("loVol"), tsIndex0.rename("maxSR"),
                      left_index=True, right_index=True).plot(style=[".", "-"])

   Out[26]: <AxesSubplot:xlabel='Date'>
```

Table 2.1 illustrates the difference in weights derived by following the different systematic approaches mentioned above. The underlying member universe used for all is the set of member stocks of EURO STOXX 50 as of January 2010.

TABLE 2.1 Difference in weights derived by systematic approaches.

	Equal-Weighted	Capitalization-Weighted	Global Minimum Variance (Unconstrained)	Most Diversified Portfolio (Unconstrained)	Global Minimum Variance (10% Upper Bound)	Most Diversified Portfolio (10% Upper Bound)	Global Minimum Variance (5% Upper Bound)	Most Diversified Portfolio (5% Upper Bound)
Total	2	6.1	–	–	–	–	5.0	–
Banco Santander	2	5.8	–	–	–	–	–	–
Telefonica SA	2	5.0	31.2	–	10.0	–	5.0	5.0
Sanofi-Aventis	2	3.6	12.1	15.5	10.0	10.0	5.0	5.0
E.On AG	2	3.6	–	–	–	–	–	1.4
BNP Paribas	2	3.4	–	–	–	–	–	–
Siemens AG	2	3.2	–	–	–	–	–	–
BBVA (Bilb-Viz-Arg)	2	2.9	–	–	–	–	–	–
Bayer AG	2	2.9	–	3.7	2.2	5.0	5.0	5.0
ENI	2	2.7	–	–	–	–	–	–
GDF Suez	2	2.5	–	4.5	–	5.4	5.0	5.0
BASF SE	2	2.5	–	–	–	–	–	–
Allianz SE	2	2.4	–	–	–	–	–	–
Unicredit Spa	2	2.3	–	–	–	–	–	–
Soc. Generale	2	2.2	–	3.9	–	3.7	–	5.0
Unilever NV	2	2.2	11.4	10.8	10.0	10.0	5.0	5.0
France Telecom	2	2.1	14.9	10.2	10.0	10.0	5.0	5.0
Nokia OYJ	2	2.1	–	4.5	–	4.8	–	5.0
Daimler AG	2	2.1	–	–	–	–	–	–
Deutsche Bank AG	2	1.9	–	–	–	–	–	–
Deutsche Telekom	2	1.9	–	2.6	5.7	3.7	5.0	5.0
Intesa Sanpaolo	2	1.9	–	–	–	–	–	–
AXA	2	1.8	–	–	–	–	–	–
Arcelor Mittal	2	1.8	–	–	–	–	–	–
SAP AG	2	1.8	21.0	11.2	10.0	10.0	5.0	5.0
RWE AG (Neu)	2	1.7	2.7	–	7.0	–	5.0	–
ING Groep NV	2	1.6	–	0.4	–	–	–	–
Danone	2	1.6	1.9	1.8	8.7	3.3	5.0	5.0
Iberdrola SA	2	1.6	–	–	5.1	–	5.0	1.2

(Continued)

TABLE 2.1 (*Continued*)

	Equal-Weighted	Capitalization-Weighted	Global Minimum Variance (Unconstrained)	Most Diversified Portfolio (Unconstrained)	Global Minimum Variance (10% Upper Bound)	Most Diversified Portfolio (10% Upper Bound)	Global Minimum Variance (5% Upper Bound)	Most Diversified Portfolio (5% Upper Bound)
Enel	2	1.6	–	–	–	–	5.0	2.9
Vivendi SA	2	1.6	2.8	4.5	10.0	5.9	5.0	5.0
Anheuser-Busch INB	2	1.6	0.2	10.9	2.1	10.0	5.0	5.0
Assic. Generali Spa	2	1.6	–	–	–	–	–	–
L'Air Liquide	2	1.4	–	–	–	–	5.0	–
Muenchener Rueckve	2	1.3	–	2.1	–	3.1	5.0	5.0
Schneider Electric	2	1.3	–	–	–	–	–	–
Carrefour	2	1.3	1.0	1.3	3.7	2.5	5.0	5.0
Vinci	2	1.3	–	–	–	–	–	–
LVMH Moet Hennessy	2	1.2	–	–	–	–	–	–
Philips Elec (Kon)	2	1.2	–	–	–	–	–	–
L'Oreal	2	1.1	0.8	–	5.5	–	5.0	5.0
Cie de St-Gobain	2	1.0	–	–	–	–	–	–
Repsol YPF SA	2	0.9	–	–	–	–	5.0	–
CRH	2	0.8	–	5.1	–	5.2	–	5.0
Credit Agricole SA	2	0.8	–	–	–	–	–	–
Deutsche Boerse AG	2	0.7	–	–	–	–	–	1.9
Telecom Italia Spa	2	0.7	–	–	–	–	–	2.5
Alstom	2	0.6	–	–	–	–	–	–
Aegon NV	2	0.4	–	–	–	–	–	–
Volkswagen AG	2	0.2	–	7.1	–	7.4	–	5.0
Count of members	50	50	50	50	50	50	50	50

Source: Adapted from Paul Demey, Sébastien Maillard, and Thierry Roncalli, *Risk-Based Indexation*, March 20, 2010. Available at SSRN, https://papers.ssrn.com/sol3/papers .cfm?abstract_id=1582998.

Commercially Available Indexes. Many commercially available indexes (and exchange-traded funds [ETFs] that track them) implement the ideas described in this section. The universe of smart beta products available in the market is constantly changing; a sample as of 2021 is provided in Table 2.2. Please refer to Bloomberg (or a simple Google search) for updates.

TABLE 2.2   An overview of stock selection and weighting decisions of some alternative equity indices.

Index	Stock Selection	Stock Weighting
Indices that change only the selection compared to standard index		
Broad Dividend Achievers[1]	Positive dividend growth	
MSCI High Dividend Yield[2]	High dividend yield, positive dividend-per-share growth, low dividend payout ratio	
FTSE Active Beta Momentum and Value[3]	High price momentum, high book value-to-price ratio, high sales-to-price ratio, high flow-to-a price ratio	Market capitilization (or free float)
Russell High Dividend Yield[4]	Positive free cash flow, positive return on equity, positive forecasted earnings growth, high price momentum, low debt-to-equity ratio, low EPS variability, high dividend yield, high dividend growth	
Russell Defensive[5]	Low leverage, high return on assets, low earnings variability, low total return volatility	
Indices that change only the weighting		
FTSE GWA[6]		Net income, cash, flow, book value
MSCI Value Weighted[7]		Sales, earnings, cash earnings, book value
MSCI Risk Weighted[8]		Inverse of historical variance
MSCI Minimum Volatility[9]	Index universe remains the same as the parent market index	Volatility minimization
S&P 500 Equal-weighted[10]		Equal weighted
FTSE EDHEC-Risk Efficient[11]		Sharpe ratio maximization
FTSE TOBAM Max. Diversified[12]		Maximize diversification ratio
Lyxor SmartIX ERC[19]		Set risk contribution of constituents equal
Indices that change both selection and weighting		
Dow Jones Select Dividend[13]	Positive dividend growth, low dividend payout ratio	Dividend
FTSE RAFI[14]	High sales, high cash flow, high book value, high dividend	Sales, cash flow, book value, dividend
Intellidex[15]	High price momentum, earnings momentum, quality, value, management action	Equal weighted
S&P GIVI[16]	Low market beta	Intrinsic value
S&P 500 High Beta[17]	High market beta	Market beta
S&P 500 Low Volatility[18]	Low volatility	Inverse of volatility

[1]http://www.indxis.com/USBroad.html
[2]http://www.msci.com/products/indices/strategy/risk_premia/hdy/
[3]http://www.ftse.com/Indices/FTSE_ActiveBeta_Index_Series/index.jsp
[4]http://www.russell.com/indexes/data/dividend/russell-high-dividend-yield-indexes.asp
[5]http://www.russell.com/indexes/data/stability/russell-stability-indexes.asp
[6]http://www.ftse.com/indices/FTSE_GWA_Index_Series/index.jsp
[7]http://www.msci.com/products/indices/strategy/risk_premia/value_weighted/
[8]http://www.msci.com/products/indices/strategy/risk_premia/risk_weighted/
[9]http://www.msci.com/products/indices/strategy/risk_premia/minimum_volatility/
[10]http://www.standardandpoors.com/indices/sp-500-equal-weight-index/en/us/?indexId=spusa-500-usdew–p-us-1–
[11]http://www.ftse.com/indices/FTSE_EDHEC-Risk_Efficient_Index_Series/index.jsp
[12]http://www.ftse.com/Indices/FTSE_TOBAM_Maximum_Diversification_Index_Series/index.jsp
[13]https://www.djindexes.com/dividend/
[14]http://www.ftse.com/Indices/FTSE_RAFI_Index_Series/index.jsp
[15]https://indices.nyx.com/fr/directory/intellidex
[16]http://www.standardandpoors.com/indices/sp-givi-global/en/us/?indexId=sp-givi-global
[17]http://www.standardandpoors.com/indices/sp-500-high-beta/en/us/?indexId=spusa-500-usdw-hbp-us-1–
[18]http://www.standardandpoors.com/indices/sp-500-low-volatility/en/us/?indexId=spusa-500-usdw-Iop-us-1–
[19]http://www.ftse.com/Indices/Lyxor%20SmartIX%20ERC%20Equity%20Indices/index.jsp
Source: Amenc, Goltz, and Lodh (2012).

2.3 RISK FACTOR INVESTING

Since the original publication of CAPM theory, it has been demonstrated empirically that certain unobserved variables other than the broad market excess return had significant explanatory power over returns of individual securities. The Arbitrage Pricing Theory of Ross (1976) extends the SML equation to:

$$r_{it} = \alpha + \sum_{j=1}^{M} \beta_{ij} f_{jt} + \varepsilon_t$$

We refer to these unobservable variables f_{jt} as *risk factors*. The list of potential risk factors continues to grow as new risk factors are identified by academic and practitioners' research. It is important to note how these risk factors are assigned economic meaning, as seen below.

Well-Established Risk Factors. Most popular/most commonly quoted risk factors are summarized in Table 2.3 by MSCI.[9]

Naturally, there are many products available in the current market designed to facilitate factor investing. For a (far from exhaustive) example, Table 2.4 summarizes only the factor indexes offered by MSCI.

It is important to note that we here do not take a view on whether some risk factors are generally "beneficial," and therefore higher exposure to those risk factors necessarily leads to portfolio outperformance. This is certainly an area still hotly debated by practitioners and academics alike; a few competing theories provide an economic explanation to the attractiveness of certain factors.

TABLE 2.3 Well-known systematic factors from academic research.

Systematic Factors	What It Is	Commonly Captured by
Value	Highlights the excess returns from stocks that have low pricing if compared to their fundamental values	Price to book ratio, book value, revenues, sales, earnings, cash earnings, net profits, dividends, cash flow
Smaller size (small cap)	Focuses on the excess returns generated by small firms (measured by their market capitalization) when compared to larger companies.	Market cap (full or free float)
Momentum	Shows excess returns tied to companies with strong track records of positive past performance	Relative returns (3-month, 6-month, 12-month, potentially with last month excluded), historical alpha
Lower volatility	Focuses on the excess returns from stocks that have lower volatility, beta, and/or idiosyncratic risk if compared to the market/sector average	Standard deviation (1 yr, 2 yrs, 3 yrs), downside standard deviation, deviation of idiosyncratic returns, beta
Dividend yield	Reflects excess returns generated by firms that have higher dividend yields than average competitors	Dividend yield
Quality	Shows the excess returns that can be attributed to stocks that meet "high-quality" parameters such as low debt ratios, stable earnings growth and other similar indices	ROE, earnings stability dividend growth stability, strength of balance sheet, financial leverage, accounting policies, strength of management, accruals, cash flows

Source: Adapted from Jennifer Bender, Remy Briand, Dimitris Melas, and Raman Aylur Subramanian, "Foundations of Factor Investing," MSCI (December 2013), https://www.msci.com/documents/1296102/1336482/Foundations_of_Factor_Investing.pdf.

TABLE 2.4   MSCI family of factor indices.

Systematic Factors	MCI Indices
Value	MSCI Value Weighted Indexes: Capture value factor by weighting according to four fundamental variables (sales, earnings, cash flow, book value)
Smaller size (small cap)	MSCI Equal Weighted Indexes: Capture low size effect by equally weighting all stocks in a given parent index
Momentum	MSCI Momentum Indexes: Reflect the performance of high-momentum stocks by weighting based on 6- and 12-month momentum scaled by volatility
Lower volatility	MSCI Minimum Volatility Indexes: Reflect empirical portfolio with lowest forecast volatility using minimum variance optimization
	MSCI Risk Weighted Indexes: Capture low-volatility stocks by weighting based on the inverse of historical variance
Dividend yield	MSCI High Dividend Yield Indexes: Select high-dividend stocks with screens for quality and potential yield traps
Quality	MSCI Quality Indexes: Capture high-quality stocks by weighting based on debt to equity, return on equity, and earnings variability

Source: Jennifer Bender et al., 2013 / MSCI

For now, we will not focus on whether particular risk factors outperform others, but rather on the very fact that a set of risk factors is responsible, at least over some time horizon, for a large portion of the security's total return.

Fama-French Factors. Prof. Kenneth R. French maintains a database of key risk factors they have identified and continue to study at https://mba.tuck.dartmouth.edu/pages/faculty/ken.french/data_library.html.

The key risk factors we focus our analyses on are the following four (in addition to the broad market return risk factor of CAPM):

- SMB, or "Small Minus Big," representing a discount associated with firm size. It is computed as the average return on nine small stock portfolios minus the average return on nine big stock portfolios.

- HML, or "High Minus Low," representing a premium associated with "value" investment. It is computed as the average return on two value portfolios minus the average return on two growth portfolios.

- RMW, or "Robust Minus Weak," representing a premium associated with higher profitability. It is computed as the average return on two robust operating profitability portfolios minus the average return on two weak operating profitability portfolios.

- CMA, or "Conservative Minus Aggressive," representing a discount associated with aggressive investment as indicated by total asset growth. It is computed as the average return on two conservative investment (low annual asset growth) portfolios minus the average return on two aggressive investment (high annual asset growth) portfolios.

Fama and French create time series for these risk factors following the general method of portfolio sorting:

- On a given date (start of period), rank all member stocks according to a chosen metric, such as the Px/Book ratio.

- Group all member stocks into K portfolios according to the ranking—for example, into deciles of the ranking.

- Within each portfolio, weights are either equal or proportional to market capitalization.

- At the end of the period, record the returns of these K portfolios. Repeat all steps starting from ranking/grouping for the next period.

Each risk factor series is then constructed as a difference in returns across some of the portfolios (labeled SMB, HML, RMW, CMA above).

You can see the specifics of construction of the relevant series described in https://mba.tuck.dartmouth.edu/pages/faculty/ken.french/Data_Library/f-f_5_factors_2x3.html.

2.4 FAMA-MACBETH REGRESSIONS

Fama-MacBeth regressions are a method of constructing risk premium time series associated with specific risk factors. It is a two-step procedure:

1. For each member security, the time series of its returns are regressed against the time series of risk factors as calculated by Fama and French (previous section). This regression yields factor loadings for each member security (betas of that stock with reference to specific risk factors).
2. For each date in the sample, a cross-sectional regression is performed: Stock returns on a given date are regressed against their factor loadings (betas). This regression yields the risk premia amounts (portions of security returns) associated with each factor on that date.

EXERCISE 2.C   Estimation of Risk Premia Series

We can collect the list of S&P 500 tickers from Wikipedia: the *read_html* function in *pandas* allows us to easily extract all the tables from a particular webpage; the first table on the page contains the needed list of tickers. Prior to reading the table, we download the relevant Wikipedia page by executing the GET method implemented in the *requests* package.

```
In [1]: import pandas as pd
```

```
In [27]: import requests
         wikiPg = requests.get("https://en.wikipedia.org/wiki/List_of_S%26P_500_companies").text
         dfSpx = pd.read_html(wikiPg)[0]

         tickersSpx = dfSpx["Symbol"].tolist()
         tickersSpxMM = dfSpx[dfSpx["GICS Sector"] == "Materials"]["Symbol"].tolist()
```

We can download the full list of SPX tickers or filter them, for instance, by sector, as in the example above.

```
In [3]: import yfinance as yf
```

```
In [11]: dfPx = yf.download(" ".join(tickers), start="2000-01-01")["Adj Close"]
         [*********************100%*********************]  9 of 9 completed
```

In the rest of this example, we will assume that daily stock prices for the S&P 500 constituents beginning in 2000 have been downloaded into the *dfPxAll* data frame (e.g., using the *yfinance* package as shown above).

The *Pandas-datareader* package contains, among other functionalities, a simple utility to download risk factor series from Prof. French's webpage.

```
In [3]: import pandas_datareader.data as pdr
```

```
In [4]: ff = pdr.DataReader("F-F_Research_Data_5_Factors_2x3", "famafrench", start="2000-01-01")[0]
```

The original Fama-French risk factor names cause conflicts for two reasons. The first is that some of the risk factor names (e.g., RF) coincide with some of the tickers in the S&P 500. The second, as we will later use these risk factors in OLS regression formulas, is that some of them include a dash in the risk factor names, which is misinterpreted as a minus sign between two different variables. To resolve these conflicts, we therefore need to slightly correct the names:

```
In [5]: ff.rename(columns=lambda x: "x" + x.replace("-", "_"), inplace=True)
```

We will conduct our regressions at the monthly frequency; we therefore resample the closing price data to monthly and merge with the risk factors' *dataframe*:

```
In [6]: dfMonthly = dfPxAll.resample("M", kind="period").last().pct_change().dropna()
        dfMonthly = dfMonthly.join(ff, how="inner")
        dfMonthly
```

Out[6]:

	MMM	ABT	ABMD	ACN	ATVI	ADBE	AMD	AAP	AES	AFL	...	XLNX	ZBRA	ZBH	ZION	xMkt_RF	xSMB	xHML	xRMW	xCMA	xRF
2006-02	0.017943	0.023870	-0.050228	0.035839	-0.128312	-0.029700	-0.074880	-0.050953	0.015258	-0.012209	...	-0.028763	-0.019765	0.003336	0.048402	-0.30	-0.43	-0.37	-0.50	1.90	0.34
2006-03	0.028537	-0.038705	0.240385	-0.079302	0.103200	-0.093385	-0.142488	0.008482	-0.013873	-0.024216	...	-0.066716	0.013140	-0.022839	0.002545	1.46	3.40	0.55	0.10	-0.40	0.37
2006-04	0.126683	0.013445	0.002326	-0.033256	0.029006	0.121602	-0.024427	-0.034102	-0.005275	0.053401	...	0.086803	-0.112478	-0.069526	0.003626	0.73	-0.85	2.34	1.79	-0.01	0.36
2006-05	-0.015499	-0.000936	0.036350	-0.031648	-0.078224	-0.269643	-0.045131	-0.052213	0.084266	-0.012923	...	-0.057443	-0.110355	-0.037361	-0.019765	-3.57	-2.86	2.39	1.15	1.46	0.43
2006-06	-0.034545	0.021311	-0.032090	0.006039	-0.129969	0.060426	-0.209453	-0.240636	0.002718	-0.009616	...	-0.128846	-0.032569	-0.063253	-0.038134	-0.35	-0.22	0.80	1.33	-0.08	0.40
...	...	...	...	...	...	...	...	...	...	...	...	...	...	...	...	...	...	...	...	...	...
2021-07	-0.003474	0.047534	0.048156	0.080690	-0.123847	0.061454	0.130523	0.033733	-0.085218	0.024972	...	0.035951	0.043419	0.016167	-0.013432	1.27	-4.56	-1.75	5.37	-0.55	0.00
2021-08	-0.008656	0.044553	0.112551	0.059431	-0.014949	0.067677	0.042659	-0.043431	0.007173	0.036492	...	0.038374	0.062790	-0.079366	0.117938	2.90	-0.79	-0.13	-0.26	-1.67	0.00
2021-09	-0.099209	-0.065205	-0.105616	-0.049441	-0.060459	-0.132560	-0.070629	0.034794	-0.043569	-0.080275	...	-0.029565	-0.122196	-0.025635	0.068912	-4.37	1.25	5.09	-1.94	2.08	0.00
2021-10	0.018584	0.095299	0.020030	0.124829	0.010337	0.129646	0.168416	0.079611	0.100745	0.029541	...	0.192132	0.035951	-0.022137	0.017773	6.65	-2.69	-0.44	1.74	-1.48	0.00
2021-11	-0.040610	-0.024207	-0.051982	-0.003874	-0.250544	0.029968	0.317225	-0.021284	-0.064014	0.014573	...	0.271541	0.102688	-0.164338	0.007285	-1.55	-1.74	-0.52	7.38	1.60	0.00

190 rows × 416 columns

Next, we perform the first step of Fama-MacBeth regressions: We regress stock price return time series on risk factors. We rely on the R-inspired "formula" syntax for linear regressions, implemented in the *statsmodels.formula* package:

```
In [7]: import statsmodels.formula.api as smf

In [8]: tickers = dfPxAll.columns.tolist()
        dfTickerLoadings = pd.DataFrame({ii : smf.ols(ii + " ~ xMkt_RF + xSMB + xHML + xRMW + xCMA",
            data=dfMonthly).fit().params for ii in tickers})
        dfTickerLoadings
```

Out[8]:

	MMM	ABT	ABMD	ACN	ATVI	ADBE	AMD	AAP	AES	AFL	...	WY	WHR	WMB	WLTW	WYNN	XEL	XLNX	ZBRA	ZBH	ZION
Intercept	-0.001509	0.005528	0.015776	0.005632	0.010981	0.008077	0.001119	0.000905	-0.003868	0.001017	...	-0.005170	-0.000433	0.000156	0.002573	-0.001225	0.004365	0.006922	0.006347	-0.001260	0.007481
xMkt_RF	0.009075	0.007400	0.009411	0.010176	0.007405	0.013204	0.022125	0.008112	0.011711	0.012674	...	0.012289	0.016317	0.011576	0.008068	0.019254	0.004676	0.009592	0.011865	0.010198	0.008727
xSMB	0.002239	-0.003980	0.015431	-0.000668	-0.002989	-0.002072	0.001519	0.007273	0.000971	-0.001579	...	0.002594	0.004482	0.004448	0.000612	0.010304	-0.003541	0.004825	0.004825	0.000502	0.001466
xHML	-0.001017	-0.004202	-0.009199	-0.002754	-0.004615	-0.001401	-0.007853	-0.001681	-0.002555	0.007065	...	0.005249	0.007170	0.001786	0.001314	0.006149	-0.002444	-0.002501	-0.001850	0.001424	0.019768
xRMW	0.004866	-0.000469	0.002526	0.002785	-0.008699	-0.004045	-0.003610	0.011632	-0.001294	0.000672	...	0.001879	0.006711	-0.000086	-0.001959	0.005122	0.004169	-0.000031	0.001870	-0.003534	-0.009565
xCMA	0.004884	0.004779	0.000513	0.000031	-0.004296	-0.008523	0.001650	0.022214	0.004132	0.000401	...	-0.002602	0.006977	-0.006100	-0.001650	-0.006776	0.004899	-0.062091	-0.007417	0.001453	-0.003960

6 rows × 410 columns

We now merge the loadings *dataframe* with the original stock return data to prepare the panel for the second-stage regressions:

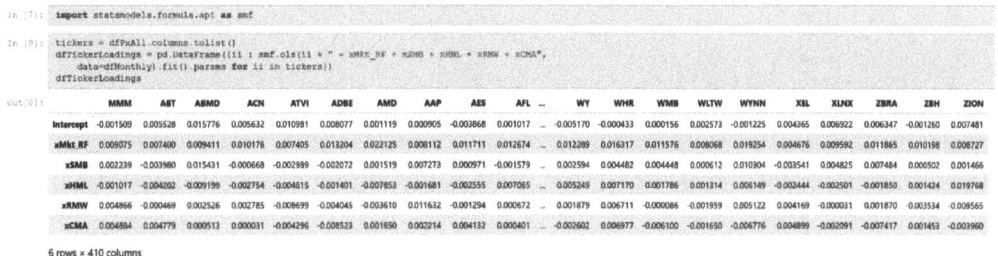

```
In [9]: idx = dfMonthly.index
        dfMonthly.index = ["z" + str(ii) for ii in range(len(idx))]
        dfJointPanel = pd.concat([dfTickerLoadings, dfMonthly[tickers]]).T
        dfJointPanel
```

Out[9]:

	Intercept	xMkt_RF	xSMB	xHML	xRMW	xCMA	z0	z1	z2	z3	...	z180	z181	z182	z183	z184	z185	z186	z187	z188	z189
MMM	-0.001509	0.009075	0.002239	-0.001017	0.004866	0.004884	0.017943	0.028537	0.126683	-0.015499	...	0.004797	0.100651	0.023147	0.037507	-0.021720	-0.003474	-0.008656	-0.099209	0.018584	-0.040610
ABT	0.005528	0.007400	-0.003980	-0.004202	-0.000469	0.004779	0.023870	-0.038705	0.013445	-0.000936	...	-0.030828	0.000501	0.005682	-0.028584	-0.006172	0.047534	0.044553	-0.065205	0.095299	-0.024207
ABMD	0.015776	0.009411	0.015431	-0.009199	0.002526	0.000513	-0.050228	0.240385	0.002326	0.036350	...	-0.068055	-0.017932	0.006275	-0.112712	0.096739	0.048156	0.112551	-0.105616	0.020030	-0.051982
ACN	0.005632	0.010176	-0.000668	-0.002754	0.002785	0.000031	0.035839	-0.079302	-0.033256	-0.031648	...	0.037120	0.101036	0.052914	-0.026934	0.044762	0.080690	0.059431	-0.049441	0.124829	-0.003874
ATVI	0.010981	0.007405	-0.002989	-0.004615	-0.008699	-0.004296	-0.128312	0.103200	0.029006	-0.078224	...	0.050659	-0.027298	-0.014715	0.066455	-0.018612	-0.123847	-0.014949	-0.060459	0.010337	-0.250544
...	...	...	...	...	...	...	...	...	...	...	...	...	...	...	...	...	...	...	...	...	...
XEL	0.004365	0.004676	-0.003541	-0.002444	0.004169	0.004899	-0.004284	-0.010522	0.038017	-0.003716	...	-0.084388	0.143644	0.072019	-0.005891	-0.064380	0.035975	0.007326	-0.084659	0.033440	-0.013315
XLNX	0.006922	0.009592	0.004825	-0.002501	-0.000031	-0.062091	-0.028763	-0.066716	0.086803	-0.057443	...	-0.002068	-0.049117	0.032768	-0.007502	0.138698	0.035951	0.038374	-0.029565	0.192132	0.271541
ZBRA	0.006347	0.011865	0.007484	-0.001850	0.001870	-0.007417	-0.019765	0.013140	-0.112478	-0.110355	...	0.287755	-0.028533	0.005276	0.019088	0.065265	0.043419	0.062790	-0.122196	0.035951	0.102688
ZBH	-0.001260	0.010198	0.000502	0.001424	-0.003534	0.001453	0.003336	-0.022839	-0.069526	-0.037361	...	0.061105	-0.016781	0.106697	-0.049842	-0.043218	0.016167	-0.079366	-0.025635	-0.022137	-0.164338
ZION	0.007481	0.008727	0.001466	0.019768	-0.009565	-0.003960	0.048402	0.002545	0.003626	-0.019765	...	0.212613	0.033666	0.015284	0.043336	-0.086731	-0.013432	0.117938	0.068912	0.017773	0.007285

410 rows × 196 columns

(Continued)

Then we perform the second stage of Fama-MacBeth regressions:

```
In [10]:  dfRiskFactors = pd.DataFrame({"z" + str(ii) : smf.ols(
              "z" + str(ii) + " ~ xMkt_RF + xSMB + xHML + xRMW + xCMA",
              data=dfJointPanel).fit().params for ii in range(len(idx))})
          dfRiskFactors.columns = idx
```

We observe now how the RMW and CMA risk factors appear more stable than the rest (note the different *y*-axis scale):

```
In [11]:  dfRiskFactors = dfRiskFactors.T.iloc[:, 1:]
          dfRiskFactors.plot(subplots=True)

Out[11]:  array([<AxesSubplot:>, <AxesSubplot:>, <AxesSubplot:>,
                 <AxesSubplot:>], dtype=object)
```

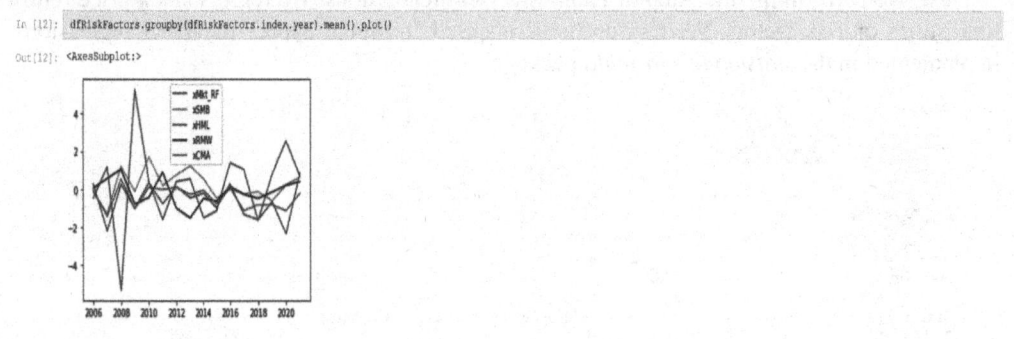

Now we look at the same time series averaged by year; observing annual averages makes the same series slightly easier to interpret on a longer time scale by eliminating short-term noise. Volatility has increased again since 2016 or so after several quieter years. Value stocks (HML) are outperforming in 2021 after underperforming in the previous few years:

```
In [12]:  dfRiskFactors.groupby(dfRiskFactors.index.year).mean().plot()

Out[12]:  <AxesSubplot:>
```

Finally, we attempt to test our set of risk factors for parsimony, that is, we test whether any of the risk factors on the list are redundant and can be replaced by a combination of other factors. The minus sign in the OLS regression formula removes the risk factor in question to the list of all regressors that precede it:

```
In [13]:  dols = {ii : smf.ols(ii + " ~ xMkt_RF + xSMB + xHML + xRMW + xCMA - " + ii,
                     data=ff).fit() for ii in ff.columns}
          pd.DataFrame({ii : (dols[ii].params.Intercept, dols[ii].pvalues.Intercept)
                     for ii in dols}, index=["Intercept", "pvalue"]).T[:-1]
```

Out[13]:	Intercept	pvalue
xMkt_RF	1.039087	0.000499
xSMB	0.118284	0.480474
xHML	-0.446894	0.014310
xRMW	0.382221	0.002285
xCMA	0.154308	0.123438

High *p*-values indicate that we can reject the null hypotheses that risk factors are redundant for SMB and CMA, but not the other risk factors. Fama and French's original analysis (on a different historical sample) indicated that the HML risk factor may be redundant, but others are not.

We strongly encourage the reader to examine our analyses in this exercise for robustness by repeating it on other stock portfolios (e.g., specific industry sectors within S&P or indexes for overseas markets) and different time frames. Depending on the parameters chosen, the conclusions will inevitably vary.

2.5 EXPANDING THE RISK FACTOR UNIVERSE

As mentioned earlier, while we have so far focused our analysis on just a handful of risk factors, avid research by both academics and practitioners has led to a proliferation of identified risk factors. This phenomenon is sometimes referred to (maybe somewhat disparagingly) as the "risk factor zoo." It is however not unreasonable that new data processing techniques (such as deep learning) and a significant increase in data availability have led to a large number of new, and potentially useful, risk factors being identified.

Successful commercial risk factor models exist which are based on many identified risk factors. The most prominent of those are models by BARRA, such as its Global Equity Model.[7]

Deep Learning in Search of Risk Factors. Machine learning is, and has been, instrumental in the search for new risk factors as it is able to efficiently process a large number of "features." Furthermore, we no longer need to restrict ourselves to linear dependence in the risk factor definition equation; we can more generally think of risk factors as the space of features in a supervised ("deep" i.e., having hidden layers) learning problem with security returns as output. As a matter of fact, new studies exist that combine the deep learning approach with the problem of search for new ESG risk factors.[8]

Alternative Data. While traditional fundamental indexes and smart beta indexes relying on systematic portfolio rebalancing of the same universe of stocks have been popular for years, and both offer a rich variety of commercially available indexes, indexes that rely on "alternative data," that is, nontraditional data sources – not securities' market data or firm financials – are still somewhat rare. Without doubt, the hedge fund industry does make extensive use of alternative data, but few indexes so far are calculated leveraging those data sources.

In general, alternative data can be roughly categorized into four types (these are discussed in more detail in Chapter 4):

- *Sentiment:* Social media feeds, news flow, corporate announcements, and other published media are monitored and analyzed for clues to sentiment on stocks, products, and the economy. This category includes the analysis of language used by executives on earnings calls, etc.
- *Other web scraping:* Involves compiling data from targeted websites in a bid to gain information on brands and products. This includes job listings and employee-satisfaction rankings, which can offer clues to a company's growth prospects.
- *Credit card data:* Some data providers put together large panels of consumers who agree to share their credit and debit card activity. These data are used for real-time tracking of retail revenue.
- *Satellites and aerial surveillance:* Used to track ships en route, monitor crops, and detect activity in ports and oil fields. Also, cars in parking lots are often counted as a proxy for retailer sales activity.

---

[7] Yohsuke Miki, Paul Green, and Pamela Brougham, eds., *Global Equity: Risk Model Handbook* (BARRA, 1998), https://www.alacra.com/alacra/help/barra_handbook_GEM.pdf.

[8] For example, Carmine de Franco, Christophe Geissler, Vincent Margot, and Bruno Monnier, "ESG Investments: Filtering versus Machine Learning Approaches," October 22, 2018, https://arxiv.org/pdf/2002.07477.pdf

Examples of available indexes do exist, though; particularly noteworthy are indexes of sentiment from the list above that leverage natural language sources (to be covered in more detail in Chapter 5). Many of these offerings are from recent startup companies, as this is still a very novel and rapidly developing field. To name a few:

- *Indexica* (http://indexica.com/) offers customized index solutions applying NLP techniques to public text data sources.
- *Refinitiv* (https://www.refinitiv) publishes sector-based news sentiment indices.

It is highly likely that we will see numerous new offerings in this field emerge in the near future.

ESG Risk Factors. It is entirely possible to construct risk factors following the Fama-French portfolio sorting approach for an arbitrary metric used to rank the underlying member securities. For instance, we can use ESG scoring (environmental, social, and corporate governance score, or a combination thereof) to rank the portfolios. For example, we can rank all member securities by carbon emissions and define our risk factor as the difference in returns between "high-carbon polluting" and "low-carbon polluting" quartile portfolios.

In practice, there is no uniform standard approach to ESG scoring; therefore, performance of ESG risk factors is highly dependent on the choice of underlying data and the choice of scoring methodology.

This discussion, of course, only scratches the surface of the alternative data topic, as well as how it applies to ESG. We return to discussing alternative data sources and their applications in much greater detail in subsequent chapters.

CHAPTER 3

ESG Ratings

3.1 INTRODUCTION

The recent growth in ESG investments has brought to life a variety of market utilities that provide third-party assessment of ESG performance quality (how exactly this quality is defined varies greatly among these utilities and will be discussed in more detail below) using a uniform methodology across the spectrum of companies being rated. The function these utilities perform is very similar to that performed by credit rating agencies for fixed income markets.

Purpose of ESG Ratings. In a similar fashion as credit ratings, ESG ratings – if reliable – provide a consistent and cost-effective framework for comparing different companies in terms of their ESG "quality." ESG ratings for corporates may be used in a number of ways, such as:

- Companies use their ESG scores to benchmark their ESG performance and demonstrate their commitments to stakeholders.
- Companies increasingly rely on ESG ratings to gain access to specialized financing for sustainability projects.
- Investors gain transparency from ESG ratings on how exposed companies are to specific risks and how well companies are managing those risks.
- Fund managers use ratings to screen companies for inclusion in sustainable investment funds.

Unfortunately – as is currently the case with many areas within the not-yet-mature and rapidly developing ESG sphere – there are still inconsistencies in the approaches that the rating agencies use.

As we start this chapter with a discussion on the general approach to ESG ratings construction, we should keep in mind, though, that individual implementations of ESG rating methodologies diverge, at times very significantly, among rating providers.

ESG Rating Providers. Three of the more popular ESG rating providers, as this book is being written, are listed below. We are fully aware that the ESG rating business may evolve rapidly and significantly, along with the rest of the ESG field, and new dominant providers may continue to emerge:

- *MSCI.* MSCI, an S&P 500 member, is a global provider of equity, fixed income, and real estate indexes, multi-asset portfolio analysis tools, as well as ESG and climate products. It operates the MSCI World, MSCI All Country World Index (ACWI), and MSCI Emerging Markets Indexes, among others. MSCI is an active participant in the ESG field; its ESG rating methodology has been developed in-house and is one of the first ones to achieve commercial popularity/recognition.

- *S&P.* S&P Global Ratings is an American credit rating agency and a division of S&P Global, an S&P 500 member, which publishes financial research and analysis on stocks, bonds, and commodities. S&P is considered the largest of the Big Three credit rating agencies, which also include Moody's Investors Service and Fitch Ratings. In its expansion beyond credit rating services, S&P Global acquired the RobecoSAM ESG ratings business from Robeco, a Dutch asset management company. The acquisition included the widely followed RobecoSAM Corporate Sustainability Assessment – an annual evaluation of companies' sustainability practices. RobecoSAM assessment is recognized as one of the more popular and advanced ESG scoring methodologies, as it draws on 20 years of experience analyzing sustainability impact on a company's long-term value creation.

- *Morningstar.* Morningstar is a publicly traded financial services company that provides an array of investment research and investment management services. In 2020, Morningstar acquired Sustainalytics, a company that rates the sustainability of listed companies based on their ESG performance following their proprietary methodology.

Let us start with some exploratory data analysis, taking a closer look at samples of actual ratings.

EXERCISE 3.A   Exploratory analysis of rating samples

As usual, we leverage the *pandas* built-in functionality:

```
In [1]:  ▶ import pandas as pd
```

The current ratings from three providers have been collected for all constituents of the S&P 500 index into a single file. Note that MSCI ratings use a letter rating scale (AAA, AA, A, BBB, BB, B, CCC); for the purpose of this comparison exercise, we convert the letter rating into a 0–100 range using a linear scale.

We read the collected ratings for S&P 500 constituents from a CSV file:

```
In [2]:  ▶ df = pd.read_csv("esg notebooks/Bbg Data/esg rating comparison.csv")
           df
```

Out[2]:

	Ticker	S&P	SA	MSCI
0	LYB	60	54.341007	50.000
1	SBNY	30	61.445797	21.430
2	AXP	76	44.416560	78.570
3	VZ	0	36.469057	64.285
4	AVGO	41	55.494303	35.715
...	...	...	...	...
500	ZTS	65	39.695082	78.570
501	DLR	91	28.423965	64.285
502	EQIX	83	32.113465	78.570
503	LVS	97	39.117467	50.000
504	DISCK	57	37.901856	50.000

505 rows × 4 columns

A basic histogram of the three rating samples combined on the same chart provides a useful comparison. For instance, we can observe that the empirical distribution of the S&P ratings is heavily skewed toward better ratings (i.e., there are more highest-rated in S&P 500 than those within any other ratings band).

Parameter alpha specifies the degree of how transparent we want the histogram bars to be; otherwise, the bars from one distribution would completely obscure the histograms plotted behind them.

```
In [33]:  ▶  df[df.columns[1:]].plot(kind="hist", alpha=0.5)
     Out[33]:  <AxesSubplot:ylabel='Frequency'>
```

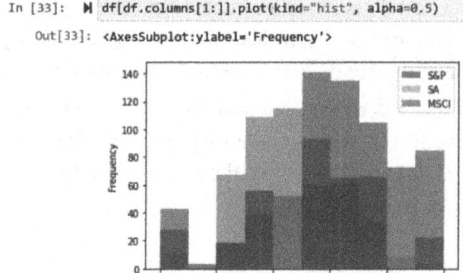

As an alternative to using histogram bar charts, we can fit smooth curves to the three rating distributions instead.

3.2   OVERVIEW OF ESG RATING METHODOLOGIES

As we have mentioned in the initial paragraphs of this chapter, there are several different providers of ESG ratings on the market, each of which has its own specific methodology used to generate the ratings. As it would be too long, and beyond the scope of this book, to detail each and every one of the major methodologies currently in use, we shall simply provide an overview of the S&P methodology, at a high level, to provide an example and to highlight areas of commonality and differences. The reader is encouraged to review other ones, which are available online, such as the one by Bloomberg, the one from Morningstar, and the MSCI one, to name a few.

High-Level Overview of S&P ESG Rating Methodology. The S&P ESG rating is cross-sectional and focuses on a corporation's capability to successfully operate in the future, while assessing how ESG factors could potentially affect stakeholders, specifically in regard to material direct or indirect financial impacts. The ESG factors measure the corporation, or entity, in terms of what impact it would have on the natural and social environment would be, and the quality of its governance structure. The concept of stakeholders is used, as opposed to shareholders alone, as proposed by Edward Freedman (see Chapter 1), and is set to include the corporation employees, customers, lenders, borrowers, the local community, government, regulators, policyholders, voters, members, suppliers, and any other affected party.

A high ESG evaluation score indicates a low chance of experiencing negative material ESG-related events and a better positioning to capitalize on ESG-related growth opportunity, while lower ESG evaluation scores indicate the inverse.

Steps in the methodology:

1. *Create the ESG profile for the entity.* A profile is generated to assess the exposure of the entity and the entity's operations to known ESG risks and opportunities, and how the entity is proceeding with risk mitigation and opportunity capitalization. The analysis begins with ESG-related exposure by sector and location.

2. *Assess long-term preparedness*. The capacity to anticipate and adapt to long-term plausible disruptions and regime changes, linked to ESG-linked factors, is assessed. These factors are not strictly environmental or social, but also include technological and regulatory changes that might impact the entity and other factors.

3. *Generate final ESG evaluation ranking*. The final ranking is prepared by combining the ESG profile with the long-term preparedness opinion scores. This score indicates S&P's overall view on the relative exposure to known ESG-related risks and opportunities, and its opinion on long-term sustainability and readiness in the face of emerging trends and potential disruptions.

4. *Live monitoring and updates*. The ESG evaluation score is monitored and updated, to account for new data, updates in strategies, and any material event that affects the entity. This can lead to the entity being temporarily rated as "Under Review" (UR) when some of the ESG evaluations used in the rating are potentially under impact by ongoing world events.

Overview of ranking metrics and approach:
1. *ESG evaluation scale*. The ESG evaluation is done on a linear ranking scale between 0 and 100, with higher rankings signifying a higher likelihood of sustainability when exposed to ESG-related risks and opportunities and lower values correlating to lower capability to handle risk or exploit opportunities.

2. *Preparedness opinion metrics*. The preparedness opinion is a qualitative metric that can take one of five values (best in class, strong, adequate, emerging, and low). It is based on expert opinion calls by S&P analysts.

Combination of metrics (i.e., what effects do preparedness scores have on overall ratings):
1. *Best-in-class preparedness*. This is a rare score and generally has a strong positive effect on the overall evaluation. Tends to correlate with highest ESG evaluations. If paired with a very low ESG profile score, it will not provide a significant offset on the overall evaluation.

2. *Strong preparedness*. This is a relatively rare score and typically has a positive effect on the overall evaluation. If paired with a very low ESG profile score, it will not provide a measurable offset on the overall evaluation.

3. *Adequate preparedness*. This is a relatively common score and has a minimal impact on the overall evaluation, unless the ESG profile score is above 85.

4. *Emerging preparedness*. This score has a negative impact on the overall evaluation.

5. *Low preparedness*. This score is rare and has a significantly negative impact on the overall evaluation.

Materiality and value chain:
1. *Materiality*. When addressing the ESG evaluation, the impact of ESG factors is graded on how meaningful these are expected to be on business operations, cash flows, legal or regulatory liabilities, access to capital, reputation, or relationships with key stakeholders and society more generally, either directly or through the value chain (upstream or downstream).

2. *Value chain*. Exposure is evaluated both directly and as coming via the value chain, including partially owned subsidiaries, suppliers, franchisees, licensees, lenders or underwriters, customers, taxpayers, and residents.

Metrics used to build the ESG profile:
1. *Environmental profile*. When addressing the environmental profile, the following subitems are assessed:
   a. Weighted sectoral and regional analysis of material ESG exposures
   Climate hazards and natural disasters
   Labor disputes

Financial restatements

Misdeeds of management

Other disruptions to operational activities

b. Entity-specific ESG exposure

Greenhouse gas (GHG) emissions

Waste data

Water usage data

Land usage data

c. Qualitative and quantitative analysis of entity effectiveness at managing ESG-related risks and opportunities

d. Additional risks and opportunities not captured under factor scores

e. The forward-looking effects of material ESG events

2. *Social profile.* When addressing the social profile, the following subitems are assessed:

   a. Sector-region score, weighted by the entity's business mix

   b. Entity-specific factors (compared to peers):

   Workforce and diversity

   i. Labor standards, pay, benefits, and rewards

   ii. Employee engagement

   iii. Proportion of contracted and unionized labor

   iv. Engagement in promoting fair and humane labor standards across the value chain

   Safety management

   i. Occupational health and safety for all employees (permanent, temporary, and contractors)

   ii. Product safety

   iii. Engagement in promoting safety management across the value chain

   Customer engagement

   i. Trends in customer satisfaction, retention, and complaints

   ii. Anticipation of changing customer preferences

   iii. Ability to ensure reliability and affordability of products

   iv. Protection of customer information

   v. Potential for misleading or misselling to customers

   Communities

   i. Direct operations and suppliers' engagement with local communities

      (a) Contributions to and support of local communities

      (b) Local hires

      (c) Donations

   ii. Exposure to war, other conflicts, and terrorism

3. *Governance profile.* When addressing the governance profile, the following sub-items are assessed:

   a. Jurisdiction-based score, calculated on location of Headquarters

   b. Entity-specific factors (compared to peers):

   Structure and oversight

   i. Composition, skills, tenure, diversity, and independence of the governing body

   ii. Committee structures and their membership

   iii. Degree of commitment to board duties

   iv. Succession planning and unexpected changes

    v. Comprehensiveness of board oversight

    vi. Auditors' independence

Code and values

    i. Comprehensiveness of the policy framework

    ii. Code of conduct and its application across the value chain

    iii. Public statements about ethics and values

    iv. Extent of training in code and values

    v. Executive remuneration and incentives

Transparency and reporting

    i. Level and quality of disclosure of ESG indicators

    ii. Publication of a detailed annual sustainability report or of an integrated report that contains detailed sustainability information

    iii. Level of disclosure regarding taxation issues

Financial and operational risks

    i. Internal controls and audit

    ii. Financial health and execution risks

    iii. Cybersecurity

    iv. Contingent liabilities

    v. Disaster recovery

    vi. General supply chain management

Factors Used to Build the Long-Term Preparedness (LTP) Assessment Score. To build the LTP assessment, the analysts from S&P meet with the management team and board representatives, to be informed on the entity's capacity to anticipate and adapt to ESG-related long-term disruptions. The dimensions measured are:

1. *Awareness.* Senior management and board capabilities in awareness of emerging trends and potential business disruptors.

2. *Assessment.* Senior management and board capabilities in assessment of emerging trends and potential business disruptors.

3. *Action plan.* How capable and effective senior management is in planning to manage, mitigate, or exploit risks and opportunities already identified in Awareness and measured in Assessment.

4. *Embeddedness.* How adaptable and agile the entity is to any change:

    a. *Culture.* How embedded and effective are strategic objectives, particularly those related to ESG, across the entire organization and its key stakeholders.

    b. *Decision-making.* How embedded and effective strategic objectives, particularly those related to ESG, are in influencing senior management decisions.

5. *Climate-related financial disclosures.* To what extent the entity has adopted the Financial Stability Board's Taskforce on Climate-related Financial Disclosures (TCFD) recommendations (no measure of quality of the disclosure or the climate change scenario assumptions, if any).

As noted earlier, as the rating methodologies are not yet mature, the results of different rating approaches differ, sometimes significantly. Furthermore, while the high-level approach (described above for the S&P methodology) is disclosed, application details are not. This is where certain machine learning techniques come to the rescue: In this book, we leverage regression trees and the random forest approach to infer empirically, where possible, relative weights of various drivers of the ESG score, as well as the list of what is potentially a large number of driver variables.

We proceed with a review of the relevant regression tree techniques before applying them to the problem at hand.

3.3   REGRESSION TREES AS AN ALTERNATIVE SCORING TECHNIQUE

In the field of machine learning, as it pertains to classification and regression, one of the most commonly used techniques is the decision tree, and most specifically the regression tree (we shall review the difference between the two shortly). Before we delve into the theory and practical applications of the coding aspects of regression trees, let us, however, spend some time understanding the basic concepts behind what a decision tree is, how it is used, and how it provides a logical and mathematical framework to thought and action formalization, which can be used to train machine learning algorithms to gain useful insights for the ESG practitioner.

We can start by providing a much-generalized definition of what a decision tree is, as exemplified in Figure 3.1, which is: "A decision support tool that uses tree-like modeling of decisions and their consequences, including random event outcomes, costs, and utility, to display an algorithm exclusively composed of conditional control statements."

Decision trees are often represented as flowchart-like objects, where each internal node is a decision on a specific attribute (i.e., the answer to a question, which has to be TRUE or FALSE) and each branch represents the effect of the specific decision. Each leaf (the end state of any branch, represented by the triangle in Figure 3.1) represents a *class label,* which is an end state (i.e., the decision taken after computation of all the attributes).

Typical uses of decision trees, outside of computational applications, are in decision analysis, where they serve as visual and analytical support tools to evaluate expected values and utility of competing alternative options.

An alternate use of decision trees, where the concept of probability enters the fray, is for them to be used as a descriptive tool to calculate conditional probabilities of specific events.

The rules that apply to decision tree nodes can be linearized (which is most convenient for use in computational applications) in a way that the outcome becomes the contents of the leaf node and the conditions in the root-to-leaf path become a series of IF/AND statements.

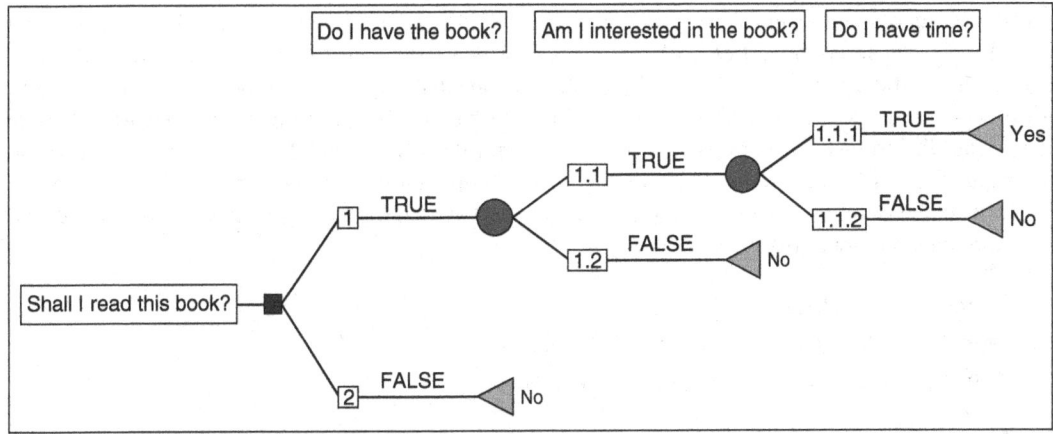

FIGURE 3.1   A generic decision tree.

In a generalized way, this linearization can be summarized, for a three-node condition with TRUE value for all three stated *conditions* leading to *outcome1*, as follows:

IF *condition1* AND *condition2* AND *condition3* THEN *outcome1*

Decision Trees to Infer Rules from Empirical Data. A major use for decision trees, and one that is central to their use in machine learning, is that of models to generate induction rules from empirical data. In this case, multiple decision trees are generated, and the optimal one is chosen algorithmically, being the one that correctly accounts for the highest amount of data with the lowest number of nodes (each node being one TRUE/FALSE question, as shown in Figure 3.1). Many different algorithms exist for the computation and selection of optimal trees, and these can be found online and in specialized textbooks, if of interest. In Python, decision trees are, of course, implemented in the *scikit-learn* library.

Decision Trees in Machine Learning and Data Mining. As we have mentioned earlier, decision tree learning is a type of predictive modeling used extensively in machine learning and data mining. The underlying concept is to utilize a decision tree as a predictive model, allowing us to transition from a set of empirical observations about a phenomenon (which are topologically represented as the branches of the tree) to overarching conclusions about the phenomenon's target states (which are topologically represented by the leaves), contingent on different pathways. Depending on whether the target (predicted) variable can take discrete values (e.g., belonging or not to a certain category) or continuous values (e.g., real numbers, the predicted value of a certain bond, in USD), the decision tree will be called either a *classification tree or a regression tree.*

When used for data mining applications, the decision tree generally represents data, while the resulting output usually is an input for a decision-making process that lies downstream. The goal of applying decision trees to data is typically to be able to predict the value of a target variable end state (e.g., the value of an asset) based on the value of several input variables (e.g., the asset's location, specific characteristics).

Nomenclature of Decision Tree Components. The input variables, also called *input features,* need to have finite and discrete values in order to be usable (i.e., they need to be *classifiable,* according to a defined and determined classification system). Within the domain of the classification, each element is called a *class.*

Within the tree, each node (with the exclusion of terminal nodes, which are called *leaf nodes*), is labeled by an *input feature,* and the possible branches that emanate from that node are labeled with each of the possible values (or groupings of values, for continuous variables) that lead to the next subordinate decision node, which will be labeled by a different input feature.

The leaf nodes, which are the terminal nodes and represent the end states for the system, are labeled with a *class*, or probability distribution over *classes*, which signifies that the population that follows the specific subset of input features that lead to the node, fall into the particular end state distribution shown. A well-built and informative tree will segregate, or at least skew, distributions of specific subsets of classes in specific nodes, while a poorly built one (i.e., one that is devoid of information) will show uniform distributions across all leaf nodes. (A uniform distribution across all leaf nodes signifies that the input features chosen have no impact on the end state for the system, and the overall distribution across the population is the same as the distribution across subpopulations that share specific input features.)

An example of an informative tree would be one that associates the risk of developing lung cancer with the following input features:

- Smoker/nonsmoker
- Smoker for less than 5 years/more than 5 years
- Smoker for less than 10 years/more than 10 years

This tree would provide a clear output where the risk of lung cancer is higher in the smoker population and increases the longer the smoking habit persists.

An example of a noninformative tree would be the same one (risk of developing lung cancer) that, however, used the following input features (notice how these are all binary variables that can assume TRUE/FALSE values, as above, but have no bearing on the actual question at hand):

- Is a baseball fan/Is not a baseball fan
- Uses public transportation/Does not use public transportation
- Voted at last general election/Did not vote at last general election

In this case, we expect that the distribution of the risk of developing lung cancer will be (barring statistical errors tied to sample size) effectively the same between the overall population and any one of the leaf nodes in the tree.

Construction of Decision Trees. To build a decision tree, we start by splitting the source set, which is the root node of the tree, into a number of subsets, which are called the *successor children*. This splitting occurs in accordance with a predetermined set of splitting rules that are based on the type of classification features that are being used (splitting rules can be either dichotomous, i.e., TRUE/FALSE, or based on some threshold value, i.e., exceed/does not exceed). The splitting process is repeated recursively on each subset, via a process called *recursive partitioning*, which ends when the subset at the node that is generated is entirely comprised of the same values as the target variable, or if there is no incremental predictive value added by further splitting. This type of algorithm that starts from the top and goes down is also called a TDIT (top-down induction of decision trees) and is one of the most used strategies for machine learning of decision trees from data (others also exist).

If we want to describe a decision tree from a formal mathematical standpoint, we can express it as:

$$(x,Y) = (x_1, x_2, x_2, x_4, ..., x_n, Y)$$

where the dependent variable Y is what we are trying to predict, or classify, while the vector x, composed of the input features $x_1, x_2, x_2, x_4, ..., x_n$, is what we are using to assist us in the categorization.

As we have seen before, decision trees can be either classification trees, if the predicted outcome is a discrete class (e.g., predicting whether a phenomena happens or not), or regression trees, when the predicted outcome is a continuous class (e.g., the predicted cost of carbon removal in dollars per ton for certain types of industries or activities, or the amount of time it will take for a certain plot of depleted land to revert to normality).

Independent of whether we are covering regression or classification trees, both fall under the generalized term of CART (classification and regression tree) analysis, as they have sufficient similarities to allow them to be treated in the same general framework. We must note, however, that they also have differences, the major of which is, unsurprisingly, in the methodologies used to decide where to split the trees.

Pros and Cons of Decision Trees vs. Other Predictors. Decision trees, as any mathematical or logical tool, have a distinct set of strengths and weaknesses, which we, as ESG practitioners, must be aware of if we want to utilize them to the fullest of their capabilities. In a nutshell, these are:

Pros:
- Ease of understanding and interpretation – minimal explanation is required.
- Value of insight is not necessarily tied to hard data – trees can be set up with descriptive conditions and preferential outcomes, without voiding the functionality of the instrument.
- Provide easy way to determine expected outcomes, as well as best- and worst-case scenarios.
- Can be easily integrated into other modeling techniques and decision tools.
- Can consider multiple decision-makers in one single tree.

Cons:

- Relative instability and high sensitivity to underlying data (small changes in data can lead to large changes in tree structure and outcomes).
- Low degree of accuracy compared to other instruments (such as random forests).
- When dealing with categorical variables with a large number of levels, the decision trees will be structurally biased in favor of attributes with more levels than others.
- Intrinsic complexity of calculation, especially when dealing with uncertainty in values and/or interlinkage of outcomes.

Selected Techniques to Optimize Decision Tree Effectiveness. Given the list of pros and cons that we have just reviewed, we can now look at a few well-known techniques and methodologies that can be applied to maximize the prior and minimize the latter.

The list we are presenting is far from complete and counts but a few major considerations that should be applied in the pursuit of better and more accurate decision trees.

We can start with an effort to increase the *accuracy* of the decision tree, which is mainly achieved via an increase in the number of nodes, or levels, of the tree itself.

In many cases, the leaf nodes in a tree are pure nodes. This means that all the data in that specific node belongs to only one class. (This is what a good tree should aim to do, as we have seen in our previous examples.)

While increasing the number of nodes can provide higher accuracy, this is not always the case, as noninformational levels can be added into the mix that provide no additional insights. Of course, one must also remember that adding nodes to the decision tree will almost always increase the amount of computational time that is required to process it. This could, therefore, produce the unwanted results of having a much slower tree-building algorithm than what would be required, and at no measurable increase in efficiency or accuracy. In fact, if the algorithm were to start splitting nodes that are pure (i.e., oversplitting), we could actually experience the opposite effect of what is being sought, with an overall *decrease* in accuracy and increase in runtime.

As with many aspects of computational modeling, it is always important to test the results of the different parameters and see what the output is, to optimize the accuracy and runtime to meet our requirements.

If we were to summarize the effects of increasing the depth (D) of a decision tree (i.e., increasing the nodes), we could break them down as follows:

Pros:

- Increased accuracy if depth is not increased beyond optimal level.

Cons:

- Runtime increases.
- Accuracy decreases if depth is increased beyond optimal level.
- Artificial deepening via splitting of pure nodes leads to reduced accuracy and classification issues.

There are multiple ways of determining how the splitting of the nodes is performed, and the choice of the node-splitting function has a strong effect on the overall accuracy of the decision tree output. The following are a few possible functions, with brief descriptions:

- *Chi-square.* Chi-square is applied to classification trees. It has the advantage of being able to generate more than two splits and is based on the statistical significance of differences between the parent node and child nodes.
- *Gini impurity.* This function is applied to classification trees. It is probably the most popular and the easiest way to split a decision tree. It is based on the Gini measure, which is the probability of

correctly labeling a randomly chosen element if it was randomly labeled according to the distribution of labels in the node.

- *Information gain function.* Also known as *reduction in entropy* function. This is a function used for classification trees and is based on the concept of entropy, which is used for calculating the purity of a node. The lower the value of entropy, the higher purity the node will have. The entropy of a homogeneous node is zero. This function tends to favor the most impactful features that are closest to the root of the tree and is generally seen as an easy tool to determine relevance/ irrelevance of select features.
- *Phi function.* Measure of "goodness" function. The phi function is generally maximized when the feature chosen splits the samples to produce homogenous splits with approximately the same number of samples in each split.
- *Reduction in variance.* This method is only used for regression trees. It uses variance to determine the feature on which node is split into child nodes.

How to Evaluate Decision Tree Performance. Once we have built a decision tree, using one of the many packages available and having selected one of the node-splitting functions we listed above, we need to be able to evaluate the performance it is producing, in order to fine-tune it as necessary.

There are multiple dimensions across which a decision tree can be measured to estimate how it performs, and they all derive from the direct measurement of the numbers and ratios of true positives, true negatives, false positives, and false negatives that are returned by the tree when running a set number of sample data through it. The most used metrics are:

- *Accuracy.* The number of correct predictions made divided by the total number of predictions made.
- *False discovery rate.* The proportion of type I errors. A type I error is where the algorithm incorrectly rejects the null hypothesis; in other words, it generates a false positive: False positives/ (False positives + True positives).
- *False omission rate.* The proportion of type II errors. A type II error is where the algorithm generates a false negative (the algorithm prediction is negative, but the true value is positive). False negatives/(False negatives + True negatives).
- *Miss rate.* Number of false negatives/(False negatives + True positives).
- *Precision.* True positives/(True positives + False positives).
- *Sensitivity.* True positives/(True positives + False negatives).
- *Specificity.* True negatives/(True negatives + False positives).

A very common way to display the performance of a decision tree is by using a confusion matrix, where the predicted condition and the actual condition are displayed, and the different types of error generated by the decision tree are clearly visible. As an example, please refer to Figure 3.2, which shows a confusion matrix for a hypothetical decision tree that classifies corporate disclosures by ESG sentiment (positive or negative).

The confusion matrix in the figure shows us 450 true positives, 320 true negatives, 130 false negatives, and 100 false positives.

Based on these values, we can calculate the performance metrics for this particular tree as follows:

- **Accuracy:** $$\frac{450+320}{1000}=0.770$$

- **False discovery rate:** $$\frac{100}{100+450}=0.181$$

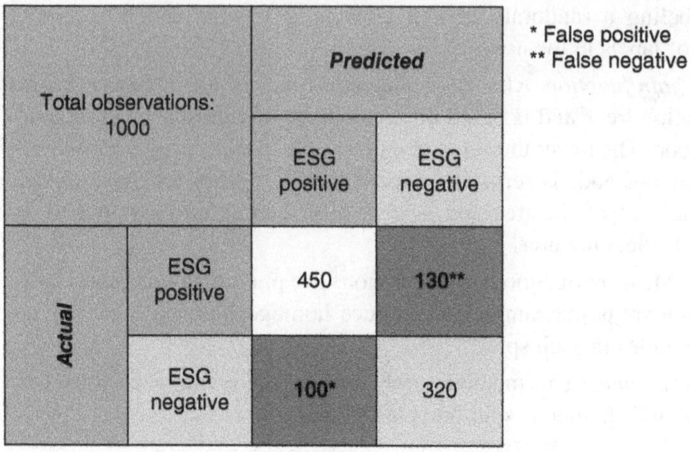

FIGURE 3.2   A decision tree confusion matrix example.

- **False omission rate:** $\dfrac{130}{130+320}=0.288$

- **Miss rate:** $\dfrac{130}{130+450}=0.224$

- **Precision:** $\dfrac{450}{450+100}=0.818$

- **Sensitivity:** $\dfrac{450}{450+130}=0.775$

- **Specificity:** $\dfrac{320}{320+100}=0.762$

What do these numbers mean in practical terms? A calculated accuracy of 77.0% is relatively good, but certainly has room for improvement. The sensitivity value of 77.5%, on the other hand, shows us how the tree correctly identifies just over three quarters of ESG positive corporate disclosures, and the specificity value of 76.2% tells us it has a similar performance in identifying ESG negative corporate disclosures.

Example of a Regression Tree Application. To better understand the use of regression trees and how they can be applied to ESG applications, we can use an example, based on synthetic data, where we try to predict the average number of years that it will take to recover degraded land back to natural state, based on a series of parameters such as number of years it has been in degraded state, whether it is used for agriculture or not, whether it has forest covering or not, and so on.

From an initial cursory review of the data, we know that the primary discriminator for the regression tree is whether the land is Agricultural or not, followed by whether it is or isn't forested, so we start by running an initial regression tree using these two variables.

Figure 3.3 shows the regression tree that is generated by the data, with node splits for Agricultural (TRUE/FALSE) and Forested (TRUE/FALSE). The predicted time to recover, expressed in years, is shown in each leaf node, and it is quite evident that while the nonagricultural leaf nodes are relatively well clustered, the agricultural one is still very dispersed, and requires us to deepen the tree to achieve some better predictive value to our analytics.

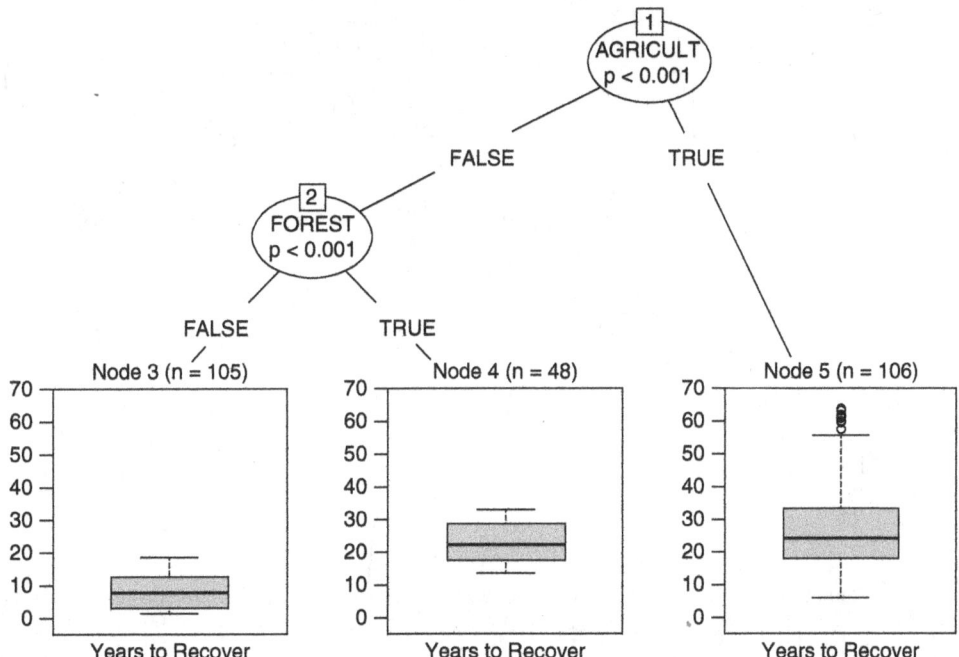

FIGURE 3.3 A regression tree to predict years required for recovery of degraded land, using status as agricultural or forested as predictor variables.

If we now add the following variables to our regression tree, we can improve our accuracy:

- Degraded for over 10 years (TRUE/FALSE)
- Degraded for over 50 years (TRUE/FALSE)
- Human assistance for recovery possible (TRUE/FALSE)
- Potential for rapid recovery alone (TRUE/FALSE)

Figure 3.4 shows us how, with the addition of these extra variables and nodes, we can get much tighter predictions and a clear and explainable understanding of which factors drive the expected duration for the recovery. There is still room for improvement, as we notice how the agricultural land with more than 10 years of degradation but less than 50 years still shows a dispersed set of outcomes (and would potentially warrant adding extra nodes and variables if we required higher accuracy in the predictions over the entire dataset).

The Concept and Application of Tree Pruning. While it might be tempting to generate trees with very large numbers of nodes, in the pursuit of accuracy on the training sets used to set the regression trees up, this way of proceeding comes with an intrinsic, and potentially deadly, flaw. This flaw is known as *data overfitting,* which is caused by trees that are so complex as to be, effectively, custom-tailored to fit the training dataset to such a perfect extent that they are no longer accurate predictors on any other set and, consequently, show poor performances when used on test sets.

The way around this issue is to use smaller trees with fewer nodes, in an effort to pursue lower variance and better interpretative flexibility, while adding some degree of bias to the tree.

One way of determining when a tree has enough nodes, as an example, is to only increase them if the residual sum of squares (RSS) decrease that is created by each new split is kept above an arbitrarily high threshold (which avoids oversplitting). While this might be a good strategy in some instances, it

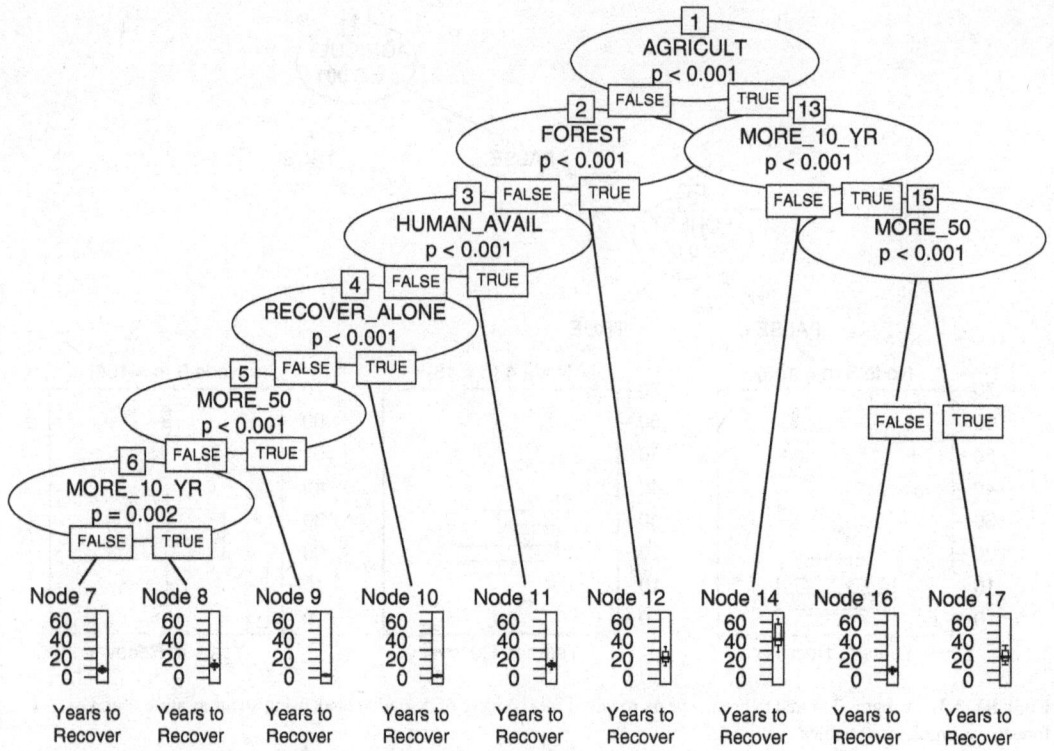

FIGURE 3.4   Enhanced regression tree to predict years required for recovery of degraded land.

faces drawbacks as it is topologically limited, since branches that start with low RSS value splits but are followed by high RSS value ones will be pruned by this methodology, as it is designed to work in a top-down fashion.

An alternative option is to simply grow the trees to a high degree of complexity and branching, and then prune them back to subtrees of adequate simplicity and accuracy. This, however, requires algorithms and methodologies that are capable of discerning between "good" and "bad" trees and branches and can figure out what to prune and what to keep.

Evaluation of all possible subtrees and their errors, especially for regression trees of considerable size, rapidly becomes an insurmountable effort, due to the computational challenge that it imposes on us, and is therefore not a practical solution.

The most effective option, and the one that is in widespread use, is cost complexity pruning (a.k.a. weakest link pruning). Cost complexity pruning creates a series of trees T_0 to T_n with T_0 being the initial tree and T_n being the tree pruned all the way to the root alone. Each tree step from 0 to n creates a new tree by removing a subtree from the previous tree $(i - 1)$ and replacing it with a leaf node.

The trade-off between the subtree's complexity and its fit to the training data is controlled by the values of the tuning parameter α. The closer α is to 0, the closer the tree will be to T_0, and the higher α becomes, the higher the number of terminal nodes will be.

There are several implementations that allow cost complexity pruning, including *scikit-learn*, providing the user with all the necessary tuning parameters required to use this methodology.

The way to choose the optimal results of the application of cost-complexity pruning can be summarized as follows:

1. Generate a large regression tree using a methodology of choice to determine the optimal level of node splitting (as previously discussed).
2. Use cost complexity pruning on the regression tree to generate a series of subtrees, testing different values for α.
3. Use a cross-validation methodology to evaluate which parameters evaluate which parameters of α minimize the average error on the training data (e.g., K-fold validation could be used).
4. Produce as output the subtree from step 2 that is generated by the chosen value of α from step 3.

3.4 · RANDOM FOREST

An alternative methodology to simple regression trees, and in certain aspects a significantly improved one, is represented by the random forest technique, which covers a learning method for classification, regression, and other tasks and focuses on the construction of multiple sets of decision trees at training level. For the purposes of classification, the output of the random forest is taken to be the class selected by the highest fraction of trees. When used for regression, the mean or average prediction that the individual trees return is the output that the forest generates.

When compared to regression trees, random forests do not present the systemic problem of overfitting to the training set that plagues the former, and overall tend to perform better, but with a loss in accuracy, when compared to gradient boosted trees. Random forests have a stronger sensitivity to data characteristics than regression trees have, as a rule of thumb.

As we have seen, regression trees that grow to have many nodes tend to learn patterns that are very irregular and training-set-specific, with the resulting overfit issues that are well known (low bias, high variance). Random forests, on the other hand, allow us to average multiple decision trees, trained on different subsets of the same training set, and therefore reduce the variance of the outputs. The result of this breakup of the set is a relatively modest increase in bias and a somewhat more significant loss of interpretability (we no longer have a single, easy to explain tree), but the overall performance of the model is greatly improved.

Conceptually, a random forest can be seen like the joining together of many separate regression trees to work on a single problem (thus the analogy between tree and forest).

Bootstrap Aggregating (or Bagging). The original training algorithm used in random forests to aggregate the results of the different trees is called *bagging* and uses the generalized methodology of bootstrap aggregation.

It works, conceptually, as follows:

Given a training set X ($x_1, x_2, x_3, x_4, \ldots, x_n$) with responses $Y(y_1, y_2, y_3, y_4, \ldots, y_n)$, the algorithm will select a random sample with replacement of the training set for B iterations and fit trees to the new sample, as follows:

For every b in [1 to B]:

- Pick, with replacement, n training examples from training set X and responses $Y(X_b, Y_b)$
- Train regression tree f_b on X_b, Y_b.

Once the training is completed, predictions for unseen samples (x') will be made by averaging the predictions from all the individual regression trees applied to the unseen sample.

The results of this method are a reduction in variance and a moderate, if not null, increase in bias. This is because, while a single tree will be highly sensitive to noise in the data of the training set it is based on, the average of many trees will not, if the trees themselves are not closely correlated with each other. The training of the trees on different subsets of the data allows us to reduce the risk of having closely correlated trees (or potentially the same tree multiple times) if we were to train on the entire dataset for every iteration. By breaking up the training set in subsets, we ensure that the trees are de-correlated between themselves, as they are exposed to different training sets.

A good measure of the uncertainty of the prediction that the random forest will generate can be determined by looking at the standard deviation of the predictions from all the individual regression trees on an unseen sample (x'):

$$\sigma = \sqrt{\frac{\sum_{b=1}^{B}\left(f_b\left(x'\right)-\hat{f}\right)^2}{B-1}}$$

where:

B is the number of samples/trees (free to choose, typically from a few hundred to several thousand)

x' is the unseen sample

$\hat{f}$ is the average prediction on x'

$f_b\left(x'\right)$ is the prediction of tree b on x'

Alternative methods for bagging are also available, such as feature bagging, which the reader can investigate in more detail if the topic is of interest.

Extra Trees. An interesting characteristic of random forest is the possibility of adding a further level of randomness to the process by generating high-level of randomization trees, via the process of *ExtraTrees*. These are trees that are trained over the whole learning sample (as opposed to a bootstrap one as in the paragraph above), but the node splitting is randomized across all possible values of each node's feature range; a set number of randomly generated splits happen for each node, and the split that yields the highest score is chosen to split the node. This procedure yields very unusual trees, which have the potential to add some extra level of insight to a more standard type of random forest implementation.

Using Random Forests to Determine Variable Importance. One of the most useful features that random forests provide the ESG practitioner with is the possibility to rank the importance of variables in a regression problem in a quantitative and comprehensible way. This is done by measuring the out-of-bag error for each data point and averaging it over the forest.

Once this measure is done for each variable feature, the value of each is permuted among the training data and the out-of-bag error is measured again, on this disrupted set.

The importance of the variable feature will then be determined by averaging the difference in out-of-bag error before and after the permutation across all trees in the random forest and normalizing the score by the standard deviation of the differences.

Any variable feature that creates a large value is ranked higher (i.e., more important) than one that produces a smaller value (i.e., this is a measure of impact). We must note that this methodology is biased toward attributes with more levels (i.e., binary categorical variables will score lower than continuous numerical ones), but methodologies do exist to mitigate this bias. Also worthy of note is the fact that in cases where the set includes correlated features that have similar influence on the output, this methodology will favor smaller groups of correlated features vs larger ones.

EXERCISE 3.B   Replicating ESG Ratings Based on Underlying ESG Data for Companies

As discussed earlier in the chapter, while the basic principles behind proprietary ratings are announced, the exact details that would allow us to reconstruct the rating from other observable variables with 100% precision are not available (or, for certain rating methodologies, do not exist, as the ratings are judgmental, at least to some degree).

In this exercise, we will attempt using decision tree/random forest machine learning techniques to approximate the actual proprietary Bloomberg rating methodology (and infer the most important driver variables behind the rating empirically).

For all S&P 500 constituents, we collect values for 53 "driver variables" that are expected to have an influence on each company's ESG rating. These values constitute our (learning) dataset.

```
In [38]:  ▶ df[df.columns[1:]].plot(kind="density", alpha=0.5).set_xlim(0, 100)
    Out[38]:  (0.0, 100.0)
```

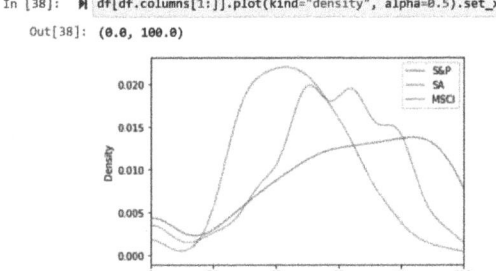

The list of Bloomberg data variables we are using is as follows ("object" data type signifies nonnumeric variables; e.g., those taking a value of "Y" or "N"):

```
In [4]:  ▶ df = pd.read_csv("esg notebooks/Bbg Data/esg variables.csv")
           df
```
Out[4]:

	nm	ESGScore	TOT_GHG_CO2_EM_INTENS_PER_SALES	CLIMATE_CHG_POLICY	ENERGY_INTENSITY_PER_SALES	WATER_INTENSITY_PER_SALES
0	LYB	24.888181	868.374590	Y	3823.406479	9343.134076
1	SBNY	28.142175	NaN	N	NaN	NaN
2	AXP	20.342784	2.871389	Y	8.175933	NaN
3	VZ	16.702828	31.884217	Y	89.073367	60.490523
4	AVGO	25.416391	NaN	Y	NaN	NaN
...	...	...	...	...	...	...
500	ZTS	18.180347	44.675055	N	124.895879	435.484660
501	DLR	13.018176	767.858646	Y	2200.374164	1380.115215
502	EQIX	14.707967	389.311083	Y	1076.927822	NaN
503	LVS	17.915800	222.979591	Y	401.493202	2365.772149
504	DISCK	17.359050	NaN	N	NaN	NaN

505 rows × 55 columns

(Continued)

In our dataset, 33 variables are numeric. Relevant machine learning techniques implemented in the *sklearn* library that we will use in this chapter require all data to be numeric; therefore, we need to preprocess our data by converting Y/N text variables into zeros and ones:

```
In [5]:  ▶  df.dtypes[2:]
```

```
Out[5]:   TOT_GHG_CO2_EM_INTENS_PER_SALES       float64
          CLIMATE_CHG_POLICY                     object
          ENERGY_INTENSITY_PER_SALES            float64
          WATER_INTENSITY_PER_SALES             float64
          WASTE_GENERATED_PER_SALES             float64
          BIODIVERSITY_POLICY                    object
          WATER_POLICY                           object
          WOMEN_MANAGEMENT_TO_EMPL_RATIO        float64
          PCT_WOMEN_EMPLOYEES                   float64
          EQUAL_OPPORTUNITY_POLICY               object
          ANTI-BRIBERY_ETHICS_POLICY             object
          EMP_PROT_WHISTLE_BLOWER_POLICY         object
          HEALTH_SAFETY_POLICY                   object
          HUMAN_RIGHTS_POLICY                    object
          POLICY_AGAINST_CHILD_LABOR             object
          FAIR_REMUNERATION_POLICY               object
          PCT_BOD_COMP_PD_IN_STK_AWD            float64
          SAY_PAY_NUMBER_OF_VOTES_FOR           float64
          PCT_NON_EXEC_DIR_ON_CMPNSTN_CMTE      float64
          CLAWBACK_PROVISION_FOR_EXEC_COMP       object
          CHG_OF_CTRL_BFIT_GOLD_CHUTE_AGR        object
          SAME_PERSON_CEO_AND_CHMN               object
          PCT_OF_NON_EXECUTIVE_DIR_ON_BRD       float64
          PCT_INDEPENDENT_DIRECTORS             float64
          INDEPENDENT_CHAIRPERSON                object
          INDEPENDENT_LEAD_DIRECTOR              object
          FORMER_CEO_OR_ITS_EQUIV_ON_BRD         object
          NUMBER_OF_DIRECTORS_ON_BOARD          float64
          PCT_IND_DIRECTORS_ON_AUDIT_CMTE       float64
          PCT_NON_EXEC_DIR_ON_AUD_CMTE          float64
          PCT_OF_AUD_CMTE_MEMBERS_3+_BDS        float64
          AUDIT_COMMITTEE_MEETING_ATTEND_%      float64
          IND_AUDIT_COMMITTEE_CHAIRPERSON        object
          YEARS_AUDITOR_EMPLOYED                float64
          DUAL_CLASS_UNEQUAL_VTG_RTS             object
          CLASSIFIED_BOARD_SYSTEM                object
          POISON_PILL_PLAN                       object
          BOD_AVERAGE_AGE                       float64
          BOD_AGE_RANGE                         float64
          CHIEF_EXECUTIVE_OFFICER_AGE           float64
          CHAIRMAN_AGE                          float64
          PCT_OF_EXECUTIVES_THAT_ARE_WOMEN      float64
          PCT_BRD_MEMBERS_THAT_ARE_WOMEN        float64
          NUM_BRD_MEMB_SERVING_OVER_10Y         float64
          BOARD_AVERAGE_TENURE                  float64
          EXECUTIVE_AVERAGE_TENURE              float64
          CHIEF_EXECUTIVE_OFFICER_TENURE        float64
          CHAIRMAN_TENURE                       float64
          PCT_OF_NON_EXECUTIVE_DIR_3+_BDS       float64
          PCT_OF_EXECUTIVE_DIR_ON_2+_BDS        float64
          NUM_BDS_CEO_SERVES_OTHER_FIRMS        float64
          NUM_BDS_CHMN_SERVES_OTHER_FIRMS       float64
          NUM_POS_CHMN_HOL_IN_OTH_FIRMS         float64
          dtype: object
```

Also, the data we have collected contains a lot of gaps: not all variables are observed for all the companies of interest. We replace NA data with mean values throughout the dataset.

```
In [7]:  ▶  import numpy as np
```

```
In [9]:  ▶  for ii in df.columns[1:]:
                 if df.dtypes[ii] == np.dtype('O'):
                     df[ii] = np.where(df[ii] == "Y", 1, 0)
```

Now we are ready to try training a simple regression tree on our dataset. Regression trees are implemented by the *sklearn.tree.DecisionTreeRegressor* class in Python's *sklearn*.

max_depth parameter specifies that we are calibrating a tree that has a maximum depth of 3 (three steps between the decision tree's root note and the farthest leaf).

```
In [10]:  ▶  df.fillna(df.mean(), inplace=True)
```

However, the resulting correlation of our generated ratings (even in-sample!) to the actual Bloomberg ESG ratings data for the S&P 500 constituent sample is present, but still quite far from 100%.

```
In [12]:  ▶ import sklearn.tree as tree
```

```
In [13]:  ▶ mdl = tree.DecisionTreeRegressor(max_depth=3)
            mdl.fit(df[df.columns[2:]], df[df.columns[1]])
```

```
Out[13]: DecisionTreeRegressor(max_depth=3)
```

The *plot_tree* method of the decision tree class allows us to visualize the decision tree calibrated to data. We enlarge the resulting figure by specifying figure size explicitly to *matplotlib*:

```
In [14]:  ▶ dfRes = pd.DataFrame({"tree": mdl.predict(df[df.columns[2:]]), "actual":df[df.columns[1]].values})
            dfRes = dfRes.sort_values("actual").reset_index(drop=True)
            dfRes.corr()
```

Out[14]:

	tree	actual
tree	1.000000	0.480324
actual	0.480324	1.000000

```
In [6]:  ▶ import matplotlib.pyplot as plt
```

```
In [15]:  ▶ plt.figure(figsize=(12, 12))
            tree.plot_tree(mdl, fontsize=10, feature_names=df.columns[2:])
            plt.show()
```

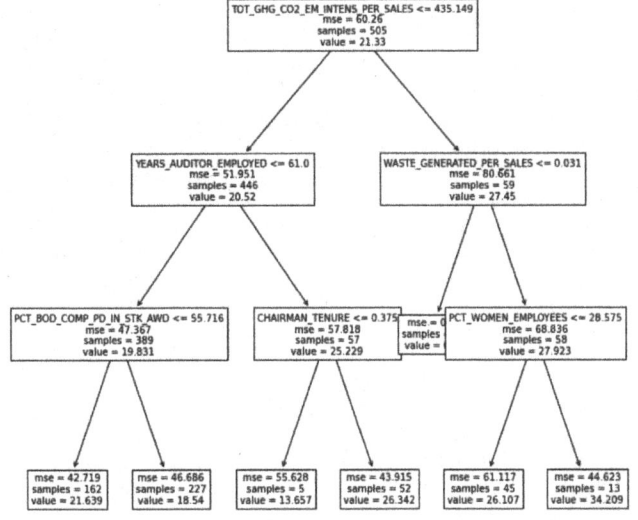

As we have seen above from our in-sample rating correlation, the quality of our rating predictions still leaves much to be desired. As the next step, we replace a single regression tree used above with a random forest implementation that trains an ensemble of decision trees simultaneously and uses their average prediction as its resulting forecast. The random forest regressor is implemented in *sklearn* by the *sklearn.ensemble.RandomForestRegressor* class.

(*Continued*)

```
In [17]:  ▶ import sklearn.ensemble as ens

In [18]:  ▶ mdlForest = ens.RandomForestRegressor(max_depth=3)
            mdlForest.fit(df[df.columns[2:]], df[df.columns[1]])

  Out[18]:  RandomForestRegressor(max_depth=3)
```

This slightly more sophisticated method results in a notable improvement in the in-sample fit, increasing in-sample correlation with the actual ratings from 48% to 61%.

```
In [19]:  ▶ dfRes = pd.DataFrame({"tree": mdl.predict(df[df.columns[2:]]),
                                   "forest": mdlForest.predict(df[df.columns[2:]]),
                                   "actual": df[df.columns[1]].values})
            dfRes = dfRes.sort_values("actual").reset_index(drop=True)
            dfRes.corr()

  Out[19]:
```

	tree	forest	actual
tree	1.000000	0.797153	0.480324
forest	0.797153	1.000000	0.605177
actual	0.480324	0.605177	1.000000

CHAPTER 4

Alternative Data

4.1 WHAT ARE ALTERNATIVE DATA AND THEIR ESG APPLICATIONS?

In the current age of information, one rule has held steady for over 15 years, and this has been the exponential growth of available data, which, in layperson's terms, is called *big data*. While it is not likely that this trend will continue indefinitely, we are already witnessing a situation where more data is available than what can be readily processed and consumed by the average practitioner.

Furthermore, the vast majority of data that is being generated falls into the "unstructured data" category, which comes with several drawbacks in terms of processing it and being able to extract useful signals that can be then turned into drivers for financial models (Figure 4.1).

Within the subject of ESG finance, the reliance on unstructured, or "alternative," data, is even stronger than in other disciplines, since the relatively recent nature of this field, coupled with the lack of established and structured reporting sources, has created a very inconsistent data landscape to navigate. ESG reporting practices are, at best, inconsistent across different industries and sectors, and data tends to be incomplete. Parameters and metrics are also typically self-reported by companies on a voluntary basis (please refer to Chapter 3 for further elaboration on the lack of standardization in ESG reporting and, by consequence, ratings). As a result of this unregulated and somewhat haphazard data landscape and standards, investors that are interested in the ESG ecosystem are largely left to rely on a plethora of "alternative" data sources, which they have to navigate based on their own experience and common sense.

Fortunately for us, as ESG practitioners, several Fintech startups have entered the fray in these early stages and have taken the lead in offering both ESG ratings (as previously discussed) and the underlying data used for the ratings' generation. Among these, without the ambition to be exhaustive in our list, we can quote the following examples (others can be seen, e.g., in the Datarade AI's "top 10" list, later in this chapter):

- Truvalue Labs: https://truvaluelabs.com/products/data
- OWL Analytics: http://owlanalytics.net/
- Arabesque: https://www.arabesque.com/s-ray/

As has frequently happened with similar startups in the field, some new players have either been rapidly acquired by well-established powerhouses in the data-providing space (Bloomberg, Reuters Eikon, etc.), or directly developed/funded in-house by them.

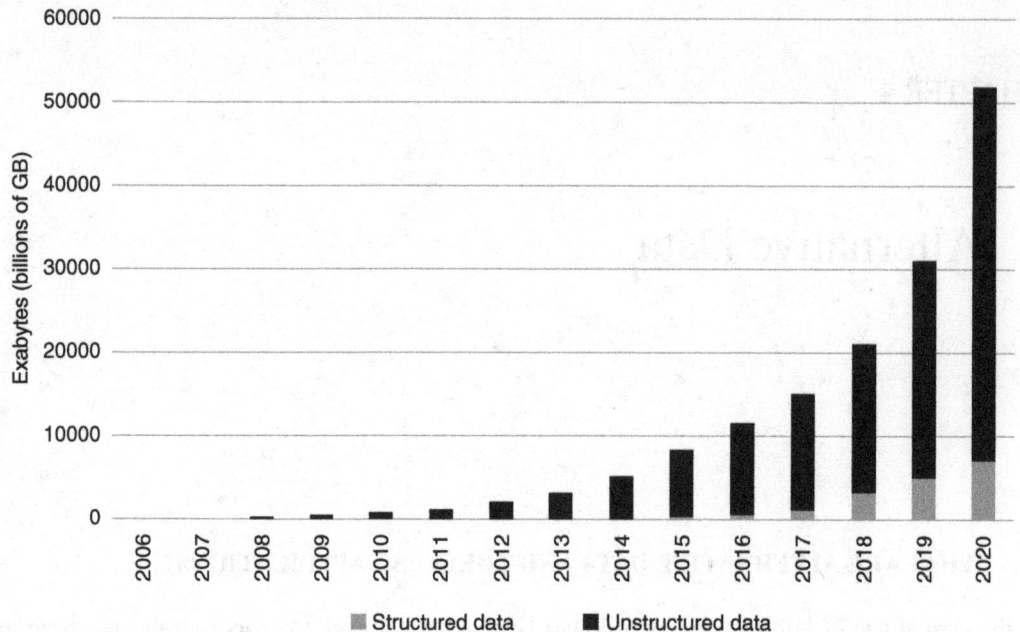

FIGURE 4.1   The Cambrian explosion of data.
Source: EETimes, "Digital Data Storage Is Undergoing Mind-Boggling Growth," September 14, 2016, https://www
.eetimes.com/digital-data-storage-is-undergoing-mind-boggling-growth/#

Alternative Data Types. Current types of alternative data can be broken down into the following
four categories. As more types of data become readily available and new ways of exploiting the data
become mainstream, we expect the categories will increase over time:

- *Sentiment.* This category of data includes content from social media feeds (of different types),
  news flows, corporate announcements, and other general published media. It is unstructured text
  that is monitored and analyzed for clues to sentiment and opinions on stocks, specific products,
  or the economy in general. This category also includes the analysis of transcripts of the language
  used by executives in earnings calls with analysts and their answers to questions by reporters.
  This type of data is typically time-sensitive and rapidly loses relevance to the practitioner (after
  all, it measures a transient feeling, which is prone to changing as the conditions change, in the
  same way an opinion poll changes, and it quickly becomes obsolete).
- *Other web scraping.* This category involves longer-persistence information that is gleaned by
  compiling data from targeted websites in an effort to gain information on companies, brands, and
  specific products. Examples of this are the analysis of company-specific job postings (number,
  type, location, trends, etc.), online feedback from clients, and employee satisfaction ratings, all of
  which are used to try to gain insight and clues on a companies' growth prospects and overall
  customer satisfaction ratings. This type of data is indicative of medium to long-term trends and
  stays relevant for longer than sentiment analysis.
- *Credit card data.* This category of data has been made available by some data providers who have
  managed to gather large enough anonymized panels of consumers with their credit and debit card
  activity. As long as the panels are of sufficient size, this type of data can be used as a real-time
  tracker for retail revenue, which can also add unprecedented levels of granularity, based on the
  composition and localization of the panel of consumers. This is a very specific type of dataset,
  and very time-sensitive, as most of this information is published by official statistics boards

within a relatively short period of time after the actual expenditures, and the data from the panels rapidly becomes stale.

- *Satellite and aerial imagery.* This category of data, depending on the type of use it is put to, can go from being very short term in focus (e.g., analysis of the number of cars in shopping malls as a real-time proxy for seasonal sales) to extremely long term (e.g., climate-related analysis, such as looking at changes in forestation/agricultural coverage in certain regions of the world). It is certainly a field that provides a vast set of different opportunities, many of which are being offered by commercial enterprises at the time of the writing of this textbook (tracking of ships en route, monitoring of crops, measurement of activity in ports and oil fields, etc.), and many more of which will certainly become available in the near future.

Alternative Data Clearinghouse. One of the problems with the burgeoning volume of data is finding a central, single location where it can be easily accessed and downloaded for the purposes of analysis and processing.

Several companies offering these services are now present in the marketplace, fulfilling this role of central clearinghouse for data, and we have chosen to take an in-depth look at Datarade AI,[1] a commercial clearinghouse for trading in alternative datasets that has been created relatively recently, as it hosts a variety of ESG-specific datasets that are of potential use for the purposes of this textbook. The data services provided by Datarade AI are by subscription (while the company does not own the data itself, it earns commissions from the owners of the data for all subscriptions that originate from the Datarade AI website) and are, by no means, required to be able to properly complete the study of this chapter or understand the topic at hand.

The website has a comprehensive description of all the types of datasets available, as well as an FAQ section that provides guidance and answers to most user questions.

The datasets that are of most interest for the purposes of this textbook are the ones focusing on the following areas.

ESG Attributes. The datasets available in this category include:

- ESG data
- ESG risk data
- ESG sentiment data
- Corporate and company ESG data
- ESG country rating data
- ESG fund-rating data
- ESG equities data
- ESG defense and weapons data
- Raw ESG data
- Sustainability data
- UN sustainable development data
- Greenhouse gas emissions data
- Energy consumption data

Types of Data. The kind of data that is found in the different datasets is diverse and covers different dimensions of the ESG spectrum, depending on the data provider. Table 4.1, while not comprehensive, provides a good overall feel for the categories of data that are available.

In addition to the "pure" ESG data, the clearinghouse also provides access to many linked series of datasets, which can have applications for the ESG practitioner, such as:

---

[1] https://datarade.ai/data-categories/esg-data

TABLE 4.1   A sample of data sources.

Supplier	Dataset Description	Environmental	Social	Governance
ACLED data	Armed conflict location and event data project – Historical data		X	
Akadia	Employee health and safety data		X	
Akadia	Energy, water, and waste data of global companies	X		
Akadia	Greenhouse gas emissions / carbon footprint data	X		
Bedrock	SEC filers – Auditor changes, restatements, control issues, going concern			X
Bedrock	SEC filers – Financial statement restatements			X
Bedrock	SEC filers with material weakness in internal control			X
Bedrock	SEC filers with substantial doubt over going concern			X
Bitvore Cellenus	Bitvore Cellenus for environmental, social, and governance (ESG)	X	X	X
Chain of Demand	Chain of demand's ESG services, products, and data coverage	X	X	X
Clarity AI	Sustainability cloud software as a service (ESG, impact, climate, regulation, etc.) for companies, governments	X	X	X
Datacie	Risk factors: North American public companies risk data			X
DataSpark	ESG, financial, and alternative key metrics for investment research	X	X	X
DataSpark	Greenhouse gas carbon emissions of global corporations	Climate dataset global coverage	X		
DataSpark	SFDR ESG portfolio reporting – Complete regulatory and data package	X	X	X
ESG Analytics	Hazardous waste emissions by sector and business	X		
ESG Data	Business location information, foot traffic, and footprint data for ESG risk	X	X	
ESGAnalytics AI	Web-based platform – ESG data for 193 countries, 60k companies, and 1200 exchange-traded funds	X	X	X
ESGAnalytics AI	Gender gap by sector and business		X	
ESGAnalytics AI	Water impacts by sector and business	X		
ESGAnalytics AI	Future climate risk by company at 5-, 10-, and 20-year forecasts	X		
Event Registry	ESG risks database related to companies, sectors, and countries worldwide	X	X	X
FACTSET	Alternative data (global coverage) – Novel ESG, market, and business intelligence	X	X	X
GIST	Traceable sustainability (ESG) data for 3500+ listed companies	X	X	X
Impact Cubed	Corporate ESG factor data for all listed companies (40,000+)	X	X	X
Impact Cubed	Sovereign ESG factor data for all sovereign debt issuers (190+ countries)	X	X	X
Impact Cubed	Sustainable products and services data for all listed equities (40,000+)	X		

Supplier	Dataset Description	Environmental	Social	Governance
ISS	ESG custom rating (develop custom ESG scoring models)	X	X	X
Knowsis	Insights Dashboard: Risk alerts, aggregated news feed, and social sentiment data. ESG and listed equities, macro topics, alerts, and anomalies	X	X	X
RegAlytics	International financial alerts for over 5000 regulators – BIS, ECB, HKMA, MAS			X
RegAlytics	US employment alerts for over 5000 regulators – DOL, EEOC, state agencies, and more			X
RegAlytics	US financial alerts for over 5000 regulators – SEC Federal Reserve state banks, securities regulators, and more			X
Sensefolio	Company ESG scores – Includes USA, China, UAE, India, UK, France, Brazil	X	X	X
Sensefolio	Sustainability raw data – Europe, Asia, North America, South America	X	X	
SG	Risk scores via API/ datafeed for companies, governments, funds and portfolios	X	X	X
SIGWATCH	Global nongovernmental (NGO) signals (ESG and reputational) – data service – corporate scores + source data	X	X	X
SIGWATCH	Global NGO signals (ESG and reputational) – data service – corporate scores	X	X	X
SIGWATCH	Global NGO signals (ESG and reputational) – data service-sector scores + source data	X	X	X
SIGWATCH	Global NGO signals (ESG and reputational) – data service-sector scores	X	X	X
Sustainable Platform	Controversial industry data across 18,000 companies, large and small, 97% global market cap		X	
Sustainable Platform	Sustainability / UN SDG sales data on 18,000+ companies to enhance ESG performance, returns and reduce risk	X	X	X
Sustainable Platform	UN SDG and ESG scores for companies and portfolios, material for forward-looking risk and return	X	X	X
Zero Trafficking	Suspected human trafficking networks – zero trafficking relational data		X	
Zero Trafficking	List of US illicit massage businesses 2021 – 30K records		X	X
ZIGRAM	Anti–money laundering penalties			X

Environmental data:
- Weather data
- Climate data
- Air quality index
- Pollen data
- Wildfires data
- Marine data

- Water data
- Land use data
- Geological data
- Surface data
- Atmosphere data
- Ionospheric data
- Thermosphere data

Political data:
- Voter data
- Political risk data
- Campaign and election data
- Fundraising and donor data
- Government and congressional data

Geospatial data:
- Location data
- Point of interest (POI) data
- Map data
- Satellite data
- Cell tower data
- Geographical Information Systems (GIS) data
- Geographic data
- Mobility data
- Geodemographic data

Transport and logistics data:
- Traffic data
- Trucking fleet data
- Aviation data
- Road data
- Freight data
- Trade data
- Maritime data

Energy data:
- Oil and gas data
- Fuel data
- Solar energy data
- Wind power data

Where Does the ESG Data Come From? Independent of whether the data is sourced from a clearinghouse, such as in Table 4.1, directly from vendors, or from freely available open sources, the majority of ESG data, ultimately, is self-reported. There is, however, a significant minority that can be sourced from third-party and real-time ESG signals that can be mined with a variety of techniques.

TABLE 4.2 **Types of data sources.**

Sources	Description	Frequency/Type	Output
Corporations	• ESG annual reports • ESG proxy reports • Corporate website press releases	Both periodic (typically quarterly) and extemporaneous (press releases) / Unstructured text	Corporate ESG statistics
Governments and NGOs	• Governmental agency websites • Governmental agency reports • NGO websites • NGO reports	Usually periodic (quarterly or annual) / Unstructured text	Governmental/NGO ESG statistics
Crowd-sourced	• Social media feeds • News/web articles • Blogs • Company reviews	Real-time / Unstructured text	ESG signals

Broadly speaking, we can break down the data in the three following categories:

1. **Self-reported:** Data from company websites, press releases, blogs, annual shareholder reports, proxy reports, regulatory filings, executive management interviews/statements
2. **Third-party statistics:** Reports/scorecards/ratings issued by NGOs and governmental agencies, government websites
3. **Real-time signals:** Live newsfeeds, social media articles/blogs, and company reviews

Each of these three categories is broadly characterized, despite the common attribute of being unstructured in nature, by having frequencies and types of output that are category-specific, as we can see in Table 4.2.

4.2 HOW TO VALIDATE AN ESG DATA PROVIDER

In the growing ecosystem of data providers, with multiple new offerings appearing with increasingly higher frequency on the marketplace, it is crucial to be able to differentiate good data from bad data and to be sure that, if you choose to pay for data subscriptions, you are purchasing something that has value, consistency, and data quality.

Data is central to any model that the ESG practitioners will build and use during their career, and the computer science adage, "Garbage In – Garbage Out," holds true.

To reiterate this point, we want to remind our readers how this concept truly was born with the idea of a digital programmable computer, by quoting a passage by Charles Babbage, who invented the first mechanical computer in 1822:

On two occasions I have been asked..., "Pray, Mr. Babbage, if you put into the machine wrong figures, will the right answers come out?"... I am not able rightly to apprehend the kind of confusion of ideas that could provoke such a question.

—Charles Babbage,
Passages from the Life of a Philosopher (1864)

Unfortunately for us, the dispersed and unstandardized nature of the data and data providers currently available on the market makes the task of sourcing solid, reliable ESG data more of an art than a science.

This current status is due to global lack of regulation on the format, content, and governance structure over the ESG data, how it is reported, and what metrics it is required to contain. Additionally, many corporations choose to selectively disclose ESG metrics that shine a positive light on them, while not disclosing the ones that would not be so benign.

These inconsistencies in data quality and reliability create obstacles and challenges for data providers, governments, NGOs, and, by extension, the ESG practitioner, to whom this book is targeted.

Luckily, this situation also creates a business opportunity for third-party data providers to collect, evaluate, and clean up ESG data, which they are subsequently able to supply as a robust dataset to investors and researchers in the field.

There are currently hundreds of different vendors (some of which are listed in the previous table) in this space. Each vendor has specific areas of expertise, and many are ESG exclusive.

There is also a growing push, within the ESG rating space, toward standardization across providers reporting on ESG factors, which is beneficial to the sector as a whole and makes life easier for the practitioner.

As many of these vendors are either topic-specific, geography-specific, or both, it is normally necessary to rely on a multitude of different providers when building models that apply to anything more than a handful of companies.

If we go back to the Datarade clearinghouse, at the time of this writing we can find a "top 10 data providers" list for ESG reported. This list has been compiled based on Datarade's experience with data providers the company engages with; we repeat the list here as a sample of well-known ESG data providers (this list is not independently verified):

- *Truvalue Labs* applies AI-driven technology to over 100,000 unstructured text sources in 13 languages, including news, trade journals, and nongovernmental organizations and industry reports, to provide daily signals that identify positive and negative ESG behavior.

- *Owl Analytics* is a data and indexing company that offers detailed data and metrics on the ESG characteristics of global equities.

- *Arabesque S-Ray* is a global data provider that focuses on advisory and data solutions by combining big data and ESG metrics to assess the performance and sustainability of companies worldwide.

- *Accern* is an AI- and ML-based platform that uses news and alternative data (historical ESG data covering the past 15 years, collected from Dow Jones News Wires and EDGAR Securities and Exchange Commission filings) to capture ESG signals and create ESG scores to understand companies' ESG behaviors.

- *Sustainalytics* rates the sustainability of listed companies based on their ESG performance.

- *Clarity AI* is a sustainability technology platform that uses machine learning and big data to deliver environmental and social insights to investors and organizations. As of December 2021, Clarity AI's platform had analyzed more than 30,000 companies, 135,000 funds, 198 countries, and 187 local governments, and had delivered data and analytics for investing, corporate research, and reporting.

- *Goldbaum* is a data provider for ESG and stock market data. It provides analysts and portfolio managers with an AI-powered research platform that automatically reconciles, aggregates, and clusters all the financial and extra financial data into one place.

- *ISS ESG* provides climate data, analytics, and advisory services to help financial market participants understand, measure, and act on climate-related risks across all asset classes. In addition, ESG solutions cover corporate and country ESG research and ratings helping to identify material social and environmental risks and opportunities.

- *Sense Folio* scans financial news, companies' financial reports, and social media data to discern and observe signals on how involved companies are toward ESG.

- *Miotech* is an AI platform that empowers financial institutions to draw actionable insights on their data. It covers ESG data for green finance and responsible investments, provides software to manage ESG reporting, improve energy efficiency, and track and reduce carbon emissions.

4.3   PROCESSING SATELLITE DATA

We now transition to taking a deeper look at the techniques and methodologies applied to processing satellite data, both by looking at existing indices and examples and by applying the methodology in our own exercise section.

A good example of a satellite data index that is readily available is the SpaceKnow Africa Night Light Index (ticker: SPCK name of the country). Publicly available macroeconomic data for many African nations are scarce. Additionally, even those countries that do have established publications of such indicators, such as gross domestic product (GDP), typically publish their data with notable lags and/or need for frequent restatement of prior data, which makes models that rely on macroeconomic variables hard to use for this continent. The SpaceKnow Africa Night Light Index is designed to allow generation of reliable real-time macroeconomic indicators for African countries, without having to count on local issuance of data, which can be erratic and potentially incorrect.

The Night Light Index is, effectively, an aggregation, at country level, of the light intensity measured by satellites during nighttime (measured in areas that have negligible cloud coverage, to ensure the data is consistent). The data is averaged over monthly aggregations and compared to the same period from a year ago (or longer) to detect increases/decreases in activity (which can be used as a proxy for GDP).

As an example, from the SpaceKnow case study on Nigeria, we can refer to Figure 4.2, which shows two curves, the light gray line representing quarterly GDP data[2] and the dark gray line representing quarterly data from the SpaceKnow Nigeria Night Light Index.

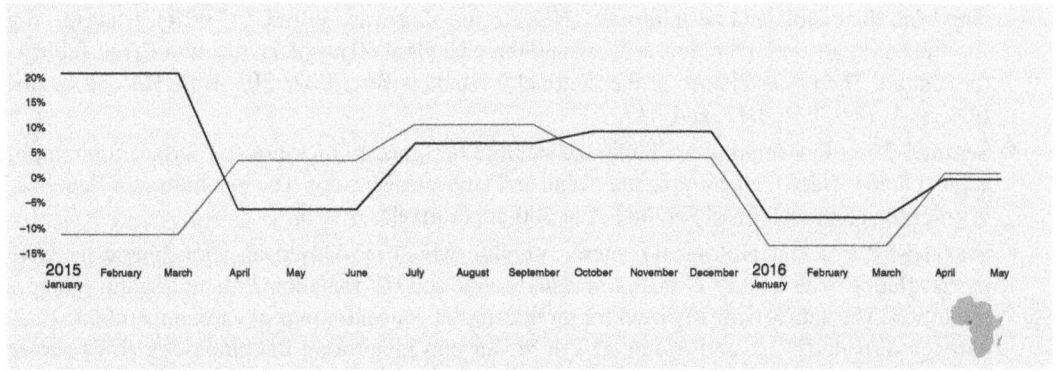

FIGURE 4.2   Night Light Index.
Source: SpaceKnow.

---

[2] http://www.tradingeconomics.com/

A similar application referencing India is available online[3] and provides interesting insight on the methodologies used for this kind of analysis.

Practical Methodologies and Indices for Satellite Imagery Processing. We shall now shift our focus to the practical methodologies that are needed to process satellite imagery in a way that allows us to gain insightful information on data that are relevant to the practitioner of ESG finance. In order to do so, we will leverage the (mostly) free imagery that has recently become available to the public in very large quantities via satellite data consortiums such as Copernicus.[4]

We debated whether to include this section in the book at all, given that it is not directly "quantitative finance" per se, but ultimately decided in favor of inclusion, as it allows understanding of fundamentals of imagery analytics, which the financial engineer will certainly be called on to use in future practical applications. Furthermore, with the increase of importance of alternative data, it is likely that these concepts and indices will become more and more mainstream and new financial and econometric models will appear in the coming years that will require the basic understanding of the topic that we hope to provide in this chapter. It is likely that, most of the time, the reader will encounter satellite imagery data in the form of processed results rather than raw imagery data, such as those being processed here. Nevertheless, it is certainly useful for the aspiring financial engineer to have at least a high-level understanding of how these processed data are generated and what underlying processes drive them.

There are a very large number of free satellite services available online, mostly because these are run by publicly funded organizations such as the European Space Agency and NASA, both of which have a mandatory commitment to making all data freely available to the scientific community and the general public. Several commercial providers of satellite data are available and allow for tailored and hard-to-retrieve data to be gathered, if required. The following list is abridged and includes content from major freely available satellite imagery sources. These sources are approximately ordered by relevance, starting from the most significant/popular:

- **Sentinel-1.** Images are generated from two polar-orbiting satellites. These satellites mostly focus on environmental change by monitoring marine environments for sea ice levels, oil spills, marine winds, waves and currents, and terrestrial environments for land-use change, land deformation, and others. They are also used for first-responder applications, such as floods and earthquakes. The satellites orbit Earth 180° apart and at an altitude of approximately 700 km, passing over the same place on Earth (revisit time) every 6 to 12 days, depending on the area.

- **Sentinel-2.** This satellite is mainly dedicated to the Copernicus services. It carries a multispectral imager with a swath of 290 km per image. The imager provides a set of 13 spectral bands spanning from the visible and near infrared (NIR) to the shortwave infrared (SWIR), featuring four spectral bands at 10 m, six bands at 20 m, and three bands at 60 m spatial resolution (see Table 4.3 for details). The nomenclature of the Sentinel-2 bands is B01, B02, B03, B04, B05, B06, B07, B08, B8A, B09, B10, B11, and B12.

- **Sentinel-3** is a low-orbiting medium-size satellite designed to measure sea surface topography, sea and land surface temperature, and ocean and land surface color. The resolution for Sentinel-3 is lower than Sentinel-1 and Sentinel-2, at 300 m per pixel.

- **Sentinel-5P** is a meteorological-centered satellite which is focused on atmospheric measurements relating to air quality, climate force, and ozone and UV radiation with high spatio-temporal resolution. The data is typically used for monitoring of concentrations of carbon monoxide (CO), nitrogen dioxide (NO_2), and ozone (O_3) in the air and monitoring the ultraviolet (UV) aerosol index. Sentinel-5P also has the capability of tracking different geophysical parameters of clouds. It covers almost the whole globe, including the far north and far south (95% coverage for latitudes in the interval [−7°, 7°]).

---

[3] http://india.nightlights.io/#/
[4] https://scihub.copernicus.eu/

TABLE 4.3 Sentinel-2 bands and descriptions.

Band	Resolution	Central Wavelength	Description
B1	60 m	443 nm	Ultra-blue (coastal and aerosol)
B2	10 m	490 nm	Blue
B3	10 m	560 nm	Green
B4	10 m	665 nm	Red
B5	20 m	705 nm	Visible and near infrared (VNIR)
B6	20 m	740 nm	VNIR
B7	20 m	783 nm	VNIR
B8	10 m	842 nm	VNIR
B8a	20 m	865 nm	VNIR
B9	60 m	940 nm	Shortwave infrared (SWIR)
B10	60 m	1375 nm	SWIR
B11	20 m	1610 nm	SWIR
B12	20 m	2190 nm	SWIR

- **Landsat 8.** The Landsat program, which has been running since 1972, represents the single longest uninterrupted run of satellite imagery acquisition of Earth as of the time of writing this textbook. The latest satellite of this family, the *Landsat 8*, launched in 2013, provides data in 11 spectral bands with spatial resolutions ranging from 15 to 60 meters. The *Landsat 8* bands are B01, B02, B03, B04, B05, B06, B07, B08, B09, B10, and B11 (note how B8A and B12 are not available).

- **Landsat 7** satellite orbits the Earth in a sun-synchronous, near-polar orbit, at an altitude of 705 km (438 mi). The satellite is multispectral, providing visible, near-infrared, mid-infrared and thermal bands, similar to Landsat 8.

- **Landsat 1–5 MSS** (Multispectral Scanner System). This online collection includes archived data from the, now retired, Landsat missions 1 through 5. It has 4 available bands in 60 m resolution – green, red, and two separate near-infrared (NIR) bands. Data is available globally starting from 1972.

- **Landsat Thematic Mapper (TM).** The TM sensor was carried onboard *Landsat 4* and *Landsat 5* and provided additional six spectral bands and one thermal infrared band in 120 m resolution, resampled to 30 meters. The data is available globally from July 1987 to December 1993 for *Landsat 4* and from March 1984 to May 2012 for *Landsat 5*. This collection is mainly used for change detection over medium time frames (change detection and the creation of land use–land cover maps) as well as monitoring of vegetation, ice, and water resources.

- **Landsat 7 ETM+.** The Landsat Enhanced Thematic Mapper + (ETM+) is currently carried on top of the Landsat 7 satellite. It includes sensing for 8 optical and 1 thermal infrared bands in 30 m resolution (with panchromatic band in 15 m resolution). Global data can be downloaded since April 1999, with a revisit time of 16 days. The data is used for the same applications as the Landsat TM above. Due to sensor failure on the satellite, there are data gaps for all images acquired since May 30, 2003.

- **MODIS.** The data for MODIS is hosted on Amazon Web Services (AWS). The dataset is updated daily and provides data from MODIS "land" bands 1–7: B01, B02, B03, B04, B05, B06, and B07.

- **DEM.** The Digital Elevation Model (DEM) is a 3D representation of the Earth's terrain's surface generated from terrain elevation data captured by satellite imagery. It is generally used for terrain analysis and orthorectification (geometrical scaling of satellite imagery to ensure that the scale is uniform). This dataset has 30 m resolution but is locally improved with additional datasets where available. This is a static set of data, which is gradually improved by improved precision of measurement (i.e., it is not date-specific).

- **Earthdata.** NASA's Earth Science Data Systems (ESDS) program is dedicated to oversight and management of the life cycle of NASA's Earth science data – from acquisition through processing and distribution. Since 1994, Earth science data have been free and open to all users for any purpose, and since 2015, all data systems software developed through research and technology awards have been made available to the public as Open Source Software (OSS). The program includes access to imagery and data from over 600 satellites made available by NASA.[5]
- **PROBA-V.** PROBA-V is a small satellite, operated by the European Space Agency (ESA), which supports applications such as land use, worldwide vegetation classification, crop monitoring, famine prediction, food security, disaster monitoring, and biosphere studies. The focus of PROBA-V is vegetation monitoring to provide a daily overview of global vegetation growth. Data generated by these instruments include the one-day Synthesis products and the 10-day Synthesis products, both with a ground resolution of about 1 km (1 km × 1 km pixel size).

A fairly comprehensive overview of online resources for satellite imagery analysis and sourcing is currently available from the Global Investigative Journalism Network at https://gijn.org/resources-for-finding-and-using-satellite-images/.

Another interesting toolbox, to become familiar with the data and the different bands from the satellites, is the Sentinelhub Playground,[6] which allows intuitive viewing and creation of specific indices online.

Intensity-Based Indexes. For use in ESG financial engineering applications, the simple images alone are seldom sufficient, and a further level of processing is often required in order to be able to perform useful analytics on the data. Some of the post processing is based on change detection (appearance or disappearance of features), which we shall not be treating in this section, while the rest is generally based on the calculation of a variety of brightness/color indexes in geographic locations of interest.

The conceptual basis behind this methodology is that different wavelengths of light are reflected/absorbed by different types of materials (e.g., plants, soil, rocks, cement, water, etc.) in material-specific ways. This difference in light absorption/reflection can be utilized to determine the prevalence of one type of groundcover vs. another, or other overall conditions of interest (level of moisture, percentage of certain types of geological materials, etc.).

As an example, if we are interested in determining the presence or absence of vegetation on any given point on the surface for which we have a satellite image available, we could use a vegetation-specific index, such as the Normalized Difference Vegetation Index (NDVI),[7] which tells us, in a quantifiable form, whether a particular point in a satellite image is covered by vegetation or not. In a similar fashion, specific indices exist that do the same for water surfaces, types of soil, and several others.

In Figure 4.3, we can see both the visible light and the NDVI index for the New York City area, with the areas where vegetation is present being displayed in lighter color in the bottom half of the image (notice how Central Park is clearly visible, as highlighted by the white arrow).

The most commonly used indices for ESG applications are the following:

Normalized Difference Vegetation Index (NDVI). This is a simple index for measuring green vegetation cover. It normalizes green leaf scattering in the NIR wavelengths with chlorophyll absorption in the red wavelengths. Vegetation strongly reflects NIR and absorbs red light, so the NDVI index is good for quantifying the amount of vegetation. The higher the index value, the more likely the location is to be covered with forest.

The values of NDVI range between –1 and 1. Negative values (approaching –1) typically represent water. Values around zero (generally between –0.1 and 0.1) usually are rocky, sandy, or snow-covered areas. Grass and shrubs are identified by low positive values (0.2–0.4), with temperate and tropical rainforests being represented by anything starting above 0.4 all the way to 1.0.

---

[5] https://search.earthdata.nasa.gov/search
[6] https://apps.sentinel-hub.com/sentinel-playground
[7] https://en.wikipedia.org/wiki/Normalized_difference_vegetation_index

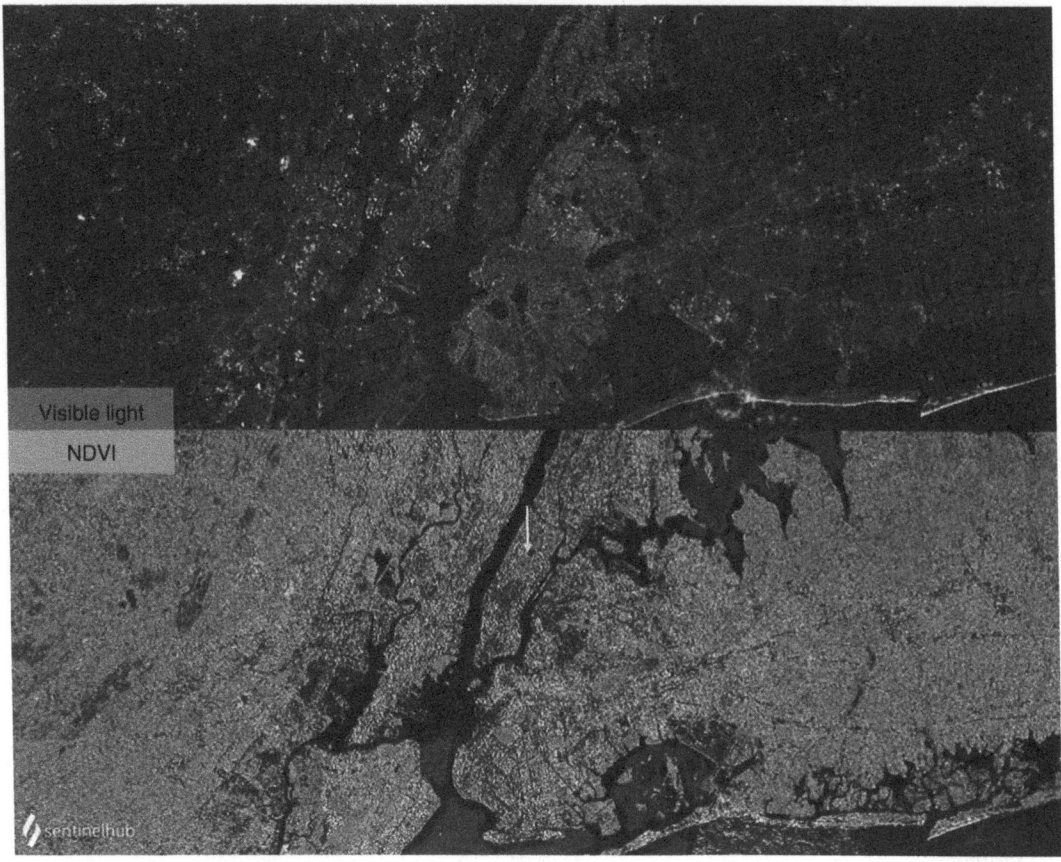

FIGURE 4.3 Visible light view vs. NDVI for the New York City area.
Source: SentinelHub

The formal definition of NDVI is the following:

$$NDVI = \frac{NIR - RED}{NIR + RED}$$

For practical use with Sentinel-2 data, it is calculated using the following bands (for use with data from other satellites please refer to https://custom-scripts.sentinel-hub.com/sentinel-2/ndvi/):

$$NDVI = \frac{B_8 - B_4}{B_8 + B_4},$$

where B_8 and B_4 refer to eighth and fourth Sentinel bands respectively.

Soil Adjusted Vegetation Index (SAVI). This index was developed to solve instability issues with NDVI that derive from variance in soil color, soil moisture, and saturation effects from high-density vegetation. The SAVI vegetation index accounts for the differential red and NIR extinction through the vegetation canopy by introducing an additional parameter (L), as follows.

The formal definition of SAVI is

$$SAVI = (1+L)\frac{NIR - RED}{NIR + RED + L}$$

FIGURE 4.4   SAVI for the New York City area.
Source: SentinelHub

For practical use with Sentinel-2 data, it is calculated using the following bands:

$$SAVI = (1+L)\frac{B_8 - B_4}{B_8 + B_4 + L}$$

Figure 4.4 shows the SAVI index for the New York City area, which can be compared to the previous NDVI image.

Visible Atmospherically Resistant Index (VARI) – This index is designed to highlight vegetation using visible light and minimize lighting differences and atmospheric effects.[8]

The formal definition of VARI is the following:

$$VARI = \frac{Green - Red}{Green + Red - Blue}$$

For practical use with Sentinel-2 data, it is calculated using the following bands:

$$VARI = \frac{B_3 - B_4}{B_3 + B_4 - B_2}$$

In Figure 4.5, we can see the VARI index for the New York City area.

Modified Normalized Difference Water Index (MNDWI). This index is used to detect and enhance open water features viz. land features. It utilizes the green and middle-infrared bands and, if compared to the NDWI from which it derives, it shows less built-up area features correlating with open water.

The difference from the NDWI is that the MNDWI is modified by substituting the MIR (middle-infrared) band for the NIR band.

---

[8] A. A. Gitelson, R. Stark, U. Grits, D. Rundquist, Y. Kaufman, and D. Derry, "Vegetation and Soil Lines in Visible Spectral Space: A Concept and Technique for Remote Estimation of Vegetation Fraction," *International Journal of Remote Sensing* 23 (2002): 2537–2562.

FIGURE 4.5   VARI for the New York City area.
Source: SentinelHub

The formal definition of the modified NDWI (MNDWI) is the following:

$$MNDWI = \frac{\text{Green} - \text{MIR}}{\text{Green} + \text{MIR}}$$

where MIR is a middle infrared band such as Landsat TM band 5 (1.55–1.75, B11 on Sentinel-2 bands). For practical use with Sentinel-2 data, it is calculated using the following bands:[9]

$$MNDWI = \frac{B_3 - B_{11}}{B_3 + B_{11}}$$

In Figure 4.6, we can see the MNDWI index for the New York City area (the light gray band in the center on the water is an artifact of the satellite data).

Normalized Difference Moisture Index (NDMI). This index detects and visualizes moisture levels in vegetation. The major applications are in forestry (fuel level monitoring of forests) and agriculture (drought assessment). The bands that it utilizes are the NIR and SWIR in a normalized ratio, which reduces illumination and atmospheric artifacts:

$$NDMI = \frac{NIR - SWIR1}{NIR + SWIR1}$$

For practical use with Sentinel-2 data, NDMI is calculated using the following bands:

$$NDMI = \frac{B_8 - B_{11}}{B_8 + B_{11}}$$

---

[9] H. Xu, "Modification of Normalized Difference Water Index (NDWI) to Enhance Open Water Features in Remotely Sensed Imagery," *International Journal of Remote Sensing* 27 (14) (2006): 3025–3033.

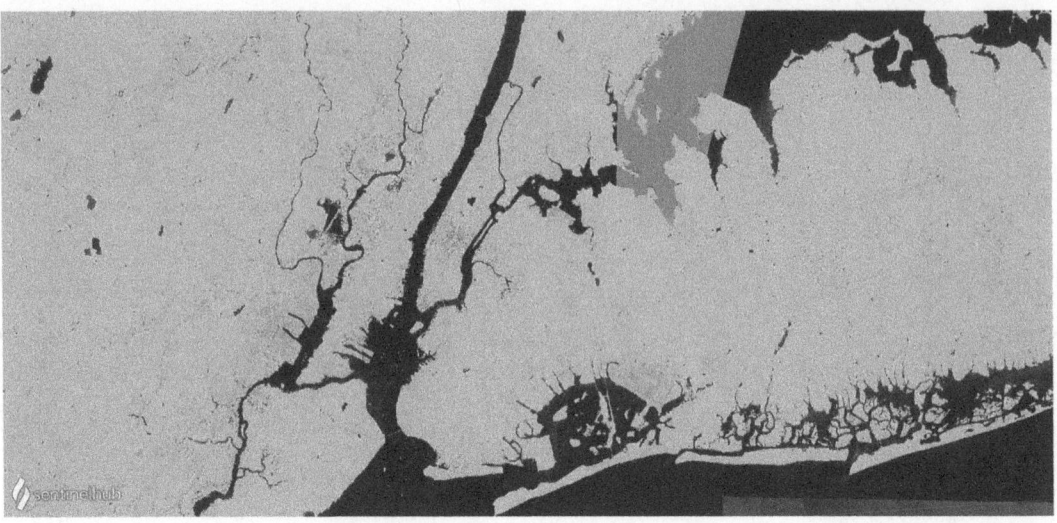

FIGURE 4.6   MNDWI for the New York City area.
Source: SentinelHub

FIGURE 4.7   NDMI for the New York City area.
Source: SentinelHub

In Figure 4.7, we can see the NDMI index for the New York City area.

Besides vegetation and moisture, satellite/aerial imagery data can also be processed for non-biosphere-related applications. A few examples of intensity-based indices used for geology applications, specifically for classification of soil types, are presented next. They are typically used for detecting fossil fuel and other mineral deposits.

Clay Minerals Ratio. The Clay Minerals Ratio index is calculated as a ratio between the SWIR1 and SWIR2 bands. The scientific basis of this index is grounded in the different absorption spectra of hydrous minerals such as clays, which typically have a specific absorption profile that peaks with radiation in the 2.0–2.3-micron portion of the spectrum.

$$Clay\ Minerals\ Ratio = \frac{SWIR1}{SWIR2}$$

FIGURE 4.8   Clay Minerals Ratio for the New York City area.
Source: SentinelHub

This ratio is originally obtained from Landsat TM band 7 (2.09–2.35) and band 5 (1.55–1.75). For Sentinel-2 data, the following bands should be used:

SWIR1 = shortwave infrared 1 band [B11]
SWIR2 = shortwave infrared 2 band [B12]

In Figure 4.8, we can see the Clay Minerals Ratio index for the New York City area.

Ferrous Minerals Ratio. This index is designed to identify areas of terrain rich in iron-bearing materials. It identifies rock features containing iron-bearing minerals using the ratio between the short-wave infrared (SWIR: 1.55–1.75 µm) and near-infrared (NIR: 0.76–0.9 µm) bands.[10]

$$Ferrous\ Minerals\ Ratio = \frac{SWIR}{NIR}$$

For Sentinel-2 data, the following bands should be used:

SWIR = shortwave infrared band [B11]
NIR = visible and near infrared band [B07]

Figure 4.9 shows the Ferrous Minerals Ratio index for the New York City area.

---

[10] For the theoretical basis behind the Ferrous Minerals Ratio definition, please refer to: Donald B. Segal, "Theoretical Basis for Differentiation of Ferric-Iron Bearing Minerals Using Landsat MSS Data," *Proceedings of Symposium for Remote Sensing of Environment,* 2nd Thematic Conference on Remote Sensing for Exploratory Geology, Fort Worth, TX (1982): 949–951.

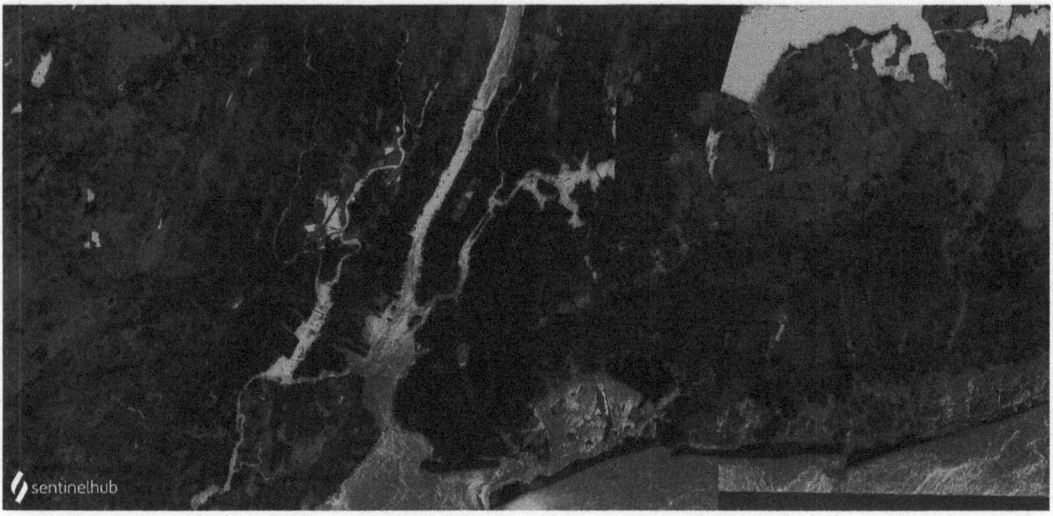

FIGURE 4.9 Ferrous Minerals Ratio for the New York City area.
Source: SentinelHub

EXERCISE 4.A   Processing Downloaded Satellite Images with EarthPy

In this first exercise, we focus on analysis and extraction of quantitative information from already-downloaded images.

As always, we start by loading relevant packages. *EarthPy* and *RasterIO* are the two packages commonly used for satellite (also aerial and generally geographic) image manipulation. Useful *EarthPy* documentation is available at https://www.earthdatascience.org/tools/earthpy/.

As the relevant names suggest, *earthpy.plot* module provides a number of useful plotting functions, while *earthpy.spatial* mainly provides calculation utilities.

```
In [1]:   ▶ import numpy as np

            import rasterio as rio

            import earthpy.plot as ep
            import earthpy.spatial as es
```

Glob is a utility package that we need to source the image file names (unsurprisingly, satellite data consists of a great many images that occupy significant disk space).

```
In [2]:   ▶ import os
            import glob

            os.getcwd()

Out[2]:   'C:\\Users\\cyril\\Documents'
```

We will work with pre downloaded images in JP2 format. Using *Rasterio*, we load image files representing different spectral (color) bands captured by the satellite and compile them into a list first.

```
In [3]:  ▶ sPath = ("esg notebooks/S2A_MSIL1C_20210827T153601_N0301_R111_T19TEK_20210827T191624.SAFE/GRANULE/"
            "L1C_T19TEK_A032283_20210827T153945/IMG_DATA")
```

```
In [4]:  ▶ bandFiles = sorted(glob.glob(sPath + "/*.jp2"))
            bandFiles
```

```
Out[4]:  ['esg notebooks/S2A_MSIL1C_20210827T153601_N0301_R111_T19TEK_20210827T191624.SAFE/GRANULE/L1C_T19TEK_A032283_202108
          27T153945/IMG_DATA\\T19TEK_20210827T153601_B01.jp2',
           'esg notebooks/S2A_MSIL1C_20210827T153601_N0301_R111_T19TEK_20210827T191624.SAFE/GRANULE/L1C_T19TEK_A032283_202108
          27T153945/IMG_DATA\\T19TEK_20210827T153601_B02.jp2',
           'esg notebooks/S2A_MSIL1C_20210827T153601_N0301_R111_T19TEK_20210827T191624.SAFE/GRANULE/L1C_T19TEK_A032283_202108
          27T153945/IMG_DATA\\T19TEK_20210827T153601_B03.jp2',
           'esg notebooks/S2A_MSIL1C_20210827T153601_N0301_R111_T19TEK_20210827T191624.SAFE/GRANULE/L1C_T19TEK_A032283_202108
          27T153945/IMG_DATA\\T19TEK_20210827T153601_B04.jp2',
           'esg notebooks/S2A_MSIL1C_20210827T153601_N0301_R111_T19TEK_20210827T191624.SAFE/GRANULE/L1C_T19TEK_A032283_202108
          27T153945/IMG_DATA\\T19TEK_20210827T153601_B05.jp2',
           'esg notebooks/S2A_MSIL1C_20210827T153601_N0301_R111_T19TEK_20210827T191624.SAFE/GRANULE/L1C_T19TEK_A032283_202108
          27T153945/IMG_DATA\\T19TEK_20210827T153601_B06.jp2',
           'esg notebooks/S2A_MSIL1C_20210827T153601_N0301_R111_T19TEK_20210827T191624.SAFE/GRANULE/L1C_T19TEK_A032283_202108
          27T153945/IMG_DATA\\T19TEK_20210827T153601_B07.jp2',
           'esg notebooks/S2A_MSIL1C_20210827T153601_N0301_R111_T19TEK_20210827T191624.SAFE/GRANULE/L1C_T19TEK_A032283_202108
          27T153945/IMG_DATA\\T19TEK_20210827T153601_B08.jp2',
           'esg notebooks/S2A_MSIL1C_20210827T153601_N0301_R111_T19TEK_20210827T191624.SAFE/GRANULE/L1C_T19TEK_A032283_202108
          27T153945/IMG_DATA\\T19TEK_20210827T153601_B09.jp2',
           'esg notebooks/S2A_MSIL1C_20210827T153601_N0301_R111_T19TEK_20210827T191624.SAFE/GRANULE/L1C_T19TEK_A032283_202108
          27T153945/IMG_DATA\\T19TEK_20210827T153601_B10.jp2',
           'esg notebooks/S2A_MSIL1C_20210827T153601_N0301_R111_T19TEK_20210827T191624.SAFE/GRANULE/L1C_T19TEK_A032283_202108
          27T153945/IMG_DATA\\T19TEK_20210827T153601_B11.jp2',
           'esg notebooks/S2A_MSIL1C_20210827T153601_N0301_R111_T19TEK_20210827T191624.SAFE/GRANULE/L1C_T19TEK_A032283_202108
          27T153945/IMG_DATA\\T19TEK_20210827T153601_B12.jp2',
           'esg notebooks/S2A_MSIL1C_20210827T153601_N0301_R111_T19TEK_20210827T191624.SAFE/GRANULE/L1C_T19TEK_A032283_202108
          27T153945/IMG_DATA\\T19TEK_20210827T153601_B8A.jp2',
           'esg notebooks/S2A_MSIL1C_20210827T153601_N0301_R111_T19TEK_20210827T191624.SAFE/GRANULE/L1C_T19TEK_A032283_202108
          27T153945/IMG_DATA\\T19TEK_20210827T153601_TCI.jp2']
```

```
In [5]:  ▶ lst = []
            for ii in bandFiles:
                with rio.open(ii, "r") as f:
                    lst.append(f.read(1))
```

Notice that the sizes of images in our list are different:

```
In [6]:  ▶ [ii.shape for ii in lst]
```

```
Out[6]:  [(1830, 1830),
          (10980, 10980),
          (10980, 10980),
          (10980, 10980),
          (5490, 5490),
          (5490, 5490),
          (5490, 5490),
          (10980, 10980),
          (1830, 1830),
          (1830, 1830),
          (5490, 5490),
          (5490, 5490),
          (5490, 5490),
          (10980, 10980)]
```

This occurs because different Sentinel-2 bands have different spatial resolution (some 10 m, some 20 m, and some 60 m). We therefore stretch less granular images to match the dimensions of those of the highest 10 m resolution. As the last preparation step, we stack all band images (now of the same dimensions) into a single *numpy* array.

The first three are 60 m bands; we stretch each pixel into six identical ones. Next, 4–6 and 10–12 are the 20 m ones; we therefore stretch them into 2 × 2 pixel groups. As a result, all our images now have the same dimensions, corresponding to the highest resolution available across all bands:

```
In [7]:  ▶ for ii in [0, 8, 9]:
                lst[ii] = np.kron(lst[ii], np.ones((6, 6)))
            for ii in [4, 5, 6, 10, 11, 12]:
                lst[ii] = np.kron(lst[ii], np.ones((2, 2)))
```

```
In [8]:  ▶ arrSt = np.stack(lst)
            arrSt.shape
```

```
Out[8]:  (14, 10980, 10980)
```

(*Continued*)

At this stage, we can plot the different bands side by side using a convenience function provided by *EarthPy*. Note that these are, of course, not natural colors but rather scalar intensities within each band; colors in the image may be specified by the color map *cmap* argument; we leave it at grayscale, which is the default setting.

```
In [9]:  M  ep.plot_bands(arrSt, figsize=(20, 12), cols=5, cbar=False, title=[ii[-7:-4] for ii in bandFiles])
```

```
Out[9]:  array([[<AxesSubplot:title={'center':'B01'}>,
                <AxesSubplot:title={'center':'B02'}>,
                <AxesSubplot:title={'center':'B03'}>,
                <AxesSubplot:title={'center':'B04'}>,
                <AxesSubplot:title={'center':'B05'}>],
               [<AxesSubplot:title={'center':'B06'}>,
                <AxesSubplot:title={'center':'B07'}>,
                <AxesSubplot:title={'center':'B08'}>,
                <AxesSubplot:title={'center':'B09'}>],
               [<AxesSubplot:title={'center':'B11'}>,
                <AxesSubplot:title={'center':'B12'}>,
                <AxesSubplot:title={'center':'B8A'}>,
                <AxesSubplot:title={'center':'TCI'}>, <AxesSubplot:>]],
              dtype=object)
```

Bands B04, B03, and B02, respectively, correspond to red, green, and blue intensities. We can plot the same image in natural color (or natural color with extra brightening, as shown here). The image is brightened by multiplying RGB intensities by $1 / (1 - str\_clip)$; brightening is, in fact, commonly needed for satellite images, depending on atmospheric conditions and time of day.

In this exercise, we chose a region in Maine. Most of the area is covered with forest; the southeastern quadrant also contains Atlantic coastline, part of the ocean waters, and several (wood-covered) islands along the coast.

```
In [10]:  ▶ ep.plot_rgb(arrSt, rgb=(3, 2, 1), stretch=True, str_clip=0.5)
```

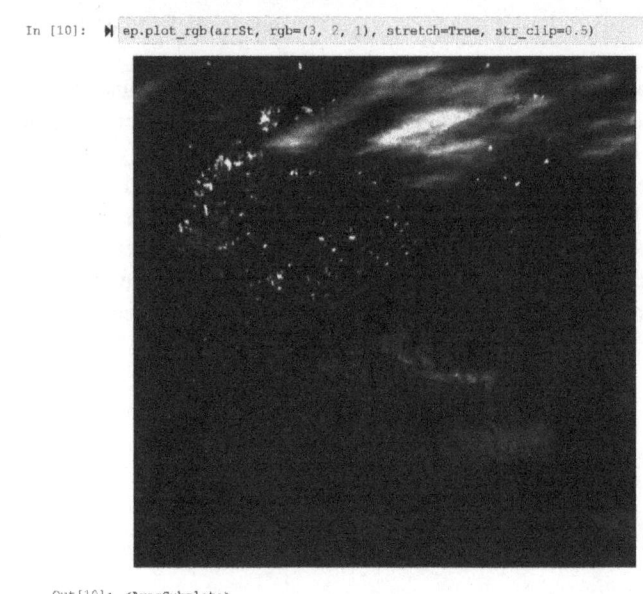

```
Out[10]:  <AxesSubplot:>
```

Furthermore, *EarthPy* library provides a handy utility to observe the spectral distribution of the image within each band:

```
In [11]:  ▶ ep.hist(arrSt, title=[ii[-7:-4] for ii in bandFiles], cols=5, alpha=0.5, figsize=(20, 12))

Out[11]:  (<Figure size 1440x864 with 15 Axes>,
           array([[<AxesSubplot:title={'center':'B01'}>,
                   <AxesSubplot:title={'center':'B02'}>,
                   <AxesSubplot:title={'center':'B03'}>,
                   <AxesSubplot:title={'center':'B04'}>,
                   <AxesSubplot:title={'center':'B05'}>],
                  [<AxesSubplot:title={'center':'B06'}>,
                   <AxesSubplot:title={'center':'B07'}>,
                   <AxesSubplot:title={'center':'B08'}>,
                   <AxesSubplot:title={'center':'B09'}>,
                   <AxesSubplot:title={'center':'B10'}>],
                  [<AxesSubplot:title={'center':'B11'}>,
                   <AxesSubplot:title={'center':'B12'}>,
                   <AxesSubplot:title={'center':'B8A'}>,
                   <AxesSubplot:title={'center':'TCI'}>, <AxesSubplot:>]],
                 dtype=object))
```

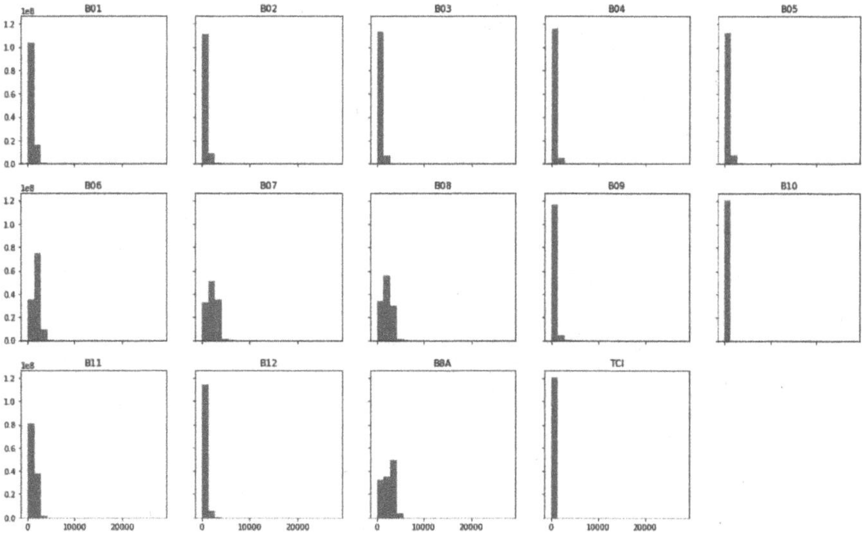

Next, we calculate a number of intensity-based image aggregation indexes defined earlier in this chapter, starting with NDVI.

As a reminder, NDVI is defined as the "normalized difference" of B08 and B04 band levels. Similar to other normalized differences, NDVI index values range from −1 to 1. Water surfaces usually result in negative NDVI readings close to −1; low positive levels usually signify urban or desert areas devoid of vegetation. Dense forests usually present NDVI levels close to 1.

We can see from the figure below that most of our chosen area of interest in the state of Maine is covered by forest, while dark areas in the bottom right correspond to the ocean waters.

We use the *plot_bands* utility function to plot the resulting index along with the legend on the side; *vmin* and *vmax* arguments define the range of accepted values for the variable represented in the plot.

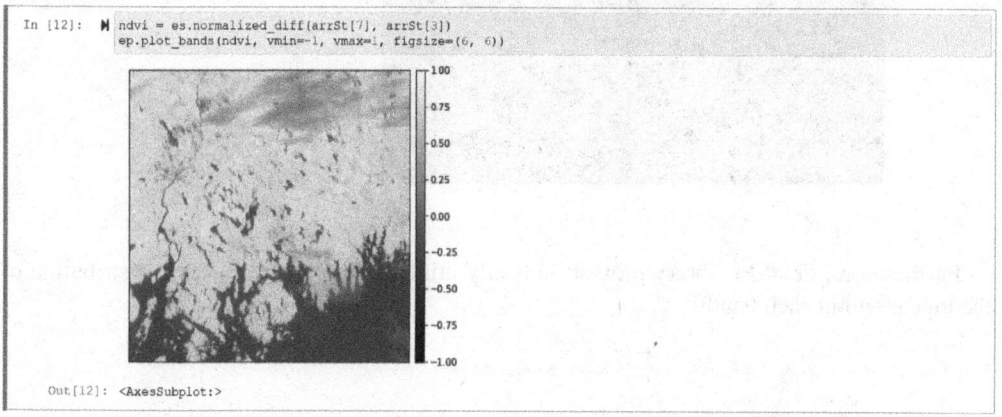

Similarly, the Normalized Difference Moisture Index (NDMI) represents the normalized difference of bands B8A and B11. High values of this index represent high-moisture vegetation (no water stress) or open water; values closer to zero represent water-stressed vegetation, and negative values usually correspond to land without vegetation.

This time, we also try applying a different-scale colormap instead of the default grayscale. Unsurprisingly, NDMI is at very high levels through the chosen region: There is no observed water stress through the forest (or the ocean, obviously).

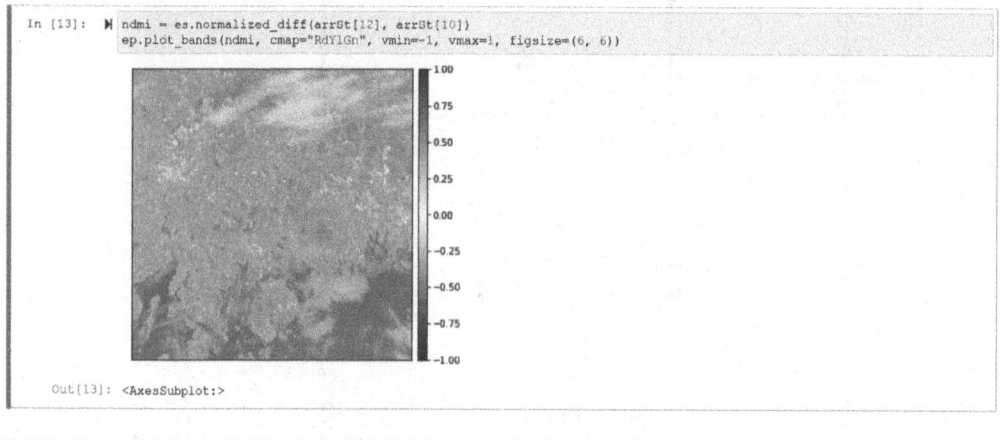

Next, we consider the Normalized Difference Water Index (NDWI) that leverages bands B3 (green) and B8, generally used to identify bodies of water. Unsurprisingly, NDWI exhibits very high levels on the ocean, but not on the continent, where the index level is mostly negative.

A related index is the, Normalized Difference Snow Index (NDSI), also shown below. (Note that the satellite images analyzed here are taken in August, so no snow is present.) We plot the two indexes side by side for ease of comparison.

```
In [15]: ▶ ndwi = es.normalized_diff(arrSt[2], arrSt[7])
           ndsi = es.normalized_diff(arrSt[2], arrSt[10])
           ep.plot_bands(np.stack([ndwi, ndsi]), cmap="RdYlGn", cols=2, vmin=-1, vmax=1, title=("NDWI", "NDSI"))
```

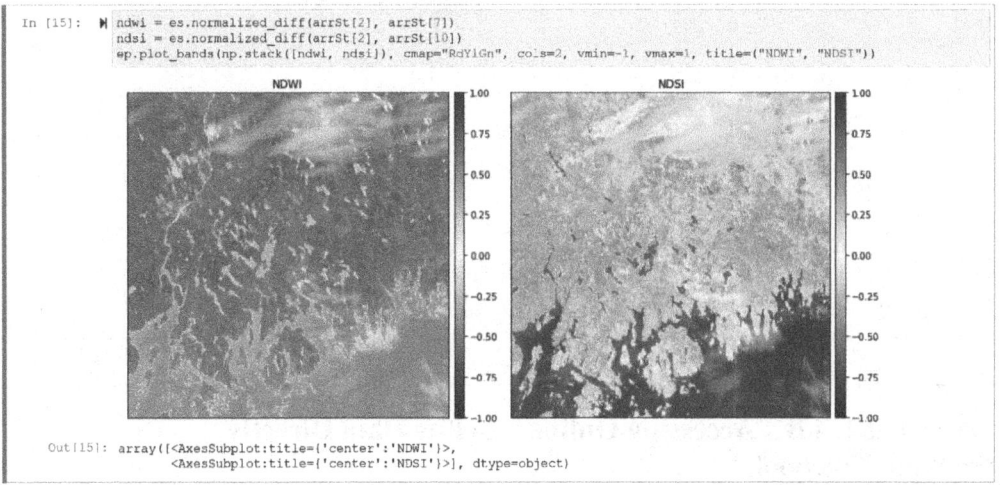

```
Out[15]: array([<AxesSubplot:title={'center':'NDWI'}>,
               <AxesSubplot:title={'center':'NDSI'}>], dtype=object)
```

The Visible Atmospherically Resistant Index (VARI) emphasizes vegetation while mitigating the effects of cloud cover variability. This index does not clearly differentiate water bodies, though.

```
In [16]: ▶ vari = (arrSt[2] - arrSt[3])/ (arrSt[2] + arrSt[3] - arrSt[1])
           ep.plot_bands(vari, cmap="RdYlGn", vmin=-1, vmax=1, figsize=(6, 6))

           <ipython-input-16-8a178e92fcf3>:1: RuntimeWarning: divide by zero encountered in true_divide
             vari = (arrSt[2] - arrSt[3])/ (arrSt[2] + arrSt[3] - arrSt[1])
```

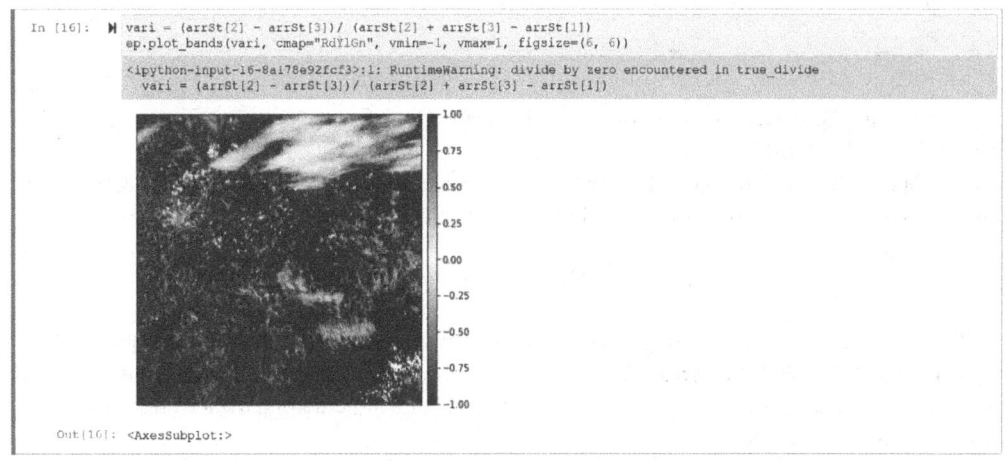

```
Out[16]: <AxesSubplot:>
```

Finally, as mentioned earlier, this type of analysis has other important applications in financial analysis. For instance, an observation of mineral ratios can be used to confirm/quantify physical assets of an oil and gas company. Mineral ratios are computed as shown below; the forest canopy (and water, of course) obscures any relevant information in our area of interest.

(Continued)

```
In [18]:  ▶ cmr = np.divide(arrSt[9], arrSt[10])
             fmr = np.divide(arrSt[11], arrSt[7])
             ep.plot_bands(np.stack([cmr, fmr]), cmap="RdYlGn", cols=2, vmin=-1, vmax=1,
                 title=["Clay Minerals Ratio", "Ferrous Minerals Ratio"])
```

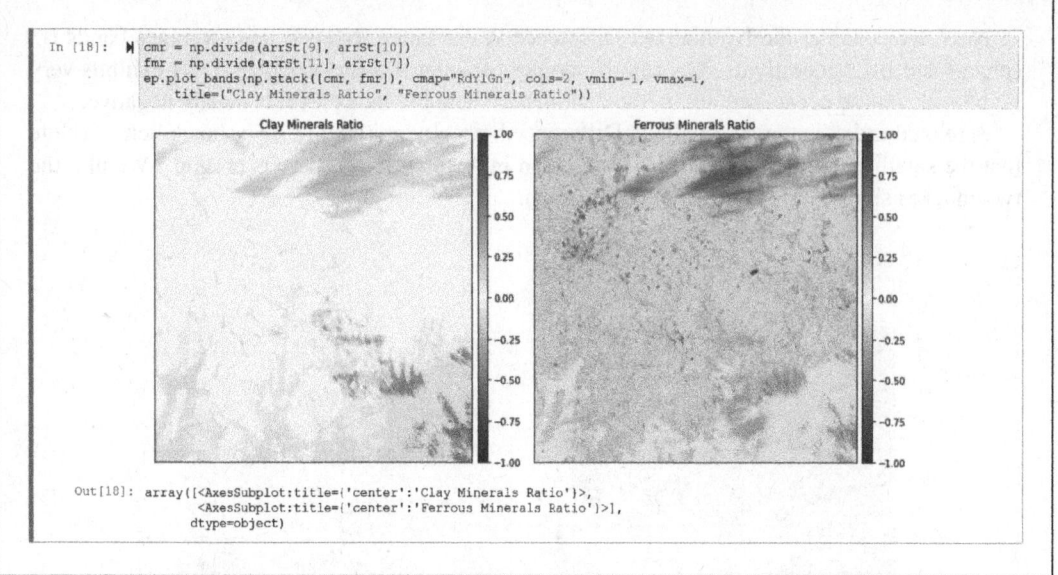

```
Out[18]:  array([<AxesSubplot:title={'center':'Clay Minerals Ratio'}>,
                 <AxesSubplot:title={'center':'Ferrous Minerals Ratio'}>],
                 dtype=object)
```

EXERCISE 4.B   Accessing Online Satellite Data Directly from the Notebook

In the previous hands-on exercise of this chapter, we studied preloaded satellite data by applying various transformations to it. This time, we will access online satellite data directly.

SentinelSat is a python package that implements an API for accessing satellite data from Sentinel-2:

```
In [19]:  ▶ from sentinelsat import SentinelAPI
```

Copernicus Open Access Hub online service provides free access to Sentinel-1, Sentinel-2, Sentinel-3, and Sentinel-5P data.

In order to access Sentinel-2 data, one must first create a free account with the Copernicus hub, and use their login credentials to establish a connection to the data service:

```
In [20]:  ▶ api = SentinelAPI("[censored]", "[censored]", "https://scihub.copernicus.eu/dhus")
```

The first (and perhaps most important) argument in the data query specifies the geographical area of interest in a "well-known text" (WKT) format. The WKT format is intuitive, and Wikipedia provides a handy cheat sheet reference: https://en.wikipedia.org/wiki/Well-known_text_representation_of_geometry.

For instance, the following string describes a rectangle in the Everglades National Park area in Florida:

```
In [21]:  ▶ aWkt = ("POLYGON ((-80.616826 25.730846, "
             "-81.105717 25.730846, -81.105717 25.166631, -80.616826 25.166631, -80.616826 25.730846))")
```

To verify this fact, we will use yet another package named *Folium*. The snippet below shows a map centered at the "first" point of our rectangle (first point in the string above).

The area shown below is slightly west of Miami (note the flipped order of coordinates in the expression below vis-à-vis the WKT string):

```
In [1]:  ▶  import folium

            m = folium.Map([25.730846, -80.616826])
            m
```

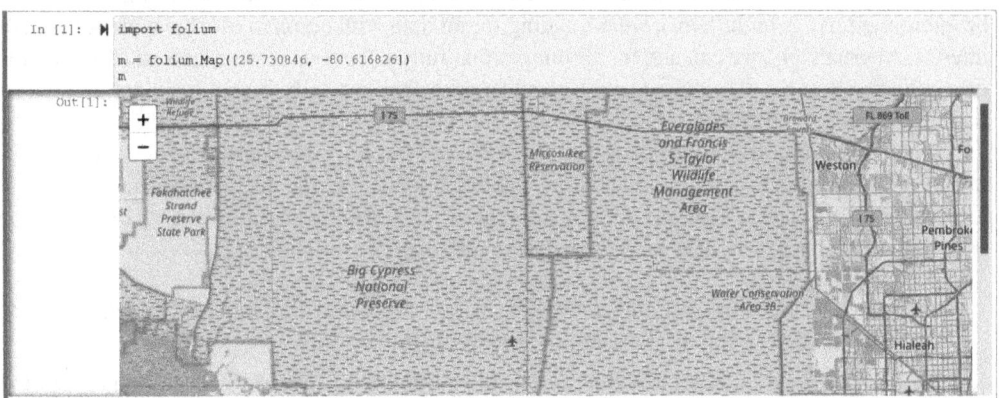

We can visualize our rectangle on top of the same map. In order to do so, we first need to convert it into a JSON representation; for this, we will need *GeoPandas*, another package dedicated to manipulating geographic data:

```
In [2]:  ▶  import geopandas as gpd
```

```
In [5]:  ▶  jWkt = gpd.GeoSeries.from_wkt([sWkt]).to_json()
            jWkt
```

```
Out[5]:  '{"type": "FeatureCollection", "features": [{"id": "0", "type": "Feature", "properties": {}, "geometry": {"type": "
         Polygon", "coordinates": [[[-80.616826, 25.730846], [-81.105717, 25.730846], [-81.105717, 25.166631], [-80.616826,
         25.166631], [-80.616826, 25.730846]]]}, "bbox": [-81.105717, 25.166631, -80.616826, 25.730846]}], "bbox": [-81.1057
         17, 25.166631, -80.616826, 25.730846]}'
```

The statement above generates a JSON string corresponding to our earlier WKT representation. Note that the *from_wkt* method expects a list or array of strings, not a single WKT string.

Now we can add our rectangle to the map:

```
In [6]:  ▶  folium.GeoJson(jWkt).add_to(m)
            m
```

```
Out[6]:
```

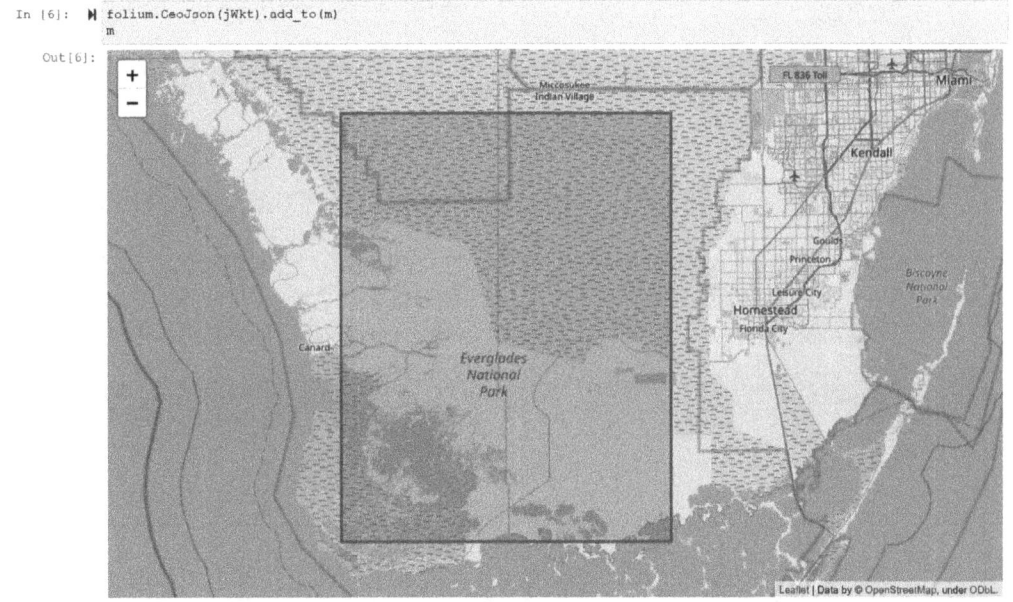

(Continued)

Next, we are ready to query the data service for the list of images available for our area of interest within a particular date range. We receive a dictionary with file links in it.

We can also pass an additional argument that specifies how exactly the "area of interest" is to be interpreted. By default (here), we are asking for all data with nonzero overlap with our area of interest. Alternatively, we can ask for all images that fully cover our area of interest (if we set the *area_relation* argument to "*Contains*") or all images that are fully inside our area of interest (*area_relation* is "*IsWithin*").

We are, however, explicitly specifying the satellite of interest, "processing level," which determines parameters such as spatial resolution, and percentage of cloud coverage in images (we are requesting only images with cloud coverage below 10% to ensure sufficient visibility of the ground below). There are, of course, many more parameters available:

- Please refer to https://scihub.copernicus.eu/twiki/do/view/SciHubUserGuide/WebHome for a detailed description of the Sentinel capabilities and data.
- https://sentinel.esa.int/web/sentinel/user-guides/sentinel-2-msi/overview contains further details on Sentinel-2.

```
In [10]:  ▶ products = api.query(area=sWkt, date=("20210901", "20210930"), platformname="Sentinel-2",
                                  processinglevel="Level-2A", cloudcoverpercentage=(0, 10))
```

For ease of data handling, we convert the returned dictionary into a *GeoData Frame*, a generalization of a data frame defined by the *GeoPandas* package that holds geographic data in tabular form. We sort the returned results by cloud coverage and download the data files from the first row – the batch with the lowest cloud coverage (this is a ~1 Gb dataset and will take several minutes to download).

```
In [11]:  ▶ dfGeo = api.to_geodataframe(products).sort_values(["cloudcoverpercentage"], ascending=[True])
            dfGeo
```

Out[11]:

	title	link	link_alternative	link_icon	
6cc876e0-6035-476b-83ab-09cc7080ca4e	S2B_MSIL2A_20210927T160509_N0301_R054_T17RMJ_2...	https://scihub.copernicus.eu /dhus/odata/v1/Pro...	https://scihub.copernicus.eu /dhus/odata/v1/Pro...	https://scihub.copernicus.eu /dhus/odata/v1/Pro...	2(
475a6722-8a5d-4f8a-a2ac-ae22428920ec	S2B_MSIL2A_20210927T160509_N0301_R054_T17RMH_2...	https://scihub.copernicus.eu /dhus/odata/v1/Pro...	https://scihub.copernicus.eu /dhus/odata/v1/Pro...	https://scihub.copernicus.eu /dhus/odata/v1/Pro...	2(
9f65f014-53c0-4214-b03e-d1f9ca747734	S2B_MSIL2A_20210917T160509_N0301_R054_T17RMH_2...	https://scihub.copernicus.eu /dhus/odata/v1/Pro...	https://scihub.copernicus.eu /dhus/odata/v1/Pro...	https://scihub.copernicus.eu /dhus/odata/v1/Pro...	2(
01c036d0-596b-45bd-ae4f-5907a69a15fc	S2B_MSIL2A_20210927T160509_N0301_R054_T17RNJ_2...	https://scihub.copernicus.eu /dhus/odata/v1/Pro...	https://scihub.copernicus.eu /dhus/odata/v1/Pro...	https://scihub.copernicus.eu /dhus/odata/v1/Pro...	2(
b235e5e8-fdd5-4852-af96-3011869b12cc	S2B_MSIL2A_20210027T160509_N0301_R054_T17RNH_2...	https://scihub.copernicus.eu /dhus/odata/v1/Pro...	https://scihub.copernicus.eu /dhus/odata/v1/Pro...	https://scihub.copernicus.eu /dhus/odata/v1/Pro...	2(
a53fd353-2076-4f17-bb05-f4dd899884d4	S2A_MSIL2A_20210905T155901_N0301_R097_T17RMH_2...	https://scihub.copernicus.eu /dhus/odata/v1/Pro...	https://scihub.copernicus.eu /dhus/odata/v1/Pro...	https://scihub.copernicus.eu /dhus/odata/v1/Pro...	2(
5e4ab73a-f14a-4861-962d-6adb17e3bc21	S2B_MSIL2A_20210917T160509_N0301_R054_T17RNH_2...	https://scihub.copernicus.eu /dhus/odata/v1/Pro...	https://scihub.copernicus.eu /dhus/odata/v1/Pro...	https://scihub.copernicus.eu /dhus/odata/v1/Pro...	2(
24906978-abcb-41c7-b2f2-5b2cf57bf51f	S2A_MSIL2A_20210925T160021_N0301_R097_T17RMH_2...	https://scihub.copernicus.eu /dhus/odata/v1/Pro...	https://scihub.copernicus.eu /dhus/odata/v1/Pro...	https://scihub.copernicus.eu /dhus/odata/v1/Pro...	2(

8 rows × 41 columns

```
In [31]:   ▶  retInfo = api.download(dfGeo.index[0])
              retInfo

              Downloading:     0%|              | 0.00/464M [00:00<?, ?B/s]

              MD5 checksumming:    0%|          | 0.00/464M [00:00<?, ?B/s]

Out[31]:  {'id': '6cc876e0-6035-476b-83ab-09cc7080ca4e',
           'title': 'S2B_MSIL2A_20210927T160509_N0301_R054_T17RMJ_20210927T201814',
           'size': 464441085,
           'md5': '3ce922fc2d25bd20aef769608c615318',
           'date': datetime.datetime(2021, 9, 27, 16, 5, 9, 24000),
           'footprint': 'POLYGON((-81.51181 25.226535529136566,-81.494354 25.298807545252696,-81.458496 25.44699327556766,-8
           1.4227 25.595120074594007,-81.38696 25.743221494603684,-81.351135 25.891328504151385,-81.315186 26.03943686526273
           3,-81.279236 26.187538702515648,-81.27164 26.218735424925782,-80.90228 26.219896197155975,-80.90311 25.2283813853489
           4,-81.51181 25.226535529136566))',
           'url': "https://scihub.copernicus.eu/dhus/odata/v1/Products('6cc876e0-6035-476b-83ab-09cc7080ca4e')/$value",
           'Online': True,
           'Creation Date': datetime.datetime(2021, 9, 27, 23, 9, 10, 503000),
           'Ingestion Date': datetime.datetime(2021, 9, 27, 23, 8, 51, 632000),
           'quicklook_url': "https://scihub.copernicus.eu/dhus/odata/v1/Products('6cc876e0-6035-476b-83ab-09cc7080ca4e')/Prod
           ucts('Quicklook')/$value",
           'path': 'S2B_MSIL2A_20210927T160509_N0301_R054_T17RMJ_20210927T201814.zip',
           'downloaded_bytes': 464441085}
```

For simplicity, we have unzipped the downloaded archive manually.

Next, let us combine the different available bands from the downloaded batch into a single array. We will rely on the *glob* package utility to list the relevant files in the folder and on the *rasterio* package to manipulate bitmap files.

```
In [12]:   ▶  import glob
              import numpy as np

              import rasterio as rio

In [14]:   ▶  sPath = "".join(["S2B_MSIL2A_20210927T160509_N0301_R054_T17RMJ_20210927T201814", #retInfo["title"],
                  ".SAFE/GRANULE/L2A_T17RMJ_A023818_20210927T160542/IMG_DATA"])
              bandFiles = sorted(glob.glob(sPath + "/R10m/*.jp2"))
              bandFiles

Out[14]:  ['S2B_MSIL2A_20210927T160509_N0301_R054_T17RMJ_20210927T201814.SAFE/GRANULE/L2A_T17RMJ_A023818_20210927T160542/IMG_
           DATA/R10m\\T17RMJ_20210927T160509_AOT_10m.jp2',
           'S2B_MSIL2A_20210927T160509_N0301_R054_T17RMJ_20210927T201814.SAFE/GRANULE/L2A_T17RMJ_A023818_20210927T160542/IMG_
           DATA/R10m\\T17RMJ_20210927T160509_B02_10m.jp2',
           'S2B_MSIL2A_20210927T160509_N0301_R054_T17RMJ_20210927T201814.SAFE/GRANULE/L2A_T17RMJ_A023818_20210927T160542/IMG_
           DATA/R10m\\T17RMJ_20210927T160509_B03_10m.jp2',
           'S2B_MSIL2A_20210927T160509_N0301_R054_T17RMJ_20210927T201814.SAFE/GRANULE/L2A_T17RMJ_A023818_20210927T160542/IMG_
           DATA/R10m\\T17RMJ_20210927T160509_B04_10m.jp2',
           'S2B_MSIL2A_20210927T160509_N0301_R054_T17RMJ_20210927T201814.SAFE/GRANULE/L2A_T17RMJ_A023818_20210927T160542/IMG_
           DATA/R10m\\T17RMJ_20210927T160509_B08_10m.jp2',
           'S2B_MSIL2A_20210927T160509_N0301_R054_T17RMJ_20210927T201814.SAFE/GRANULE/L2A_T17RMJ_A023818_20210927T160542/IMG_
           DATA/R10m\\T17RMJ_20210927T160509_TCI_10m.jp2',
           'S2B_MSIL2A_20210927T160509_N0301_R054_T17RMJ_20210927T201814.SAFE/GRANULE/L2A_T17RMJ_A023818_20210927T160542/IMG_
           DATA/R10m\\T17RMJ_20210927T160509_WVP_10m.jp2']

In [15]:   ▶  lst = []
              for ii in bandFiles:
                  with rio.open(ii, "r") as f:
                      lst.append(f.read(1))
              arrStack = np.stack(lst)
              arrStack.shape

Out[15]:  (7, 10980, 10980)
```

Visualize the RGB image (visible bands) using *EarthPy*:

(*Continued*)

```
In [16]:  ▶  import earthpy.plot as ep

In [24]:  ▶  ep.plot_rgb(arrStack, rgb=(3, 2, 1), stretch=True)
```

```
Out[24]:  <AxesSubplot:>
```

As the last step, we save the visible RGB array in a file and clip the local image to the original shape of interest.

We continue to rely on the *rasterio* package to read and write bitmap files. We combine three JP2 band files downloaded from the Copernicus hub service into a single RGB file, preserving the metadata from one of the original band files:

```
In [20]:  ▶  b4 = rio.open(bandFiles[3])
             b3 = rio.open(bandFiles[2])
             b2 = rio.open(bandFiles[1])

             with rio.open("rgb0.tiff", "w", driver="Gtiff", width=b4.width, height=b4.height,
                           count=3, crs=b4.crs, transform=b4.transform, dtype=b4.dtypes[0]) as f:
                 f.write(b2.read(1), 1)
                 f.write(b3.read(1), 2)
                 f.write(b4.read(1), 3)
```

In order to use our area of interest defined earlier, we need to convert the area coordinates to the coordinate system used by the downloaded files. In order to do so, we first specify coordinate reference system (CRS) used in our WKT above and subsequently use the *to_crs* method to convert to a new CRS system:

```
In [77]:  ▶  msk = gpd.GeoSeries.from_wkt([sWkt]).set_crs(epsg=4326)
             msk = msk.to_crs(epsg=32617)
             msk.crs

Out[77]:  <Projected CRS: EPSG:32617>
          Name: WGS 84 / UTM zone 17N
          Axis Info [cartesian]:
          - E[east]: Easting (metre)
          - N[north]: Northing (metre)
          Area of Use:
          - name: Between 84°W and 78°W, northern hemisphere between equator and 84°N, onshore and offshore. Bahamas. Ecuador
          - north of equator. Canada - Nunavut; Ontario; Quebec. Cayman Islands. Colombia. Costa Rica. Cuba. Jamaica. Nicarag
          ua. Panama. United States (USA).
          - bounds: (-84.0, 0.0, -78.0, 84.0)
          Coordinate Operation:
          - name: UTM zone 17N
          - method: Transverse Mercator
          Datum: World Geodetic System 1984 ensemble
          - Ellipsoid: WGS 84
          - Prime Meridian: Greenwich
```

Finally, we clip the image we had saved in the TIFF file using the mask we just defined.

```
In [80]:  ▶ with rio.open("rgb0.tiff") as f:
               img = rio.mask.mask(f, msk, crop=True)
```

The resulting image we cropped is the intersection of the downloaded image and the rectangle defined by our WKT string. This intersection is the bottom right portion of the image.

This time we do not highlight the image artificially and show natural colors instead (reproduced here in grayscale, of course):

```
In [87]:  ▶ ep.plot_rgb(img[0], rgb=(2, 1, 0))
```

```
Out[87]:  <AxesSubplot:>
```

Finally, it is important to note that, these days, much of the "industrial-grade" data processing conducted by alternative data providers relies on machine learning techniques where a neural network or another classification model is trained to recognize and find specific image patterns in large sets of satellite imagery. Deep learning is obviously a very broad (and deep!) topic of its own, which we do not cover here. There are now many excellent textbooks dedicated to deep learning models and, more specifically, image recognition.

CHAPTER 5

Alternative Text Data

5.1 ALTERNATIVE TEXT DATA ON ESG

As discussed in the previous chapter, while it is often possible to find some amount of ESG data in the more traditional processed form of ESG indexes and corporate rating scores, or in a form similar to standard GAAP (Generally Accepted Accounting Principles) or IFRS9 (International Financial Reporting Standard 9) disclosures, the overwhelming majority of ESG data is unstructured and comes in what is generally described as "alternative" forms. These forms are typically neither numeric nor tabular in nature and are often embedded in seemingly random sets of potentially unrelated information.

Within this category of alternative data, the most common type at the moment is simple unstructured text data, which is typically collected from a disparate set of sources ranging from institutional ones, such as corporate reports, to external vis-à-vis the institution in question, such as media reports, to crowd-sourced, such as social media.

The more the field progresses, however, the more we expect to see other alternative sources of data become available to the mainstream practitioner and provide further insight into ESG aspects to monitor. A good example of such sources is, again, satellite and aerial imagery, which was scarce and hard to procure in the recent past but for which there is already a growing number of market participants that have started exploring and exploiting it.

One of the major challenges that a student of ESG finance faces is intrinsic to the nature of the data itself, which is extremely large in volume, making any effort to try to manually process it impractical at best and impossible at worst.

Additionally, given the nature of the data dispersed within a much larger corpus of texts that often have little or no bearing on the topic of interest, the task is made much harder, as there is an additional layer of data mining/cleanup needed beyond the data processing and signal extraction – the core objective of the exercise. According to a recent analysis of news content, as of October 2018 (Deutsche Bank research, see Figure 5.1), on average, only 2% of the financial news text is ESG-related, leaving the ESG practitioner to deal with a 1:49 signal to noise ratio.

Natural Language Processing. Given the core nature of unstructured text within the ESG data, it is not surprising that one of the key techniques that are to be used is, in general terms, what is known as Natural Language Processing (NLP). More specifically, within the broad confines of NLP, the subsection of most relevance for our purposes is topic modeling, which is the discipline that focuses on extracting relevant "topics" from large amounts of text data.

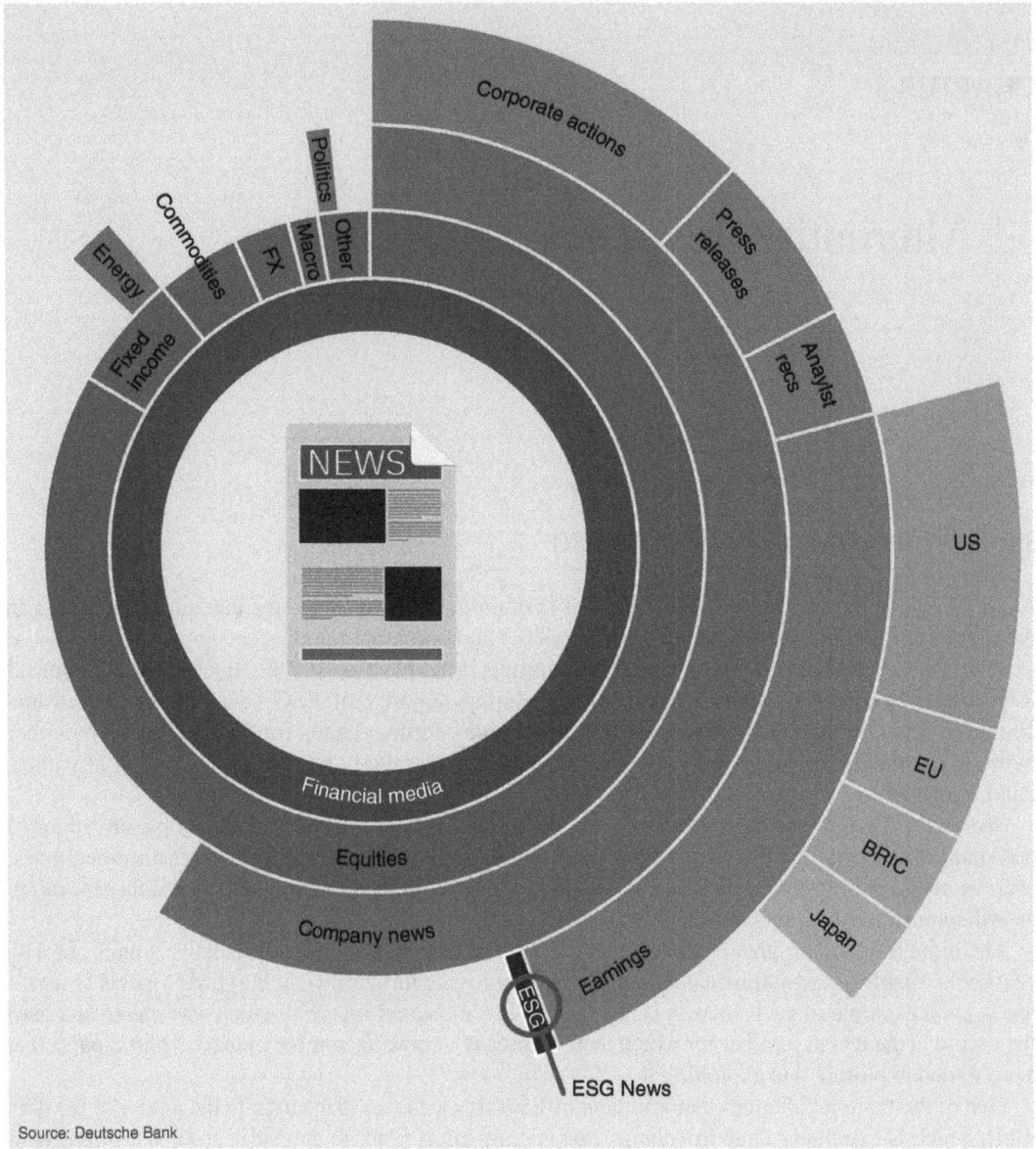

FIGURE 5.1 Illustration of financial media news by topic.
Source: Deutsche Bank Research, "Big Data Shakes Up ESG Investing," *Konzept* (October 2018): 14.

NLP is a vast and expanding area of academic and practitioner research, and we will not be able to do it justice in the amount of space allotted. We choose to focus here on giving a brief introduction to topic modeling, as arguably the most critical area for applied ESG data analysis. For a more comprehensive introduction to NLP, we recommend, for example, *Natural Language Processing and Computational Linguistics: Speech, Morphology and Syntax*,[1] *Getting Started with Natural Language Processing*,[2] or numerous other available NLP textbooks.

---

[1] Mohamed Zakaria Kurdi, *Natural Language Processing and Computational Linguistics: Speech, Morphology and Syntax* (Hoboken, NJ: John Wiley & Sons, 2016), ISBN: 978-1-848-21848-2.
[2] Ekaterina Kochmar, *Getting Started with Natural Language Processing* (New York: Manning, 2022).

Python's set of ML libraries, *scikit-learn*, provides a standard implementation of NLP models which we apply here. More cutting-edge NLP implementations also exist, of course, especially those leveraging deep learning methodologies; a most prominent recent example with wide practical applications is the Bidirectional Encoder Representations from Transformers (BERT)[3] by Google, which has processed, effectively, every English-language Google search since 2020.

We do not cover BERT in this textbook, as it is beyond the scope of what is required. However, for our readers who have an interest in more advanced NLP implementations, we recommend an example of BERT being trained on ESG reports, similar in scope to the exercise being demonstrated in this chapter, at the following GitHub link: https://github.com/mukut03/ESG-BERT.

Text Preparation. Prior to performing any kind of NLP analytics on the corpus of text, it is necessary for us preprocess it in two ways, the first being tokenization and the second lemmatization.

Tokenization is the splitting of the unstructured text into individual words separated by whitespace and punctuation.

Lemmatization is the conversion of words from their composite forms into their basic forms (conversion of plural form to singular form, removing conjugation of verbs, etc.).

Both tokenization and lemmatization are language-specific and not necessarily applicable in the same way (if at all) to different languages and language constructs. For example, tokenization by whitespace would not work for many East Asian languages, which make widespread use of composite words, or even for European languages such as German (for the same reason).

For the purposes of this textbook and the exercises wherein, we focus our attention on analysis of text in American English, with the assumption that our readers will have to make the necessary adjustments if they choose to apply the concepts and methodologies discussed here to another language.

In addition to tokenization and lemmatization, some other required secondary standard preprocessing steps are:

- *Exclusion of very short words, as they do not contain any relevant information.* Words composed of one or two characters are removed from the corpus (i.e., *I, at, me, to, go, am,* etc.).

- *Standardization to lowercase.* As the words are now taken out of order and context, the uppercase/lowercase distinction is no longer required or necessary; therefore all words are converted to lowercase.

- *Minimum/maximum frequency threshold setting and filtering.* Words that appear in either too many or too few documents in the corpus are excluded as they contain too little information content to be of use.

- *Removal of "stop words."* Stop words are words that are common in the English language, to the extent that they do not contain any informational value for the topic of interest. Examples of these words are *have, and, when, where, the,* and other similar ones. This removal is achieved via the use of a predefined list of words (typically a generic list of English-language stop words), which often is supplemented with application-specific words as well. An example of application-specific words could be the names of companies, if the corpus of documents we are reviewing are all corporate documentation, as they would appear often through the document and do not contribute in any way to the information content. In other contexts, however, a company name should not be removed (e.g., social media data), as it would indeed be part of the "topic" of interest (the name could be listed as the "biggest client" or "biggest polluter," and we would not want to remove the information). This step is a critical one, and requires careful analysis and setup, to ensure that no relevant information is lost. The *scikit-learn* set includes the *sklearn.feature_extraction.text. ENGLISH_STOP_WORDS* preset list.[4]

---

[3] See "BERT (language model)," https://en.wikipedia.org/wiki/BERT_(language_model)

[4] Note: This list has several known issues, as detailed by Joel Nothman, Hanmin Qin, and Roman Yurchak, "Stop Word Lists in Free Open-Source Software Packages," *Proceedings of Workshop for NLP Open Source Software*, pp. 7–12, Melbourne, Australia, July 20, 2018. © 2018 Association for Computational Linguistics, https://www.aclweb.org/anthology/W18-2502.pdf

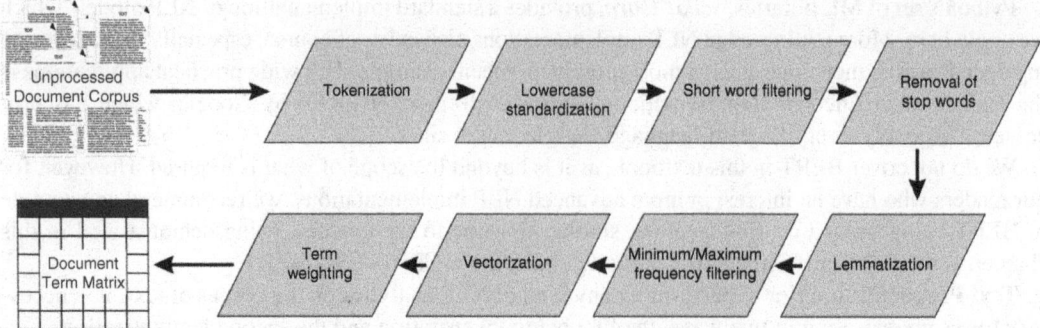

FIGURE 5.2   Steps for preprocessing in NLP analysis

Figure 5.2 summarizes the set of preprocessing steps that are required for a typical text, before NLP analysis can start.

The steps in the preprocessing diagram are covered by *scikit-learn*, except for lemmatization. Within Python, *spaCy* is capable of lemmatization; however, the capabilities and inner workings of it are beyond what can be covered in this text. If the reader has an interest in learning about parsing English in Python using *spaCy*, there is a useful post by M. Honnibal providing a comprehensive view of what can be achieved.[5]

5.2   CORPORATE ESG REPORTS

As we have seen, a predominant portion of the ESG finance data that requires processing is in the form of unstructured text from corporate disclosures (accounting reports, as well as sustainability/ESG reports and press releases, etc.), government-issued reports, news media articles about corporations and governments, social media postings of diverse nature and characterization, and other written sources of disparate kind.

At the time of writing of this book, the disclosure of ESG information by corporations remains entirely a voluntary exercise, with the proportion of firms choosing to do so steadily rising. It is the general consensus that these disclosure requirements will eventually become mandatory, which will also cause the typology and detail of the disclosures to become more standardized.

For some insight on the views of regulators on this topic, please refer to the footnote link by the Securities and Exchange Commission (SEC), which evaluates the approach and pros and cons of implementation of ESG disclosures for publicly traded US corporations as of March 2021.[6] Additionally, in March 2022, the SEC issued a press release proposing "Rules to Enhance and Standardize Climate-Related Disclosures for Investors."[7]

In the remainder of this chapter, we shall demonstrate a variety of applied text analyses of corporate ESG reports to familiarize the reader with the toolkits available to them. The exercises in this chapter draw inspiration from a Databricks seminar[8] that provides an interesting additional read.

---

[5] Matthew Honnibal, "Parsing English in 500 Lines of Python," *Explosion*, December 17, 2013, https://explosion.ai/blog/parsing-english-in-python.

[6] John Coates, "ESG Disclosure – Keeping Pace with Developments Affecting Investors, Public Companies and the Capital Markets," US Securities and Exchange Commission, March 11, 2021, https://www.sec.gov/news/public-statement/coates-esg-disclosure-keeping-pace-031121.

[7] "SEC Proposed Rules to Enhance and Standardize Climate-Related Disclosures for Investors," US Securities and Exchange Commission, March 21, 2022, https://www.sec.gov/news/press-release/2022-46

[8] Antoine Amend, "A Data-Driven Approach to Environmental, Social and Governance," Databricks, July 10, 2010, https://databricks.com/blog/2020/07/10/a-data-driven-approach-to-environmental-social-and-governance.html

EXERCISE 5.A   Preprocessing of Corporate ESG Reports

Just as in previous chapters, we load relevant libraries prior to their first use.

Pandas is very familiar to the reader; it provides common tools for data manipulation and analysis, specifically data structures and operations for manipulating numerical tables and time series.

```
In [2]:  ▶ import pandas as pd
```

In earlier chapters, we have discussed how a list of S&P 500 constituent stocks may be downloaded directly from Wikipedia. Here, our focus will be on analyzing a corpus of ESG reports from S&P 500 constituents. Given that, at the time of writing of this book, there is no centralized repository online for ESG reports (along the lines of the EDGAR database that centralizes corporate accounting reports), we have had to assemble a list of individual URLs for each report that will need to be downloaded directly from each company's investor relations website. We will make this file available to the public as an online appendix to this book (with the understanding that it represents a reporting snapshot as of December 2021, of course).

```
In [3]:  ▶ dfSpxData = pd.read_csv("spx.csv", index_col=0)
           dfSpxData
```

Out[3]:

ticker	name	sector	subindustry	location	report	latest
MMM	3M	Industrials	Industrial Conglomerates	Saint Paul, Minnesota	https://multimedia.3m.com/mws/media/2006066O/2...	2021.0
ABT	Abbott Laboratories	Health Care	Health Care Equipment	North Chicago, Illinois	https://dam.abbott.com/en-us/documents/pdfs/ab...	2020.0
ABBV	AbbVie	Health Care	Pharmaceuticals	North Chicago, Illinois	https://www.abbvie.com/content/dam/abbvie-dotc...	2020.0
ABMD	Abiomed	Health Care	Health Care Equipment	Danvers, Massachusetts	https://investors.abiomed.com/static-files/3fa...	2021.0
ACN	Accenture	Information Technology	IT Consulting & Other Services	Dublin, Ireland	https://www.accenture.com/_acnmedia/PDF-149/Ac...	2020.0
...	...	...	...	...	...	...
YUM	Yum! Brands	Consumer Discretionary	Restaurants	Louisville, Kentucky	https://www.yum.com/wps/wcm/connect/yumbrands/...	2020.0
ZBRA	Zebra Technologies	Information Technology	Electronic Equipment & Instruments	Lincolnshire, Illinois	NaN	NaN
ZBH	Zimmer Biomet	Health Care	Health Care Equipment	Warsaw, Indiana	https://investor.zimmerbiomet.com/~/media/File...	2020.0
ZION	Zions Bancorp	Financials	Regional Banks	Salt Lake City, Utah	https://s26.q4cdn.com/483754055/files/doc_down...	2020.0
ZTS	Zoetis	Health Care	Pharmaceuticals	Parsippany, New Jersey	https://www.sustainability.zoetis.com/_Assets/...	2020.0

500 rows × 6 columns

We will need a number of libraries to download and read the reports: *Requests* allows accessing and downloading files from online locations, *IO* allows reading of the received data as a byte stream, and finally *PyPDF2* provides the conversion from PDF to plain text.

```
In [13]:  ▶ import requests, io, PyPDF2
```

The following function reads the content of all reports into memory, importing each one of them as a single very large string (the largest one is over 160K characters in length!). First, we check the address argument for "*NaN*" values and skip them (NAs in the S&P 500 table indicate that we were not able to locate an ESG report for that particular company; not all companies publish them, as this is not a hard requirement at this time).

Then a "response" object is downloaded online, and *BytesIO* and *PdfFileReader* classes are successively instantiated with the response content. Finally, text is extracted page by page from

(Continued)

the PDF file (by calling the *extractText* method), and the resulting strings are all concatenated with a new line character as a separator between them.

Note that it is important to provide a finite time-out argument to *requests.get*; otherwise, the *get* function may get stuck indefinitely waiting for the server to respond.

Also, unfortunately, not all PDFs can be successfully accessed and fully read, which results in a few exceptions (see the printout below). These exceptions are caught by our function so as not to terminate the rest of the process.

```
In [14]:  def downloadPdfReportContents(addr, nm=""):
              if addr != addr:
                  print(" : ".join([nm, "NA"]))
                  return ""
              try:
                  response = requests.get(addr, timeout=5)
                  f = PyPDF2.PdfFileReader(io.BytesIO(response.content))
                  lstText = [x.extractText() for x in f.pages]
                  print(nm)
                  return "\n".join(lstText)
              except BaseException as e:
                  print(" : ".join([nm, str(type(e)), str(e)]))
                  return ""
```

We call the function above for all **S&P 500** constituents to download their reports one by one and form a giant dictionary as a result:

```
In [15]:  contentMap = {x: downloadPdfReportContents(dfSpxData["report"][x], x) for x in dfSpxData.index}
```
```
          AWK
          AMP
          ABC
          AME
          AMGN
          APH : <class 'PyPDF2.utils.PdfReadError'> : EOF marker not found
          ADI
          ANSS
          ANTM
          AON
          AOS : <class 'PyPDF2.utils.PdfReadError'> : EOF marker not found
          APA : <class 'PyPDF2.utils.PdfReadError'> : Could not read malformed PDF file
          AAPL
          AMAT
          APTV
          ADM
          ANET
          AJG
          AIZ
```

Remove stocks with zero-length report strings: Those are an indication of reports whose downloads have failed. Finally, we print out the lengths of all successfully downloaded reports (just to confirm that our resulting dictionary is indeed quite large).

```
In [16]:  contentMap = {x: contentMap[x] for x in contentMap if len(contentMap[x]) > 0}
          {x: len(contentMap[x]) for x in contentMap}
```
```
Out[16]:  {'MMM': 610535,
           'ABT': 458698,
           'ABBV': 148557,
           'ABMD': 26383,
           'ACN': 127513,
           'ATVI': 78936,
           'AES': 116985,
           'AFL': 179067,
           'A': 205848,
           'APD': 143131,
           'ALB': 167770,
           'LNT': 164596,
           'GOOG': 4152,
           'AMZN': 257683,
           'AMCR': 142486,
           'AEE': 101140,
           'AAL': 39726,
           'AEP': 17856,
           'AXP': 275426,
```

String and *RE* are standard Python libraries for string manipulation, which will be required for multiple steps in the preparation of data.

SpaCy is a powerful Python NLP library that leverages machine learning to find structure in the supplied text. Discussion of its impressive abilities is beyond the scope of this text; however, we strongly encourage everyone to acquaint themselves with *SpaCy*; more information is available to allow the reader an overview at https://explosion.ai/blog/introducing-spacy.

We proceed to load one of *SpaCy*'s pretrained models before using it in our text preprocessing (*en_core_web_sm*):

```
In [17]:  ▶ import string, re, unicodedata
             import spacy
```

```
In [18]:  ▶ spacy.cli.download("en_core_web_sm")
             spc = spacy.load("en_core_web_sm")

             ✓ Download and installation successful
             You can now load the package via spacy.load('en_core_web_sm')
```

The following function parses each string by removing whitespace and a few items "contaminating" plain text (section and figure numbers, URLs, etc.) by making heavy use of regular expressions. We encourage you to familiarize yourselves with regular expressions using https://developer.mozilla.org/en-US/docs/Web/JavaScript/Guide/Regular_Expressions/Cheatsheet or Wikipedia, or a number of other excellent online and print sources. Unfortunately, it would take more than a whole chapter to discuss *regexp* in any detail, and thus it is beyond the scope for this book.

```
In [19]:  ▶ def cleanStringOne(s):
               s = re.sub(r"^\s?\d+(.*)$", r"\1", s)  # remove leading (section, etc.) numbers
               s = s.strip()
               s = re.sub("\s?-\s?", "-", s)          # shrink word breaks
               s = re.sub(r"\s?([,:;\.])", r"\1", s)  # remove spaces preceding punctuation marks
               s = re.sub(r"((http|https)\:\/\/)?[a-zA-Z0-9\.\/\?\:@\-_=#]+\.([a-zA-Z]){2,6}([a-zA-Z0-9\.\&\/\?\:@\-_=#])*",
                   r" ", s)                            # remove web addresses
               s = re.sub(r"\d{4,}", r" ", s)         # remove long numbers
               s = re.sub('\s+', ' ', s)              # shrink contiguous whitespaces
               return s
```

The next function performs the second stage of preprocessing. First, it "deaccents" the *unicode* text by normalizing it and subsequently removing extra modifications to each letter (such as extra dots above the letter, etc.). This step may not be very critical considering that all reports are written in English; nevertheless, we include it for generality/completeness.

Second, this function parses the string into alphabetic tokens (words) and keeps those of reasonable length (between 2 and 15 characters).

For the return value, all the words are merged again into a single space-delimited string.

```
In [20]:  ▶ def cleanStringTwo(s):
               s = s.lower()

               s = unicodedata.normalize("NFD", s)
               s = "".join(x for x in s if unicodedata.category(x) != "Mn")
               s = unicodedata.normalize("NFC", s)

               tokens = re.findall(r"(((?![\d])\w)+)", s)
               tokens = list(zip(*tokens))[0] if len(tokens)>0 else []
               return " ".join([x for x in tokens if 2 <= len(x) <= 15 and not x.startswith("_")])
```

(Continued)

The following code applies text preprocessing steps consecutively to every report in our report dictionary. It is included here as a single contiguous block, but in the next few cells below, we step through distinct portions of this code one by one, applying them to a single stock for a closer look.

```
In [25]:  dfReports = pd.DataFrame()
          for ii in contentMap:
              txt = "".join([x for x in contentMap[ii] if x in set(string.printable)])

              lines = []
              prev = ""
              for line in txt.split("\n"):
                  if prev.endswith("."):
                      lines.append(prev)
                      prev = line
                  else:
                      prev = "".join([prev, " ", line])
              lines.append(prev)

              lines = [str(x) for s in lines for x in spc(cleanStringOne(s)).sents]

              lines2 = []
              for line in lines:
                  lemmas = " ".join([x.lemma_ for x in spc(line) if x.lemma_ not in ["-PRON-"]])
                  lines2.append(cleanStringTwo(lemmas))
              lines2 = [x for x in lines2 if len(x) > 100]
              newDf = pd.DataFrame({"name": ii, "lemmas": lines2})
              dfReports = dfReports.append(newDf, ignore_index=True)
```

Download the PDF report for Zions Bancorp as a single string (this is the same string we could retrieve from the reports' dictionary):

```
In [29]:  txt = downloadPdfReportContents(dfSpxData["report"]["ZION"])
          PdfReadWarning: Xref table not zero-indexed. ID numbers for objects will be corrected. [pdf.py:1736]
```

The first pair of preprocessing steps is then:

- Only keep printable characters in the string.
- Re-split the string into (tentative) sentences delimited by period instead of a new line character.

```
In [30]:  txt = "".join([x for x in txt if x in set(string.printable)])

          lines = []
          prev = ""
          for line in txt.split("\n"):
              if prev.endswith("."):
                  lines.append(prev)
                  prev = line
              else:
                  prev = "".join([prev, " ", line])
          lines.append(prev)
```

Next, have these tentative sentences (stored in *lines*) cleaned by *cleanStringOne*. We feed them to the *SpaCy* model to be further split into "sents" based on grammatical structure.

```
In [31]:  lines = [str(x) for s in lines for x in spc(cleanStringOne(s)).sents]
```

We now leverage the *SpaCy* model one more time to "lemmatize" words (turn words into their infinitive forms by removing conjugation suffixes). All pronouns (converted by *SpaCy* to the "-PRON-" literal) are removed as they hold limited value for subsequent report analysis.
Finally, preprocessing is concluded by the following set of steps:

- Lemmatized strings are subjected to the "second-stage" cleaning by *cleanStringTwo*.
- We remove sentences that are too short (shorter than 100 characters).

- The last step allows us to assemble the resulting statements into a *dataframe* that we will use for analytics purposes next.

Note that for many of the subsequent analyses we do not need to store lemmatized sentences separately and could convert them into a single processed string for each company report, similar to how the original report strings are stored in the *contentMap* dictionary. However, in the final hands-on exercise of this chapter (Exercise 5.C), we will count the sentences attributed to a particular topic in each company's report; therefore, we keep the sentences separate, in order to count them then.

In the output *dataframe*, we keep two columns: a ticker that identifies the report each sentence originated from and a string that contains the lemmatized sentence (rather, processed lemmas joined into a single string delimited by spaces).

```
In [32]:  ▶  lines2 = []
              for line in lines:
                  lemmas = " ".join([x.lemma_ for x in spc(line) if x.lemma_ not in ["-PRON-"]])
                  lines2.append(cleanStringTwo(lemmas))

              lines2 = [x for x in lines2 if len(x) > 100]
              pd.DataFrame({"name": "ZION", "lemmas": lines2})
```

Out[32]:

	name	lemmas
0	ZION	corporate responsibility report corporate resp...
1	ZION	our product covid response for customers fair ...
2	ZION	remote deposit capture focused conservation an...
3	ZION	the event of recent month have remind we all o...
4	ZION	customer employee states total assets corporat...
5	ZION	our community banking model be focus on local ...
6	ZION	communicate with our stakeholders corporate re...
7	ZION	noninterest expense income before income taxis...
8	ZION	year end assets net loan and lease deposits lo...
9	ZION	equity weighted average diluted share outstand...
10	ZION	common dividend pay plus dollar amount use for...
11	ZION	to help protect our frontline employee our bra...
12	ZION	we believe that success require an environment...
13	ZION	middle management professional overall corpora...
14	ZION	in response to the covid pandemic our branch b...
15	ZION	the commerce bank of washington design and imp...
16	ZION	throughout the year nevada state banks souther...
17	ZION	it will accommodate more than reduce related o...
18	ZION	the company have replace paper account opening...
19	ZION	uphold strong governance corporate responsibil...
20	ZION	zions bank ownership and legal form values pri...
21	ZION	engagement employees social risk and impact bo...

We save a copy of the processed reports' *dataframe* locally, so that we can retrieve it quickly later without repeating the download of 500 reports.

```
In [34]:  ▶  dfReports.to_csv("1.csv", index=False)
              dfReports
```

Out[34]:

	name	lemmas
0	MMM	sustainability report science for community sc...
1	MMM	our value our strategic sustainability framewo...
2	MMM	how we work introduction corporate governance ...
3	MMM	our customer innovation management our product...
4	MMM	it have also be time to recommit to our value ...
...	...	...
179292	ZTS	hazardous waste recycle intensity kilograms mm...
179293	ZTS	the process identie opportunity for datum proc...
179294	ZTS	packaging to provide further focus and support...
179295	ZTS	this team will also develop tool to align with...
179296	ZTS	we will also engage with our supplier on their...

179297 rows × 2 columns

5.3   TOPIC MODELING

In machine learning, topic modeling is an unsupervised learning approach that allows us to highlight the abstract "topics" that occur in a corpus of unstructured text documents. It does not require, or account for, any explicit preexisting structure in the underlying data to analyze. The output of topic modeling is a structured list of topics, matched with probability values that a particular document is linked to a particular topic. (We are choosing to use the probabilistic definition in this book; there is also an alternative definition based on topic importance, which uses the properties of bag-of-words matrices that we will discuss in the following section.)

The topics themselves are defined by a limited number of top-ranked words, the ranking methodology for which shall be explained in the upcoming sections.

Bag-of-Words. In NLP, any text (such as this very sentence, a document, or an entire book) can be represented as the set (the "bag") of its words, where grammar and word order are discarded but multiplicity is retained. In practical terms, each document is represented by an n-dimensional vector, where n is the number of different words across all documents in the corpus. Typically the bag-of-words conversion occurs after document preprocessing, once tokenization, lemmatization, and all other steps of document standardization and simplification have occurred. The metric thus produced is referred to as *term frequency*. Class *sklearn.feature_extraction.text.CountVectorizer* implements the bag-of-words counting (term frequency) in the *scikit-learn* library; in the subsequent exercises in this chapter we apply it to our corpus of documents of interest.

Consider an example where we apply a bag-of-words count to the unprocessed paragraph above and obtain the result presented in Table 5.1 (limited to words that appear at least twice; also note the limited informational value due to not having removed short words and stop words).

TABLE 5.1   Bag-of-words count illustration.

Order	Unfiltered word count	Occurrences	Percentage
1	the	9	7.0
2	of	7	5.4
3	in	5	3.9
4	is	5	3.9
5	document	4	3.1
6	words	4	3.1
7	as	3	2.3
8	this	3	2.3
9	and	3	2.3
10	bag	3	2.3
11	n	2	1.5
12	an	2	1.5
13	to	2	1.5
14	book	2	1.5
15	term	2	1.5
16	text	2	1.5
17	frequency	2	1.5
18	corpus	2	1.5
19	represented	2	1.5
20	documents	2	1.5
21	all	2	1.5
22	where	2	1.5

TF-IDF. While the *term frequency* (TF) metric is straightforward and easy to understand, it tends to be too generalized to be useful for topic-specific searches and insight. This is because it mixes informational content about the overall structure of the language (which has an average frequency of words, independent of the topic being discussed) together with topic-specific information, and the former, being a much stronger signal, can easily drown out any topic-specific signal that we might be interested in highlighting. This is exemplified by the fact that TF, by nature of simply looking at the *absolute frequency of a word*, does not account for whether the word itself is common (both across a wider corpus of documents or in the language in general). In order to address this issue and gain meaningful insight from this type of analysis, it is therefore necessary to measure the relative frequency of words in the document being analyzed, compared to the frequency of the same word within the corpus of documents of reference (be this the entire language or a specific subset). This goal is achieved by the introduction of a frequency-corrected metric, called TF-IDF (term frequency – inverse document frequency), defined as

$$tf\text{-}idf = tf\left(w, d\right) \cdot \left(1 + \log_{10} \frac{N}{DF\left(w\right)}\right),$$

where

- *tf-idf* stands for term frequency – inverse document frequency; note that the dash is not a minus sign but part of the metric name!
- *tf(w,d)* is the term frequency of word *w* (number of times it appears) in document *d*
- *DF(w)* is the document frequency of word *w* in the corpus of documents of reference (i.e., the number of documents in which *w* appears at least once within the total corpus of *N* documents of reference).

To exemplify, let us assume we were to find the word "climate" 5 times in a given document d, part of a corpus of 10,000 other documents, and the word "water" 13 times; we would calculate a TF of 5 and 13, respectively. Once we look across the entire corpus of 10,000, we notice, however, that "water," being a generally more common word, appears in 5,033 documents while "climate" only appears in 100.

We can therefore calculate the TF-IDF for climate as follows:

$$tf\text{-}idf\left(\text{"climate"}\right) = 5^{*}\left(1 + \log_{10}\left(10^4 / 10^2\right)\right) = \mathbf{15}$$

and the one for "water" as follows:

$$tf\text{-}idf\left(\text{"water"}\right) = 13^{*}\left(1 + \log_{10}\left(10^4 / 5^{*}10^3\right)\right) \cong \mathbf{16.9}$$

This calculation shows us how, despite "climate" being almost three times less frequent in the document that we are analyzing, because of the more infrequent nature of it in the corpus, it is effectively as significant as the word "water."

EXERCISE 5.B   Term Occurrence in ESG Reports

We will rely on the *sklearn.feature_extraction* collection of libraries that implements TF and TF-IDF word-counting classes along with a number of other useful utilities.

We will utilize the standard implementation of a word cloud.

```
In [5]:  ▶  import sklearn.feature_extraction as skfe
            import wordcloud
```

As usual, we will also use *matplotlib* to generate any figures and *numpy* as a numerical utility.

```
In [6]:  ▶  import matplotlib.pyplot as plt
            import numpy as np
```

Stop words are the most common words that we exclude from any subsequent calculations; these are the words that are so common and generic that we deem them not useful to the determination of topics. Examples include, for instance, pronouns and words such as "be," "can," "become," and so on. We use the standard *skfe.text.ENGLISH_STOP_WORDS* set as a starting point (despite a number of known weaknesses of this set).

We add the word *page* to the set of stop words based on an empirical finding: If not excluded, the word *page* features prominently in most reports and, therefore, lists of most common bigrams, etc. Obviously, the word *page* does not reveal any relevant ESG information.

We also add words that appear in the S&P 500 companies' names after splitting them by spaces and hyphens. Naturally, company names tend to appear quite often in a company's own ESG report (or any other report, for that matter).

```
In [16]:  ▶  stopWords = [ii for nm in dfSpxData.name.unique() for ii in nm.replace("-", " ").split(" ")]
             stopWords = stopWords + ["page"]
             stopWords = skfe.text.ENGLISH_STOP_WORDS.union(stopWords)
             stopWords

Out[16]:  frozenset({'&',
                      '3M',
                      '66',
                      'A.O.Smith',
                      'ADM',
                      'AES',
                      'APA',
                      'AT&T',
                      'AbbVie',
                      'Abbott',
                      'Abiomed',
                      'Accenture',
                      'Activision',
                      'Adobe',
                      'Advanced',
                      'Aerospace',
                      'Aflac',
                      'Agilent',
                      'Air',
```

A word cloud is a common visual representation of text data used to highlight the relative importance of specific words. In most implementations, words that appear in the text more often are drawn using a larger font size.

WordCloud is a standard class implementation of a word cloud (a set of stop words to be excluded and an upper limit of the words to consider are parameters); *generate* method is used to, yes, generate the *wordcloud* based on frequency of occurrence of specific words in our *lemmas* strings, joined together into a single long string.

```
In [8]:  ▶  wordCloud0 = wordcloud.WordCloud(stopwords=stopWords, max_words=1000, background_color="white")
            wordCloud0.generate(" ".join(dfReports.lemmas))

Out[8]:  <wordcloud.wordcloud.WordCloud at 0x2455a325a90>
```

Once generated, the word cloud is drawn by the *imshow* function in *matplotlib* just like many other 2D plots. We also turn off the axes on this figure as they are not relevant and do not add value to the cloud representation (the font size matters, but the location of words does not have specific meaning).

```
In [9]:  ▶ plt.figure(figsize=(10, 10))
           plt.axis("off")
           plt.imshow(wordCloud0)
```

Out[9]: <matplotlib.image.AxesImage at 0x2455a325b50>

Instead of running our analyses on the full universe of S&P 500 stocks (or at least the subset we can retrieve ESG reports for), it is often useful to restrict our attention to, say, a specific sector, as the findings certainly do vary considerably between different sectors or industries.

To be able to drill down in a particular sector, we add a new column by looking up the sector by the "name" field (ticker).

```
In [10]:  ▶ dfReports["sector"] = dfReports.apply(lambda row: dfSpxData.sector[row["name"]], axis=1)
            dfReports[dfReports["sector"] == "Industrials"]
```

Out[10]:

	name	lemmas	sector
0	MMM	sustainability report science for community sc...	Industrials
1	MMM	our value our strategic sustainability framewo...	Industrials
2	MMM	how we work introduction corporate governance ...	Industrials
3	MMM	our customer innovation management our product...	Industrials
4	MMM	it have also be time to recommit to our value ...	Industrials
...	...	...	...
178867	XYL	disclose whether you have set or have commit t...	Industrials
178868	XYL	recommendation of the tcfd cdsb and sasb scien...	Industrials
178869	XYL	average training and development expenditure p...	Industrials
178870	XYL	gri sasb hc xylem sustainability report messag...	Industrials
178871	XYL	how we make progress serve our customers build...	Industrials

24262 rows × 3 columns

For instance, let us plot a word cloud guided by the term frequency in ESG reports for the Energy sector. "Include" and "employee" continue to dominate, but sector-specific "operation," "safety," and "risk" also feature prominently now:

```
In [12]:  ▶ wordCloud0.generate(" ".join(dfReports[dfReports["sector"] == "Energy"].lemmas))

            plt.figure(figsize=(10, 10))
            plt.axis("off")
            plt.title("Health Care")
            plt.imshow(wordCloud0)
```

Out[12]: <matplotlib.image.AxesImage at 0x2455a3bc220>

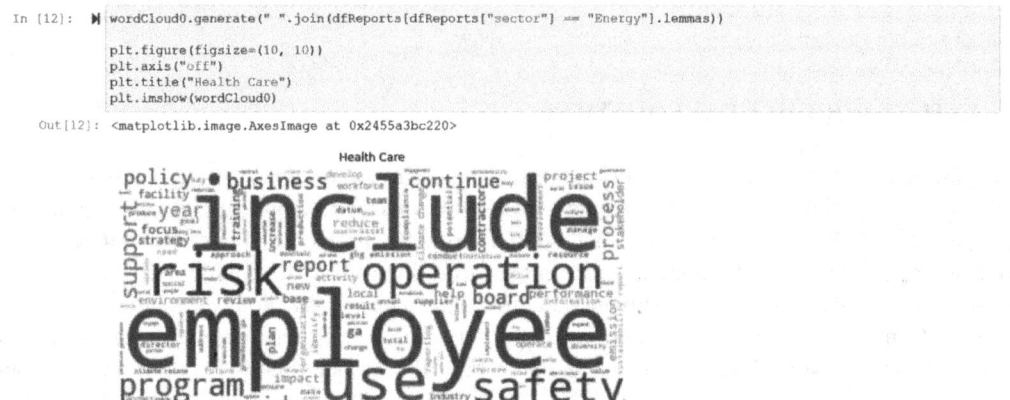

The word cloud technique has provided us with a single-word word cloud visualization, which gives us some level of insight into the content of the document corpus, but it is still very much a high-level, generic type of output. As our next step, we shall utilize the *text.TfidfVectorizer* class that implements TF-IDF frequency counting to generate bigram (combinations of two words) frequencies, to find and highlight more advanced and, potentially, meaningful data.

The *ngram_range* argument in the function represents a (min length, max length) tuple for the bigram of interest (i.e., a parameter choice of 2, 2 means that nothing shorter than two words or longer than two words will be counted).

We define a function that will count TF-IDF frequencies for bigrams within a subset of reports belonging to a sector of choice. Vectorized results are sorted by frequency before the *nTop* most frequent bigrams are returned (of course, this function may be easily generalized further; for instance, to handle longer sequences of words, or perhaps single words instead).

```
In [13]:    def CreateSectorBigrams(sSector="Industrials", nTop=6):
                tfidfVectorizer = skfe.text.TfidfVectorizer(stop_words=stopWords, ngram_range=(2, 2))
                tfidf = tfidfVectorizer.fit_transform(dfReports[dfReports["sector"] == sSector].lemmas)

                bigrams = tfidfVectorizer.get_feature_names()
                counts = np.zeros(len(bigrams))
                for ii in tfidf:
                    counts += ii.toarray()[0]

                counts = sorted(zip(bigrams, counts), key=lambda x: x[1], reverse=True)[0:nTop]
                return [x[0] for x in counts]
```

The function defined above identifies several most common bigrams within each sector. It is instructive to compile resulting bigram sequences into a single *DataFrame* as a means to observe and compare different sectors' specifics. While considerably less colorful, this *DataFrame* provides an excellent representation of sector differences. For example, greenhouse gas (GHG) emissions are an important topic for Energy, Industrials and Materials sectors, but for Health Care, for example, supply chain and health and safety concerns are more central.

```
In [17]:    pd.DataFrame({x : CreateSectorBigrams(x) for x in dfReports.sector.unique()})
```

Out[17]:

	Industrials	Health Care	Information Technology	Communication Services	Utilities	Financials	Materials	Consumer Discretionary	Real Estate	Consumer Staples	Energy
0	supply chain	supply chain	supply chain	renewable energy	natural gas	risk management	health safety	supply chain	management approach	supply chain	natural gas
1	health safety	health safety	corporate responsibility	supply chain	clean energy	climate change	sustainability report	team member	ghg emission	csr report	climate change
2	sustainability report	clinical trial	health safety	climate change	climate change	long term	human right	human right	renewable energy	general mills	oil gas
3	climate change	sustainability report	human right	corporate governance	renewable energy	environmental social	ghg emission	health safety	climate relate	human right	climate relate
4	climate relate	covid pandemic	team member	datum center	long term	small business	climate change	human rights	long term	climate change	ghg emission
5	ghg emission	long term	management approach	corporate responsibility	social governance	bny mellon	supply chain	sustainability report	corporate governance	palm oil	sustainability report

5.4   LATENT DIRICHLET ALLOCATION

While TD-IDF provides a basic level of insight on the content and topics of a document within a corpus, it has several drawbacks that make its widespread use for NLP applications less than optimal. These drawbacks all stem from the fact that TD-IDF provides a relatively limited amount of reduction in description length of the content of documents. Additionally, it does not highlight hardly any of the inter-documental and intra-documental statistical structures of potential relevance and interest (the TF-IDF metric is incapable of differentiating between, e.g., a document with an association between "climate change" and "hoax" and one where the association is "climate change" and "reversal").

In order to take our analysis of texts to the next level and solve this inadequacy of TD-IDF, we resort to a slightly more advanced approach referred to as Latent Dirichlet Allocation (LDA).

LDA is a statistical model that can be applied to a corpus of documents to classify them into similar groups by postulating the existence of unobserved groups (topics) that explain why some parts of the data are similar. Each topic is represented by a distribution of words and each document is represented by a distribution of topics, thus reducing the entire corpus to a much smaller set of matrices of topics.

The way LDA works for NLP is through discovering topics within the corpus of documents and then automatically classifying an individual document based on probability of a topic being covered in it. A topic is interpreted as a distribution of words that, taken together, suggest a shared theme. (Please note that "topic" here is used in terms of *set of words that are statistically associated with each other within the documents in the corpus,* and not in the epistemological sense of "topic," in the way that words such as "sports" or "science" are understood to be topics.)

Now, before proceeding to the analysis of corporate ESG reports using LDA, let us illustrate the concepts behind the LDA approach on a decidedly "non-ESG" themed text (rather a corpus of texts)!

If we were to look at a corpus that pertains, for example, to American sports, we could see that the words *bat, strike, pitch, inning, shortstop, base, homerun* would all fall into the topic of BASEBALL, while *touchdown, kickoff, quarterback, linebacker, scrimmage,* and *punt* would fall within the topic of FOOTBALL, and other words such as *score, umpire, win, fans,* and *game* could belong to both. As we can see in Figure 5.3, the simple classification of the documents by word content alone provides little useful information, due to the very large number of connections that rapidly become evident.

Given a sufficiently large corpus of documents, the LDA methodology will discover naturally occurring topics that are present within it, but the task of naming them will have to be performed by the user, as these will appear as distributions of probability similar to Table 5.2 (which would be the one for BASEBALL from our example above).

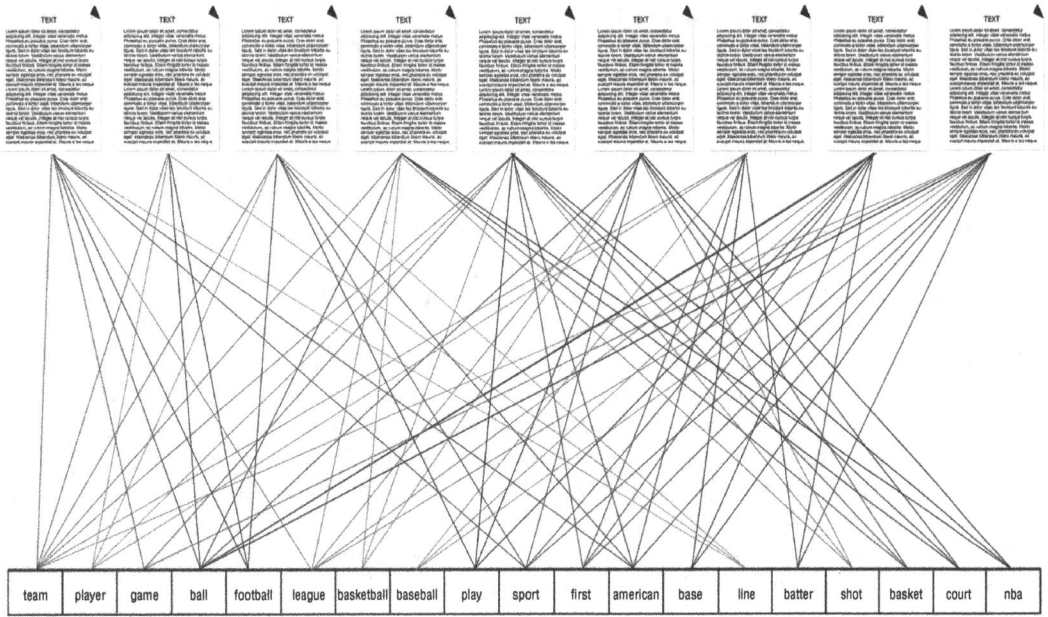

FIGURE 5.3 Classification of American sports documents by word content.

TABLE 5.2   Term distribution.

Term	Percentage of occurrence
baseball	1.7
league	**1.0**
team	**0.9**
base	0.9
game	**0.8**
player	**0.7**
play	**0.7**
batter	0.6
ball	**0.5**
first	**0.5**
out	**0.4**
pitcher	0.4
field	**0.4**
national	**0.3**
batting	0.3
home	**0.3**
run	0.3
inning	0.3
hit	0.3
major	**0.3**
professional	**0.3**
american	**0.3**
runner	0.3
fielding	0.3
plate	0.2
world	**0.2**
bat	0.2
sports	**0.2**
statistics	**0.2**
united states	**0.2**
major league	**0.2**
mlb	0.2
park	**0.2**
pitch	0.2

While the LDA can identify that the above distribution of frequency exists within the corpus for a subset of sports articles, it is up to the experimenter to be able to understand and label this distribution as being the topic "BASEBALL" as opposed to the topic "FOOTBALL."

By observing the list above we can see that, while some of the words are topic-specific, others (in bold) can be common to other related topics within the corpus (common with the topic FOOTBALL, e.g.), and can be found with different probabilities in both topics. In these cases, what allows the LDA to determine the most likely topic for the document is the co-occurrence of the ambiguous words together with topic-specific ones (e.g., while the word *park* could apply both to a football stadium as well as to a baseball stadium, the association of the term *MLB* in the document makes it likely that the topic being covered is BASEBALL and not FOOTBALL).

We can now see, conceptually, how the previous, disorganized graph in Figure 5.3 is cleaned up by the emergence of the previously hidden topics (see Figure 5.4), which reduce the number of threads to a much more manageable dimension.

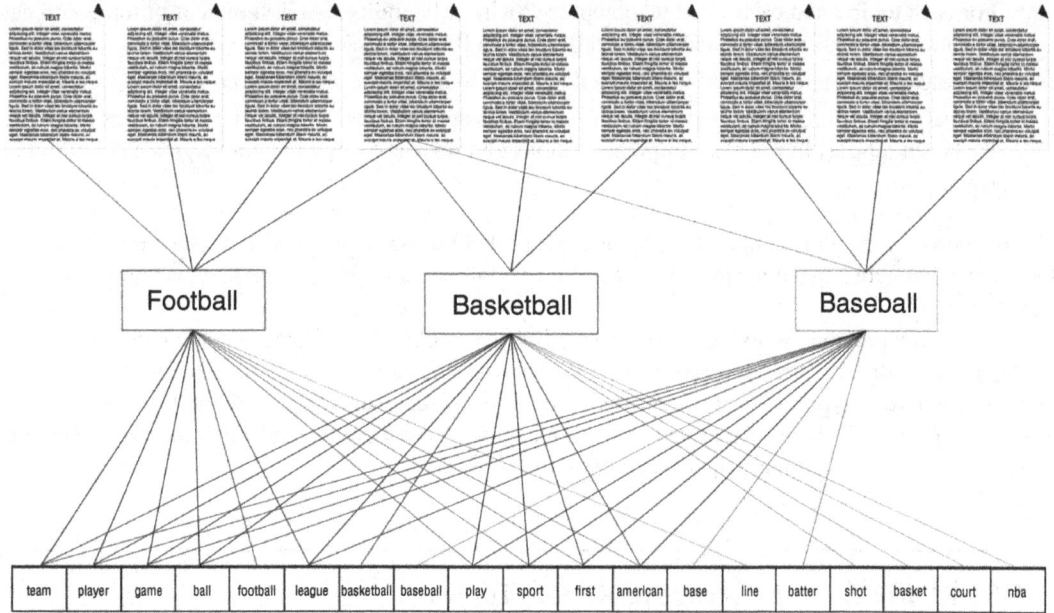

FIGURE 5.4 Classification of American sports documents by word content with latent topics made visible.

Note how, for the sake of this example, we highlighted topic-specific connections (i.e., terms that are only present in one topic and not in the others) in the shade of gray of the box around the topic, while shared ones are marked in black.

This last determination is based on the (relatively frequent) assumption that the majority of documents in a corpus will cover a small number of topics (i.e., each document will be fairly topic-specific) and, within the corpus, the different topics will appear with their own specific frequencies. In mathematical terms, this is expressed as a probability distribution, where each document has a higher likelihood, a priori, of covering certain topics as opposed to others (based on the frequency of such topics in the corpus).

Within the topic itself, the distribution of terms, as seen above, is what allows for the matching of the document with the topic (i.e., the closer the term distribution in the document is to the word topic distribution, the more likely it is that the document covers the topic under consideration).

The assumptions that LDA makes in order to function are that words in the documents are distributed multinomially, conditional on a small number of topics which are not observable a priori and are also multinomially distributed. The topics are assumed preexisting and limited in number. The LDA methodology derives the joint distribution parameters by analyzing the overall sample provided in the corpus.

The optimal functioning of this methodology is dependent on the choice of the right number of topics in the corpus, as well as being able to run enough iterations to allow the results to converge to stable values.

The way the LDA algorithm operates is by moving through the following steps:

- Choose the fixed total number of topics K.
- Randomly make an initial assignment of one of K topics to each word in the document corpus.
- For each topic t and each document d, compute $P(t|d)$, a proportion of words in document d assigned topic t.

- For each topic *t* and each word *w*, compute $P(w|t)$, probability that assignment of topic *t* comes from word *w* (this is computed not directly but via Bayes' rule).
- Reassign topics to each word *w* in each document to maximize $P(t|d) * P(w|t)$.
- Repeat the last three steps many times (until the assignments stabilize). The number of iterations is chosen a priori in practical implementations and does not rely on a convergence condition of some kind.

The output of the algorithm will be the inferred probability value $P(t|d)$ that document *d* belongs to topic *t* coupled with a list of the most likely words that fall under each topic, ranked by their probability values, $P(w|t)$.

As we have previously noted, these probability distributions are expressed numerically (in our example: baseball 1.7%, league 1.0%, team 0.9%, base 0.9%, game 0.8%), and we need to rely on our own judgment to interpret what the identified topic actually represents (*Baseball*, in this example). We are referring, specifically, to the topic's applied meaning rather than its conceptual meaning, which is an unobservable multinomially distributed random variable.

EXERCISE 5.C   Inference of Report Topics

sklearn.decomposition.LatentDirichletAllocation class is the standard implementation of the Latent Dirichlet Allocation (LDA) algorithm discussed here.

```
In [12]:  ▶ from sklearn.decomposition import LatentDirichletAllocation
```

LDA uses data from a simple term frequency (TF) vectorizer to calibrate the underlying distribution of topics. The TF vectorizer counts frequencies for words in the *lemmas* column of our reports' repository *DataFrame*. This time we are interested in counts of unigrams (single words).

The first parameter passed to the *LatentDirichletAllocation* constructor is the number of topics that we must choose prior to fitting the joint distribution. We postulate that the number of topics is six; in practice, choosing the appropriate value for this hyperparameter may require some trial-and-error iterations, as the correct number is usually not known a priori with any certainty.

random_state is the random number generator seed that we arbitrarily set to 1; we fix it at the outset for reproducibility (understanding the inherent uncertainty, we prefer our estimate not to change randomly every time we recalculate the relevant cell).

```
In [13]:  ▶ tfVectorizer = skfe.text.CountVectorizer(stop_words=stopWords, ngram_range=(1, 1))
            wordTF = tfVectorizer.fit_transform(dfReports.lemmas)

            lda = LatentDirichletAllocation(6, random_state=1)
            lda.fit(wordTF)

Out[13]:  LatentDirichletAllocation(n_components=6, random_state=1)
```

The *get_feature_names* method returns all words for which frequencies are calculated. For each of the six topics, enumerated by *x*, we sort the words based on their weights stored in *components_* to isolate the 10 most common words for each topic:

```
In [57]:  ▶ featureNames = tfVectorizer.get_feature_names()
            [" ".join([featureNames[ii] for ii in x.argsort()[:-11:-1]]) for x in lda.components_]

Out[57]:  ['water supplier human right code conduct total supply chain business',
           'report sustainability governance corporate management esg board gri environmental social',
           'emission risk climate change scope ghg relate include target year',
           'energy waste use product reduce customer renewable new carbon material',
           'safety health employee product program management work include process provide',
           'employee community support program work provide help business people diversity']
```

We judgmentally name topics based on the most common words associated with each (above). Of course, the topics will get reshuffled and likely require renaming if we choose a different number of topics (or restrict the text corpus to, e.g., reports in only some of the sectors).

```
In [59]:  topics = ["supply chain", "ESG", "emissions", "renewables", "health and safety", "employees"]
```

To get a slightly richer sense for which words are attributed to which topic, we generate separate word clouds for each topic in a loop. Note that we must invoke the *generate_from_frequencies* method instead of the previously applied *generate* as the *topicWords* array lists each word only once; we are providing preassigned frequencies to the word cloud object directly rather than having the word cloud object infer frequencies from the text sample.

The output of this snippet is beautiful greenish art assembled in a 2 × 3 grid:

```
In [60]:  nTopics = len(lda.components_)
          fig = plt.figure(figsize=(20, 20))
          for ii, topic in enumerate(lda.components_):
              topicWords = {x[0]: x[1] for x in zip(featureNames, topic)}

              ax = fig.add_subplot(nTopics, 3, ii + 1)
              ax.set_title(topics[ii])
              ax.axis('off')
              ax.imshow(wordcloud.WordCloud(background_color="white").generate_from_frequencies(topicWords))
```

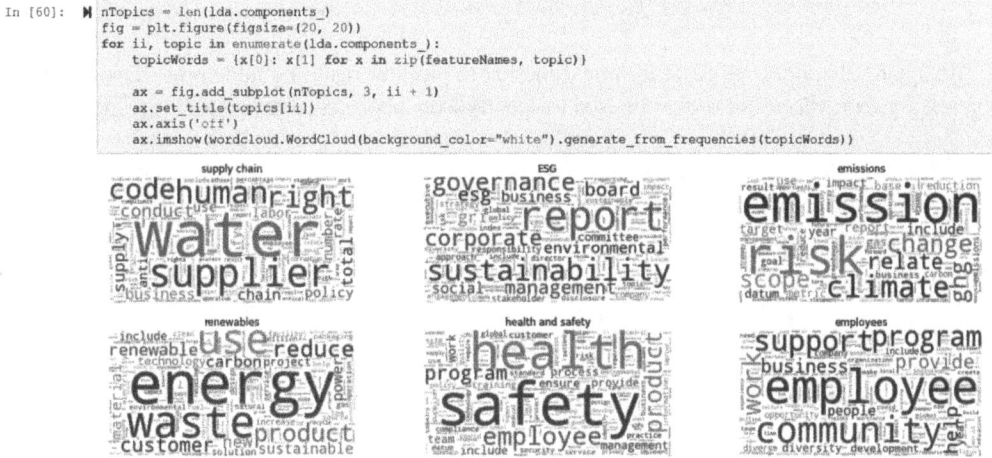

We can now assign topics to each statement in the reports. The probability that a statement belongs to each of the six topics is implied by the LDA allocation algorithm; below we append the probability matrix to the reports *dataframe*.

The "Topic" is chosen among the six topic names we defined earlier based on the highest probability reading among the six.

```
In [72]:  probs = lda.transform(wordTF)
          dfReports["topic"] = [topics[np.argmax(x)] for x in probs]
          pd.concat([dfReports, pd.DataFrame(probs, columns=["(p) " + x for x in topics])], axis=1)
```

Out[72]:

	name	lemmas	sector	topic	(p) supply chain	(p) ESG	(p) emissions	(p) renewables	(p) health and safety	(p) employees
0	MMM	sustainability report science for community so...	Industrials	ESG	0.007270	0.577944	0.007361	0.131376	0.007326	0.268722
1	MMM	our value our strategic sustainability framewo...	Industrials	ESG	0.012874	0.935425	0.012858	0.012839	0.012904	0.013100
2	MMM	how we work introduction corporate governance ...	Industrials	ESG	0.215559	0.553572	0.006732	0.098707	0.118709	0.006721
3	MMM	our customer innovation management our product...	Industrials	ESG	0.006201	0.815042	0.082253	0.006256	0.006252	0.083997
4	MMM	it have also be time to recommit to our value ...	Industrials	employees	0.018593	0.018713	0.018568	0.018576	0.018600	0.908948
...	...	...	...	...	...	...	...	...	...	...
179292	ZTS	hazardous waste recycle intensity kilograms mm...	Health Care	renewables	0.006758	0.006752	0.190597	0.491829	0.297357	0.006707
179293	ZTS	the process identie opportunity for datum proc...	Health Care	emissions	0.015182	0.015206	0.923836	0.015226	0.015359	0.015191
179294	ZTS	packaging to provide further focus and support...	Health Care	ESG	0.005984	0.291360	0.005988	0.263891	0.228200	0.204576
179295	ZTS	this team will also develop tool to align with...	Health Care	health and safety	0.008801	0.008868	0.339798	0.143212	0.490473	0.008849
179296	ZTS	we will also engage with our supplier on their...	Health Care	renewables	0.127869	0.197440	0.016783	0.411222	0.016795	0.229892

179297 rows × 10 columns

As the final part of the exercise, we count (lemmatized) statements at the intersection of industry sector and "topic"; *pandas.crosstab* is a handy utility for this very purpose.

Our objective for the creation of this pivot table is to identify which topics are prevalent (and therefore, in a sense, "important") to any particular industry segment. We do not want the overall length of the reports in a sector (i.e., absolute number of statements) to skew our results. Therefore, we normalize rows by the total number of report statements in a sector. This way, each sector's row represents a distribution of statement topics across the six choices we have identified above (each row sums up to 100%).

```
In [83]:  ▶ dfTopicBySector = pd.crosstab(dfReports.sector, dfReports.topic)
             rowSums = dfTopicBySector.sum(axis=1)
             dfTopicBySector = dfTopicBySector / rowSums[:, np.newaxis]

             <ipython-input-83-3c978d73ecd5>:3: FutureWarning: Support for multi-dimensional indexing (e.g. `obj[:, None]`) is d
             eprecated and will be removed in a future version.  Convert to a numpy array before indexing instead.
               dfTopicBySector = dfTopicBySector / rowSums[:, np.newaxis]
```

We again rely on the versatile *imshow* function to plot our resulting table on a 2D surface, in shades of green; *xticks* and *yticks* are used to specify axis labels (sectors and topics respectively).

```
In [30]:  ▶ plt.figure(figsize=(14, 8))
             plt.imshow(dfTopicBySector, cmap="Greens", aspect="auto")
             plt.xticks(range(len(dfTopicBySector.columns)), dfTopicBySector.columns)
             plt.yticks(range(len(dfTopicBySector.index)), dfTopicBySector.index)

   Out[30]:  ([<matplotlib.axis.YTick at 0x16a303cea60>,
               <matplotlib.axis.YTick at 0x16a303ce6d0>,
               <matplotlib.axis.YTick at 0x16a303cb520>,
               <matplotlib.axis.YTick at 0x16a303fc220>,
               <matplotlib.axis.YTick at 0x16a303fc730>,
               <matplotlib.axis.YTick at 0x16a303fcc40>,
               <matplotlib.axis.YTick at 0x16a30402190>,
               <matplotlib.axis.YTick at 0x16a304026a0>,
               <matplotlib.axis.YTick at 0x16a303fc970>,
               <matplotlib.axis.YTick at 0x16a303f6940>,
               <matplotlib.axis.YTick at 0x16a304022b0>],
              [Text(0, 0, 'Communication Services'),
               Text(0, 1, 'Consumer Discretionary'),
               Text(0, 2, 'Consumer Staples'),
               Text(0, 3, 'Energy'),
               Text(0, 4, 'Financials'),
               Text(0, 5, 'Health Care'),
               Text(0, 6, 'Industrials'),
               Text(0, 7, 'Information Technology'),
               Text(0, 8, 'Materials'),
               Text(0, 9, 'Real Estate'),
               Text(0, 10, 'Utilities')])
```

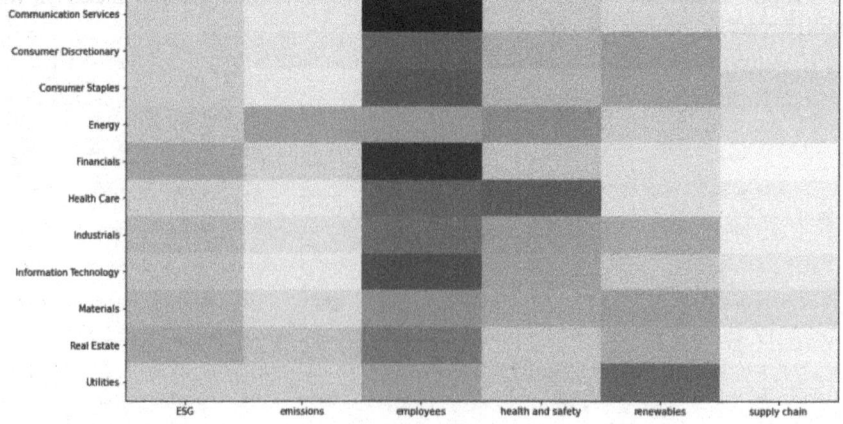

Repeating the approach we followed earlier in this exercise, instead of performing the analysis of sector differences, we can consider how the statement topic distributions vary across particular companies (whether within the same sector or not).

For example, below we restrict the corpus of reports to the energy sector names, instead of the full corpus of ESG reports for S&P 500 companies. We then follow the same steps as above (relying on the *crosstab* function) to generate the table of topic frequencies and plot them in a new table:

```
In [31]:    dfReportsEnergy = dfReports[dfReports["sector"] == "Energy"]

            dfTopicByName = pd.crosstab(dfReportsEnergy.name, dfReportsEnergy.topic)
            rowSums = dfTopicByName.sum(axis=1)
            dfTopicByName = dfTopicByName / rowSums[:, np.newaxis]

            plt.figure(figsize=(14, 8))
            plt.imshow(dfTopicByName, cmap="Greens", aspect="auto")
            plt.xticks(range(len(dfTopicByName.columns)), dfTopicByName.columns)
            plt.yticks(range(len(dfTopicByName.index)), dfTopicByName.index)
```

```
<ipython-input-31-cfe7ad21cd8d>:5: FutureWarning: Support for multi-dimensional indexing (e.g. `obj[:, None]`) is d
eprecated and will be removed in a future version.  Convert to a numpy array before indexing instead.
  dfTopicByName = dfTopicByName / rowSums[:, np.newaxis]
```

```
Out[31]:    ([<matplotlib.axis.YTick at 0x16a30429700>,
             <matplotlib.axis.YTick at 0x16a304292e0>,
             <matplotlib.axis.YTick at 0x16a304261c0>,
             <matplotlib.axis.YTick at 0x16a304550a0>,
             <matplotlib.axis.YTick at 0x16a30455550>,
             <matplotlib.axis.YTick at 0x16a30455ac0>,
             <matplotlib.axis.YTick at 0x16a30455fd0>,
             <matplotlib.axis.YTick at 0x16a30455610>,
             <matplotlib.axis.YTick at 0x16a3044d5e0>,
             <matplotlib.axis.YTick at 0x16a30449640>,
             <matplotlib.axis.YTick at 0x16a3045b6d0>,
             <matplotlib.axis.YTick at 0x16a3045bbe0>,
             <matplotlib.axis.YTick at 0x16a30461130>,
             <matplotlib.axis.YTick at 0x16a30461640>,
             <matplotlib.axis.YTick at 0x16a30461b50>,
             <matplotlib.axis.YTick at 0x16a304670a0>],
             [Text(0, 0, 'BKR'),
             Text(0, 1, 'COP'),
             Text(0, 2, 'CVX'),
             Text(0, 3, 'DVN'),
             Text(0, 4, 'EOG'),
             Text(0, 5, 'FANG'),
             Text(0, 6, 'HAL'),
             Text(0, 7, 'HES'),
             Text(0, 8, 'MPC'),
             Text(0, 9, 'MRO'),
             Text(0, 10, 'OKE'),
             Text(0, 11, 'PXD'),
             Text(0, 12, 'SLB'),
             Text(0, 13, 'VLO'),
             Text(0, 14, 'WMB'),
             Text(0, 15, 'XOM')])
```

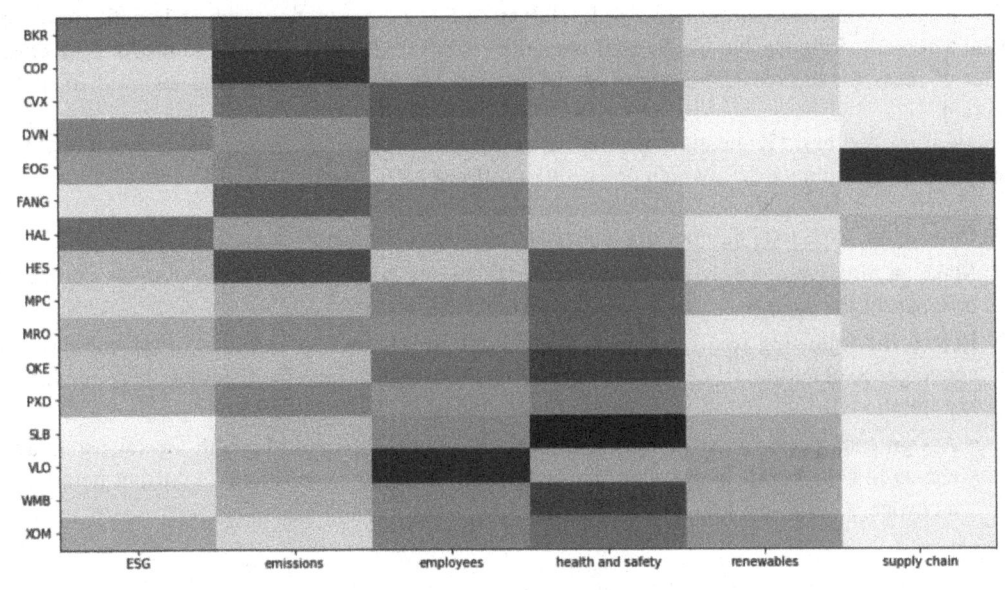

5.5 OUTLIER TOPICS

The topic modeling exercise that we just saw allowed us to generate a classification of the corporate statements across our corpus of documents and infer what different topics were covered in each document. It did not, however, tackle the question of how specific such topics are to a particular company (after all, we expect certain companies to have higher sensitivity/involvement in ESG topics than others, and this difference would reasonably show in a higher frequency of coverage of such topics in their documentation). A practical way to provide us with this type of insight on this topic specificity is to detect statement "anomalies," or outlier topics. From the initial analysis, we know the inferred probabilities of belonging to a specific topic, for each statement across our corpus, and we can group similar statements into clusters. If we notice clusters that segregate from the rest of the statements (i.e., are made up of statements that are close to each other but distant from the rest of the statements), we can confidently detect these as anomalies. These statements are anomalies in the sense that they stand apart from the rest of the statements within each topic that are specific/unique to the company whose report the statement belongs to.

There are many possible clustering algorithms that can be used to perform this type of analysis and, for the purposes of this brief exposition, we have chosen the fairly simple k-means clustering,[9] as it provides adequate performance for the task at hand without adding unnecessary complexity.

K-Means Clustering. This algorithm falls within the general category of clustering within the unsupervised machine learning problems, which are not strictly specific to NLP. The advantage of K-means is its simplicity and ease of implementation, which often makes it the go-to choice for similar problems. K-means is a method of vector quantization, dividing n observations into k clusters, assigning each observation to the cluster with the nearest mean (based on either the cluster centers or the cluster centroid). The resulting output is a division of the observations space into a partition of Voronoi[10] cells for which K-means clustering minimizes within-cluster variances.

For our purposes, K-means clustering solves the problem of categorizing a number of points in n-dimensional space into "clusters" by distance, defined by a metric function. Any function of two vectors would do, provided it is nonnegative, symmetric, and satisfies the triangular inequality:

$$d(x, y) \leq d(x, z) + d(z, y)$$

We are not trying to limit ourselves to Euclidean distance computations, which benefit from more specialized methodologies, but we do need the ability to compute the "average" points for each cluster (center of mass for the cluster) as these are to be used for calculation of distances used for outlier detection.

We will use the basic K-means algorithm, also known as "naïve" K-means (since much faster and sophisticated algorithms exist), which proceeds as follows:

- Choose the fixed total number of clusters K.
- Make an initial assignment of cluster "centroid" points $m_1, \ldots, m_K$ (these points do not have to be a part of the dataset).
- Repeat the following two steps many times until cluster choices stabilize (a typical choice of convergence condition is: centroids move by no more than a predefined amount between the two last iterations):
  - Assign each point in the dataset to the nearest centroid (centroid i with the lowest value of $d(x, m_i)$). Data points assigned to the same centroid together constitute (a current iteration of) a cluster.

---

[9] https://en.wikipedia.org/wiki/K-means_clustering
[10] https://en.wikipedia.org/wiki/Voronoi_diagram

○ Redefine new centroids to equal the averages (centers of mass) for each cluster:

$$m_i = \frac{1}{|\mathbf{M}_i|} \sum_{j \in \mathbf{M}_i} x_j$$

As mentioned, more efficient variants exist; also, a more efficient initial choice of centroids can improve performance considerably.

In *scikit-learn*, K-means clustering is implemented as class *sklearn.cluster.KMeans*. We leave the actual application of K-means (or a more sophisticated) clustering algorithm to the interested reader as an insightful exercise.

Similar to the previous chapter dealing with alternative imagery data, this chapter barely scratches the surface of the NLP body of knowledge – already a very expansive and rapidly developing area of study. We have focused here on only the most relevant NLP techniques, particularly Latent Dirichlet Allocation and its application to topic modeling. Due to space constraints, we have omitted the discussion of numerous other relevant NLP areas, such as, for instance, deep learning applications. Again, interested readers are strongly encouraged to continue their study of NLP and its applications using more specialized literature.

CHAPTER 6

Introduction to Agent-Based Modeling for ESG Finance

6.1 PREFACE

The current climate change emergency that the world and consequently the global economy are facing is certainly an unprecedented event in the relatively brief history of economic modeling and forecasting. Most of the models that are currently in use rely, in broad terms, on the concepts of looking at past events to predict the future (by regressions, correlations, reversions to mean, etc.). While this is a (relatively) practical way of looking at things in a stable, or meta-stable, set of conditions, and over a short period of time, it is, admittedly, not adequate to deal with changing conditions, stress events, or regime changes.

The reasons for using these kinds of models in economics and finance over the past century have mostly been due to the need to simplify a set of very complex interactions and adapt existing techniques from abstract fields such as physics and mathematics to the very real-world problematics of the economy and the markets.

A good example of this way of thinking, and overly simplified approaches to modeling complex systems, is the well-known joke about spherical cows to remind us of the risks of oversimplification:

> Milk production at a dairy farm was low, so the farmer wrote to the local university, asking for help from academia. A multidisciplinary team of professors was assembled, headed by a theoretical physicist, and two weeks of intensive on-site investigation took place. The scholars then returned to the university, notebooks crammed with data, where the task of writing the report was left to the team leader. Shortly thereafter the physicist returned to the farm, saying to the farmer, "I have the solution, but it works only in the case of spherical cows in a vacuum."

Looking at more mainstream quotes, we can see that, when Robert Solow, who won the Nobel Prize in Economics in 1987, was asked to testify at the 2010 congressional hearing on macroeconomic modeling aiming to investigate why macroeconomists failed to foresee the financial crisis of 2007–2010, his commentary was very much aligned to the Spherical Cow critique:

> I do not think that the currently popular DSGE models pass the smell test. They take it for granted that the whole economy can be thought about as if it were a single, consistent person or dynasty carrying out a rationally designed, long-term plan, occasionally disturbed by unexpected shocks, but adapting to them in a rational, consistent way. [. . .] The protagonists of this idea make a claim

to respectability by asserting that it is founded on what we know about microeconomic behavior, but I think that this claim is generally phony. The advocates no doubt believe what they say, but they seem to have stopped sniffing or to have lost their sense of smell altogether.

—Robert Solow, *"Building a Science of Economics for the Real World,"* July 20, *2010, House Committee on Science and Technology, Subcommitee on Investigations and Oversight*

There are several reasons that underpin this failure of neoclassical economics models to predict regime changes and shifts, both of which are critical features of ESG and climate change modeling. The most relevant of these inadequacies is that all these models have biases and assumptions that are so far removed from practical conditions to make the entire modeling exercise not applicable to the world in which we live.

Some examples of these assumptions, for what is called *economic man*, are:

- Perfect rationality
- Possession of complete information about all prices, now and in the future
- Living in a world with perfect competition

As it is immediately clear to any of our readers, all three assumptions above fail the most basic of tests, as irrational behavior is widespread, information about prices is far from complete, and competition is nowhere near perfect in most of the markets and countries in the world (thanks to the existence of monopolies, tariffs, barriers to entry, etc.).

If we take a cursory look at the most used models in the econometric space, we notice how both dynamic stochastic general equilibrium (DSGE) models and computable general equilibrium (CGE) models share the same major flaws (based on the design of the models and the equations that govern them) that result in:

- Incapability of predict
- Incapability of account for
- Incapability of describe

Current approaches, overall, try to predict the future by looking at the past, and regularly fail to foresee crisis events ahead of time.

While it is easy to understand where this kind of modeling and academic school of thought derives from, it is also quite clear that it cannot be of much use for work in the ESG space. The reason for this lack of applicability lies in the fact that ESG requires modeling of entirely novel situations, interactions, and emerging properties, brought into existence by the complex and generally unpredictable interactions of many different agents engaged in a real-time exercise on the global stage.

The traditional paradigm that has been applied in modeling economic and financial systems has generally been one of predetermined relationships, correlations, and strict laws (with strong assumptions underpinning the models). This is a framework that postulates intelligence, intelligent behavior, and complex mathematics to solve it, and does not allow for detection of chaotic, unusual events, and/or emerging properties. Recent studies in multiple fields, however, have shown how most of these assumptions and postulates do not hold true, or are not strictly necessary to optimally solve complex problems in an efficient manner. In fact, there is fascinating new research by Boussard,[1] which shows that single-celled organisms with no nervous system can solve complex problems such as mazes and network optimization, which were previously thought to require high-level intelligence and/or massive computational power.

---

[1] A. Boussard et al., "Adaptive Behaviour and Learning in Slime Moulds: The Role of Oscillations," *Philosophical Transactions of the Royal Society B,* January 25, 2021, https://doi.org/10.1098/rstb.2019.0757

6.2   USE OF AGENT-BASED MODELS IN OTHER FIELDS AND THEIR APPLICABILITY TO ESG FINANCE

Luckily for us as ESG practitioners, we can look to other fields of science, to see how similar highly complex problems are tackled and solved, and utilize the lessons learned from decades of field experience in areas such as biology, engineering, social sciences, climate science, ecology, medicine, and computer science to aid us in our endeavor. Figure 6.1 shows us examples of applications of agent-based models to different fields, organized by spatial scale and temporal scale, for ease of visualization.

If we look across the spectrum of the sciences, we notice how complex, nonlinear systems, such as the economy and the markets, exist in several different areas. Some examples include:

- Climatology
- Ecology
- Evolutionary biology
- Molecular biology
- Medicine
- Social sciences
- Engineering
- Computer science

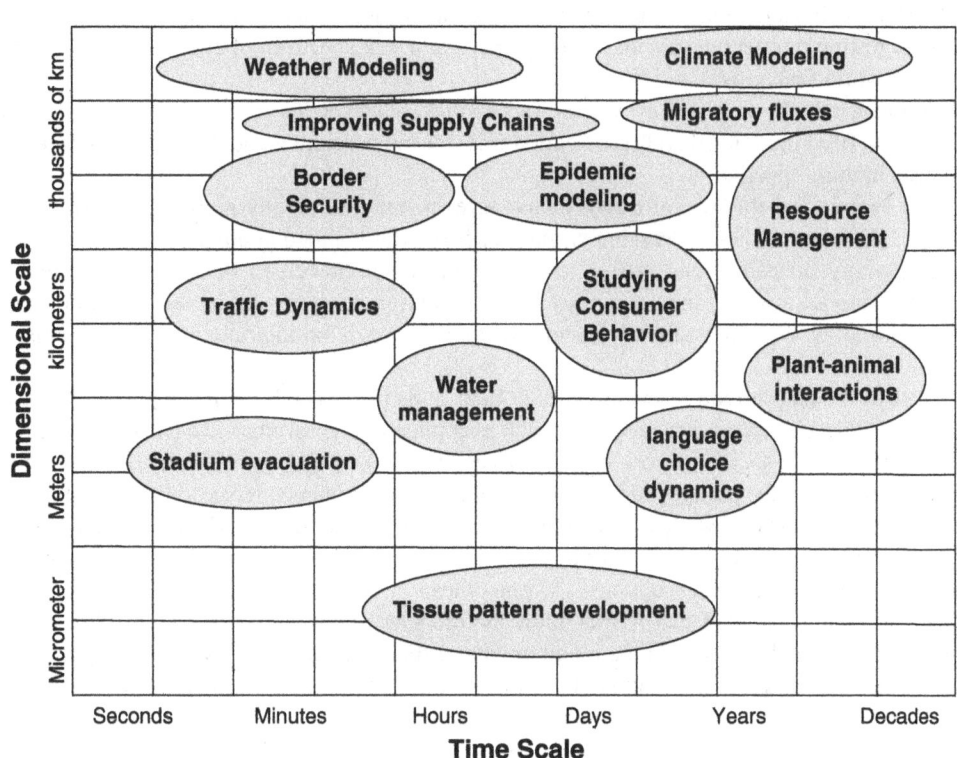

FIGURE 6.1   Examples of applications of agent-based modeling to varying temporal and spatial scales.

In all these fields, multiple different methodologies for modeling are in use, with agent-based models (ABMs) being used across the board. ABMs typically solve complex problems and provide insight in chaotic and otherwise unpredictable systems, generally characterized by high degrees of freedom, complex networks, and loose interactions.

6.3   USE OF ABMS IN THE ESG FIELD

Within the field of ESG finance, one of the most challenging areas for modeling purposes has been the subject of policies and strategies to tackle climate change, which is an unprecedented challenge and event, and how to come up with suitable methods to evaluate the potential impact and effects of proposed policies and combinations of policies.

Historically, models used for climate-energy policy design have always assumed the human population as being composed of rational, self-interested, and socially isolated individuals, for the purposes of providing simplified modeling and analytics. In reality, the economic agents that compose mankind, such as consumers, producers, investors, and innovators, have challenged these assumptions, sometimes in spectacular ways. Proof of deviation from these theoretical assumptions can be easily provided both by behavioral economics as well as by social psychology.

These realities of human behavior require, therefore, a richer and deeper treatment, if proper climate policy studies are to be undertaken. Specifically, it is necessary to integrate the diverse and relevant behavioral patterns that are typical of modern-day societies, such as the diversity of incomes and preferences, the presence of irrational behavior, and the different levels of influence that social networks, both local (family/friends) and virtual (news/social media), exert on everyone. The integration of these behaviors by agent-based models is what provides the ESG practitioner with this fundamental capability of linking behavioral analysis to systemic policy analysis in a useful and synergic manner. It then allows the testing of effectiveness and consequences of a vast spectrum of climate and energy policies under real-world scenarios.

This linkage is the reason why we see increasingly widespread acceptance and growing use of ABMs in the ESG field in general (see Section 6.10 for more details), and the climate mitigation policies space in more specificity.

As an example of this recent trend, please refer to the 2020 study in *WIREs Climate Change*[2] (where 61 different ABMs addressing climate-energy policy aimed at emissions reduction, product and technology diffusion, and energy conservation are reviewed in detail). This review covers ABMs that model a wide range of policy implementation simulations, including carbon taxation, emissions trading, adoption subsidies, and information provision instruments such as smart meters and ecolabels.

The ABM models currently used in the ESG field, and covered in the *WIREs* review, share core features required for climate-energy modeling, such as application types, empirical basis, featured markets, agent behaviors, and social network configurations as well as policy-specific metrics and properties, such as the problems the policies address, their objectives, instruments, scenarios, and insights.

The overall findings prove that, when compared to traditional models, ABMs offer the ESG practitioner much greater flexibility in pathways of emissions reduction, by allowing a more realistic modeling of individual choices, options, and outcomes.

Another notable aspect is that ABMs allow the modeler to control the overall level of complexity embedded in the model, based on the requirements of the simulation. This strikes an optimal balance between realistic results, minimization of errors, and interpretability of output.

---

[2] Jeroen van den Bergh et al., "A Review of Agent-Based Modeling of Climate-Energy Policy," *WIREs Climate Change* 11 (4) (July/August 2020).

6.4 GENERAL OVERVIEW OF ABMS

An agent-based model (ABM) is defined as a class of computational models for simulating the actions and interactions of autonomous agents (both individual and collective entities) with a view to assessing their effects on the system as a holistic entity. It differs from standard analytical solutions in the fact that the behaviors are simulated and studied using an algorithmic or mechanistic approach, as opposed to simplified and solved via generalized equations and/or mathematical processes.

ABMs combine elements of:

- Game theory
- Complex systems/Chaos theory
- Emergence
- Computational sociology
- Multi-agent systems
- Evolutionary programming
- Randomness
- Cellular automata
- Recursion

One remarkable feature of ABMs, among others, is their capability of reliably and repeatedly producing great complexity from extremely simplistic basic rules. Given that the rules by which the ABM operates are extremely simple by design, where does the complexity come from? We try to provide some background and understanding of this question in the following paragraphs. In addition we also show how to leverage this complexity for use in building models that are applicable to ESG finance, via simple examples in the code 6.A of this chapter.

To begin with, let's look at how, in general terms, ABMs are structured. ABMs can be seen as structurally composed of the following parts:

- Numerous agents specified at various scales (agent-granularity)
- Decision-making heuristics (the "rules" or "strategies")
- Learning rules or adaptive processes (evolutionary aspect, learning)
- An interaction topology (influences and geographical effects)
- An environment (the playing field)

In practical terms, they are run as computational simulations on one of two options:

- Custom software (coded in Python, R, C++, etc.)
- ABM toolkits (Netlogo, RePast, AnyLogic, GAMA, etc.)

If we were to find an intuitive parallel in the online world, we could say that they are similar, at least conceptually, to massively multiplayer online role-playing games (MMORPG), with the difference that all the players are bots that follow specific sets of rules, rather than being actual human players logged into the game.

The main shared characteristics of all ABMs are as follows:

- *Emerging properties*. The sum is greater than the parts.
- *Bounded rationality*. Agents act in what they perceive as their best interest.
- *Adaptive behavior/path-dependency*. Past experience will shape future decisions.

- *Irreducible complexity.* Real-world complexity, unbound by generalizations (computational irreducibility).
- *Radical uncertainty.* There is no underlying theory and expectation of where the system is supposed to be headed.

If we look at an ABM from a functional perspective, we see that it is usually built and organized around a framework of elements that can be summarized by the acronym PARTE:

- **Properties**
- **Actions**
- **Rules**
- **Time**
- **Environment**

Each of these elements, as shown in Figure 6.2, is an integral part of the model and is interconnected into a single, cohesive framework, which is what is used to drive the computational simulations that constitute the output of the model.

Specifically, we see how:

1. **P**roperties, **A**ctions and **R**ules define the *agents*.
2. **T**ime and **E**nvironment define the *context*.

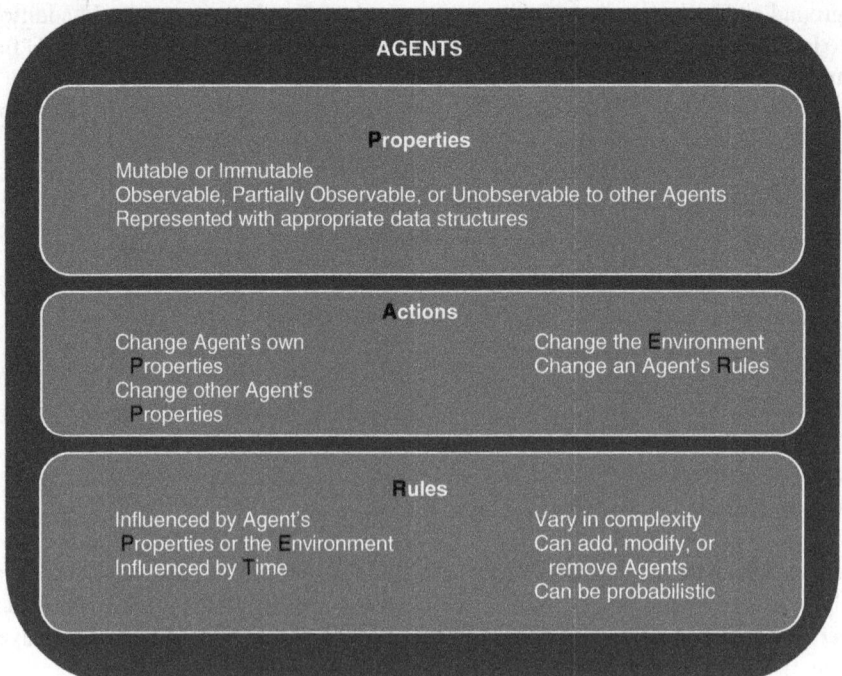

FIGURE 6.2   A general framework of agent-based models.

The *agents*, if we go back to our online gaming example, are all the different players engaged in the simulation, and have a series of predetermined properties and rules at the beginning of the computation, which are subject to modification in each round of simulation.

The *context* is, effectively, the union of the Environment component and the Time component in which the agents are engaged in the simulation, and is part of what drives the overall outcome of the model. Specifically, the two components of context, as shown in Figure 6.3, have the following characteristics:

Time

- Unit in which **Rules**, **Actions**, and changes in **Properties** or **Environment** are defined (equivalent of a round in game theory)
- Abstract or calibrated to specific real-world time scale (*rounds* as opposed to seconds, minutes, days, years, etc.)
- Phenomena can be tracked at multiple *speeds* within a model (from milliseconds, for example if simulating high-speed trading, to years or decades, if simulating climate change effects on cities and coastlines)
- Specifying different orders of events can influence model operation and outcomes (e.g., if we are simulating a marketplace, the order in which trades are placed)

Environment

- Represented with varied amount of geometric/network complexity (from simplistic uniformly mixing single populations, to highly granular, geolocated populations with barriers and movement rules and limitations)
- Can contain elements with their own **Properties**, **Actions**, and **Rules** (both fixed and mobile within the environment)
- Can change over time endogenously (as result of *agent* action) or exogenously (as result of user-specified external shocks)

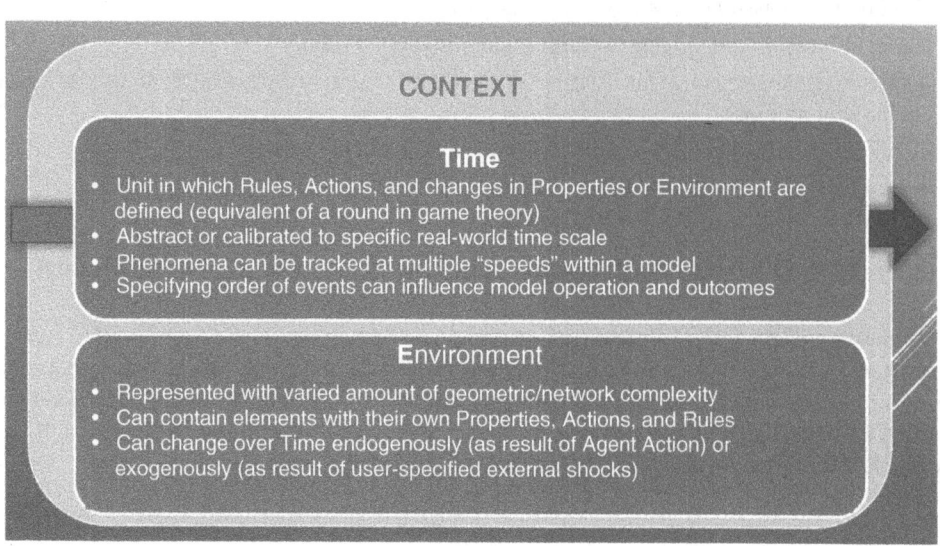

FIGURE 6.3   An overview of the context component of a generalized ABM.

6.5 GENERAL OPERATING PRINCIPLES OF ABMS

In a generalized fashion, ABMs work according to the following set of steps, which occur after the definition of the initial PARTE (Properties, Actions, Rules, Time, and Environment) setup:

- Select the number of rounds to run the simulation (n).
- Run the simulation for n cycles:
  - Apply **Rules** and calculate new **Properties** of *agents*.
  - Calculate **Environment** and emerging variables arising from *agent* activity in round (e.g., prices of assets, GDP).
  - Update/recalibrate **Properties**, **Rules**, and **Environment**.
  - Update population of *agents* as per results of round.
  - Log changes and emerging aggregate **Properties**, including **Rules** that have generated **Actions**.
  - Repeat.

Please note how this is a generic algorithm, which could, theoretically, be executed with pen and paper and not require a computer and software per se, but clearly benefits from the speed, accuracy, and consistency of applied computational methods.

The result of running a set of n rounds of simulation, as per the algorithm just described, is usually a time series of the environment variables and the modeled variables metrics that will allow the modeler to evaluate two critical aspects of the model:

1. The path that the model took from the starting state to the end state
2. Highlighting of unexpected emerging properties and phenomena (including tail events)

Some very typical use case scenarios for the output of ABMs are:

- Repeat running of the model with differing initial conditions to evaluate likelihoods of end states based on initial assumptions ("what if?" analysis)
- Testing of sensitivity to changes in rules and initial conditions
- Quantitative assessment of likelihoods of events of interest (estimates of "1 in 100" events or similar assumptions)
- Highlighting of intrinsic vulnerabilities and fragilities in the system
- Detection of opportunities and areas of unmet demand

6.6 EXAMPLE OF THE PARTE FRAMEWORK APPLIED TO AN ESG SCENARIO

To better clarify how the PARTE framework operates, and how we could use it for an ESG application, let us see how we would apply it if we were to model a climate change impact scenario analysis.

If we were to ask ourselves what the impact on a specific sector of the economy (e.g., food packaging in the USA) would be if climate change leads to a rise in sea level of 3 m over 20 years, the following ABM PARTE framework could be an adequate starting point for an extremely simplified, proof-of-concept model:

Agents
1. All major food-packaging companies in the USA
2. All major suppliers of item 1 (domestic and foreign)
3. All major clients of item 1 (domestic and foreign)

Properties

1. Geographical coordinates of all agents (including altitude above sea level)
2. Basic starting balance sheet data, if available for all agents (otherwise use, as proxy, average balance sheet data based on the size of company)
3. Basic starting creditworthiness data, if available for all agents (otherwise use average for sector)
4. Estimated cost of facilities for agents in category 1 (tied to size of agent)
5. List of clients and suppliers for each agent in category 1 (i.e., this will be two separate lists for each agent in category 1, one populated with agents from category 2 and one with agents from category 3)

Actions

1. Begin the round with raising the sea level by the amount indicated by the scenario.
2. Determine which agents in categories 1, 2, or 3 are affected (set a rule by which agents in category 1 within 1.5 m of sea level enter an emergency state and have to look for a new location, which can only be secured if creditworthiness is better than an arbitrary threshold level X and takes Y years to move into).
3. Determine which agents are flooded and remove them from the simulation.
4. Reallocate clients and suppliers of flooded category 1 agents among remaining category 1 agents.
5. Calculate impact on category 1 agents from flooding of category 2 and 3 agents.
6. Recalculate balance sheets and creditworthiness of remaining agents as a result of preceding actions.
7. Determine whether any category 1 agents are bankrupt as a result of 6 and remove from simulation.
8. Re-allocate clients and suppliers of bankrupt agents from Action 7.
9. For all "Pending Relocation" agents in category 1, reduce counter to facility being ready by one quarter.
10. For any agent in category 1 that meets creditworthiness criteria and is within 1.5 m of sea level, mark as "Pending Relocation" (i.e., they have started building/sourcing a new facility) and remove one quarter from the counter of "time to facility being ready."
11. For any agents in category 1 that are building a new facility and for which counters of "time to facility being ready" have reached zero, relocate at beginning of next round to the new location, and update their altitude setting to +10 m above sea level from current (this will remove them from risk of flooding). When counter reaches zero, keep counting (for creditworthiness) but stop tracking agent as "Pending Relocation."
12. For all agents with active "time to facility being ready" counters (either pre-move or post-move) reduce creditworthiness score by one notch from what the balance sheet/model would estimate, to account for the extra burden of the new facility costs (ensure this is not additive at each round).
13. Repeat for next round.

Rules

1. Simulation runs for 20 years.
2. Companies that are not creditworthy cannot fund a move to new facilities (creditworthiness to be determined by balance sheet or credit rating, or mix of both).
3. Disruptions to supply and demand chain cause losses that affect balance sheets proportionally to the percentage that the supplier/customer represents for the food-packing agent.

4. Producers (suppliers, i.e., category 2 agents) cannot relocate (i.e., supply will be permanently reduced if they get flooded).

5. Customers can relocate and are out of scope of model (assumed not to go bankrupt).

6. A food-packing agent (category 1) that is underwater will be removed from simulation.

7. Any food-packing agents (category 1) that lose suppliers will be impacted in profits and will have reduced creditworthiness (specifics of rule to be decided).

8. Any agent that goes below a predetermined creditworthiness threshold is considered bankrupt and removed from the pool, and suppliers and clients are distributed between the remaining agents (specific distribution rule to be decided).

9. Agents below a certain threshold of creditworthiness have a set risk of losing clients and suppliers to more creditworthy competitors (specifics to be decided).

10. Companies that relocate to higher ground (increase elevation value by 10 m) will have lower creditworthiness for a set number of years (until loans are repaid).

11. Companies that acquire suppliers and customers from other companies will increase profits and increase creditworthiness (specifics to be determined).

Time

Modeling is on a quarterly basis (aligned to corporate reports); that is, one round is one quarter.

Environment

1. All agents are geolocated in real-world environment.

2. Sea-level rise uses inputs from Intergovernmental Panel on Climate Change (IPCC) scenarios (choose appropriate scenario to model), with rises tied to specific pathway in time.

We can then run the model multiple times, to test different assumptions and scenarios, and quantitatively assess the likelihood and impact of each one.

6.7   WHY WE SHOULD LOOK CLOSELY AT ABMS

As ESG practitioners, we should focus closely on ABMs for use in our field, for several of the reasons previously stated. They are as follows:

- ABMs work extremely well for complex systems such as the ones that we need to model for climate change impact and other ESG concerns.
- The economy and the markets are messy, imperfect, nonlinear systems, like biological systems, for which ABMs are the proven gold standard for modeling.
- A well-calibrated ABM can provide insight and probabilistic assessments that surpass current correlation and statistical-based models (in ABMs *correlation is an emerging property* and not an *ab initio* given variable).
- This type of modeling represents a growing and booming field that is still in the initial stages, providing ample opportunities for early adopters.
- Access to big data required to set up behavioral rules is increasingly available (see Chapter 5 on alternative text data for more details).
- Computing power gets cheaper by the day (Moore's law still holds! See Figure 6.4).

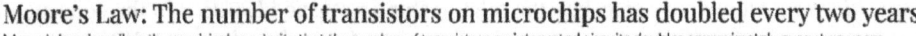

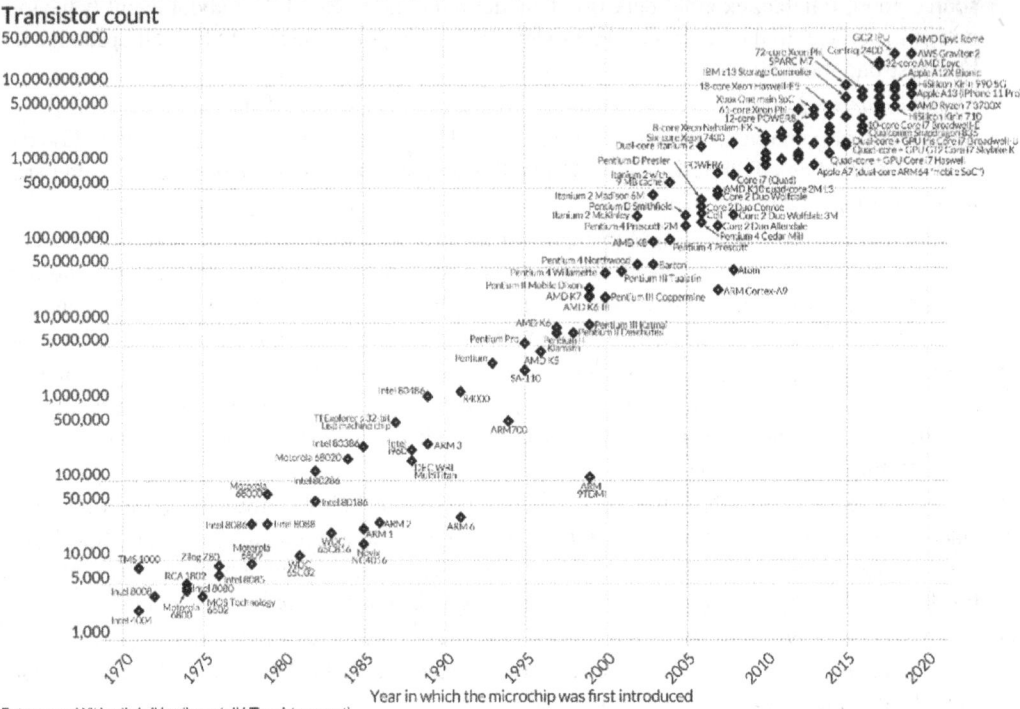

FIGURE 6.4 Moore's law says that the number of transistors on integrated circuits doubles every two years (1970–2020).

6.8 CHALLENGES IN THE USE OF ABMS

While ABMs provide a powerful and versatile tool for modeling complexity and chaotic systems, they do have a set of challenges and requirements that need to be overcome, in order to avoid some well-known pitfalls and risks that will arise by improper development and implementation.

In order to successfully develop, implement, and gain useful insight from ABMs, it is important that they be developed in accordance with these key steps:

- *Clear definition of a question or goal.* Why is the model being developed? What are we trying to model, and what is the variable(s) we are interested in evaluating? It is critical that the developer set up a very clear question or goal for the model from the beginning of the development process. As long as we design clear experiments, we will be able to yield clear insights.

- *Model scope and conceptual design.* What are the variables we are interested in designing into the model and how are they linked to one another by elementary relationships? What is the overall scope of our modeling (PARTE)? What time frame are we creating the model to simulate? What externalities are we including?

- *Model specification.* How do we translate the relationships we have identified in the conceptual design stage into rules that we can integrate in the computational framework? Where do we source good, reliable, external data if our model requires it? Good data about agent behavioral patterns is crucial to the success of the model, and each assumption should be well grounded and have a strong motivation.
- *Model implementation.* Implementation and rule setting are key (garbage in, garbage out)! Start with (relatively) simple models and build up complexity iteratively, one step at a time. Use care in translation of an ABM design into computational code and conduct error-checking and partial testing as models are implemented.
- *Testing and calibration.* Run multiple runs of testing, with many different starting parameters (it is recommended to run this as batch processes where many permutations of starting conditions are simulated, with many iterations for each permutation) to test and calibrate the model, and gain insight on how it reacts to changes in environment and specific variables.
- *Designing experiments and conducting analysis.* Carefully design the experiments and analysis that you are interested in performing, so that they can provide clear and accurate responses to the original question, and the results are not affected by other variables that you might have identified in the testing and calibration phase.
- *Sensitivity analysis.* Conduct thorough and appropriate sensitivity analysis, to get a solid understanding of which variables and rules affect the behavior of the model, to the extent of the experiment of interest, and in which conditions. Make sure you validate your conclusions by running ad hoc tests where you keep all parameters static except the one you are looking to study.
- *Synthesis and reporting.* Draw appropriate conclusions from the model analysis, and always investigate surprising results. Make sure that you understand how they arise and which conjunction of rules and variables led to them.

6.9 EXAMPLE: BUILDUP OF A POPULATION MODEL ABM

As an example of how to start building up an ABM framework, from a very basic model to a more complex one, we look at a population model and the emerging population dynamics that we are able to detect. In the last section of this chapter, we provide a hands-on exercise through which will demonstrate, in practice, how to apply these methodologies to a real-world scenario and allow our reader to build a COVID-19 epidemiology ABM model, using Python.

For this case study we focus on the theory and emerging properties of the model, while the coding and implementation part will be left to the practical section. The population model that we describe, *ABM-Economica*, was developed by the authors and runs on a typical desktop/laptop machine of average computational power in a matter of a few minutes, as a point of reference.

Let's start by stating the goals for the model.

Case Study: Emerging Population Dynamics

Goals:

1. Discover well-known population dynamics (currently represented by traditional equations) from underlying basic rules and properties.
2. Highlight emerging properties and complexity that cannot be detected by the generalized ordinary differential equations that describe the simplified population dynamics that are traditionally used.

3. Validate the use of an ABM approach as opposed to the currently used simplification and theorization approach.

We follow up by defining the PARTE for the case study:

Properties

500 agents used to start the simulation, with the following Properties (initial round):

- Agent ID
- Live/dead (binary)
- Age (increases at each round)

Actions

- Survive/die is based on mortality rates for age cohort.
- Reproduce creating a new clone with age set at 0, based on natality rates for age cohort.

Rules

- Each agent has a mortality probability, which is age-dependent (and updates every round to reflect changes in age). A random number generator is used to determine whether the agent dies in the current round or survives.
- Each agent has a natality probability, which is age-dependent (and updates every iteration to reflect changes in age). A random number generator is used to determine whether the agent procreates in the current round.

Time

- *Time is expressed in rounds.* For practical purposes, these are taken to be years, as the mortality and natality rates used are yearly ones from the US Census data.

Environment

- Initial population is uniformly distributed across ages 0–100 (we could also use the actual census distribution for any given country, and would achieve different results).
- The environment is uniform and not geographically separated.
- All agents can see and interact with other agents if required.
- All agents are assumed to be co-located and equidistant.
- The model postulates no changes in the environment during the simulations.
- The following aggregate variables are generated and tracked:
  - Population total.
  - Total breeding population (sum of agents that have potential to reproduce, i.e., are in age brackets with nonzero natality rates in the US Census data).

Multiple different scenarios are tested, to evaluate sensitivity and effects of changes in assumptions, with focus on:

1. Mortality rates (what happens if we increase/decrease them by different factors).
2. Natality rates (what happens if we increase/decrease them by different factors).

(Continued)

3. Number of repetitions of the same scenario (to observe tail events).

4. The results of these initial simulations are shown in Figure 6.5 (*note that the dip in population at the beginning is due to the random distribution of population* that we have assumed for the starting population, which leads to an initial die-off of nonbreeding members of the population, providing us insight on how the model works).

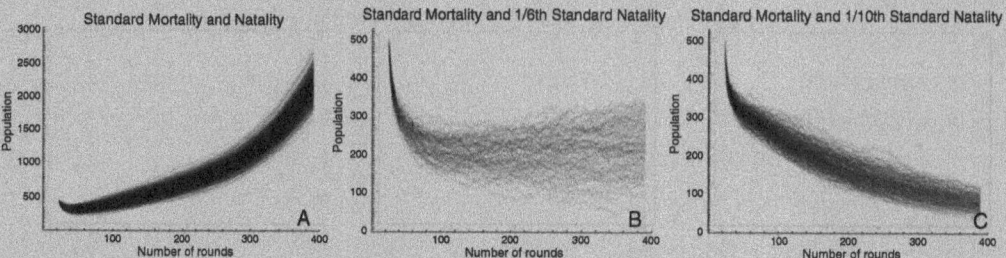

FIGURE 6.5 *ABM Economica* population runs at variable natality rates assumptions: (A) Standard mortality and natality; (B) Standard mortality and one-sixth of standard natality; (C) Standard mortality and one-tenth of standard natality.

If we look at case A, which is the aggregated view of 1000 runs of 400 rounds each at standard mortality and natality rates, we observe exponential growth, with the average population hitting around 2200 individuals by the 400th round of simulation (from the 500 initially postulated).

Case B, on the other hand, is standard mortality coupled with one-sixth of the standard natality rates, and shows an unusually wide band of outcomes that appear to be uniformly distributed around a median value of ~200 individuals in the population and some tail events that go well below 100. The system appears to fall into a highly dispersed set of possible outcomes, with large variability and no clustering/normal distribution around the mean value, making it very hard to predict with any degree of certainty.

Case C, where the natality is decreased to one-tenth of the normal, shows a stable and predictable outcome where the population declines asymptotically to extinction (which occurs in a longer time frame than the 400 rounds shown in this simulation). The outcomes are now, yet again, consistently distributed around the mean pathway, and the overall system behavior and outcome has become eminently predictable.

Having run these basic simulations on a most stylized and simplified population model, the question we need to ask ourselves is: "Do we see this in nature?"

The answer to this question, as we can see in Figure 6.6, is a resounding yes, as what our model shows is seen in the following cases:

1. Bacterial populations (exponential growth population model, a.k.a. Malthusian model)

2. Non-resource-constrained populations in early stages (e.g., the rabbit population in Australia when first introduced)

3. Non-predator-constrained populations (invasive species) in early stages

4. Current human population curve

5. Radioactive decay curves (negative exponential)

Now that we have seen that the model can re-create phenomena that occur in nature, we need to evaluate whether it provides any useful insight. Once again, the answer is positive.

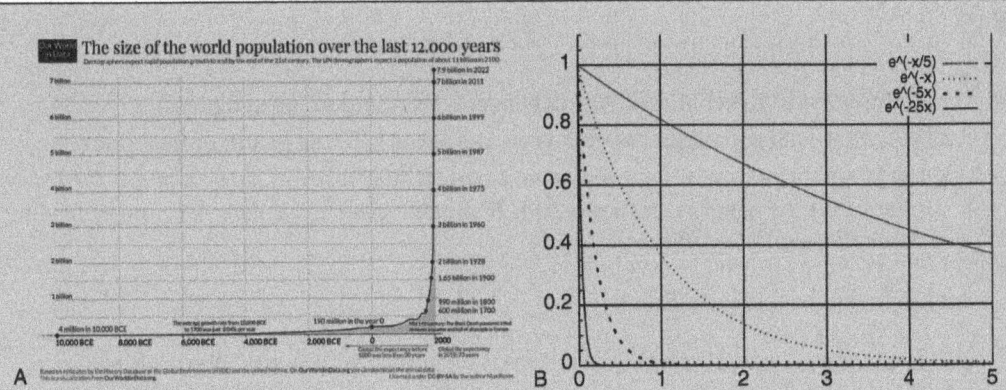

FIGURE 6.6   Examples of exponential curves in nature: (A) Human population in last 12,000 years; (B) Exponential decay curves.

We observe that the ABM is capable of predicting the likelihood of extinction of populations when natality cannot keep up with mortality. This is thanks to the characteristic of realistic modeling based on individual agents and random effects, which the mathematically simplified model (i.e., the exponential growth equation shown in Figure 6.7) is incapable of doing, as, in its mathematical simplification and elegance, it never actually goes to zero (it has an asymptote to zero).

While the exponential growth equation is incapable of providing insight and predictions of when extinction is likely to occur, the ABM provides useful insight and statistical predictions about likelihood and time frames for extinction events in specific conditions.

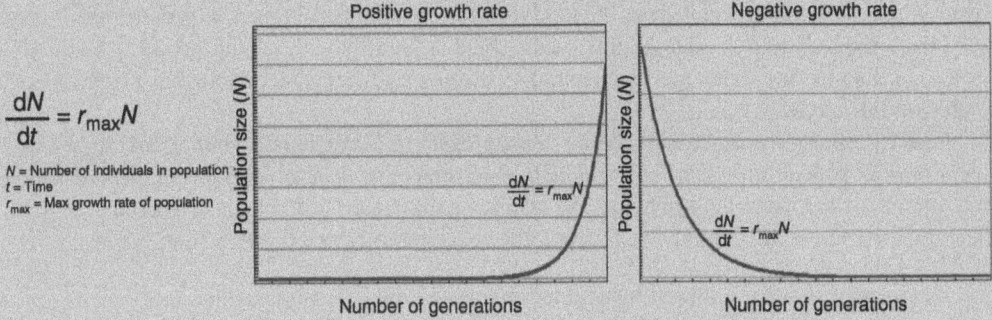

FIGURE 6.7   Exponential population growth equation (in positive and negative growth rate cases).

This characteristic of strong impact from random fluctuations, which can have far-reaching consequences, is typical of deterministic nonlinear systems (such as populations) and, in chaos theory, is generally known as the *butterfly effect*. This represents the sensitive dependence on initial conditions in which a small change in one state can result in large differences in a later state.

Addition of Calories Requirements

Let's kick our model up one notch, as real-world populations are rarely able to achieve exponential growth since resources are the limiting factor. We can easily achieve this in our ABM by making the following additions to the model:

(Continued)

We begin by implementing three new Properties **for the agents:**

1. CALORIE REQUIREMENT. **Age dependent, refreshes as agent ages.**
2. MALNOURISHED. **True/False; if True, the agent will lose health in this round.**
3. HITPOINTS. **Set to 10 for every new agent. It decreases by a set amount for every round that the agent is malnourished. If negative, the agent dies. A round of feeding resets the counter to full value (10).**

We then add the following **Rules:**

1. The food production (*calorie production*) is divided equally among all live agents.
2. If an agent receives less than its calorie requirement, it becomes malnourished.
3. No stashing of food is allowed (unconsumed food is lost).
4. Each round an agent is malnourished will cost it four hitpoints.

Finally, we edit the **Environment:**

1. Set a *calorie production* level (fixed for the duration of the simulation, but we could also set it to change over time or based on population parameters, if required).

Given we have already seen what happens with different mortality and natality rates, we choose to run this simulation at standard values, and review both a single run and a batch of 500 simulations. (We also extend the number of rounds to 1500 to evaluate longer term patterns and/ or extinction events better.)

Figure 6.8 shows us the results of these simulations, which are extremely different from what we were seeing from our model without the food requirements implementation, as was run previously.

Figure 6.8A shows us a single run, where we can identify exponential growth phases, followed by population crashes and exponential recoveries, with a regular pattern, but a very "spiky" nature to the curves.

Figure 6.8B, on the other hand, being the aggregate of 500 separate simulations, shows us a very evident plateau line (marked K), which is not immediately visible in the single simulation but becomes obvious in the aggregate. We also see a maximum level plateau (marked O), which is consistent across all simulations. Overall, the characteristics that hold true are:

Exponential growth, followed by population crashes, cyclical but irregular.

Despite random fluctuations, patterns and projections hold strong for very long periods of time.

Two distinct plateaus of population are clearly visible (**K** and **O**).

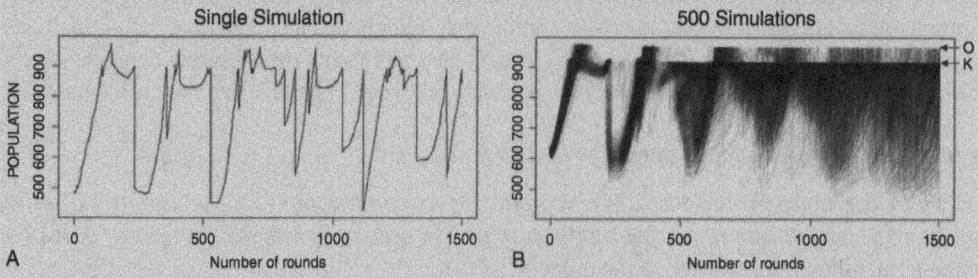

FIGURE 6.8 ABM results with fixed food supply, 1500 rounds: (A) Single simulation results; (B) Aggregate of 500 simulations.

We now, once again, ask ourselves "Do we see this in nature?" and, yet again, we do. These waves align with multiple observed cases of typical population boom-and-bust cycles which are well known and documented. In these natural population fluctuations, K is called the *carrying capacity* for a population and O the *overshoot* level that can be achieved for short periods of time. Some notable examples are:

1. Lemmings in the Arctic tundra (Figure 6.9B)
2. Snowshoe hares and Canadian lynx in the Arctic (Figure 6.9A)
3. Typical of populations that are exclusively resource-controlled

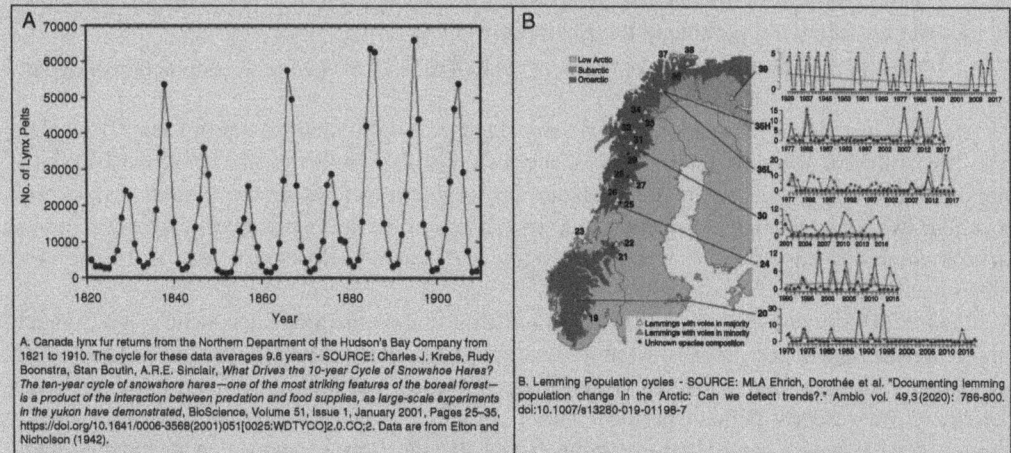

FIGURE 6.9 Boom-and-bust population cycles in nature: (A) Canadian lynx 1820–1920; (B) Scandinavian lemmings, twentieth century.

The next step in our analysis is to see if the model gives us any useful insight, and the answer is again a positive one, as it allows us to determine:

- Periodicity of boom/bust crashes
- Likelihood of crash by current population level and resource level
- Carrying capacity (K)
- Maximum overshoot value (O)
- Likelihood of extinction events
- Sensitivity to changes in resource availability
- Combined effects of changes in:
  - Mortality rates
  - Natality rates
  - Carrying capacity (K)

Addition of Calorie Stashing Capability

Let's tweak our model again, moving from the world of wildlife to human societies, and ask what would happen if we allowed stashing away of uneaten calories for future use by individual agents.

(Continued)

To implement this change to the model, we proceed as follows:

1. Add the following **P**roperty to each *agent*:
   - CALORIE STASH – Starts at zero, is updated every round.
2. Add the following **R**ules:
   - If an agent receives more calories than its current calories consumption, the unconsumed calories are added to CALORIE STASH.
   - If an agent receives less calories than its current calories consumption, the balance is taken from the CALORIE STASH. The agent can only become MALNOURISHED once it has exhausted the CALORIE STASH.
3. Add the following variable to the **E**nvironment:
   - Distribution (for histogram) of the asset CALORIE STASH across the population of *agents*.

As for our previous simulation run, we use standard natality and mortality values, to isolate the effect of these new rules on the system, and review both a single run and a batch of 100 simulations. To allow us to even better evaluate the long-term effects of the periodic boom-bust cycling, we extend the number of rounds up to 4,500, and we run two scenarios, one at standard natality/mortality rates and one at accelerated rates, to gauge the different effects that these variables can have on the system stability.

Figure 6.10 shows us the results of these simulations, at accelerated rates, which show a much more regular pattern compared to what we observed without the stashing capability. The system becomes a lot more predictable in terms of the harmonic oscillation between boom-and-bust cycles of very clearly defined periods. These periods between crashes are also significantly longer than the ones observed in the previous model, and the drops in population are more gradual.

Figure 6.10A, again, shows us a single run where we can identify exponential growth phases, followed by population crashes and exponential recoveries, but the pattern is very regular, and the "spiky" nature that we observed in the unstashed model has vanished altogether.

Figure 6.10B further compounds this finding, as we see that, even after 4,500 cycles, there is a substantial overlap of the 100 different simulations, with a very small portion of them having gone out of sync. It is worth noting how the carrying capacity and population overshoots are much less visible due to cyclical pattern and the interference that the stashing of calories now exerts on the overall effects.

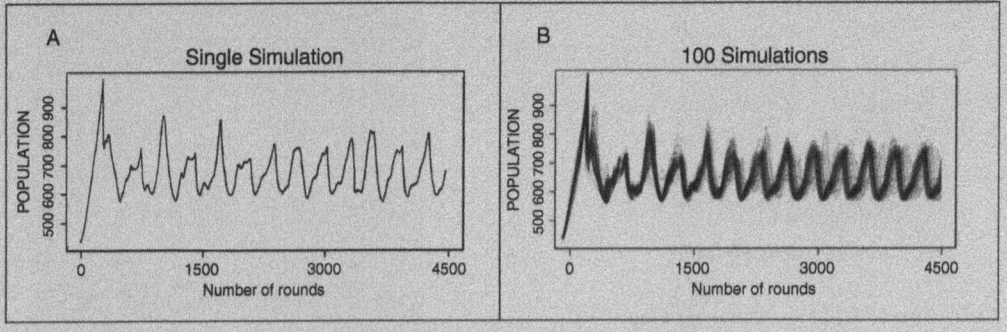

FIGURE 6.10 Simulation results with calorie stash (both at accelerated natality/mortality): (A) single run; (B) 100 simulations.

We can now also look at the histogram for the calorie stash distribution among populations, as seen in Figure 6.11, and see how the following emerging properties have appeared:

1. Calorie stashing generates **the appearance of stratification of wealth** within the *agent* society (i.e., not everyone has the same amount of food; there are "rich" agents and "poor" agents).
2. The stratification changes depending on which point in the cycle we look at (the example in Figure 6.11 is from the **exponential growth phase**).
3. The agent's place within the stratification (i.e., whether the agent is calorie-poor or calorie-rich) is only dependent on at which point of the boom/bust cycle the individual agent was born.

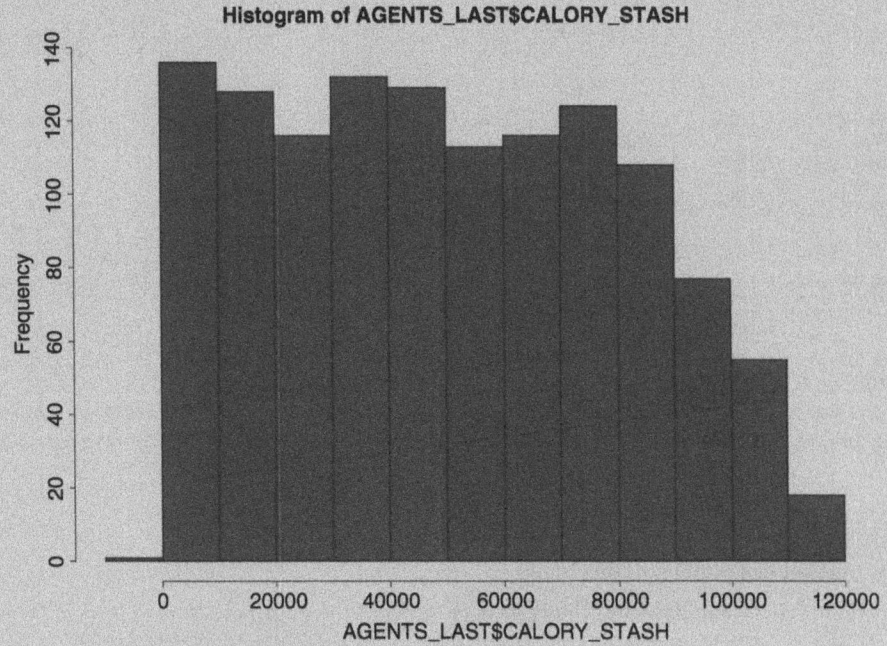

FIGURE 6.11   Example of distribution of Asset "Calories" among population (non-crash state).

If we look at how the population evolves over time, as shown in Figure 6.12, which portrays histograms of population age distributions over ~370 rounds, we notice how there is a clear

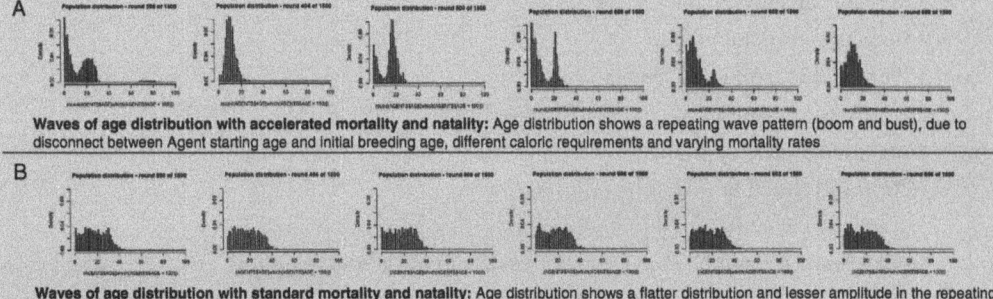

FIGURE 6.12   Cyclical waves in population age distribution: (A) at accelerated mortality and natality rates; (B) at standard rates.
Source: Ashley et al., 2020 / Frontiers Media S.A / CC BY-4.0

(*Continued*)

pattern of waves that travel through the population across time. These waves are much stronger if natality and mortality rates are higher (the lower the rates, the more stable the system is).

The wave pattern is present both in the accelerated natality/mortality scenario (Figure 6.12A) and in the standard natality/mortality one (Figure 6.12B), albeit in a dampened state.

The question, again, is whether these patterns are observed in nature or human societies. Yet again, the answer is yes.

The model is generating the typical population fluctuations around Carrying Capacity, which is a textbook case typically used to explain **logistic growth curves** in natural populations (see Figure 6.13).

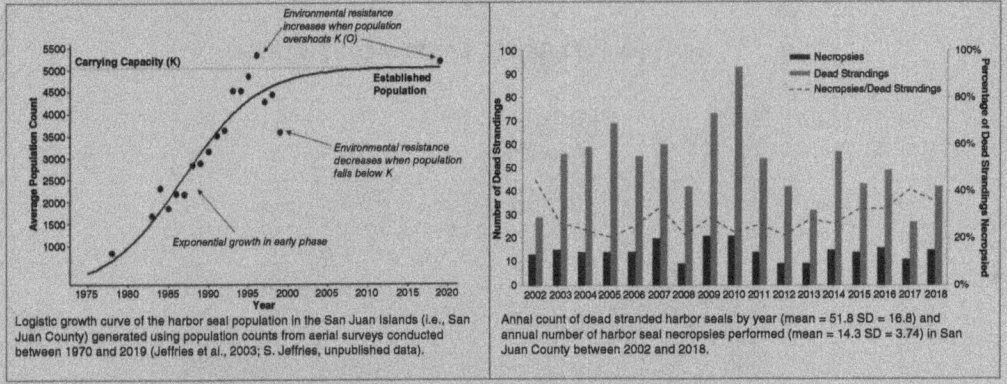

FIGURE 6.13 Logistic growth curve in the population of harbor seals in nature.
Source: Elizabeth Ashley, Jennifer Olson, Tessa E. Adler, and Stephen Raverty, "Causes of Mortality in a Harbor Seal (*Phoca vitulina*) Population at Equilibrium," *Frontiers in Marine Science* 7 (319) (2020), DOI:10.3389/fmars.2020.00319.

These types of equilibria are generally seen in:

- Undisturbed populations in stable environments
- Stable species in dynamic equilibrium

The model again provides us with useful insight. This current set of changes allows us to determine the following:

- Periodicity of boom/bust crashes (longer if compared to no calorie stashing model)
- Likelihood of crashes
- Carrying capacity
- Maximum overshoot value
- Likelihood of extinction events
- Sensitivity to changes in resource availability
- Combined effects of changes in:
  - Mortality/Natality
  - Carrying capacity
- Changes and dynamics of asset (calories) distribution in population

Another Tweak: What Happens if We Add Parental Care to Our Model?

Let's tweak our model again, second to last time in this case study. We can see what happens to our artificial society if we postulate a typical characteristic of human societies: parental care for their offspring. We do this by assuming that the parent agent will transfer half of the calorie stash to the new agent at birth.

To allow for this additional modeling capability, we simply need to implement transfer of calorie stashes in our framework, which requires the following changes:

- No changes to the **Properties**
- Adding the following **Rules**:
  ○ Every time an *agent* procreates, it hands half of its CALORIE STASH to the progeny *agent*.
- No changes to the **Environment**

We use standard natality and mortality values and keep the accelerated natality and mortality rates from the last run, which allowed us to amplify the visibility of the wavelike patterns in the population (we could also choose to run at standard rates, obviously). Given that we expect tight clustering of our simulations, we only run 50 iterations, rather than 100 as previously done, but extend it to 18,000 rounds to determine the long-term stability of the system. Given that we start with a randomly distributed population, we also add a new variable to plot, which is the BREEDING POPULATION (the population of agents within the age of reproduction). This eliminates the artificial dip at the beginning of the simulation due to the die-off of very old agents from the seeding of the population in round 1.

Figure 6.14 shows us the results of these new sets of simulations, which are characterized by a dampened oscillator pattern at the beginning of the simulation, with an extremely predictable trajectory, followed by a cyclical, periodic, and chaotic stable state, which is bound between upper and lower extremes.

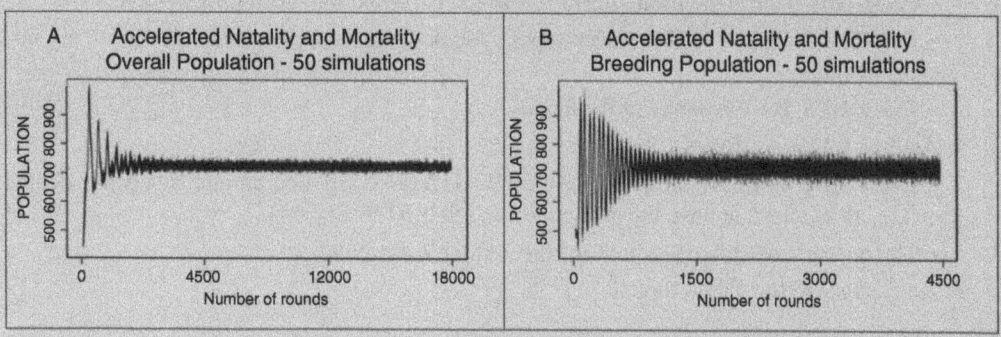

FIGURE 6.14   Simulations with parental care: (A) Overall population; (B) Breeding population.

The dampened oscillator behavior is most clearly visible in Figure 6.14B, which shows the breeding population.

If we look at the steady state for the system, once the oscillations have dampened to a stable range, as shown in Figure 6.15A, we notice how the qualitative nature of the population dynamics

(Continued)

becomes unpredictable at any given point, while being predictable in terms of overall band in which it will be contained. The population oscillations in steady state show periodic behavior and similar morphology to other complex systems such as markets (Figure 6.15B), with periods of autocorrelation, trends, crashes, and cyclicality all detectable in the system. It is interesting to note how these properties are entirely endogenous, as we did not consciously change the Environment and Rules in a way designed to engineer them in.

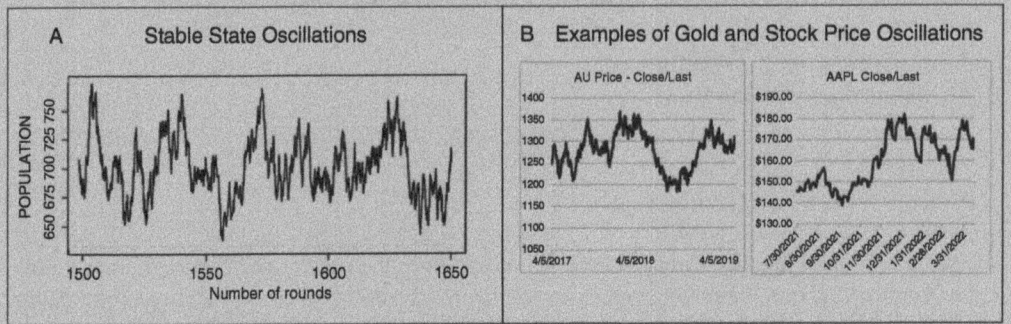

FIGURE 6.15 Simulations with parental care: (A) Detail of steady state; (B) Price of gold in 2017–2019, AAPL price in 2021.

Addition of Inheritance to the Model

We now finally proceed to one last tweak of our model by implementing one of the most human characteristics in an economic system: the capability of inheriting assets from one generation to the next. The way we proceed to edit the model and integrate this new feature (the inheritance of calorie stashes) is as follows:

1. We add the following **Properties** to the *agents*:
   - FAMILY – This is the initial *agent* ID, which is copied into each progeny *agent*
   - INHERITS FROM – The parent *agent*, for newborn *agents*, otherwise itself (for initial *agents*)
   - INHERITS TO – Progeny of the *agent*
2. Add the following **Rules**:
   - Every time an *agent* dies, the CALORIE STASH is divided among inheriting *agents* (i.e., all *agents* that have the dead *agent* as INHERITS FROM).
   - The progeny of each *agent* inherits the FAMILY attribute.
3. No changes to the **Environment**

In Figure 6.16, the results of 10,000 rounds of simulation are represented, with the same parameters as the previous run. The general behavior of the population does not seem to be affected in a particularly evident manner by the newly implemented changes.

We notice the dampened oscillator behavior is detectable, and the period of cycles and nature of fluctuations seems to have remained unchanged.

Luckily, we have a few new variables we can look at to see what else is going on in the system, besides the overall population numbers.

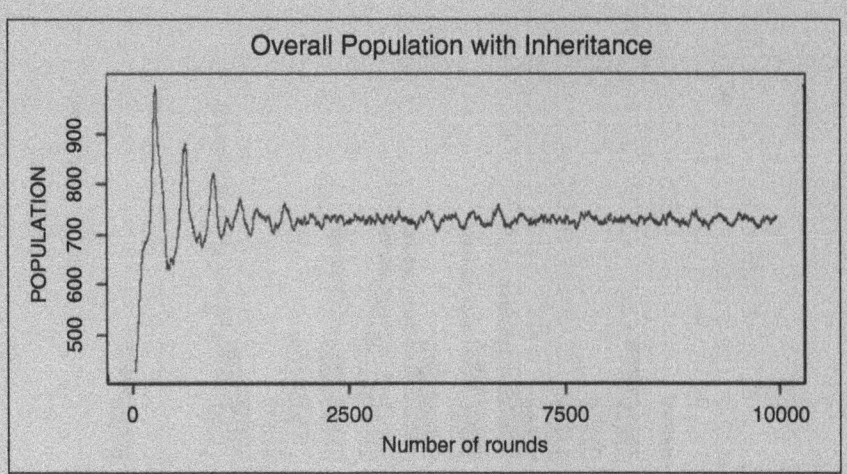

FIGURE 6.16   Simulation with inheritance: 10,000 rounds; overall population.

If, for example, we observe the FAMILIES variable, and their assets, as shown in Figure 6.17, we notice how:

1. *A novel pattern of stratification of assets* appears (despite no differences in skills/activities between agents), with certain FAMILIES accumulating vast amounts of calories (Figure 6.17A).
2. FAMILIES start at 500 and winnow down to 60 on *inverse exponential curve* after 10,000 cycles (in line with expectations from population genetics) (Figure 6.17B).
3. There appears to be *no correlation* between number of family members and per-capita assets (Figure 6.17C).

We now ask ourselves, one final time, whether these patterns are observed in nature or human societies. Unsurprisingly, the answer is positive.

The emerging properties that we see in our rudimentary population model with inheritance are clearly present, well established, and recognized in the real world, namely in:

- Social stratification in human societies
- The rise of aristocracy in feudal systems
- Current income stratification in modern economies (see Figure 6.18)

Potential Next Steps for Model Expansion

Now that the model has proven capable of providing interesting insight and highlighting well-known properties of complex systems such as societies and economies, it could very well be expanded to include a higher degree of PARTE components, such as:

- Multiple assets (labor, currency, etc.)
- Market making cycles
- Influences

(Continued)

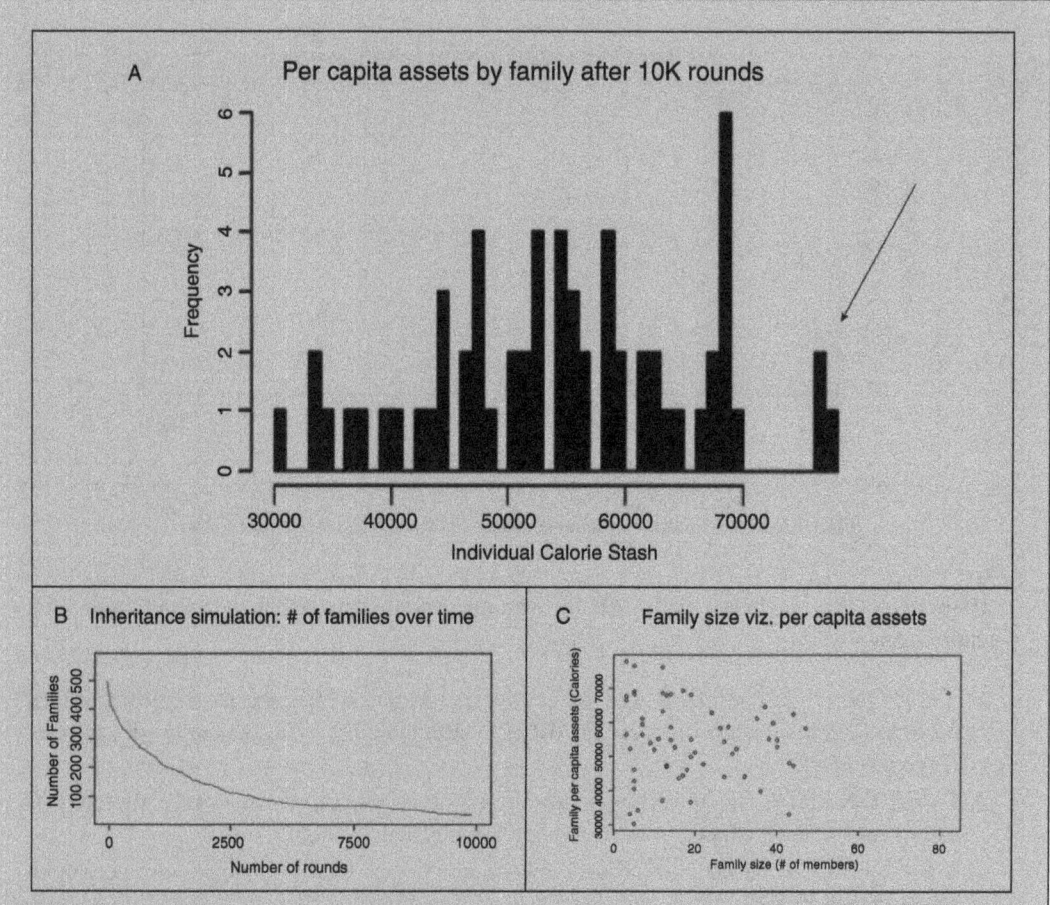

FIGURE 6.17   Family distribution: (A) Stratification of assets; (B) Number of families over time; (C) Family
members/per capita assets.
Source: (A) CRS Report 2021 / Congressional Research Service / Public domain.

- Geographical networks
- Dependencies
- Employer/Employee agents
- Loans/Interest
- Government
- Taxes
- Banks

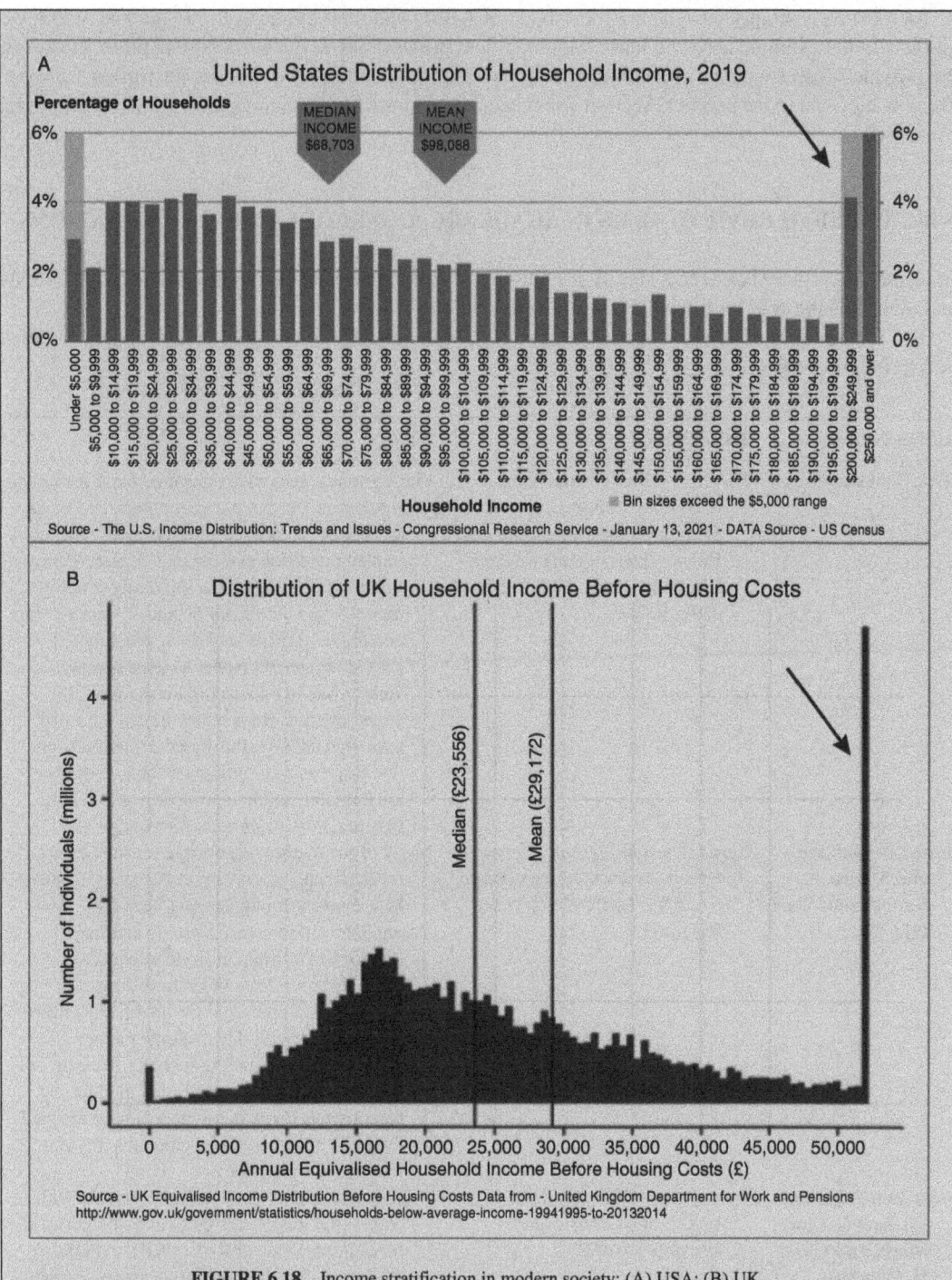

FIGURE 6.18   Income stratification in modern society: (A) USA; (B) UK.

As this text is simply introducing the subject of ABMs and their applicability to the ESG field, we end this initial example here and leave the theoretical possibilities to our readers to explore. However, we provide readers with an in-depth review of existing publications and sources for further learning. We now move on to the practical section where we demonstrate how to build a COVID-19 ABM model using Python.

6.10   IN-DEPTH REVIEW: ABMS IN ACADEMIC AND REGULATORY PUBLICATIONS

In recent years, there has been a significant amount of regulatory and academic publications on ABMs and their growing role for financial and ESG applications.

The following table provides a cursory list of sample noteworthy works for our readers to delve deeper into the topic.

Author/Source	Title/Citation	Notes
Rick Bookstaber	*The End of Theory: Financial Crises, the Failure of Economics, and the Sweep of Human Interaction* (Princeton University Press, 2017). ISBN 0691169012	Our economy may have recovered from the Great Recession, but not our economics. In *The End of Theory,* Bookstaber discusses why the human condition and the radical uncertainty of our world renders the standard economic model – and the theory behind it – useless for dealing with financial crises. What model should replace it? None. At least not any version we've been using for the past 200 years. Instead, Bookstaber argues for a new approach called agent-based economics, one that takes as a starting point the fact that we are humans, not the optimizing automatons that standard economics assumes we are.
Jean-Luc Gaffard and Mauro Napoletano, eds. / OFCE	*Agent-Based Models and Economic Policy* – www.ofce.sciences-po. fr – 2012. ISBN 978-2-312-00316-0	Many of the factors responsible for the financial crisis (financial innovation and securitization; heterogeneity of agents, markets, and regulatory frameworks) are by and large overlooked by standard macroeconomic models, which have failed to forecast the advent of the crisis and are unable to restore economic growth. This volume gathers contributions of leading scholars working on agent-based and computational models and demonstrates how these models have reached the point where they can guide macro- and microeconomic policy.
Sebastian Poledna, Michael Gregor Miess, and Cars H. Hommes	February 24, 2020. Available at SSRN: https://ssrn.com/abstract=3484768	Presentation of an ABM that can compete with and, in the long run, significantly outperform benchmark Value at Risk (VAR) and DSGE models in out-of-sample forecasting of macro variables. This ABM for a small open economy uses micro and macro data from national sector accounts, input-output tables, government statistics, and census data. The model incorporates all economic activities as classified by the European System of Accounts as heterogeneous agents.

Author/Source	Title/Citation	Notes
		The detailed structure of the ABM allows for a breakdown into sector-level forecasts. In a recent application, it was used to forecast the medium-run macroeconomic effects of lockdown measures taken in Austria to combat the COVID-19 crisis. Other potential applications of the model include stress-testing and predicting the effects of monetary or fiscal macroeconomic policies.
Mitja Steinbacher et al.	"Advances in the Agent-Based Modeling of Economic and Social Behavior," *SN Business & Economics* 1, no. 99 (2021). https://doi .org/10.1007/s43546-021-00103-3	This review discusses advances in the agent-based modeling of economic and social systems. It focuses on the state of the art of the heuristic design of agents and how behavioral economics and laboratory experiments have improved the modeling of agent behavior. It highlights how economic networks and social systems can be modeled and covers novel methodologies and data sources. It also includes an overview of estimation techniques to calibrate and validate agent-based models.
Grzegorz Hałaj / ECB	"Agent-Based Model of System-wide Implications of Funding Risk" – ECB Working Paper Series No. 2121, January 2018	Liquidity has its systemic aspect that is frequently neglected in research and risk management applications. This publication by the European Central Bank builds a model that focuses on systemic aspects of liquidity and its links with solvency conditions accounting for pertinent interactions between market participants in an ABM fashion. The model is confronted with data from the 2014 EU stress test covering all the major banking groups in the EU. The potential amplification role of asset managers is considered in a stylized fashion. In particular, the model investigates the importance of the channels through which the funding shock to financial institutions can spread across the financial system.
Jorge Antonio Chan-Lau, / IMF	"ABBA: An Agent-Based Model of the Banking System" (June 2017). IMF Working Paper No. 17/136, Available at SSRN: https://ssrn.com/ abstract=3014047	A thorough analysis of risks in the banking system requires incorporating banks' inherent heterogeneity and adaptive behavior in response to shocks and changes in business conditions and the regulatory environment. ABBA is an ABM for analyzing risks in the banking system in which banks' business decisions drive the endogenous formation of interbank networks. It allows for a rich menu of banks' decisions, contingent on banks' balance sheet and capital position, including dividend payment rules, credit expansion, and dynamic balance sheet adjustment via risk-weight optimization. The platform serves to illustrate the effect of changes on regulatory

(Continued)

Author/Source	Title/Citation	Notes
		requirements on solvency, liquidity, and interconnectedness risk. It could also constitute a basic building block for further development of large, bottom-up agent-based macro-financial models.
Ibrahim Ari and Muammer Koc / Hamad bin Khalifa University	"Sustainable Financing for Sustainable Development: Agent-Based Modeling of Alternative Financing Models for Clean Energy Investments," *Sustainability* 11(7) (2019): 1967. https://doi.org/10.3390/su11071967	Renewable energy investments require a substantial amount of capital to provide affordable and accessible energy for everyone in the world, and finding the required capital is one of the greatest challenges faced by governments and private entities. In a macroeconomic perspective, national budget deficits and inadequate policy designs hinder public and private investments in renewable projects. This study presents a quantitative and comparative proof of concept analysis of alternative financing models in a solar farm investment simulation to investigate the change in wealth inequality and social welfare by reducing debt-based financing and increasing public participation. This paper develops simulation models for conventional and alternative financing systems.
Atesmachew Hailegiorgis, Andrew Crooks, and Claudio Cioffi-Revilla George Mason University and Center for Social Complexity	"An Agent-Based Model of Rural Households' Adaptation to Climate Change," *Journal of Artificial Societies and Social Simulation* 21(4) (2018): 4. DOI: 10.18564/jasss.3812; URL: https://www.jasss.org/21/4/4.html	This paper presents an agent-based model, called OMOLAND-CA, which explores the impact of climate change on the adaptive capacity of rural communities in the South Omo Zone of Ethiopia. The purpose of the model is to answer research questions on the resilience and adaptive capacity of rural households with respect to variations in climate, socioeconomic factors, and land-use at the local level. Results from the model show that successive episodes of extreme events (e.g., droughts) affect the adaptive capacity of households, causing them to migrate from the region.
Juana Castro et al.	"A Review of Agent-Based Modeling of Climate-Energy Policy," *WIREs Climate Change* 11(4), April 1, 2020: e647; https://doi.org/10.1002/wcc.647 e647	ABMs have recently seen much application to the field of climate mitigation policies. They offer a more realistic description of micro behavior than traditional climate policy models by allowing for agent heterogeneity, bounded rationality, and nonmarket interactions over social networks. This enables the analysis of a broader spectrum of policies. This article reviews 61 ABM studies addressing climate-energy policy aimed at emissions reduction, product and technology diffusion, and energy conservation. This covers a broad set of instruments of climate policy, ranging from carbon taxation and emissions trading through adoption subsidies to information provision tools such as smart meters and eco-labels. The review pays specific attention to behavioral assumptions and the structure of social networks.

EXERCISE 6.A Modeling COVID Spread via a Custom ABM

We shall now proceed to an example of building an ABM to model the spread of COVID-19 across a uniformly interacting idealized population. As for the other exercises in this book, the reference material and datasets used can be found in the online appendix (the entire code for this exercise is also available in the online appendix).

We begin by importing the relevant libraries required for the code (which are similar to what we used in other exercises).

In [185...
```
import pandas as pd
import numpy as np
import matplotlib.pyplot as plt

from datetime import datetime
```

The next step is to import some statistical data about age distribution (taken from the US Census data), COVID-19 mortality rates by age cohort (taken from published data), average number of daily encounters per day, based on age cohorts (taken from published data), and severity statistics of COVID contagion (again, based on published data, specifically for the original variant of COVID-19).

In [186...
```
dt_us_pop = pd.read_csv("us_population_dist_11.csv")
dt_us_mort = pd.read_csv("us_covid19_mortality.csv")
dt_us_encount = pd.read_csv("us_encounters_per_day.csv")
dt_us_severity = pd.read_csv("us_contagion_severity.csv")

dt_us_pop["pct_n"] = dt_us_pop.Number / dt_us_pop.Number.sum()
```

We now start setting up the PARTE framework for our model, selecting the number of agents (12,010), the number of simulations for the individual runs (10), the number of rounds/days (CYCLES) (120), and a series of environmental variables that are necessary for the model. These include parameters such as:

- UNREPORTED: Fraction of positive cases that are not reported and go unaccounted for, (These can be modified to see the effect of higher/lower testing, e.g.. In the current case we assume a very high level of unreported cases, due to asymptomatic cases and shortage of testing, as this model was developed at the beginning of the pandemic.)
- UNDERREPORTED: Factor of cases that are not picked up at hospital facilities (again, a variable that can be modified to evaluate the effects on total number of cases).
- BEDS: Available hospital beds. (This is a percentage of the population and is a determinant in when the quarantine is enacted.)
- SPARE_CAPACITY_AVAILABILITY: Fraction of beds that are available at beginning of pandemic.
- SHED_MEDIAN: Median time to shed virus for positive cases (from literature, can be modified to evaluate what mutations in this parameter would entail).
- SHED_SD: Standard deviation for viral shedding, for positive cases (from literature, can be modified to evaluate what mutations in this parameter would entail).

(Continued)

- **STATE_RESPONSE:** Parameter tied to how fast Quarantine Response is decided.
- **QUARANTINE_IMPLEMENTATION:** Number of days the quarantine will be in force for, where the social interaction multiplier will be decreased from 1.00 (normal) to MIN_QUAR_LVL.
- **MIN_QUAR_LVL:** Multiplier to social interactions to account for efficiency of quarantine; the lower the number, the higher the effectiveness of quarantine. A value of 0 would represent total isolation of the entire population and effectively stop any spread. A value of 1 is normal interactions. (Values larger than 1 can be used to simulate increased social interactions, if needed.)
- **MAX_TIME_INFECTED:** Maximum time, in days, that a positive agent remains infectious (from literature).
- **N_COHORTS:** The number of age cohorts in the population of agents (based on the US Census segmentation).

```
In [17]:   N_AGENTS = 12010
           SIMULATIONS = 10
           CYCLES = 120
           TRANSMISSION_RATE = .03
           INITIAL_SAMPLE = N_AGENTS * 0.0001
           INIT_CYCLES = 10
           UNREPORTED = 0.95
           UNDERREPORTED = 4
           BEDS = N_AGENTS * 0.02648
           SPARE_CAPACITY_AVAILABILITY = 0.2
           SHED_MEDIAN = 20
           SHED_SD = 4
           STATE_RESPONSE = 1
           QUARANTINE_IMPLEMENTATION = 10
           MIN_QUAR_LVL = 0.34
           MAX_TIME_INFECTED = 22
           INI_STATE_RESPONSE = STATE_RESPONSE

           N_COHORTS = len(dt_us_pop)
           dt_us_pop["n_agents"] = round(dt_us_pop.pct_n * N_AGENTS)
```

We continue by setting up some overall environment variables, which we shall use to track the overall system evolution over the repeating sets of simulations:

- **OVERALL:** Total living population counter
- **OCONTAGION:** Total counter of active contagions
- **ODEATHS:** Total counter of deaths
- **ORECOVERED:** Total counter of recoveries
- **CASES_OVERALL:** Total counter of positive cases overall from day 0 (monotone function)
- **SIMTOT:** Variable to merge all plots of cases into one (for ease of visualization)

Concurrently, we also create variables for individual simulation tracking:

- POPULATION
- CONTAGION
- DEATHS
- RECOVERED
- CASES
- L_PARAMETERS
- THRESHOLD (calculated on spare capacity)

```
In [19]:  ▶  OVERALL = pd.DataFrame()
             OCONTAGION = pd.DataFrame()
             ODEATHS = pd.DataFrame()
             ORECOVERED = pd.DataFrame()
             CASES_OVERALL = pd.DataFrame()
             SIMTOT = pd.DataFrame()

             POPULATION = np.zeros(CYCLES)
             CONTAGION = np.zeros(CYCLES)
             DEATHS = np.zeros(CYCLES)
             RECOVERED = np.zeros(CYCLES)
             CASES = np.zeros(CYCLES)

             L_PARAMETERS = list(np.zeros(SIMULATIONS))
             THRESHOLD = BEDS / (1 - UNREPORTED) * SPARE_CAPACITY_AVAILABILITY
```

In the next step, we set up a loop to decide the number of runs we want the loops of simulation to be performed. (This allows to run a set of T simulations for P times, to gain sufficient data to view tail events.)

```
In [189...  #for P in range(30):
           #    for T in range(SIMULATIONS):
           P = 0
           T = 0
```

We now proceed to set up the agents by defining the Properties that they have and populating the system with the starting conditions for the Environmental variables. Note how this is achieved by using random normal distributions, where necessary.

```
In [190...  AGENTS = pd.DataFrame({
               "ID" : list(range(1, N_AGENTS + 1)),
               "LIVE" : [True] * N_AGENTS,
               "ACTIVE" : [True] * N_AGENTS,
               "DICE_THROW" : [0] * N_AGENTS,
               "AGE" : list(range(1, N_AGENTS + 1)),
               "TIME_INFECTED" : [0] * N_AGENTS,
               "CONTAGION" : [0] * N_AGENTS,
               "RECOVER" : [False] * N_AGENTS,
               "DEATH" : [False] * N_AGENTS,
               "SHEDDING" : np.random.normal(SHED_MEDIAN, SHED_SD, N_AGENTS),
               "COHORT" : np.nan
           })

           STATE_RESPONSE = 1
           TRIGGERED = False
           QUARANTINE = 0
           QUARANTINE_START = 0
           QUARANTINE_END = 0
           MAX_DAY = np.nan
           RET_NORM = 0
           RET_NORM_TIME = 0
           CORMAX = 0

           AGENTS
```

(Continued)

The output of this code is a list of 12,010 agents, which range in age from 1 to 12,010 years (!), which is clearly unrealistic and will be addressed in the next step.

Out[190...

	ID	LIVE	ACTIVE	DICE_THROW	AGE	TIME_INFECTED	CONTAGION	RECOVER	DEATH	SHEDDING	COHORT
0	1	True	True	0	1	0	0	False	False	25.735082	NaN
1	2	True	True	0	2	0	0	False	False	25.620919	NaN
2	3	True	True	0	3	0	0	False	False	22.152116	NaN
3	4	True	True	0	4	0	0	False	False	16.032194	NaN
4	5	True	True	0	5	0	0	False	False	14.686608	NaN
...	...	...	...	...	...	...	...	...	...	...	...
12005	12006	True	True	0	12006	0	0	False	False	9.876944	NaN
12006	12007	True	True	0	12007	0	0	False	False	23.955080	NaN
12007	12008	True	True	0	12008	0	0	False	False	22.030535	NaN
12008	12009	True	True	0	12009	0	0	False	False	26.075051	NaN
12009	12010	True	True	0	12010	0	0	False	False	20.174654	NaN

12010 rows × 11 columns

We proceed now to populate the age attribute for our agents, using the age distribution from the US Population file that we loaded at the beginning, thus obtaining a realistically age-distributed population of agents.

In [191...
```python
nOff = 0
for nr in range(N_COHORTS):
    n_age = int(dt_us_pop.loc[nr, "n_agents"])
    r_age = dt_us_pop.loc[nr, "min_age":"max_age"]

    n_mult = pd.to_numeric(round(n_age / len(r_age)) + 1, downcast="integer")
    ages = (list(r_age.values) * n_mult)[0:n_age]

    AGENTS["AGE"][nOff:(nOff + n_age)] = ages
    AGENTS["COHORT"][nOff:(nOff + n_age)] = nr

    nOff = nOff + n_age
```

The next step – which we present as separate portions of code but will have to be run as a series of nested loops – is the setting up of the loop for the number of rounds/days that the simulation will run for (120 in this specific case), as follows. Note how we print out the state of the simulation, to provide assurance that the code is running and a general idea of the progress. (Depending on the machine, it can take a few minutes to run.)

In [192...
```python
N = 0 # for N in range(CYCLES):
print(f"CYCLE {N} of ITERATION {T} of {SIMULATIONS} @ {datetime.now()}")
print(STATE_RESPONSE)
```

```
CYCLE 0 of ITERATION 0 of 10 @ 2022-04-22 22:32:55.946668
1
```

We start by running some conditional statements, beginning with an initial one that works on the idea that, at the very beginning of the pandemic (INIT_CYCLES), there are no cases, and seeding needs to occur. At this stage, a random number of agents are infected with the virus, effectively starting the epidemic.

```
In [193...   if N < INIT_CYCLES:
                 AGENTS["CONTAGION"][np.random.choice(N_AGENTS, size=int(INITIAL_SAMPLE), replace=False)] = 1

             G_tot_Pop = sum(AGENTS.DEATH == 0)
             G_pct_Contagion = sum((AGENTS.CONTAGION > 0) & (AGENTS.DEATH == 0) & ~AGENTS.RECOVER) / G_tot_Pop
```

We now cycle through the age cohorts for agents that are COVID positive, and apply both the mortality calculations and the contagion calculations (i.e., will they infect some other agent?).

```
In [194...   for mm in range(N_COHORTS):
                 bet = (AGENTS["COHORT"] == mm) & (AGENTS["DEATH"] == 0) & (AGENTS["CONTAGION"] == 0)
                 n_cohort = len(AGENTS.loc[bet])

                 n_daily_contacts = dt_us_pop.loc[mm, "daily_contacts"]
                 prob_contagion = 1 - (1 - TRANSMISSION_RATE * STATE_RESPONSE) ** (G_pct_Contagion * n_daily_contacts)
                 eps = np.random.uniform(size=n_cohort)

                 AGENTS.loc[bet, "CONTAGION"] = [1 if jj <= prob_contagion else 0 for jj in eps]
```

We also update the environment variables as needed:

```
In [195...   for mm in range(N_COHORTS):
                 bet = (AGENTS["COHORT"] == mm) & (AGENTS["DEATH"] == 0) & (AGENTS["TIME_INFECTED"] < AGENTS["SHEDDING"]) \
                     & (AGENTS["CONTAGION"] > 0)
                 n_cohort = len(AGENTS.loc[bet])

                 d_mort_rate = 1 - (1 - dt_us_pop.loc[mm, "case_fatality"]) ** (1 / MAX_TIME_INFECTED)
                 eps = np.random.uniform(size=n_cohort)
                 i_exclude = np.random.choice(n_cohort, size=int(round(n_cohort * UNREPORTED)), replace=False)
                 eps[i_exclude] = 99999
                 AGENTS.loc[bet, "DEATH"] = [1 if jj <= d_mort_rate else 0 for jj in eps]
```

Overall parameters are also updated and logged:

```
In [196...   AGENTS.loc[AGENTS["TIME_INFECTED"] >= AGENTS["SHEDDING"], "RECOVER"] = 1
            AGENTS.loc[AGENTS["DEATH"] > 0, "LIVE"] = False

            POPULATION[N] = sum(AGENTS["DEATH"] == 0)
            DEATHS[N] = sum(AGENTS["DEATH"] > 0)
            RECOVERED[N] = sum(AGENTS["RECOVER"] > 0)
            CASES[N] = sum((AGENTS["CONTAGION"] == 1) & (AGENTS["TIME_INFECTED"] < AGENTS["SHEDDING"]))
```

Quarantine response rules start to be run, conditional on initial parameters being met (see above), providing data to us in form of printed statements on the quarantine status:

```
In [14]:    if (CASES[N] > THRESHOLD) and not TRIGGERED and (QUARANTINE <= QUARANTINE_IMPLEMENTATION):
                 print("TRIGGERING QUARANTINE")
                 TRIGGERED = True
                 QUARANTINE_START = N
                 QUARANTINE = QUARANTINE + 1
                 STATE_RESPONSE = INI_STATE_RESPONSE - QUARANTINE / QUARANTINE_IMPLEMENTATION * (INI_STATE_RESPONSE - MIN_QUAR_LVL)
                 print(STATE_RESPONSE)
```

```
In [15]:    if (CASES[N] > THRESHOLD) and TRIGGERED and (QUARANTINE < QUARANTINE_IMPLEMENTATION) and (N > QUARANTINE_START):
                 print("IMPLEMENTING QUARANTINE")
                 QUARANTINE = QUARANTINE + 1
                 STATE_RESPONSE = INI_STATE_RESPONSE - QUARANTINE / QUARANTINE_IMPLEMENTATION * (INI_STATE_RESPONSE - MIN_QUAR_LVL)
                 print(STATE_RESPONSE)
```

```
In [16]:    if (QUARANTINE <= (10 + P)) and TRIGGERED and (QUARANTINE >= QUARANTINE_IMPLEMENTATION):
                 print("QUARANTINE IN FULL SWING")
                 QUARANTINE = QUARANTINE + 1
                 print(STATE_RESPONSE)

            print(f"{TRIGGERED}, {QUARANTINE} > {QUARANTINE_IMPLEMENTATION}, {QUARANTINE} > 10+{P}")

            False, 0 > 10, 0 > 10+0
```

(Continued)

As the next step, we assume that quarantine rules will be lifted and a return to normal will be implemented. (This can be done by presetting a duration of the quarantine or conditionally writing a piece of code that ties it to some system parameter—for example, a certain number of days of declining cases).

```
In [17]:   if (QUARANTINE > (10 + P)) and TRIGGERED and (QUARANTINE > QUARANTINE_IMPLEMENTATION):
               print("TRIGGERING STATE RESPONSE RETURN TO NORMAL")
               TRIGGERED = False
               QUARANTINE_END = N
               RET_NORM = True
               STATE_RESPONSE = 1
               STATE_RESPONSE = (INI_STATE_RESPONSE + STATE_RESPONSE) * .5
               RET_NORM_TIME = RET_NORM_TIME + 1

           if RET_NORM and RET_NORM_TIME <= 1:
               RET_NORM_TIME = RET_NORM_TIME + 1
               print(f"{RET_NORM_TIME} SLOW RETURN TO NORMAL")

           if RET_NORM and RET_NORM_TIME > 1:
               RET_NORM_TIME = 0
               print(f"{RET_NORM_TIME} FULLY RETURNED TO NORMAL")
               STATE_RESPONSE = 1
               RET_NORM = False
```

At the end of the iteration (day) we print the contagion percentage (This can be commented out to speed up the code.)

```
In [201...   AGENTS.loc[AGENTS["CONTAGION"] > 0, "TIME_INFECTED"] += 1
             print(f"CONTAGION PERCENTAGE = {G_pct_Contagion}")
             # end loop for N in range(CYCLES)

             CONTAGION PERCENTAGE = 8.326394671107411e-05
```

The Overall Environment variables are now updated:

```
In [19]:   OVERALL = pd.concat([OVERALL, pd.Series(POPULATION)], axis=1)
           OCONTAGION = pd.concat([OCONTAGION, pd.Series(CONTAGION)], axis=1)
           ODEATHS = pd.concat([ODEATHS, pd.Series(DEATHS)], axis=1)
           ORECOVERED = pd.concat([ORECOVERED, pd.Series(RECOVERED)], axis=1)
           CASES_OVERALL = pd.concat([CASES_OVERALL, pd.Series(CASES)], axis=1)
```

This is followed by a notation of the maximum cases and day at which they occurred (and the closure of the loop for *T*):

```
In [20]:   print(f"FINISHED CYCLE {T} OF {SIMULATIONS}")
           MAX_CASES = max(CASES)
           MAX_DAY = np.where(CASES == MAX_CASES)

           L_PARAMETERS[T] = {
               "ITERATION" : T,
               "MAX_CASES" : MAX_CASES,
               "MAX_DAY" : MAX_DAY,
               "QUARANTINE" : QUARANTINE,
               "QUARANTINE_START" : QUARANTINE_START,
               "QUARANTINE_END" : QUARANTINE_END
           }
           # end loop for T in range(SIMULATIONS)

           FINISHED CYCLE 0 OF 10
```

Once the loop is done, the plotting of the individual simulation is generated, where the observed cases are plotted against the day of simulation:

```
In [22]:  ▶  DETECTED = CASES_OVERALL * (1 - UNREPORTED)
             OBSERVED = DETECTED / UNDERREPORTED
             SIMTOT = pd.concat([SIMTOT, OBSERVED], axis=1)
```

```
In [23]:  ▶  plt.plot(OBSERVED)
             plt.xlabel("Days from event start")
             plt.ylabel("OBSERVED")
             plt.title(f"VARIABLE QUARANTINE DURATION TEST - CYCLE {P} OF 60\n\
                 AVG. QUARANTINE START AT DAY {QUARANTINE_START} ENDED AT {QUARANTINE_END} TOT. AVG DURATION {QUARANTINE} DAYS")
```

Out[23]: Text(0.5, 1.0, 'VARIABLE QUARANTINE DURATION TEST - CYCLE 0 OF 60\n   AVG. QUARANTINE START AT DAY 17 ENDED AT 26 TOT. AVG
          DURATION 11 DAYS')

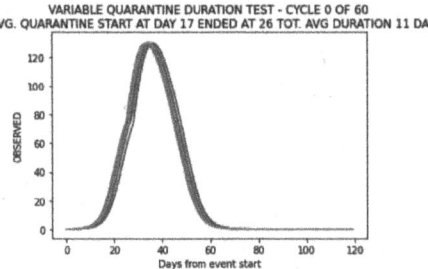

At the end of all the simulations, SIMTOT is plotted, which is the superimposed plots of OBSERVED cases for each set of *T* simulations in an individual run. (*P* loops are to be used to generate volumes and/or to provide the possibility to implement batch runs with varying variables.)

```
In [24]:  ▶  plt.plot(SIMTOT)
             plt.xlabel("Days from event start")
             plt.title(f"VARIABLE QUARANTINE DURATION TEST - TOTAL CYCLES")
```

Out[24]: Text(0.5, 1.0, 'VARIABLE QUARANTINE DURATION TEST - TOTAL CYCLES')

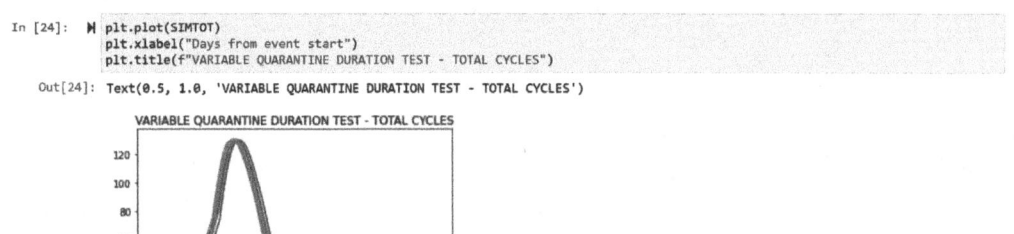

CHAPTER 7

Climate Risk: Macro Perspective

7.1 CLIMATE CHANGE: BACKGROUND INFORMATION AND DEFINITIONS

The subject of climate change, and crucially the average temperature of the globe, has been at the center of public opinion and attention in the recent decades, and indeed since mankind evolved consciousness of weather patterns and cyclicality. Back in the early twentieth century and well into the 1970s, there were competing views in the scientific community – one arguing for global warming (due to exponential increases in greenhouse gases) and the other being concerned with global cooling, caused by aerosols and orbital forcing, which were the likely cause of the dip in overall temperatures observed between the end of the Second World War and the late 1970s.

Since the early 1970s, however, both the climate data and the published studies by climatologists[1] have shown that global warming was the direction the planet was heading in, and at an increasingly fast pace (Figure 7.1).

The observation of the atmospheric temperatures on Earth, which have been logged directly at meteorological stations around the world, with reliable and sufficiently granular data starting in the early nineteenth century (the oldest series of temperature measurements on record is the central England temperature data series, which starts in 1659 and can be freely downloaded at https://www.metoffice .gov.uk/hadobs/hadcet/cetml1659on.dat), has shown a marked and steady increase of approximately 1.1° Celsius from 1880 to 2020.

The increase in temperature might seem, in and of itself, modest and protracted over a relatively (by human standards) long period of time. This proves, however, not to be the case, if we look at the shape of the average temperature curves, as shown in Figure 7.2, taken from the Berkeley Earth project, as we rapidly notice how the entirety of the temperature increase has occurred between 1980 (when the temperature was, effectively, very similar to the late 1700s) and 2021, and that the slope of this increase is distinctly different from previous changes in the record.

Additionally, it is important to notice how this is an *average temperature for all land-based meteorological stations*, and the local changes are larger in scope. It is key to note how, as the Earth is in a meta-stable equilibrium, as will be discussed in later paragraphs, changes in base conditions of seemingly small magnitude can catalyze much larger chains of events via feedback and feed-forward mechanisms, which are typical of complex, chaotic systems.

---

[1] Thomas C. Peterson, William Connelly, and John Fleck, "The Myth of the 1970s Global Cooling Scientific Consensus," *Bulletin of the American Meteorological Society* 89(9) (2008): 1325–1337, http://www.jstor.org/stable/26220900

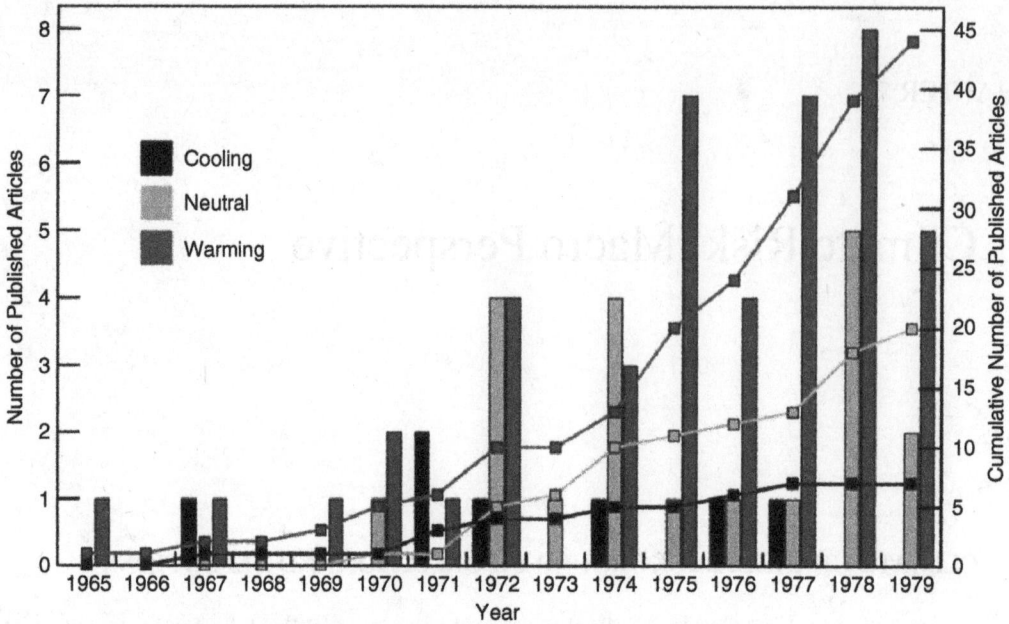

FIGURE 7.1 The number of papers classified as predicting, implying, or providing supporting evidence for future global cooling, warming, and neutral categories during the period from 1965 through 1979.
Source: Paterson, Connelly, and Fleck, 2008.

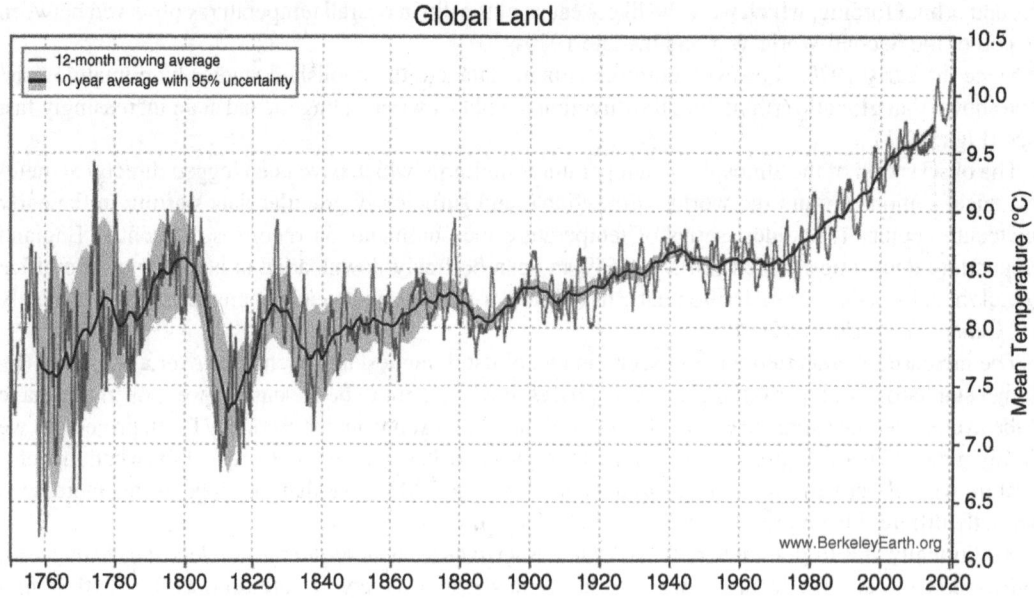

FIGURE 7.2 The average temperature on land: Global 1750–2020.
Source: BerkeleyEarth.org

The data at this point no longer allows for viable alternative hypotheses and conjectures to deny the measured facts that the planet has indeed entered an accelerated warming stage, and the question shifts to the causes behind it and what action, if any, can, and should, be taken to mitigate or reverse this trend.

As this text focuses on quantitative methods for ESG finance, we shall keep the discussion of the topic of climate change to a very brief and cursory level, conscious that we will not be able to do it justice or address it in any way that is even close to being as thorough as it deserves. However, given the vast amount of resources, published research, and data freely available from academic and NGO sources globally, we trust that our readers will be able to do more research into the topic, if they feel so inclined.

For the purposes of this textbook, we have chosen to source some of our data from the Global Change Data Lab, a nonprofit organization that publishes *Our World in Data* (www.ourworldindata .org), a freely accessible online resource focused on increasing the use of data and evidence to make progress against the world's largest problems.

We will intentionally keep this discussion brief so we can focus more directly on the financial aspects of this problem and how to apply the concepts that we have shown in the rest of the book to these topics.

As a general rule, the atmospheric concentration of CO_2 is directly correlated with the average global temperature, with increasing concentrations correlating to increases in temperatures and decreasing concentrations correlating to decreases in temperatures, as can be seen in the 800,000-year record from Antarctic ice-cores, shown in Figure 7.3.

The first question to ask is, where is this CO_2 coming from, and how have the atmospheric profiles of CO_2 concentration changed over geological eras? We can easily answer both questions by taking a cursory look at the basic concepts of the carbon cycle and the historical record of atmospheric CO_2 over the last 40 million years.

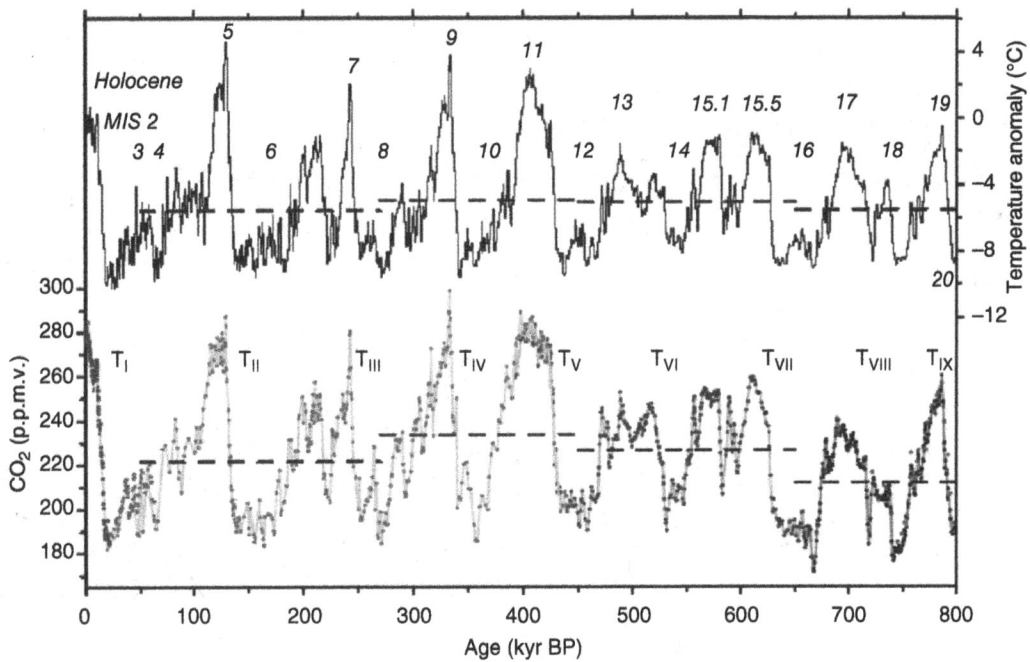

FIGURE 7.3   Compilation of CO_2 records and EPICA Dome C temperature anomaly over the past 800 kyr.
Source: D . Lüthi et al., "High-Resolution Carbon Dioxide Concentration Record 650,000–800,000 Years before Present," *Nature* 453 (7193), May 15, 2008: 379–382, https://pubmed.ncbi.nlm.nih.gov/18480821/

The Carbon Cycle. The amount of carbon atoms on the planet is finite, with each and every one of them having been generated in the furnaces of red giant stars in the brief time before they exploded into supernovae billions of years ago (the exception to this rule being the tiny amounts of carbon generated by nuclear reactions either by decay of heavier elements or via human-caused nuclear reactions, neither of which is a large enough source to be significant).

All these atoms of carbon, therefore, have been present on (or, more precisely, in) the planet since Earth was formed, over 4.5 billion years ago, and cycle between different states, based on the effects of organic (biological) and inorganic (weathering, geological) processes.

In Figure 7.4, we can see a simplified version of the carbon cycle on Earth, which can provide useful insight on how the entire process works at a very broad level (see, e.g., "In-Depth Review: The Carbon Cycle" for more details).

The Historical Record of Atmospheric CO_2. Atmospheric CO_2 has varied with cycles of different periodicity over the last 600 million years (for which there is accurately reconstructed data), through the effects of multiple naturally occurring cycles and processes. As a data point, the highest estimated value on record (for life-bearing epochs) for CO_2 in the atmosphere is ~5,000 ppm during the Cambrian period (~500 million years ago), and the lowest is ~170 ppm during the Pleistocene glaciation (approximately 2 million years ago). It is estimated by experimental results that a level of atmospheric CO_2 of around 150 ppm or lower would no longer allow plant life to survive, as there would not be enough carbon in the air to sustain photosynthesis and plants would go dormant and start dying out rapidly.[2]

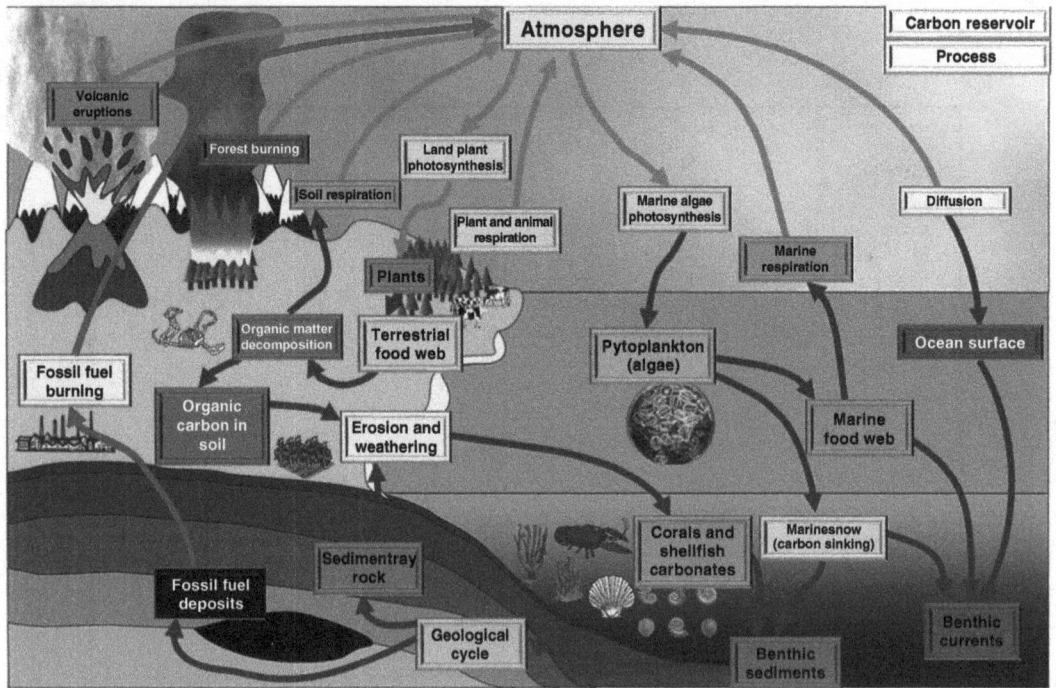

FIGURE 7.4   Simplified carbon cycle.

---

[2]L. Gerhart and J. Ward, "Plant Responses to Low [CO_2] of the Past," *New Phytologist*, 188(3) (2010): 674–695; and N. Tolbert, C. Benker, and E. Beck, "The Oxygen and Carbon Dioxide Compensation Points of C3 Plants: Possible Role in Regulating Atmospheric Oxygen," *Proceedings of the National Academy of Sciences* 92(24) (1995): 11230–11233.

In-Depth Review: The Carbon Cycle

The carbon cycle, as shown in Figure 7.4, has two types of constituents, processes and reservoirs, which have the following characteristics.

Carbon Cycle Processes

These processes can be either biological or inorganic in nature and represent phenomena where carbon atoms are made to undergo chemical transformations from one state to another. These processes generally involve transitions in chemical state, but not necessarily, as they also include simple weathering, where, for example, large blocks of carbonaceous rock are weathered down by erosion from wind and water and enter the rivers and oceans, where they then undergo chemical processes (which are a separate process). Some notable examples of carbon cycle processes are shown in the following table:

Process	Effect	Notes
Volcanic eruptions	Releases CO_2 in atmosphere	From geological reservoirs
Soil respiration	Releases CO_2 in atmosphere	From organic processes in soil (bacteria, microorganisms, fungi, etc.)
Organic matter decomposition	Releases CO_2 in atmosphere	From decomposing organic matter on land (decomposes to CO_2 and H_2O)
Fossil fuel burning	Releases CO_2 in atmosphere	From fossil fuel deposits, mostly due to human activity
Geological cycle	Removes carbon from atmosphere and other reservoirs	Via subduction and other geological processes. Includes creation of fossil fuel deposits
Erosion and weathering	Transports carbon from ground-based reservoirs to marine reservoir	Via the effect of wind, sun, and rain. Affects surface carboniferous rock that is eroded into small particles and ends into the riverine systems and into the oceans, where it undergoes further processes.
Plant and animal respiration	Releases CO_2 in atmosphere	Due to the energy consumption of living beings (converting sugar to CO_2 and H_2O). Plants also have photosynthesis, which offsets the amount of CO_2 that they emit by respiration.
Land plant photosynthesis	Removes carbon from the atmosphere and fixes it into plants as biomass	Fixes CO_2 into sugars using energy from sunlight to fuel the reaction. The sugars are used to build the structure of cells for all plants. This is the first step of all land-based food pyramids (primary producers).

(Continued)

Process	Effect	Notes
Marine (water) algae photosynthesis	Removes carbon from the atmosphere and fixes it into phytoplankton as biomass	Fixes CO_2 into sugars using energy from sunlight to fuel the reaction. The sugars are used to build the structure of cells for all algae. This is the first step of all water-based food pyramids (primary producers).
Marine (water) algae and animal respiration	Releases CO_2 in water	Due to the energy consumption of living beings (converting sugar to CO_2 and H_2O). Algae also have photosynthesis, which offsets the amount of CO_2 that they emit by respiration.
Diffusion	Removes CO_2 from atmosphere into oceans and bodies of water	CO_2 is highly soluble in water (as is amply evident by carbonated beverages), and the surface of any body of water extracts CO_2 from the atmosphere to maintain the solubility equilibrium with the atmosphere, effectively removing CO_2 from it until this equilibrium is met.
Marine snow (carbon sinking)	Transports carbon from decaying marine web organisms to benthic sediments reservoirs	Remnants of decaying organisms in the water column slowly sink to the bottom of the ocean, where they then become part of the benthic sediment and slowly get recycled by the geological cycle to form sedimentary rocks.

Carbon Reservoirs. Carbon reservoirs are, effectively, locations, in an ample sense, where carbon atoms are found on Earth, in a sufficiently stable and large quantity to be relevant for the carbon cycle. These reservoirs are present in all areas of the planet, including the atmosphere, land, sea, and subterranean domains, and transfers from one reservoir to another happen via carbon cycle processes, as described. The main reservoirs for the carbon cycle on Earth are listed in the following table.

Reservoir	Speed of exchange	Estimated dimensions (gigatons)	Notes
Atmosphere	Fast	720	
Benthic currents	Slow	~40,000	
Benthic sediments	Slow	1750	
Fossil fuel deposits	Naturally extremely slow, modified by humans to be extremely fast	~4,000	Historically, fossil fuel deposits were a one-way reservoir (once deposited, it was highly unlikely that carbon in coal or underground oil would reenter the cycle).

Reservoir	Speed of exchange	Estimated dimensions (gigatons)	Notes
Land plants	Fast to medium	550–680	
Marine food web	Fast	~4	
Ocean surface	Medium	1020	
Organic carbon in soil	Medium	1580	Includes methane in permafrost, fungi, and bacteria
Phytoplankton	Fast to medium	50	
Sedimentary rock	Slow	75,000,000	
Terrestrial food web	Fast	~4	Includes all animals (wild and domestic)

There are several methodologies available to accurately determine the atmospheric CO_2 concentration in the distant past, the easiest one being the direct measurement of air bubbles trapped in ice cores in Antarctic ice, which is only available up to approximately 800,000 years ago. The longest-ranging method is the alkenone–pCO_2 methodology used to reconstruct the partial pressure of ancient atmospheric carbon dioxide (pCO_2) measured by stable carbon isotope compositions of algal biomarkers (alkenones) in the fossil record.

Other available techniques, all of which provide data that is, in broad terms, consistent with each other, are:

- Measurement of stomatal indices of fossil leaves
- The carbon isotopic compositions of paleosol carbonate nodules
- The boron isotopic compositions of shallow-dwelling foraminifera

By looking at the data from all the various sources, as summarized in Figure 7.5, we can see how the CO_2 concentration in the atmosphere has changed dramatically over time, as was originally pointed out in the nineteenth century by John Ball.[3] He noted how "all the coal in the Carboniferous deposits that were being mined at the time, must have been extracted from the atmosphere."

Figure 7.5 summarizes in a single, easy-to-comprehend graph the record of the last 600 million years, with three separate detailed windows for the last 800,000 years, last 2,000 years, and last 100 years. Please note how the graph shows the emergence of major plant adaptations over geological time (appearance of embryophytes, or land plants, evolution of stomata, or leaf pores, emergence of angiosperms, or flowering plants, and arrival of grasses).

The amplitude of the fluctuations has declined significantly since the Carboniferous period (~360 to ~300 million years ago) that Ball referred to in his paper, due in part to the large depositions of fossil fuels, with fluctuations around the 1,000 ppm level during the Cretaceous period (~100 million years ago) and then decreasing constantly through the entire Cenozoic era (66 million years ago to today). As we have seen in previous data, for the last several million years, the concentration has

---

[3] John Ball, *Proceedings of the Royal Geographical Society and Monthly Record of Geography*, Vol. 1, No. 9 (New York: John Wiley & Sons, 1879), pp. 564–589.

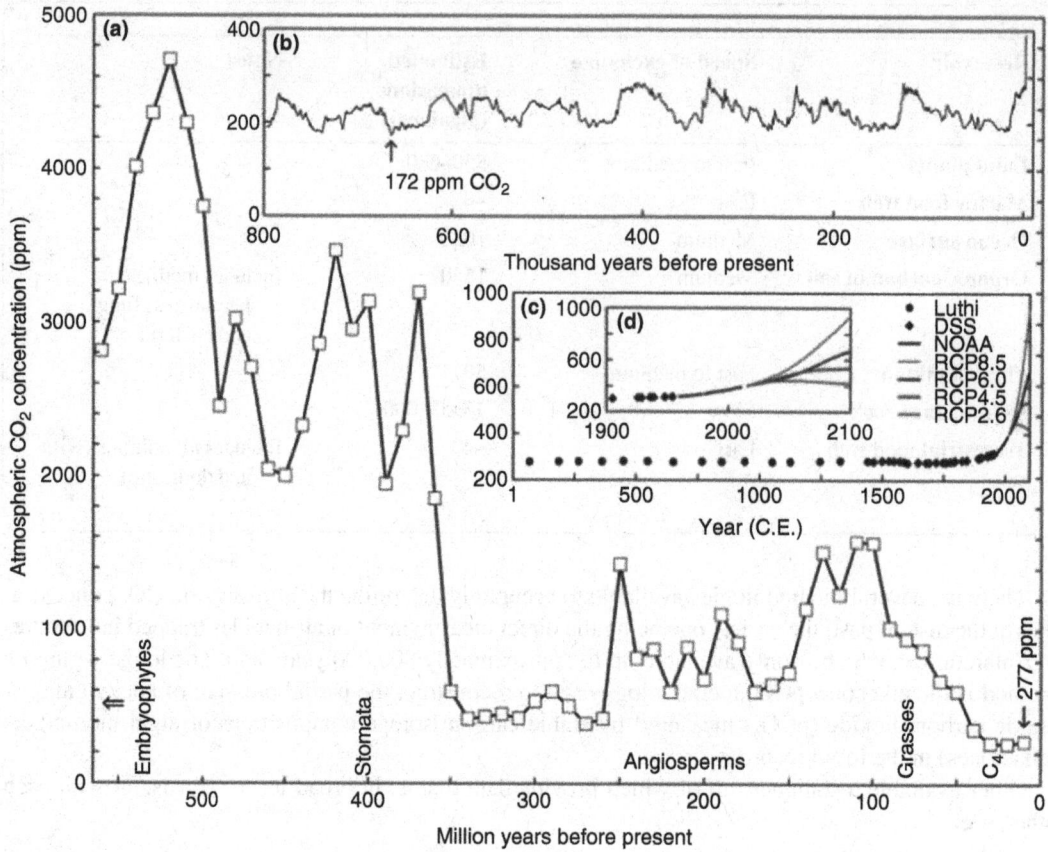

FIGURE 7.5 Atmospheric CO$_2$ concentration (ca) through time.
Source: Peter J. Franks et al., "Sensitivity of Plants to Changing Atmospheric CO$_2$ Concentration: from the Geological Past to
the Next Century," *New Phytologist*, January 25, 2013, https://doi.org/10.1111/nph.12104.

been fluctuating periodically between a minimum recorded level of 172 ppm and ~300 ppm, with a
series of nine glacial periods, where it remained steady at the lowest values for tens of thousands of
years at a time.

If we look at the more granular data, taken from the direct measurement of the trapped atmosphere
in the ice core samples from Antarctica, we can zoom into the last 800,000 years, as shown in Figure 7.6,
within the oscillating equilibrium period (Milankovitch cycles), and clearly see the cyclical oscillation
between ~170 ppm and ~280 ppm, which is tied to the ice age cycles, and the very recent spike up to
400+ ppm, which starts with the industrial revolution in the 1700s (which happened to coincide with a
peak in the ice age cycle).

If we look at a much shorter time scale – for example, at the data measured at the Mauna Loa observatory between 1958 and 2021 (Figure 7.7) – we can see, besides the seasonal variation pattern that is
clear and provides a sigmoidal change of +/–3% over the yearly average, a clear and monotone increase
of approximately 100 ppm (or roughly one-third of the starting level) in atmospheric CO$_2$ concentration
over the last 60 years.

The Impact of Human Activities on Atmospheric CO$_2$ Levels. If we observe the recent record of
CO$_2$ in the atmosphere (1700s to today) and couple it with the lack of obvious and sustained alternative and evident geological processes that are releasing CO$_2$ in the atmosphere (such as widespread
volcanic activity, e.g.), it is clear that the observed spike is due to the only major change in the carbon
cycle, which is the consequence of anthropogenic mining and extraction of fossil carbon to use as fuel
for human use (either for heating or for technological activity).

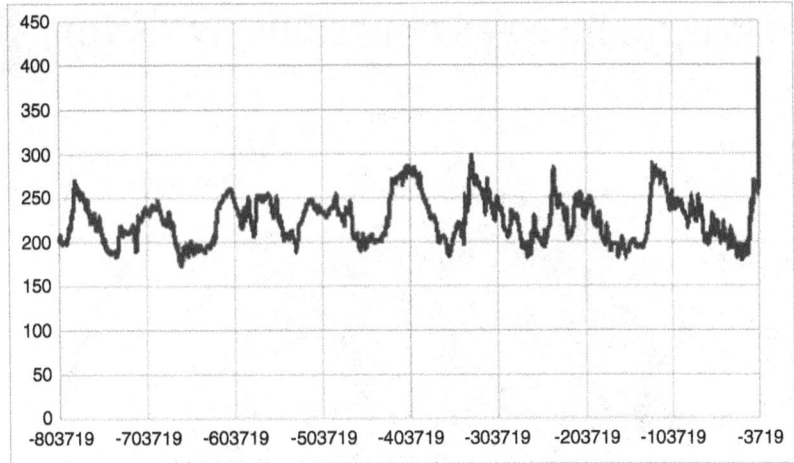

FIGURE 7.6 Global CO_2 concentrations in the last 800,000 years.
Source: NOAA / U.S. Department of Commerce / Public domain: https://data.noaa.gov/dataset/dataset/noaa-wds-paleoclimatology-antarctic-ice-cores-revised-800kyr-co2-data

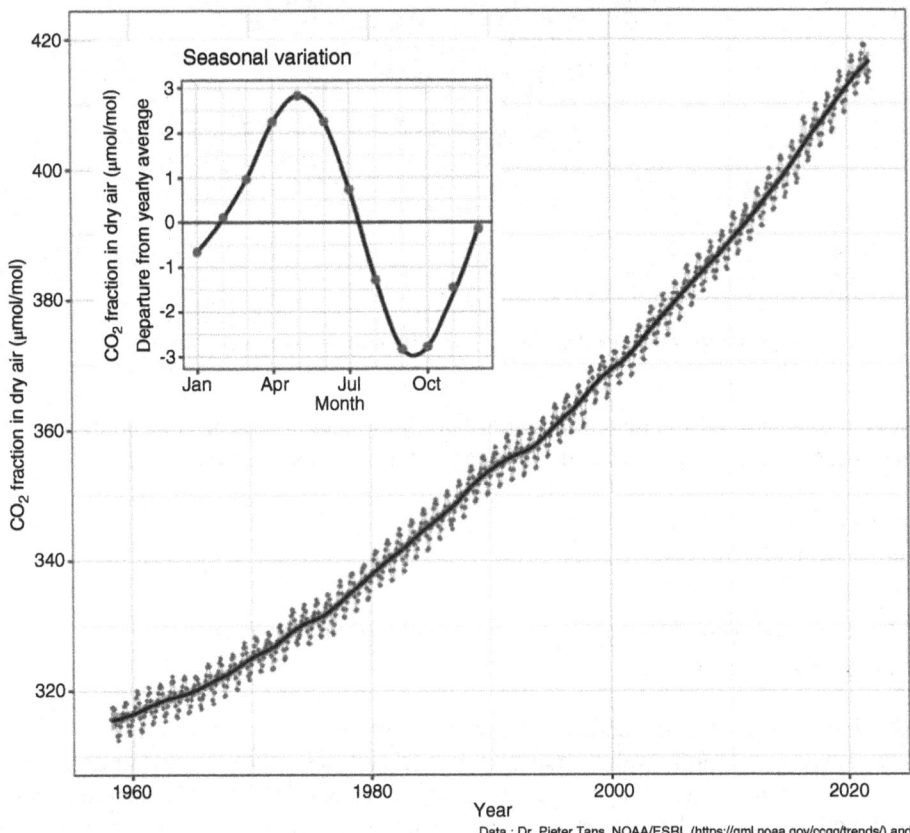

Data : Dr. Pieter Tans, NOAA/ESRL (https://gml.noaa.gov/ccgg/trends/) and
Dr. Ralph Keeling, Scripps Institution of Oceanography (https://scrippsco2.ucsd.edu/). Accessed 2021-12-16
https://w.wiki/4ZWn

FIGURE 7.7 Monthly mean CO_2 concentration at Mauna Loa observatory, 1958–2021.

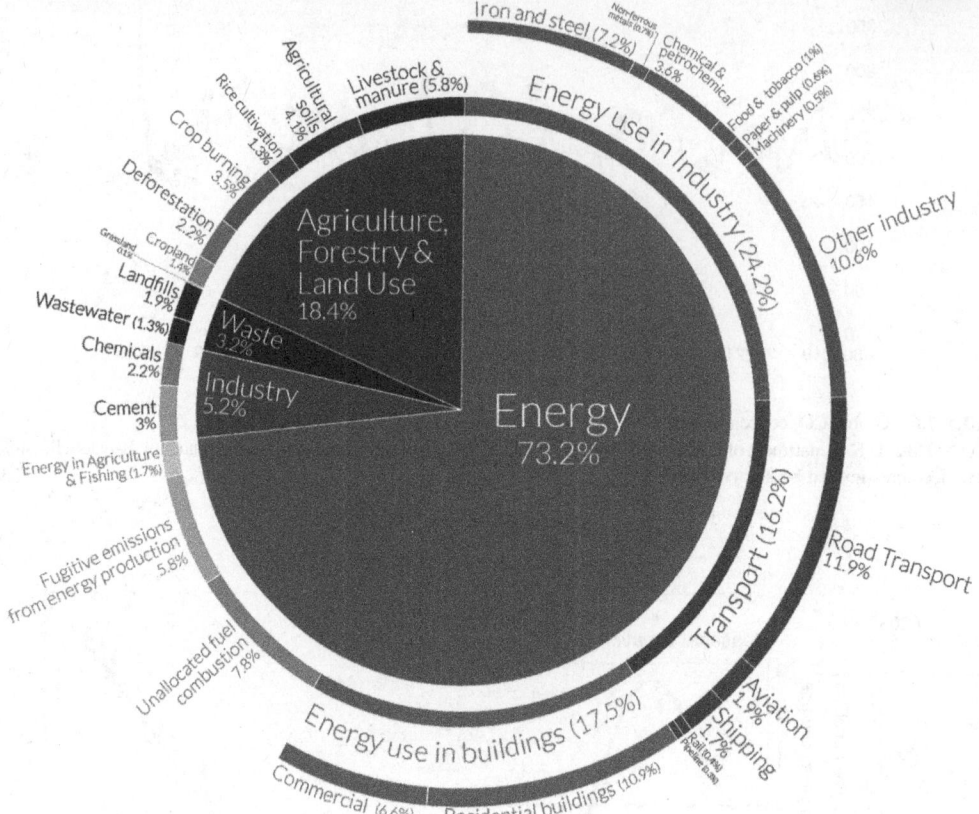

FIGURE 7.8   Global greenhouse gas (GHG) emissions by sector (2016).

In addition to releasing CO_2, human activities have been releasing other greenhouse gases (GHG), which have been further compounding the warming of the atmosphere, such as:

- Methane (CH_4)
- Nitrous oxide (N_2O)
- Ozone (O_3)
- Chlorofluorocarbons (CFCs) and hydrochlorofluorocarbons (HCFCs)
- Hydrofluorocarbons (HFCs)

Besides the well-known, and well-discussed, process of fossil fuel burning as a driver of increased global greenhouse gas (GHG) levels in the atmosphere, methane and CO_2 levels have also increased significantly due to the large number of cattle being farmed globally. (Cattle produce significant amounts of methane in their digestive systems, via methanogen microbes in their gut microbiome.)

By observing the range of human activities and their relative emissions by sector, we see that energy, as a widespread category, accounts for almost three quarters of emissions (73%); agriculture, forestry, and land use account for over 18%; and the rest is industry (5%) and waste (3%). More details about the breakdown of each of these categories can be seen in Figure 7.8.

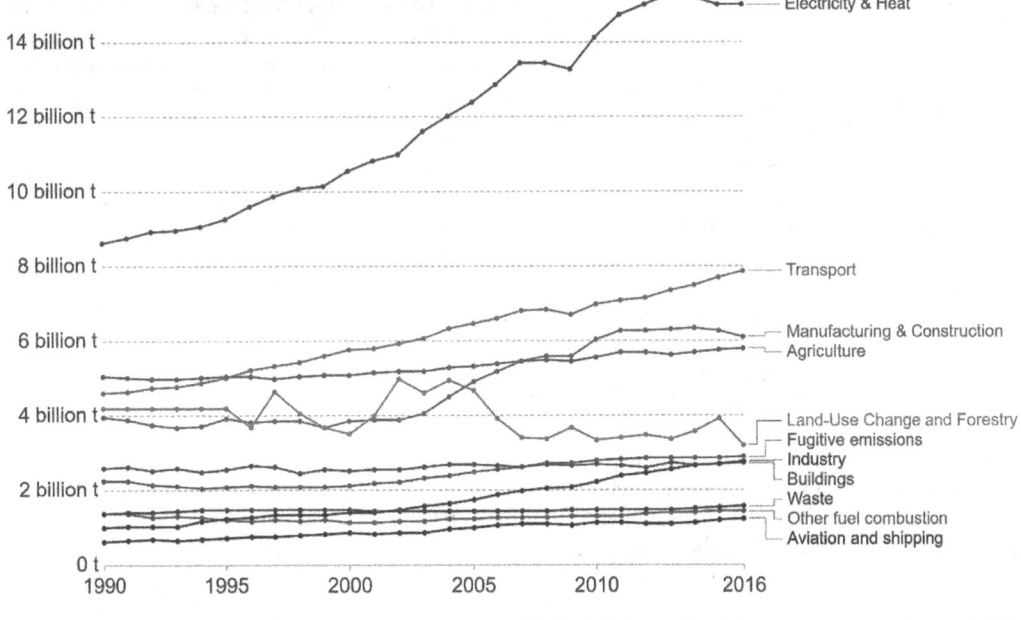

Greenhouse gas emissions by sector, World
Greenhouse gas emissions are measured in tonnes of carbon dioxide-equivalents (CO₂e).

FIGURE 7.9   Global greenhouse gas (GHG) emissions by sector (2016).

Most of the activities listed in the GHG emissions Figure 7.9, except for residential heating and vehicle use, are generally performed and managed by corporate entities around the globe.

Once we look at how these trends have been evolving since 1990, as we can see in Figure 7.9, we can highlight an overall gradual increase, with a couple of outliers, namely the electricity and heat sector (flat), manufacturing and construction (flat), and land-use change and forestry (in decline). While these stationary or slightly declining trends are a positive sign, the overall total GHG emissions are steadily increasing.

Looking at the emissions data and slicing them by the type of activity that drives them, we notice how over a quarter of all GHG emissions are directly linked to food production activities, as detailed in Table 7.1.

The data is presented in chart form in Figure 7.10, they make the underlying data freely available in a repository (https://github.com/owid/co2-data), which we recommend as a source of data for exercise and further study.

Future Evolution of CO₂ Levels and Global Temperature. The steady rise of CO_2 levels and global thermal anomalies is clear, but the situation becomes harder to assess once we pose the question of CO_2 and temperature in a future tense. Specifically, the question should not be "Will they continue to rise" – to which the answer, at least in the short term, is an obvious yes, but rather "Which profile of rising will they follow?" Finally, the most poignant question for the ESG practitioner is "What impact can current and future policy have on GHG and temperature levels in the decades and centuries to come?"

The answer to the last two questions is strongly predicated on a series of scenario assumptions that can be modeled such as:

- How much fossil fuel will be burned in the coming years?
- How much more will the world rely on renewable energy sources?

TABLE 7.1 Global greenhouse gas emissions from food production.

General category	Subcategory	Subcategory % of total food-related GHG emissions	General category % of total food-related GHG emissions	General category % of overall GHG emissions
Supply chain	Retail	3%	18%	5%
	Packaging	5%		
	Transport	6%		
	Food processing	4%		
Livestock and fisheries	Wild-catch fisheries	1%	31%	8%
	Livestock and fish farms	30%		
	• Methane from cattle's digestion			
	• Emissions from manure management			
	• Emissions from pasture management			
	• Fuel use from fisheries			
Crop production	Crops for animal feed	6%	27%	7%
	Crops for human food	21%		
Land use	Land use for human food	8%	24%	6%
	Land use for livestock	16%		

- How more efficient will processes become?
- Which policies will be enacted, and how successful will governments worldwide be at enforcing them?

Several other assumptions exist that either cannot yet be modeled accurately or are, at the moment, highly speculative or present large margins of error in the current models (e.g., the amount, speed, and feed-forward effect of the release of methane and CO_2 trapped in Arctic permafrost that is undergoing accelerated thawing).

As a result, multiple scenarios are being proposed that predict, based on a series of assumptions that we shall look at later in this chapter, global temperature rises between 1.3°C and 5.1°C, on average, by the year 2100.

While this data alone is worthy of concern, as practitioners of ESG finance, we must be able to identify and quantify what risks such scenarios would bring to the financial and economic systems. This practice allows us to better understand the differential impact that these climate-related risks might have on one corporation or entity vs. another. We first require a common taxonomy of climate-related risks, which we take from the "Recommendations of the Task Force on Climate-Related Financial Disclosures."[4] Although the recommendations are not focused specifically on financial risks, they provide very good classification for financial and nonfinancial entities alike.

Physical Risks and Transition Risks. All climate-related risks are divided in two categories, "physical" risks and "transition" risks, based on the nature of their action.

1. *Physical Risks*. These are risks resulting from direct action due to changes in climate patterns. They can be immediate and event-driven, in which case they are characterized as *acute risk*; or they can be long-term climate-pattern shift driven, in which case they are characterized as *chronic risk*.

---

[4] "Final Report: Recommendations of the Task Force on Climate-related Financial Disclosures," TCFD (June 2017), https://assets.bbhub.io/company/sites/60/2020/10/FINAL-2017-TCFD-Report-11052018.pdf

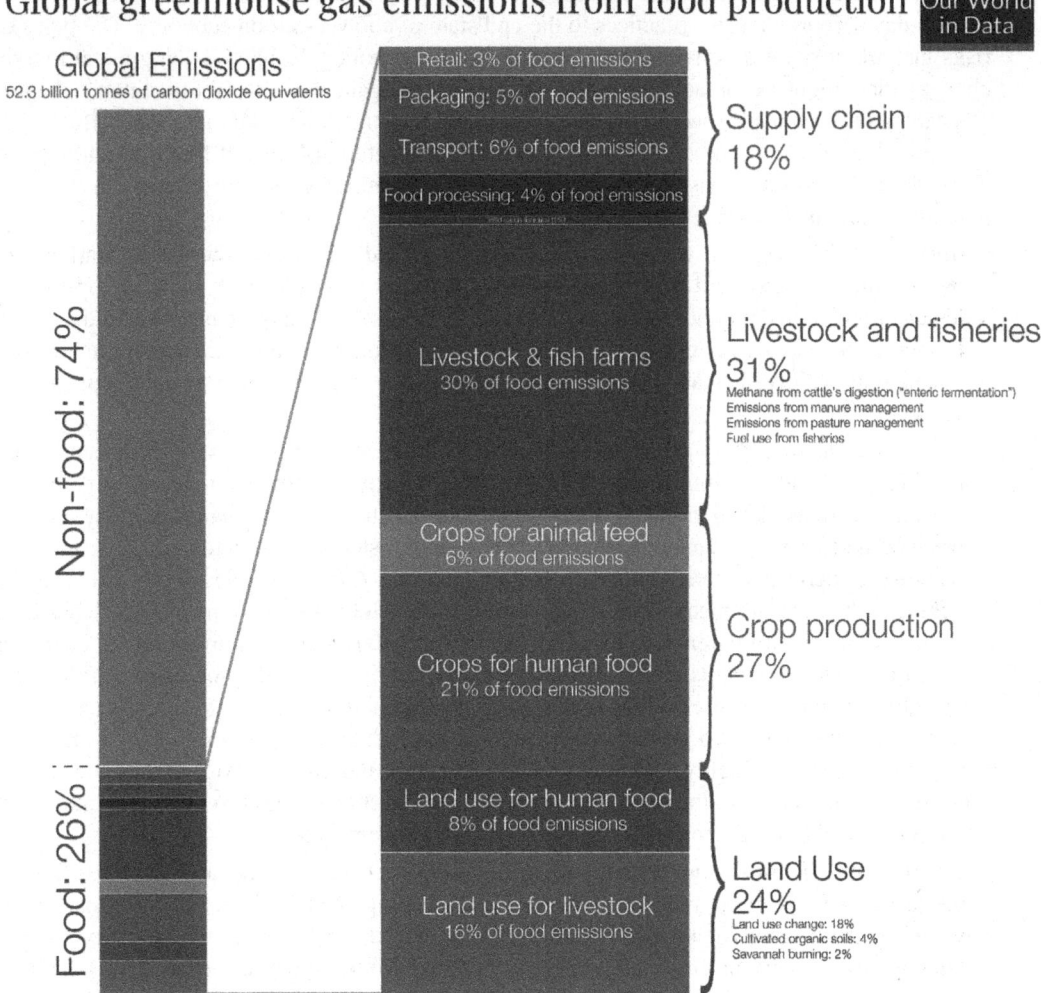

Data source: Joseph Poore & Thomas Nemecek (2018). Reducing food's environmental impacts through producers and consumers. Published in *Science*.
OurWorldinData.org – Research and data to make progress against the world's largest problems.   Licensed under CC-BY by the author Hannah Ritchie.

FIGURE 7.10   Global greenhouse gas (GHG) emissions from food production (2016).
Source: *Our World in Data* (www.ourworldindata.org).

The way physical risks manifest is typically through direct action on assets owned by organizations, such as damage to facilities and infrastructure, or by indirect action, such as impact on supply chains. In a similar fashion, physical risks can also disrupt an organization's financial performance by changing the underlying conditions that are necessary for it to be a viable business, for example by reducing or changing the availability and quality of water supply, reducing the availability of food supplies for workforce needs, and/or extreme temperature events affecting premises, storage facilities, operations, supply chains, transport needs and employee safety. Specifically:

○ *Acute risk*. Examples of acute physical risks include increased severity of extreme weather events, such as cyclones, tornadoes, hurricanes, or floods, as well as heat/cold waves and seasonal drought.

○ *Chronic risk*. Examples of chronic physical risks include protracted higher temperatures leading to sea level rise; seasonal pattern shifts making fertile areas turn into deserts; winter warming of ski resorts, which does not allow persistent snow cover; changes in ocean currents/temperature disrupting fisheries; or chronic heat waves leading to crop failures.

2. *Transition Risks.* These are risks resulting from the requirements due to the transition from present-day carbon-intensive practices to the end state of a lower-carbon economy. The types of risks that are covered by this category include extensive policy, legal, technology, and market changes that might occur as a response to, and to mitigate the effects of, climate change. Depending on what these specific risks are, how fast they materialize and make their effects felt, and what they focus on, these transition risks may pose different levels of financial and reputational threat to organizations. A few examples of transition risks that are relevant to the ESG practitioner are the following:

○ *Market risk.* The ways in which climate change can, and will, affect the global markets are varied, complex, and hard to predict. These include the appearance of shifts in supply and demand for certain commodities, products, and services as the climate changes and old patterns disappear while new ones emerge. It is expected that risks and opportunities that are climate-related will rapidly increase over time, as we explore in more detail in later portions of this textbook.

○ *Policy risk.* The regulatory environment regarding climate change is in a state of constant flux, as policies and laws continue to rapidly evolve. The objectives of these policies are generally of two kinds: actions that attempt to reduce the adverse effects of climate change (e.g., by limiting the amount of GHG emissions) and actions that seek to foster adaptation to impending changes in climate patterns in different countries and jurisdictions. A few examples of the first category include carbon-pricing mechanisms (aimed to reduce GHG emissions); incentives to shifts in energy sources toward renewable energy/lower emission sources; imposition of stringent energy efficiency standards for construction of new buildings; introduction of laws, rules, and regulations to improve efficiency in water usage; and promotion of sustainable land-usage practices. The risks associated with policy risks, and the financial impact that they can have on corporations, can be highly dependent on the nature of the policy measures that are implemented and the timing of the implementation (i.e., major change with fast implementation will have much higher cost than minor change with slow implementation).

○ *Litigation risk.* This category of risk covers litigation and legal risks that are linked to climate-related issues. In the recent years there has been an increasing trend in climate- and environmental-related litigation claims against corporations, having been brought forward by property owners, municipalities, states, insurers, shareholders, and public interest organizations (NGOs). Often these claims have been based on failure of corporations to mitigate impacts of climate change, adapt to climate change, and/or fully disclose materially relevant financial risks related to climate/environmental risks to shareholders and the general public. Given the expectation of continued and accelerated climate change in the years to come, the nature, size, and quantity of these claims is likely to increase significantly soon.

○ *Technology risk.* This category of risk covers technological innovation requirements that will be needed by corporations to adapt to a lower-carbon, more energy-efficient economic system. These improvements and innovations will come at a cost and are likely to have significant impacts on how organizations operate and turn profits. As an example of technology risk, we can highlight the development and use of emerging technologies such as renewable energy sources that will require a significant investment in batteries and other energy storage infrastructure. These improvements in energy efficiency and potentially carbon capture and storage will affect the competitiveness and bottom line of many organizations by adding to production and distribution costs, and impacting the demand for their products and services by the customers. Often, as was the case with the emergence of the automobile, which replaced the horse and buggy industry, new technologies will displace older ones and disrupt some portions of the incumbent economic systems, leading to the emergence of winners and losers from this process of *creative destruction*. While these transitions need to occur, the timing of the development of the technologies required, and their fielding, is still unclear. This lack of clarity on when the transition will occur adds to the uncertainty and exacerbates the potential impact of this type of risk on corporations.

○ *Reputation risk.* As climate change is a very visible and high-priority topic in most countries, many corporations, especially publicly traded ones, will be under tight scrutiny from public opinion on how they manage the challenges and requirements deriving from it. As a result, there is significant reputational risk if a corporation is perceived, by customers or the general public, as being lax in the way it handles the climate change transition and/or too slow/uncommitted to transition to a lower-carbon economy.

Table 7.2 provides some more detailed examples of physical risks and transition risks.

TABLE 7.2   Examples of climate risks from the TCFD report.

Type	Climate-related risks	Potential financial impacts
Transition risks	**Policy and legal**	
	Increased pricing of GHG emissions	Increased operating costs (e.g., higher compliance costs, increased insurance premiums)
	Enhanced emissions-reporting obligations	Write-offs, asset impairment, and early retirement of existing assets due to policy changes
	Mandates on and regulation of existing products and services	Increased costs and/or reduced demand for products and services resulting from fines and judgments
	Exposure to litigation	
	Technology	
	Substitution of existing products and services with lower emissions options	Write-offs and early retirement of existing assets
	Unsuccessful investment in new technologies	Reduced demand for products and services
	Costs to transition to lower emissions technology	Research and development (R&D) expenditures in new and alternative technologies
		Capital investments in technology development
		Costs to adopt/deploy new practices and processes
	Market	
	Changing customer behavior	Reduced demand for goods and services due to shift in consumer preferences
	Uncertainty in market signals	Increased production costs due to changing input prices (e.g., energy, water) and output requirements (e.g., waste treatment)
	Increased cost of raw materials	Abrupt and unexpected shifts in energy costs
		Change in revenue mix and sources, resulting in decreased revenues
		Repricing of assets (e.g., fossil fuel reserves, land valuations, securities valuations)
	Reputation	
	Shifts in consumer preferences	Reduced revenue from decreased demand for goods/services
	Stigmatization of sector	Reduced revenue from decreased production capacity (e.g., delayed planning approvals, supply chain interruptions)
	Increased stakeholder concern or negative stakeholder feedback	Reduced revenue from negative impacts on workforce management and planning (e.g., employee attraction and retention)
		Reduction in capital availability

(Continued)

TABLE 7.2 (*Continued*)

Type	Climate-related risks	Potential financial impacts
Physical risks	**Acute**	Reduced revenue from decreased production capacity (e.g., transport difficulties, supply chain interruptions)
	Increased severity of extreme weather events such as cyclones and floods	Reduced revenue and higher costs from negative impacts on workforce (e.g., health, safety, absenteeism)
	Chronic	Write-offs and early retirement of existing assets (e.g., damage to property and assets in "high-risk" locations)
	Changes in precipitation patterns and extreme variability in weather patterns	Increased operating costs (e.g., inadequate water supply for hydroelectric plants or to cool nuclear and fossil fuel plants)
	Rising mean temperatures	Increased capital costs (e.g., damage to facilities)
	Rising sea levels	Reduced revenues from lower sales/output
		Increased insurance premiums and potential for reduced availability of insurance on assets in high-risk locations

Source: Task Force on Climate-Related Financial Disclosures (TCFD) report 2021 / CDP, https://www.tcfdhub.org/risk-management/

If we look at the published works from the Bank of England, we see how Mark Carney, the former governor of the bank, classified the risks slightly differently in a 2018 speech (using three types instead of two), as "three channels through which climate risk affects financial stability":[5]

- *Physical risks* arise from the increased frequency and severity of climate- and weather-related events that damage property and disrupt trade.
- *Liability risks* stem from parties who have suffered loss from the effects of climate change seeking compensation from those they hold responsible.
- *Transition risks* can arise through a sudden and disorderly adjustment to a low-carbon economy.

Independent of whether we consider liability risks as part of transition risks or as their own self-standing category, the transition risks for markets and financial entities deserve a more focused discussion, which we shall undertake in this book. We shall also define *carbon risk* as the risk of financial losses resulting from GHG emissions (generally as a result of any, or combination of, channels identified by Carney).

Another important definition is that of *stranded assets*. These are a risk category defined as "assets that have suffered from unanticipated or premature write-downs, devaluations, or conversion to liabilities."[6]

Among the most significant environment-related drivers that can result in stranded assets are:

- *Direct environmental drivers* (climate change, ecosystem degradation, changes in marine currents/temperatures, droughts, etc.)
- *Drivers that derive from changes to resources,* either via scarcity or modification of equilibria (e.g., shale-gas abundance, phosphate scarcity)

---

[5] Mark Carney, Governor of the Bank of England, "A Transition in Thinking and Action," April 6, 2018, https://www.bis.org/review/r180420b.pdf.

[6] "Stranded Assets Programme," Smith School of Enterprise and the Environment, March 25, 2014, https://web.archive.org/web/20140327230917/http://www.smithschool.ox.ac.uk/research/stranded-assets/

- *Policy and regulatory drivers* (new laws, carbon pricing, air pollution standards, etc.)
- *Changing costs for renewable energies* (reducing costs for solar, eolic, electric vehicles, etc.)
- *Social/behavioral drivers* (divestment campaigns from fossil fuels, changes in consumer habits and behaviors, increased demand for sustainable products, etc.)
- *Litigation drivers* (GHG liabilities) and changing interpretations of corporate statutory duties (e.g., fiduciary duties, disclosure requirements, social responsibilities, etc.)

A good example of stranded assets risk due to drivers in this list is one of the large underground deposits of fossil fuels, which are currently on the balance sheets of oil and gas companies as untapped assets. These deposits might have to remain underground if their extraction becomes uneconomical or unpalatable to shareholders in the future (whether due to direct regulation or a shift in demand for these fuels), and thus would have to be written down on the balance sheet.

Projected Scenarios for CO_2 and Temperature for the Remainder of the Century. As we have seen earlier in this chapter, there are several different assumptions used to calibrate the models that provide the possible pathways for CO_2 and temperature for the next 80 years.

Most of these assumptions, as well as the models and the science behind them, fall under the mandate of the Intergovernmental Panel on Climate Change (IPCC), which is the United Nations' body for assessing the science related to climate change, and is one of the international organizations most relevant to climate change analysis. The IPCC was created to provide policymakers with regular scientific assessments on climate change, its implications and potential future risks, as well as to put forward adaptation and mitigation options.

Using many parallel climate models, the IPCC gathered a working group to project representative concentration pathways (RPCs) to describe several different GHG emissions trajectories, and consequent average surface temperatures, which could take place over the next 80 years. The workgroup resulted in a projection of five separate pathways, spanning a relatively broad range of outcomes between 2020 and 2100, all of which were purposefully published without the inclusion of socioeconomic narratives (as these were beyond the scope of the panel).

A parallel and complementary IPCC effort, called shared socioeconomic pathways (SSPs), analyzed five different ways in which the world might evolve in the absence of shared climate policies, as well as how different levels of climate change mitigation results might be achieved if the mitigation targets from the RCPs were to be combined with the SSPs (Figure 7.11). The SSPs have specific narratives that describe which socioeconomic trends and policies are required for the pathway to occur and how these would affect future societies (Table 7.3). The goal of these different narratives is to cover the range of plausible, if not all the possible, future outcomes.[7]

In order to visualize the amount of mitigation challenge and adaptation challenge that is required in each of the five SSPs, it is helpful to visualize them in a bidimensional graph, with mitigation requirements being the vertical axis (low to high) and adaptation requirements being the horizontal (low to high from left to right), as we can see in Figure 7.12.[8]

The IPCC periodically issues reports covering aspects of scientific, technical, and socioeconomic relevance on the topic of climate change. The Sixth Assessment Report (AR6) is structured in three working groups (WG) that assess three major aspects of climate change. The first WG study was published in 2021 (*Physical Science Basis*), the second WG report was published in February 2022 (*Impacts, Adaptation, and Vulnerability*), and the third is planned for later in 2022 (*Vulnerability and Mitigation of Climate Change*). The final synthesis report is due to be finished by late 2022.

---

[7] Keywan Riahi et al., "The Shared Socioeconomic Pathways and Their Energy, Land Use, and Greenhouse Gas Emissions Implications: An Overview," *Global Environmental Change* 42 (2017): 153–168, ISSN 0959-3780, https://doi.org/10.1016/j.gloenvcha.2016.05.009.

[8] "Analysis: UK's 'Jet Zero' Plan Would Allow Demand for Flying to Soar 70%," *Carbon Brief*, (July 21, 2022, https://www.carbonbrief.org/analysis-uks-jet-zero-plan-would-allow-demand-for-flying-to-soar-70/.

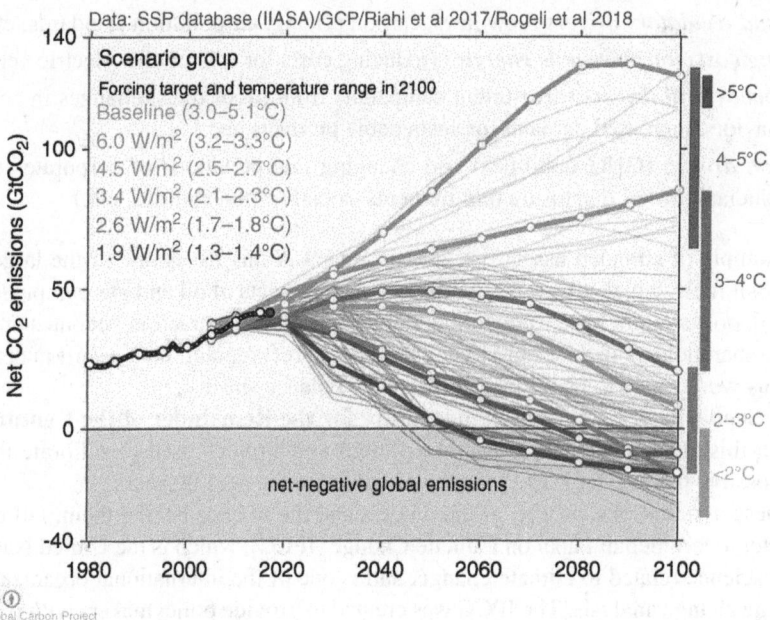

FIGURE 7.11   Aggregate view of SSP pathways.
Source: Zeke Hausfather 2018 / Carbon Brief

TABLE 7.3   SSPs and relative narratives.

Shared socioeconomic pathway	Narrative
SSP1	**Sustainability (Taking the Green Road)** The world shifts gradually, but pervasively, toward a more sustainable path, emphasizing more inclusive development that respects perceived environmental boundaries. Management of the global commons slowly improves, educational and health investments accelerate the demographic transition, and the emphasis on economic growth shifts toward a broader emphasis on human well-being. Driven by an increasing commitment to achieving development goals, inequality is reduced both across and within countries. Consumption is oriented toward low material growth and lower resource and energy intensity.
SSP2	**Middle of the road** The world follows a path in which social, economic, and technological trends do not shift markedly from historical patterns. Development and income growth proceeds unevenly, with some countries making relatively good progress while others fall short of expectations. Global and national institutions slowly but steadily work toward achieving sustainable development goals. Environmental systems experience degradation, although there are some improvements and, overall, the intensity of resource and energy use declines. Global population growth is moderate and levels off in the second half of the century. Income inequality persists or improves only slowly and challenges to reducing vulnerability to societal and environmental changes remain.

Shared socioeconomic pathway	Narrative
SSP3	**Regional rivalry (a rocky road)** A resurgent nationalism, concerns about competitiveness and security, and regional conflicts push countries to increasingly focus on domestic or, at most, regional issues. Policies shift over time to become increasingly oriented toward national and regional security issues. Countries focus on achieving energy and food security goals within their own regions at the expense of broader-based development. Investments in education and technological development decline. Economic development is slow, consumption is material-intensive, and inequalities persist or worsen over time. Population growth is low in industrialized and high in developing countries. A low international priority for addressing environmental concerns leads to strong environmental degradation in some regions.
SSP4	**Inequality (a road divided)** Highly unequal investments in human capital, combined with increasing disparities in economic opportunity and political power, lead to increasing inequalities and stratification both across and within countries. Over time, a gap widens between an internationally connected society that contributes to knowledge- and capital-intensive sectors of the global economy, and a fragmented collection of lower-income, poorly educated societies that work in a labor intensive, low-tech economy. Social cohesion degrades and conflict and unrest become increasingly common. Technology development is high in the high-tech economy and sectors. The globally connected energy sector diversifies, with investments in both carbon-intensive fuels like coal and unconventional oil, but also low-carbon energy sources. Environmental policies focus on local issues around middle- and high-income areas.
SSP5	**Fossil-fueled development (taking the highway)** This world places increasing faith in competitive markets, innovation, and participatory societies to produce rapid technological progress and development of human capital as the path to sustainable development. Global markets are increasingly integrated. There are also strong investments in health, education, and institutions to enhance human and social capital. At the same time, the push for economic and social development is coupled with the exploitation of abundant fossil fuel resources and the adoption of resource and energy intensive lifestyles around the world. All these factors lead to rapid growth of the global economy, while global population peaks and declines in the twenty-first century. Local environmental problems like air pollution are successfully managed. There is faith in the ability to effectively manage social and ecological systems, including by geo-engineering if necessary.

Source: Zeke Hausfather 2018 / Carbon Brief

The SENSES Toolkit. A good online resource to provide context and comprehension of climate scenarios is the SENSES Project (http://senses-project.org/), a nonprofit organization dedicated to the popularization of climate change scenarios. SENSES supports the understanding of climate change scenarios through sharing of data and visualization tools, which include an online "toolkit" composed of three main portions:

1. *Projections of climate change.* This portion provides quantitative information (i.e., temperature, precipitation, frequency of extreme climatic events) on how the climate is expected to evolve in response to specific projected levels of atmospheric CO_2.
2. *Projections of climate change impact on the economy.* This portion describes the potential impacts that the different scenarios would have on specific sectors. These can include water economy, agriculture, fisheries, marine ecosystems, coastal infrastructure sectors, etc. The climate change

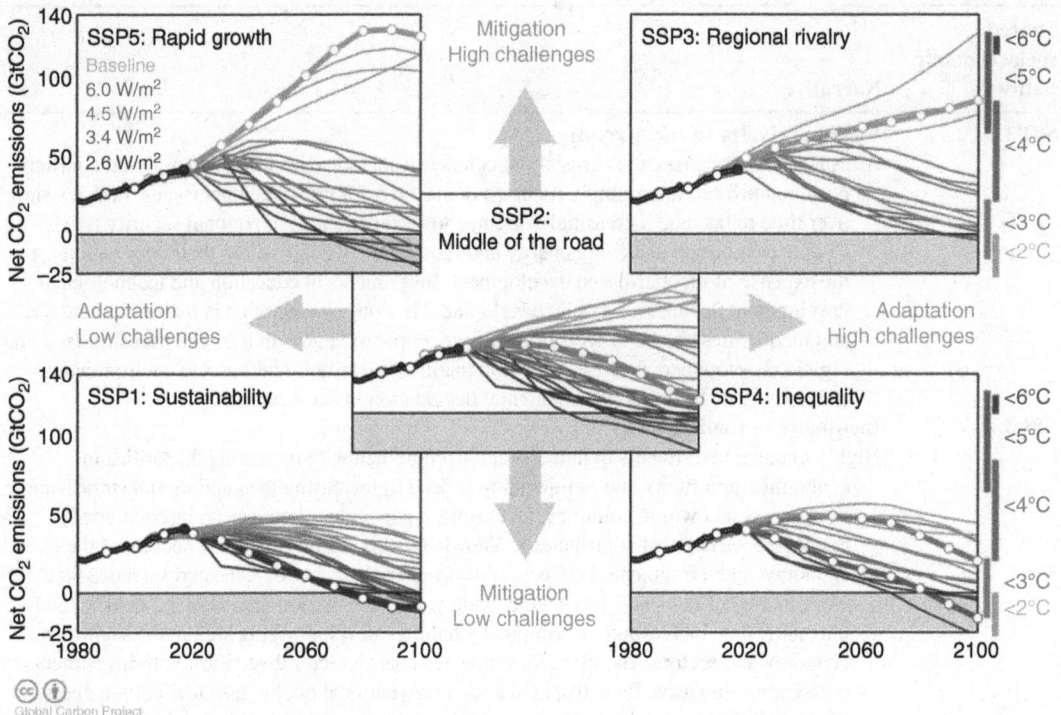

FIGURE 7.12   SSPs by mitigation and adaptation challenge levels.
Source: Zeke Hausfather 2018 / Carbon Brief

projections from the first portion of the toolkit are used as input for impact models to calculate, for example, changes in agricultural production, which, subsequently, can be drivers of other downstream models. The climate impact scenarios, additionally, are dependent on a series of assumptions about future socioeconomic developments (population, policy, technological developments, etc.), and the climate impact projections provide estimated impacts of the climate change pathways on specific sectors of the economy in a quantitative and measurable way.

3. *Mitigation scenarios.* The third portion of the toolkit describes possible countermeasures that can be implemented to mitigate climate change. These mitigation scenarios are based on plausible projections that include the development of energy sources, economies, changes in land use, and emissions across the globe. They are constrained by the goal of not allowing the global mean temperature to exceed a particular temperature threshold (i.e., the model first postulates the threshold and then what mitigation is required to achieve the goal, if the goal can be achieved). Again, all the projections depend on a series of assumptions on future socioeconomic developments, and the mitigation scenarios describe the macroeconomic investments, technology costs, changes in land use, and other postulated requirements needed to remain within specific set levels of climate change.

SENSES also curates a "finance track" online resource at https://climatescenarios.org/finance-portal/, which, as an example, discusses impact to the power industry under different possible climate change scenarios. Figure 7.13 shows a sample of projections on how volumes of power generation from different sources are expected to change under the assumptions of the 2°C warming scenario.

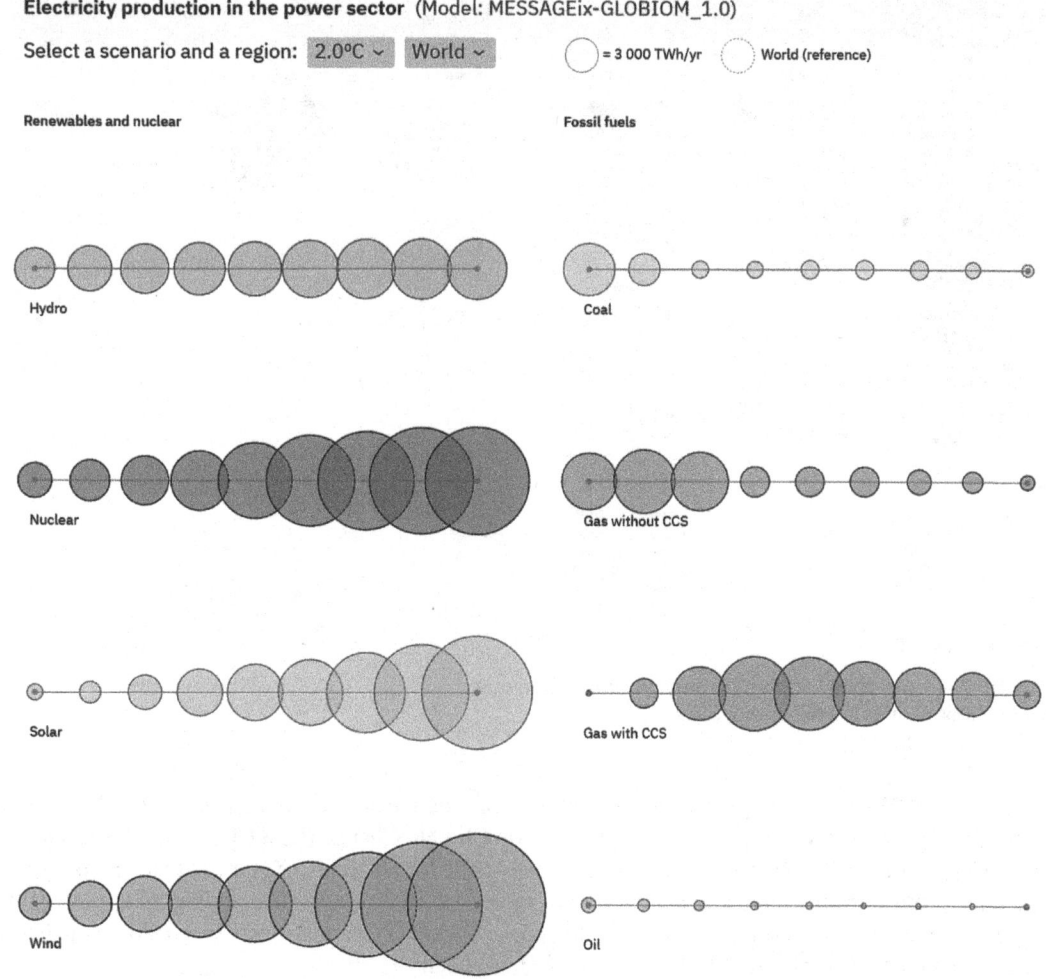

Electricity production in the power sector (Model: MESSAGEix-GLOBIOM_1.0)

Select a scenario and a region: 2.0°C ⌄   World ⌄   ◯ = 3 000 TWh/yr   ◯ World (reference)

Renewables and nuclear   Fossil fuels

Hydro   Coal

Nuclear   Gas without CCS

Solar   Gas with CCS

Wind   Oil

FIGURE 7.13   Changes in power production by climate change scenario.
Source: "Transition Risks Power Sector Transformation," https://climatescenarios.org/power-sector/.

7.2   REGULATORY RESPONSE TO CLIMATE CHANGE

The regulatory and policy response to climate change challenges across the globe involves a variety of players at different levels, each of which is involved in specific relevant regulatory initiatives.

These players can be, broadly, grouped as follows:

- United Nations
- Other international bodies and agencies
- Individual nation governments
- Nongovernmental organizations (NGOs)
- Industry regulatory bodies (including financial regulators)

Given the scope of this book and the vast nature of the regulation in place that pertains to climate change, we will not cover all existing regulations and regulators but will rather focus on a few topics and areas of interest to the practitioner of ESG finance, inasmuch as they pertain to the main focus of this text.

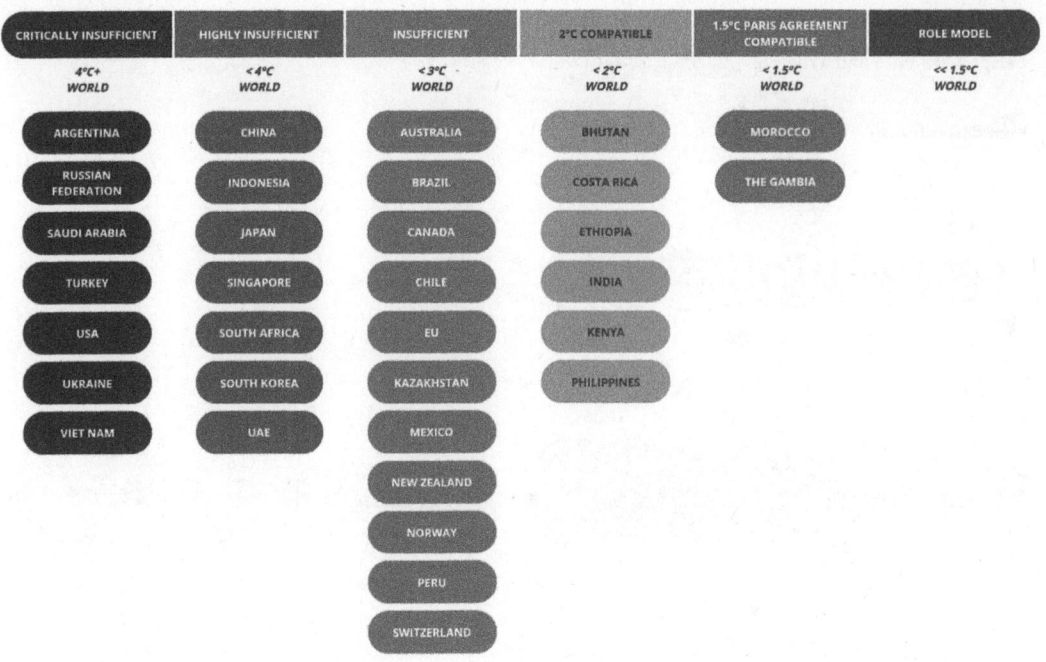

CRITICALLY INSUFFICIENT	HIGHLY INSUFFICIENT	INSUFFICIENT	2°C COMPATIBLE	1.5°C PARIS AGREEMENT COMPATIBLE	ROLE MODEL
4°C+ WORLD	< 4°C WORLD	< 3°C WORLD	< 2°C WORLD	< 1.5°C WORLD	<< 1.5°C WORLD
ARGENTINA	CHINA	AUSTRALIA	BHUTAN	MOROCCO	
RUSSIAN FEDERATION	INDONESIA	BRAZIL	COSTA RICA	THE GAMBIA	
SAUDI ARABIA	JAPAN	CANADA	ETHIOPIA		
TURKEY	SINGAPORE	CHILE	INDIA		
USA	SOUTH AFRICA	EU	KENYA		
UKRAINE	SOUTH KOREA	KAZAKHSTAN	PHILIPPINES		
VIET NAM	UAE	MEXICO			
		NEW ZEALAND			
		NORWAY			
		PERU			
		SWITZERLAND			

FIGURE 7.14 Alignment to Paris Agreement, aviation and shipping.
Source: Adapted from Climate Action Tracker

The United Nations hosts yearly United Nations Climate Change Conferences, within the framework of the United Nations Framework Convention on Climate Change (UNFCC). These conferences, called Conference of Parties (COP), serve as a formal venue for all UNFCCC parties to assess progress on dealing with climate change and, in the more recent venues, to negotiate and agree upon legally binding obligations for developed countries to reduce their GHG emissions (Kyoto Protocol, Paris Agreement). The most relevant COP events to date have been:

- COP 1 (1995, Berlin): First COP.
- COP 3 (1997, Kyoto): Signature of the Kyoto Protocol. This treaty formalized the intent of the signatories to reduce GHG emissions based on consensus that global warming is occurring and it is caused primarily by human-made CO_2 emissions.
- COP 21 (2015, Paris): Signature of the Paris Agreement, committing parties to a goal of limiting temperature increase under 2°C and taking consistent measures to effect change in relevant industries, including finance. The United States withdrew in 2020 and rejoined in 2021.
- COP 26 (2021, Glasgow): Adoption of the Glasgow Climate Pact. This includes an agreement to revisit emission reduction plans in 2022 in order to try to keep the 1.5°C Paris Agreement target achievable. It also commits to limit (*phase down*) the use of unabated coal and includes a commitment to climate finance for developing countries.

Under the stipulations of the Paris Agreement, each signatory country has committed to national goals toward GHG emissions reductions, which are being tracked at a country level and reported upon. Participating countries have different levels of compliance by industry type, and their current alignment can be tracked in Figure 7.14. Each country is aligned to the warming scenario that their current emissions profile has them tracking closest to, by specific industry type assessments (in the figure, this is based on the assessment of aviation and shipping).

Compliance data by country can be retrieved both from the Climate Action Tracker website (https://climateactiontracker.org/countries/) as well as from the World Bank:

- *Climate Action Tracker*. This independent scientific analysis organization tracks government climate action and measures it against the agreed-upon Paris Agreement aims of "holding global warming well below 2°C and pursuing efforts to limit warming to 1.5°C." It tracks 36 countries and the European Union, which, collectively, are currently responsible for 80% of the GHG emissions on the planet.
- *World Bank Climate Change Knowledge Portal (CCKP)*. This is a central resource for information and data that is managed by the World Bank (https://data.worldbank.org/topic/climate-change). It includes data and reports focused on climate change from all countries in the world. The CCKP provides global data on historical and future climate, vulnerabilities, and impacts. It contains climate, disaster risk, and socioeconomic datasets as well as Climate Risk Country Profiles.

A significant number of ongoing international programs have a stated goal to combat climate change risk, some of which (the most relevant for the ESG finance practitioner) are listed in Table 7.4.

In addition to these international programs, there are international and prominent local financial regulators that are increasingly addressing environmental risks directly, both via their general mandate as well as through direct climate risk supervision.

Table 7.5 provides a high-level view of the major players in the financial regulatory arena and links to select publications that allow the reader to gain familiarity with their mandate and supervisory activity.

TABLE 7.4 **Examples of international programs to combat climate risk.**

Program	Description
Intergovernmental Panel on Climate Change (IPCC) https://www.ipcc.ch/	The United Nations body for assessing the science related to climate change. It was created to provide policymakers with regular scientific assessments on climate change, its implications, and potential future risks, as well as to put forward adaptation and mitigation options.
UN Environment Program Finance Initiative (UNEP FI) https://www.unepfi.org/publications/banking-publications/the-climate-risk-landscape/	UNEP FI is a partnership between UNEP and the global financial sector to mobilize private sector finance for sustainable development. It publishes Principles for Responsible Investment (PRI), Principles for Responsible Banking (PRB), etc.
Coalition of Finance Ministers for Climate Action https://www.financeministersforclimate.org/	The FMCA brings together fiscal and economic policymakers from over 50 countries in leading the global climate response and in securing a transition toward low-carbon resilient development. Finance ministers from 50 countries have signed on to the (nonbinding) Helsinki Principles, a set of six principles that promote national climate action, especially through fiscal policy and the use of public finance.
One Planet Summit https://www.oneplanetsummit.fr/en	A cross-disciplinary platform organized by UN, World Bank, and the government of France to prioritize international collaboration in the area of climate change. It includes many sovereign wealth funds among the founding organizations.
Network for Greening the Financial System (NGFS) https://www.ngfs.net/en	Network of Central Banks and Supervisors for Greening the Financial System, launched at the first One Planet Summit in 2017. It is a group of central banks and supervisors willing, on a voluntary basis, to share best practices and contribute to the development of environment and climate risk management in the financial sector and to mobilize mainstream finance to support the transition toward a sustainable economy. The NGFS also publishes NGFS climate scenarios.

TABLE 7.5 Financial regulators with significant involvement in climate risk regulation.

Authority	General mandate	Climate risk supervision	Prominent guidelines and regulation
International financial regulatory bodies			
Bank for International Settlements (BIS)	Hosts Secretariat of the Basel Committee on Banking Supervision (BCBS), a governance body that establishes Basel frameworks, a cornerstone of global banking regulation	Prescribes the role of central banks, regulators and supervisors in the age of climate change	https://www.bis.org/publ/othp31.htm
Financial Stability Board (FSB)	An international body that monitors and makes recommendations about the global financial system, hosted and funded by BIS	Focuses on systemic risks, of which climate risk is an important one	https://www.fsb.org/wp-content/uploads/P231120.pdf
FSB Task Force on Climate-Related Financial Disclosures (TCFD)	Financial Stability Board established the TCFD to develop recommendations for more effective climate-related disclosures that could promote more informed investment, credit, and insurance underwriting decisions and, in turn, enable stakeholders to understand better the concentrations of carbon-related assets in the financial sector and the financial system's exposures to climate-related risks	NA	https://assets.bbhub.io/company/sites/60/2020/10/FINAL-2017-TCFD-Report-11052018.pdf
Prominent local financial regulators			
European Central Bank (ECB)	Central bank for the Eurozone	Published final guide on climate risk and banking supervision Banks to perform self-assessment on ECB expectations in 2021 ECB to fully review banks' environmental/climate risk practices in 2022 Next supervisory stress test in 2022 to also focus on climate-related risks	https://www.bankingsupervision.europa.eu/legalframework/publiccons/pdf/climate-related_risks/ssm.202005_draft_guide_on_climate-related_and_environmental_risks.en.pdf

Authority	General mandate	Climate risk supervision	Prominent guidelines and regulation
European Banking Authority (EBA)	Financial regulator of the EU; responsibilities include regulatory stress tests of EU banks	Published a discussion paper on management of ESG risks	https://www.eba.europa.eu/sites/default/documents/files/document_library/Publications/Discussions/2021/Discussion%20Paper%20on%20management%20and%20supervision%20of%20ESG%20risks%20for%20credit%20institutions%20and%20investment%20firms/935496/2020-11-02%20%20ESG%20Discussion%20Paper.pdf
Bank of England (BoE)	Central bank of the UK, includes the regulatory function (Prudential Regulatory Authority)	Utilizes its stress-testing framework to assess the impact of climate-related risks on the UK financial system; publishes the climate biennial exploratory scenario (Climate BES) starting in 2021	https://www.bankofengland.co.uk/-/media/boe/files/stress-testing/2021/the-2021-biennial-exploratory-scenario-on-the-financial-risks-from-climate-change.pdf?la=en&hash=2E5CAECE75E701315B51B09303F99FCF8D21C8E2
Hong Kong Monetary Authority (HKMA)	Central Bank of Hong Kong	published principles of supervisory approach to climate risk management; conducts a dedicated climate stress test	https://www.hkma.gov.hk/media/eng/doc/key-information/guidelines-and-circular/2020/20200630e1a1.pdf

From Table 7.5, one of the major regulatory bodies for the purposes of this textbook is the Task Force on Climate-Related Financial Disclosures (TCFD). The TCFD originated in 2015, following the request from the finance ministers and central bank governors from the G20 nations to the Financial Stability Board (FSB) to convene public and private sector participants to come to a consensus on how the financial sector should take account of climate-related issues. As a result of this activity, the need for better information to support informed investment, lending, and insurance underwriting decisions was highlighted, specifically in the dimensions that are required to improve understanding of climate-related risks that apply to these activities. In order to identify which information is required to assess and price climate-related risks, the FSB established an industry-led task force, the TCFD, with the stated mandate to develop voluntary climate-related financial disclosures that would be useful to investors and other third parties.[9] The TCFD finalized this development work in 2017 with the release of the final set of recommendations. This document provides companies with a framework that can be used to prepare more effective climate-related financial disclosures, leveraging their existing reporting processes.

The overall recommendations from the 2017 TCFD publication include the following required disclosures grouped by type:

Governance:
- Describe the board's oversight of climate-related risks and opportunities.
- Describe management's role in assessing and managing climate-related risks and opportunities.

Strategy:
- Describe the climate-related risks and opportunities the organization has identified over the short, medium, and long term.
- Describe the impact of climate-related risks and opportunities on the organization's businesses, strategy, and financial planning.
- Describe the resilience of the organization's strategy, taking into consideration different climate-related scenarios, including a 2°C or lower scenario.

Risk Management:
- Describe the organization's processes for identifying and assessing climate-related risks.
- Describe the organization's processes for managing climate-related risks.
- Describe how processes for identifying, assessing, and managing climate-related risks are integrated into the organization's overall risk management.

Metrics and Targets:
- Disclose the metrics used by the organization to assess climate-related risks and opportunities in line with its strategy and risk management process.
- Disclose Scope 1, Scope 2, and, if appropriate, Scope 3 GHG emissions, and the related risks. Scope 1 to 3 are defined as follows:
  - *Scope 1* refers to all direct GHG emissions.
  - *Scope 2* refers to indirect GHG emissions from consumption of purchased electricity, heat, or steam.

---

[9] source: https://www.fsb-tcfd.org/about/

- ○ *Scope 3* refers to other indirect emissions not covered in Scope 2 that occur in the value chain of the reporting company, including both upstream and downstream emissions. Scope 3 emissions could include: the extraction and production of purchased materials and fuels, transport-related activities in vehicles not owned or controlled by the reporting entity, electricity-related activities (e.g., transmission and distribution losses), outsourced activities, and waste disposal.
- Describe the targets used by the organization to manage climate-related risks and opportunities and performance against targets.

At the time of writing of this textbook, five years have passed since the publishing of the initial TCFD recommendations, and recent data on the adoption and implementation of these standards and metrics are showing significant progress, with still more to be done to reach full implementation.

As of 2022, the most recent findings are:

- Nearly 60% of the world's 100 largest public companies support the TCFD, report in line with the TCFD recommendations, or both.
- Disclosure of climate-related financial information has increased since 2017, but continuing progress is needed.
- Energy companies and materials and buildings companies lead on disclosure.
- One in 15 companies reviewed disclosed information on the resilience of its strategy.
- Asset manager and asset owner reporting to their clients and beneficiaries, respectively, is still likely insufficient.

7.3   CLIMATE CHANGE MODELING

The methodologies for modeling climate change, such as those that are used for the generation of the scenarios that we have seen in the previous sections, are various and of different degrees of complexity, based on the time frames that are being modeled, the granularity of data inputs and outputs, and the kind of accuracy and sensitivity that is necessary.

Although climate models are not part of the scope of this textbook, we will take a cursory look at the most common types of methodologies used in the field, to provide a better understanding of the subject to our readers (especially considering that the climate change impact models use the output data from climate change models as their own input data and are therefore extremely interconnected to them).

While there are several qualitative models for climate, we shall focus exclusively on the quantitative ones, as these are the ones that are used for the purposes of climate change modeling as intended for ESG finance.

The common characteristic of all numerical climate models is to use quantitative methodologies, of one kind or another, to model the interactions of different drivers for climate, such as atmosphere, land surface, oceans, and ice coverage, and produce estimates of resulting effects, given initial postulated assumptions. These models can be used for multiple purposes and in different time scales, from weather predictions, all the way to overall long-term climate change.

All these models look at Earth as a closed system, with a set amount of incoming energy from the sun, in the form of shortwave electromagnetic radiation (mostly in the visible and shortwave, near-infrared, and infrared spectrum), and a set amount of outgoing radiating energy in the infrared electromagnetic spectrum. In the most simplistic of models, an imbalance between the incoming calories and the outgoing ones, in favor of the incoming ones, will lead to an increase in temperature, and the opposite will lead to a decrease.

The simplest models look at Earth as a single unified radiant heat transfer model and average outgoing and incoming energy to predict temperature changes. As can be easily imagined, these models are not very precise and can be used only for order-of-magnitude types of assessments.

There are also models that couple atmosphere-ocean-sea ice into one aggregated system and solve full equations for mass and energy transfers and radiant exchange, which provide more precise estimates and data projections.

The most used types of climate models fall into the following general categories (in increasing order of complexity):

1. *Zero-dimensional models.* The zero-dimensional (0d) energy balance model simply models the balance between incoming and outgoing radiation at Earth's surface, modeling Earth as a mathematical point in space; that is, there is no explicit accounting for latitude, longitude, or altitude. This is a very simplistic model, and includes the effective radiative temperature of Earth (including clouds and atmosphere) and provides an estimated average of Earth of 15°C. This type of model relies heavily on Earth reflectivity (albedo) and is capable of rapidly determining the impact of changes in solar output, Earth albedo (such as if we were to increase aerosols in the atmosphere), or Earth radiance on average Earth temperature. It is, however, not useful in pointing out the causes behind these changes and the temperature distribution on the planet, as it cannot address energy transfer within the global system.

2. *Box models.* These models are the simplest of climate models, excluding 0d models, and they reduce the global environment to a simplified set of boxes (also known as reservoirs) that are interconnected and exchange calories between each other. There are many assumptions in these models (homogenous mixing, free flow, uniform concentration of chemical species, etc.), to allow easy computation. Simple versions (small number of chemical species and reduced number of boxes) can be solved analytically, but most models are generally too complex for this type of approach and require solving by numerical techniques.

3. *Radiative-convective models.* Radiative-convective models add the geographical dimension to the zero-dimensional models and are capable of predicting, fairly accurately, globally and seasonally averaged surface and atmospheric temperatures. These models include the well-known and documented surface temperature/H_2O amount in the atmosphere feedback mechanism. Despite the higher degree of granularity that these models pose, they still have several significant drawbacks and are far from perfect. For a comprehensive review of these models, see Ramanathan and Coakley.[10]

4. *Higher-dimension models.* This is an expansion of the zero-dimensional model, to integrate manually specified horizontal transport of energy in the atmosphere (i.e., hot equator and cold poles, e.g.). It allows better zonal averages than a pure zero-dimensional model but is lacking in any dynamics (i.e., it is entirely static).

5. *EMICs (Earth-system Models of Intermediate Complexity).* EMICs are mainly used to investigate climate on long time scales at reduced computational cost. These models are mostly classified by their resolution, parametrization, and "integration." There are four generally recognized EMIC categories, dependent on the type of atmospheric simplification used:

   a. Statistical-dynamical models

   b. Energy moisture balance models

   c. Quasi-geostrophic models

   d. Primitive equation models

      As a data point, out of 15 models included in the IPCC's fifth assessment report, 26% were statistical-dynamic (4/15), 46% were energy moisture balance (7/15), and 13% each quasi-geostrophic and primitive equations models (2/15 each).

---

[10] V. Ramanathan and J. A. Coakley, "Climate Modeling through Radiative-Convective Models," *Reviews of Geophysics* 16(4) (1978): 465–489, doi:10.1029/RG016i004p00465.

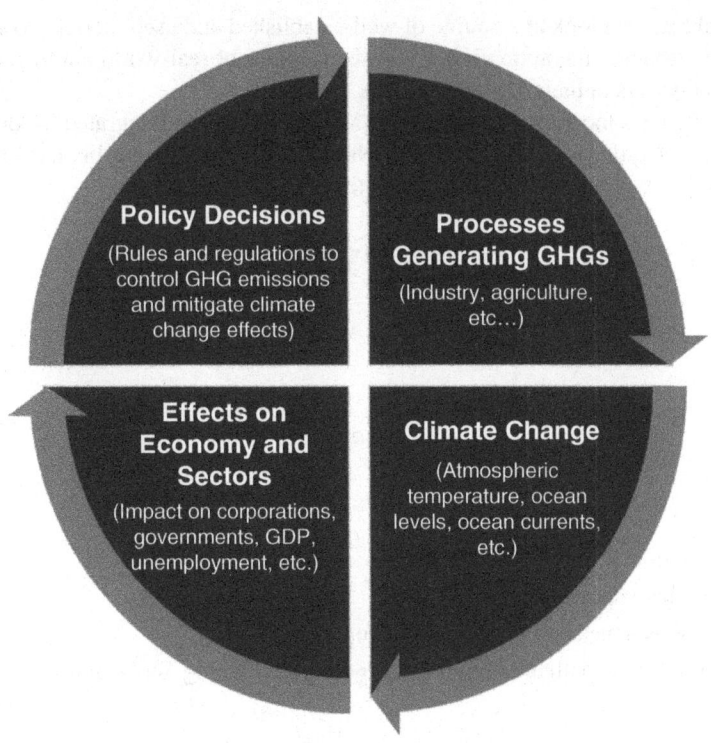

FIGURE 7.15 Workflow example of an optimization-based IAM.

6. *Global Climate Models, or General Circulation Models (GCMs).* GCMs are the most complex climate models currently in use. These models divide the atmosphere and oceans into discrete cells, each of which is treated as a separate computational unit (similar to how ABMs operate). Individual cell-level processes are modeled directly, and the interface between cells is then calculated by specific rules and boundary conditions. There are models that only focus on the atmosphere (AGCMs) and ones that couple the atmosphere with the ocean (AOGCMs).

In addition to these climate change models, there are also models that assess the impacts and damages of the changes on the economy and on specific sectors. The combination of these two types of models creates a new class of models called integrated assessment models (IAM). The IAMs are used to generate the SSP projections both for physical parameters (temperature, GHG emissions) and macroeconomic variables (GDP and similar). Most IAMs are general equilibrium (optimization) models, but there are also more traditional econometric models in use as well as ABMs (refer to Chapter 6).

A typical workflow of an optimization-based IAM is shown in Figure 7.15.

Most IAMs are built by combining two modules, an economic module and a climate module, which feed off each other and are used to maximize a specific utility function.

Typically, the modules fall along the following lines:

- *Economic module.* This defines the production function (GDP), including the impact of climate change on GDP (mitigation and adaptation costs, physical damage costs); the quantitative impact is calculated as a function of the average temperature, which is provided by the climate module.
- *Climate module.* A model of atmospheric and oceanic temperature distribution, including the dynamics of GHG emissions, based on assumptions and scenarios, some of which are exogenous (*ab initio* parameters) and others derive from the economic module.

We can now take a rapid look at a couple of well-established and used models, to allow our readers to transition from a generic, theoretic view, to some examples of real-world applications that are relevant for ESG practitioners in their day-to-day work.

DICE Model. Perhaps the most well-known IAM is the Dynamic Integrated Model of Climate and Economy (DICE) by Nordhaus,[11] who received a Nobel memorial prize for his IAM work.

The model maximizes present value of global utility, as follows:

$$\{\mu_t\} = argmax \sum_t U_t (1+r)^{-t}$$

where

$$U_t = P_t \frac{1}{1-\alpha} \left(c_t^{1-\alpha} - 1 \right)$$

and

P_t = global population at time t

c_t = consumption per capita at time t

α is close to 1 and is a measure of societal inequality aversion

μ_t is a control variable path that represents policies affecting the amount of GHG emissions (see below)

The optimization is subject to several types of constraints as outlined below.

Macroeconomic Constraints. Total output (Q) is defined by the standard Cobb-Douglas production function

$$Q_t = \Omega_t A_t K_t^\gamma P_t^{1-\gamma}$$

where

K_t^γ = capital input (a measure of all machinery, equipment, and buildings; the value of capital input divided by the price of capital) at time t

A_t = total factor productivity at time t

Ω_t = climate-related loss coefficient at time t

P_t = global population at time t

γ = elasticity of output with respect to capital

Consumption is the difference between output and gross investment:

$$c_t P_t = Q_t - I_t$$

where

c_t = consumption per capita at time t

P_t = global population at time t

I_t = gross investment at time t

---

[11] William D. Nordhaus, *"Rolling the 'Dice': An Optimal Transition Path for Controlling Greenhouse Gases,"* Cowles *Foundation Discussion Paper No. 1019,* Yale University, June 1992, https://cowles.yale.edu/sites/default/files/files/pub/d10/d1019.pdf

Capital K_t evolves according to:

$$K_t = (1 - \Delta_K) K_{t-1} + I_t$$

where

Δ_K = rate of depreciation of capital stock

Physical Constraints. GHG total emissions (E_t) are modeled by

$$E_t = (1 - \mu_t) \sigma_t Q_t$$

where

μ_t = an emissions control variable that represents policies affecting the amount of GHG emissions
σ_t = technological parameter that represents the trend in the GHG-output ratio (assumed known)
Q_t = total consumption, as defined above

The resulting GHG concentration in the atmosphere is calculated by:

$$M_t = \beta E_t + (1 - \Delta_M) M_{t-1}$$

where

M_t = atmospheric GHG concentration at time t
β = marginal atmospheric retention ratio
Δ_M = rate of transfer from the rapidly mixing reservoirs to the deep ocean

The temperature of the atmosphere T and the temperature of the deep ocean T_{DO} evolve according to:

$$T_t = T_{t-1} + \frac{1}{R_1} \left(F_t - \lambda T_{t-1} - \frac{R_2}{t} \left(T_{t-1} - T_{DO_{t-1}} \right) \right)$$

$$T_{DO_t} = T_{DO_{t-1}} + \frac{1}{t} \left(T_{t-1} - T_{DO_{t-1}} \right)$$

where

R_1 = thermal capacity of the upper stratum of the ocean
R_2 = thermal capacity of the deep ocean
λ = feedback parameter
F = rate of radioative forcing in the atmosphere at time t

Combining the burden of climate change mitigation/adaptation (numerator) and physical damages (denominator), we can therefore define Q_t (total consumption) as

$$Q_t = \frac{\left(1 - b_1 \mu_t^{b_2} \right)}{\left(1 + \theta_1 T_t^2 \right)}$$

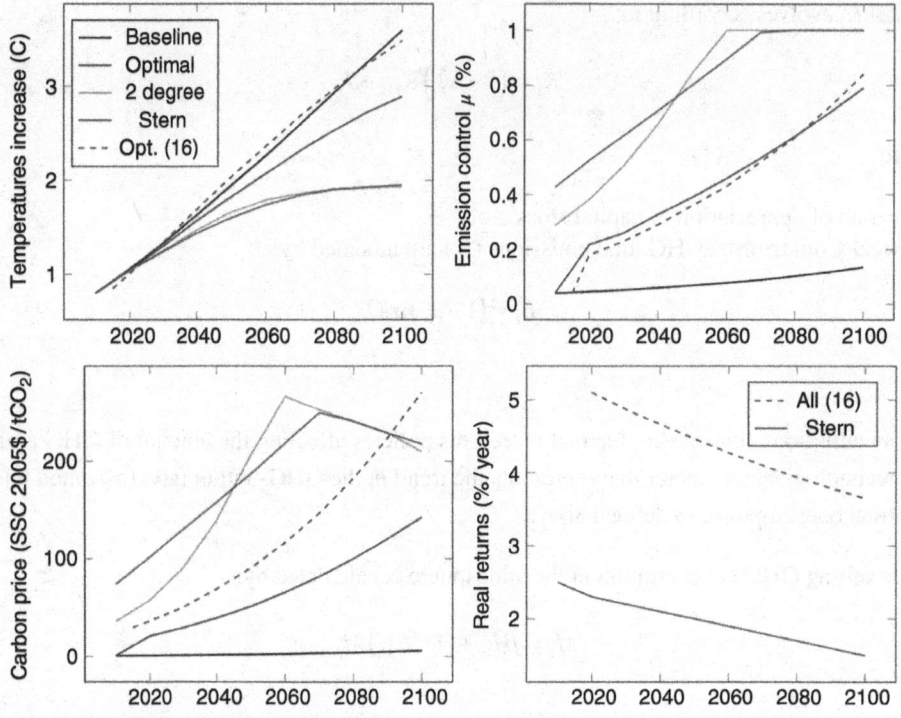

Source: DICE model 2013R (Nordhaus and Sztorc, 2013) – 2016R (Nordhaus, 2018).

FIGURE 7.16 DICE model projections on 2016 data.
Source: Theo Le Guenedal, "Economic Modeling of Climate Risks," PhD candidate (April 2019), Figure 5, p. 26, https://cdn .chappuishalder.com/wp-content/uploads/sites/18/2021/12/Climate_Economy_Modeling.pdf.

where

b_1, b_2 = parameters of emissions-reduction cost function
θ_1 = parameter of damage function
T_t = temperature at time t
μ_t = fractional reduction in GHG emissions at time t

Figure 7.16 shows DICE model solutions calibrated to 2016 data. Note that:
$T_{AT} = T_t$
$E_\tau = E_t$
and
SCC_t is the "social cost of carbon", calculated as $\dfrac{\delta C_t}{\delta E_t}$ (an incremental decrease in consumption per unit of GHG emissions). The actual value of SCC is quite sensitive to model parameters.

Most of the currently used models project the probability of average warming by more than 2°C by the end of the century as approaching 100%. It is noteworthy to notice how many of these models only include human emissions of fossil fuels and do not include releases of other GHGs (such as methane and CO_2 trapped in permafrost), which could induce a feed-forward mechanism that would result in faster and larger-scale warming. Given the high degree of uncertainty that is tied to outcomes of warming above the 2-degree level, the long time horizons involved, the large number of assumptions to be made, and the complexities of the financial markets' feedback loops into the macroeconomy, it is inherently difficult to take these projections directly into financial models and convert them to future losses.

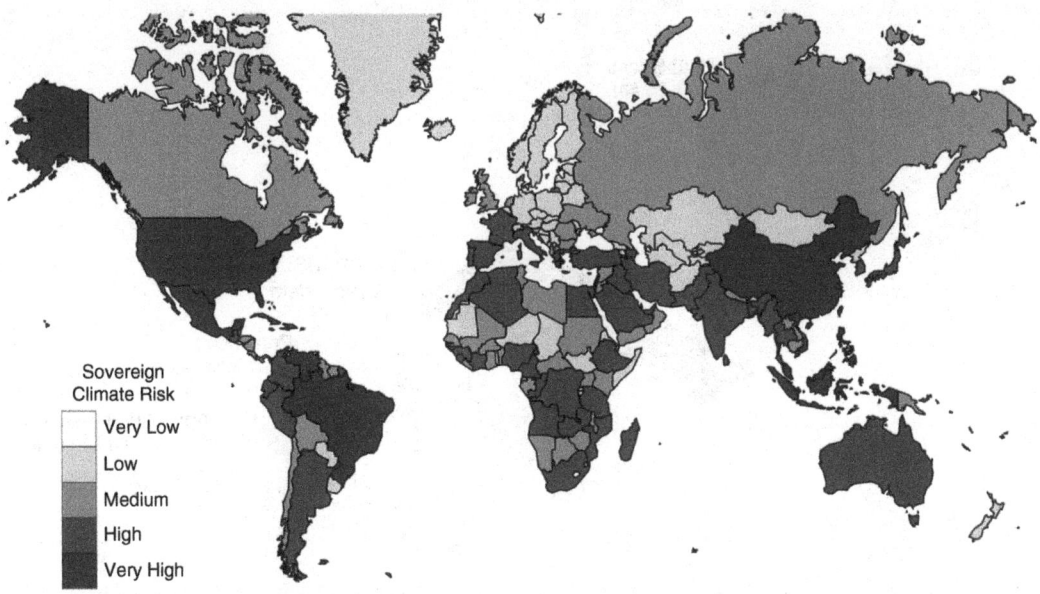

FIGURE 7.17   Sovereign climate risk model assessment.
Source: Four Twenty Seven (Moody's), https://427mt.com/

Sovereign Climate Risk Model. An alternative way of looking at the climate risk impact, which is currently in use, is to look at the climate risk at the level of sovereign nations, as is currently being done by one of Moody's affiliate startups. Figure 7.17 shows the assessment of all world countries, as generated by this model.

The Sovereign Climate Risk model assesses each country by projecting the percentage of population, GDP, and the agriculture industry exposed to dangerous levels of climate risk. The model interprets climate risk as an intersection of the following six physical risks:

1. Floods
2. Heat stress
3. Hurricanes
4. Sea level rise
5. Water stress
6. Wildfires

It then generates three maps showing projected future population, projected GDP adjusted for purchasing power parity, and current agricultural area.

For *wildfire*, *temperature*, and *precipitation-based indicators*, outputs from the NASA NEX-GDDP project are used. For *floods*, *hurricanes*, *sea-level rise*, and *water stress*, other environmental datasets are also leveraged to capture different risk dimensions. These include water stress data from the World Resources Institute Aqueduct tool[12] and hurricane data from the World Meteorological Organization. For *floods*, historical and simulated flood data considering high-resolution elevation data and data on regional flood infrastructure from Fathom, a flood analytics firm,[13] are used.

---

[12] "Aqueduct Global Maps 2.1 Data: Water," World Resources Institute, April 15, 2015, https://www.wri.org/data/aqueduct-global-maps-21-data
[13] "A New Benchmark in Global Flood Mapping," Fathom, https://www.fathom.global/

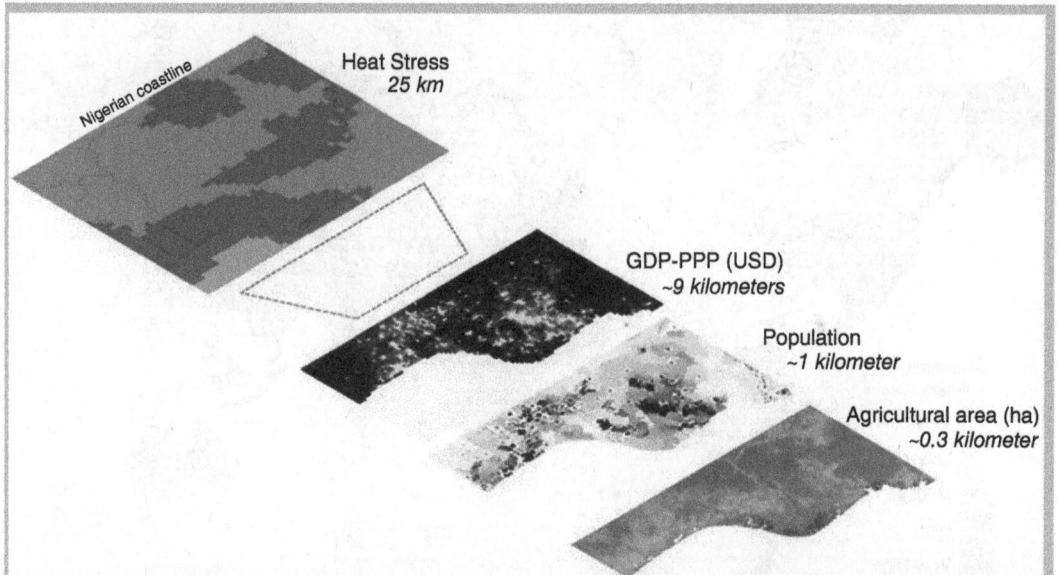

Heat stress and socioeconomic datasets mapped on the Nigerian coastline. Each dataset has a different granularity. The heat stress map shows the highest risk grid cells in dark, the GDP (PPP) map shows the largest GDP (PPP) with bright white, the population map shows the highest population densities in black, and the agriculture map shows agricultural area in light grey. © Four Twenty Seven. All Rights Reserved.

FIGURE 7.18   Heat stress and socioeconomic dataset mapped on Nigerian coastline.
Source: Four Twenty Seven (Moody's), https://427mt.com/

Once the mapping has been completed (Figure 7.18), areas are identified as high risk to each hazard if they meet the following criteria:

1. **Floods.** Exposed to at least 0.2 m of flooding during a 1-in-100-year flood event
2. **Heat stress.** Exposed to relatively high changes in temperature extremes compared to global average
3. **Hurricanes.** Situated in the regular path of cyclones
4. **Sea-level rise.** Exposed to at least some shoreline flooding during a 1-in-100-year coastal flood event
5. **Water stress.** Already has high water stress, or water supplies are diminishing and/or competition is expected to increase
6. **Wildfires.** Has high wildfire potential with sizable increases in future wildfire potential severity and number of high-risk days

The process of generating sovereign scores relies on identifying populated areas of a country that have high exposure to one or more climate hazards and calculating the total and relative portion of population, GDP, and agricultural area in these zones. The final scores are bucketed into five categories ranging from "none" to "very high" risk. By incorporating both total and relative exposure, the score provides a sense of raw amounts of social and economic capital within a sovereign that need to be safeguarded against climate hazards, as well as the sovereign's potential ability to absorb and recover from climate stress.

7.4 CARBON RISK AND CARBON PRICING

Carbon risk and carbon pricing are methodologies and tools that are used to measure future concealed impacts of current carbon usage and to make visible the "hidden" social costs of carbon emissions, thus incentivizing companies to transition to more carbon-neutral practices.

Carbon Taxes and an Emissions Trading System (ETS). A carbon tax is a tax levied on GHG emissions; it is normally denominated in dollars per ton of CO_2-equivalent emissions. Carbon taxes are special cases of so-called Pigovian taxes (named after Arthur Pigou, who developed the concept of externalities), defined as a tax on activities that produce negative externalities. In a broad sense, carbon taxes are designed to reduce Carbon CO_2 emissions by directly increasing the price of the fossil fuel that is causing the emissions, with the stated goal to incentivize alternative sources of energy and/or less power intensive methodologies to achieve the same results.

An alternative to direct carbon taxation, which is conceptually similar but allows for market trading, is emissions trading, also known as cap-and-trade. Under an emissions trading system (ETS), a central authority (usually a governmental body) allocates or sells a limited number of permits that allow discharge of a specific quantity of a specific pollutant over a set time period. The number of permits provided is usually based on recent history of emissions by each participating organization/polluter. Polluters are required to hold permits in amount equal to their emissions. Polluters that want to increase their emissions must buy permits from others willing to sell them. Figure 7.19 shows which countries/regions have implemented or are considering either direct carbon taxation or an ETS market system.

As of the date of writing of this book, the largest globally implemented ETS is the EU ETS.[14] Prices can be monitored daily at the EU Carbon Pricing Tracker,[15] and futures are traded both on EU and UK ETS permits.

Another useful resource to have a summary view of carbon prices across various initiatives is supplied by the World Bank at https://carbonpricingdashboard.worldbank.org/map_data.

From this dashboard we can generate the very informative plot shown in Figure 7.20, where current levels of carbon tax in different jurisdictions are shown vs. scope of coverage (i.e., what percentage of emissions are directly subject to tax). Note how most countries are still in very low overall percentages of coverage (only Japan, Ukraine, California, and Quebec are around or above 70% of GHGs covered by taxation).

Carbon Risk Measurement. Carbon risk for a company, or a sovereign, may be viewed as a proxy more broadly for transition risk. Carbon risk measurement quantifies corporate emissions as of today, by categorizing them into the three scopes that we saw earlier in this chapter (Scope 1, Scope 2, and Scope 3).

A commonly used form of carbon risk measurement, applicable for both corporations and sovereigns (with minor modifications), is carbon intensity, defined as:

$$\frac{CE}{R}$$

where

CE = carbon emissions (in CO_2 equivalent tons)
R = revenue (GDP for sovereigns)

---

[14] EU Emissions Trading System (EU ETS), Climate Action, https://ec.europa.eu/clima/policies/ets_en
[15] https://ember-climate.org/data/carbon-price-viewer/

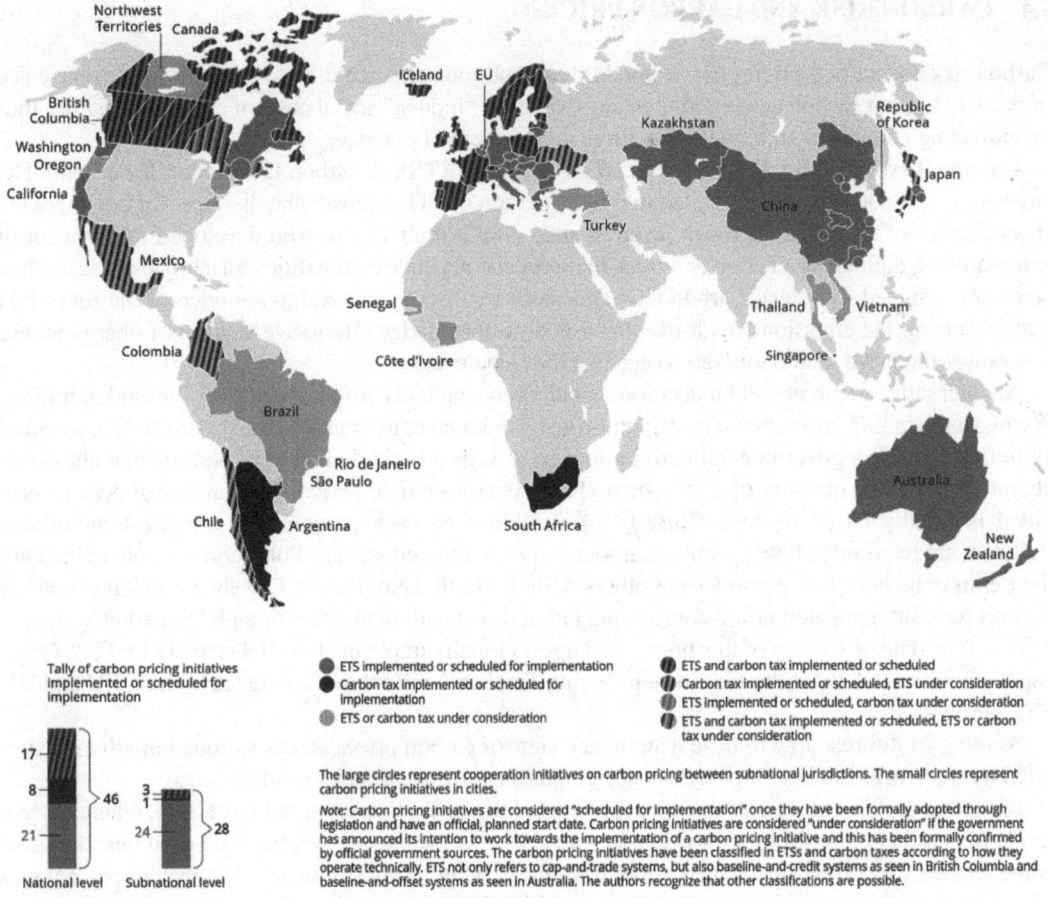

"State and Trends of Carbon Pricing 2019" *State and Trends of Carbon Pricing* (June), World Bank, Washington, DC.

FIGURE 7.19   Carbon pricing initiatives around the world.
Source: World Bank Group. 2019. State and Trends of Carbon Pricing 2019. Washington, DC: World Bank. © World Bank.
https://openknowledge.worldbank.org/handle/10986/31755. License: CC BY 3.0 IGO. http://hdl.handle.net/10986/31755

This metric allows rapid evaluation on how carbon-intense a business (or nation) is compared to others and can also act as a proxy on how sensitive such an entity would be to a forced reduction in access to fossil fuels or increased pricing/carbon taxes.

In addition to the data maintained by rating providers that we discussed earlier in the book, there are also two other dedicated data sources than can be valuable to the practitioner in ESG finance:

- *Carbon Disclosure Project (CDP),* https://www.cdp.net/en/. The CDP is a nonprofit that runs the global disclosure system for investors, companies, cities, states, and regions to manage their environmental impact. The CDP hosts, and makes available, a comprehensive dataset on corporate and city GHG emissions, etc.

- *Trucost Environmental,* https://www.marketplace.spglobal.com/en/datasets/trucost-environmental- (46). This is a subsidiary of S&P focusing on GHG emissions and other environmental data provision and analysis. It provides, to subscribing customers, access to data measuring environmental impact for approximately 15,000 companies. The data includes GHG emissions; GHG breakout; land, water, air pollutants, and waste disposal; natural resource and water use; revenue generated from each sector of a company's operations; and fossil fuel reserves, power generation capacity, and associated carbon metrics.

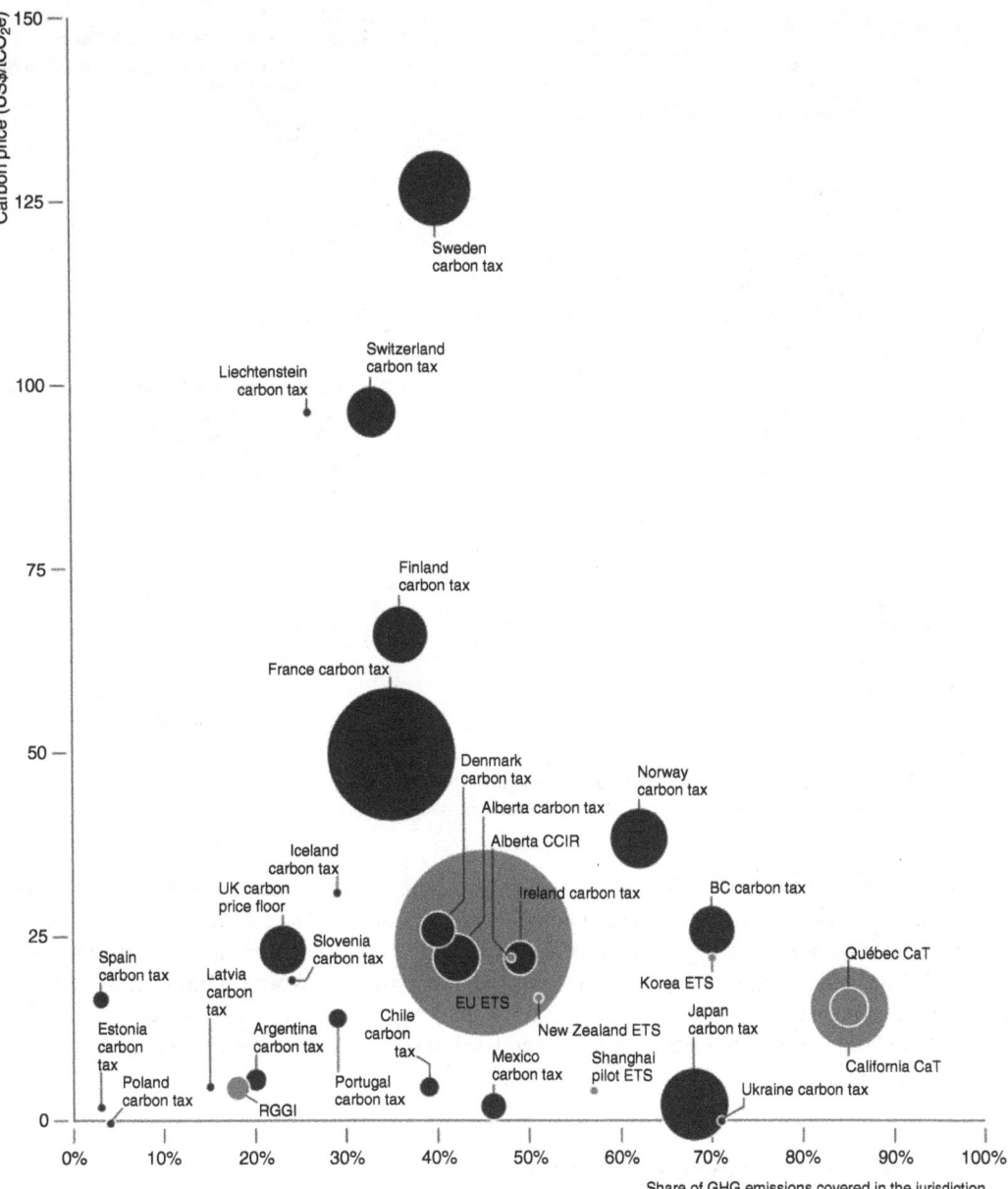

FIGURE 7.20   Carbon prices around the world today.
Source: World Bank Group. 2019. State and Trends of Carbon Pricing 2019. Washington, DC: World Bank. © World Bank. https://openknowledge.worldbank.org/handle/10986/31755. License: CC BY 3.0 IGO; http://hdl.handle.net/10986/31755 C BY 3.0 IGO."

While we review the topic of carbon risk measurement, it is also relevant to mention the Global Energy Monitor (https://globalenergymonitor.org), which is a nonprofit organization that collects and aggregates public data on polluting industries across the globe. An example of data available from their database and online dashboard is the visualization analytics on proposed new coal mines, as shown in Figure 7.21.

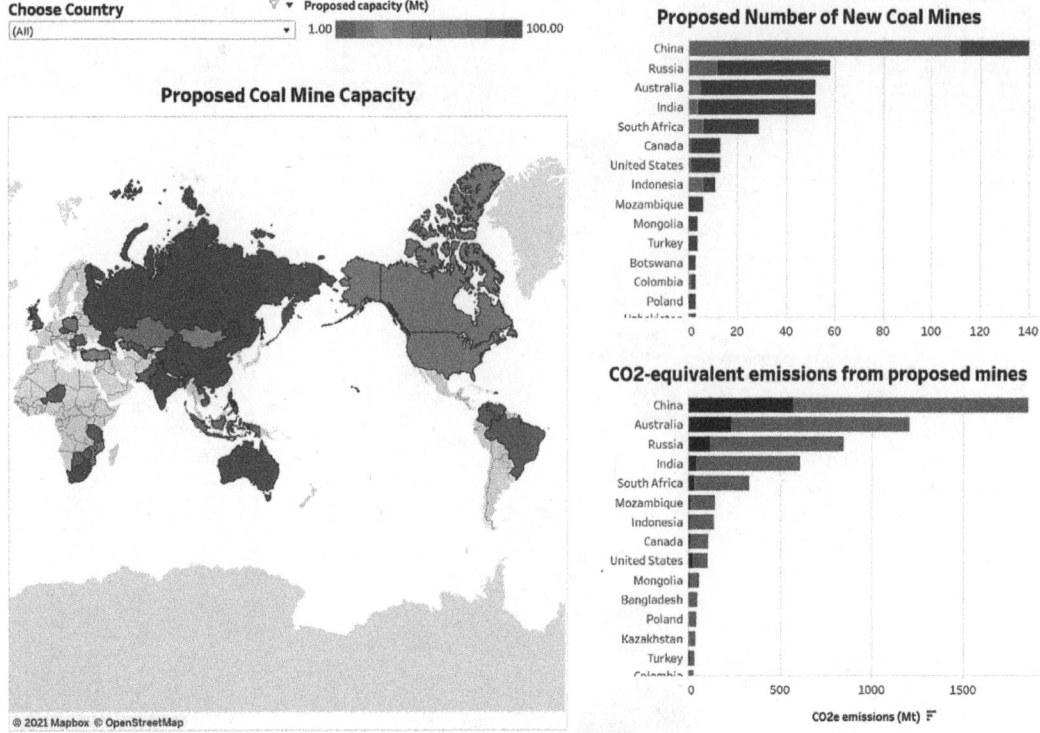

FIGURE 7.21   Coal mine tracker by the Global Energy Monitor.
Source: https://globalenergymonitor.org/projects/global-coal-mine-tracker/dashboard/

To conclude this cursory overview of carbon risk resources, we can also take a look at new technologies and initiatives in this space, a good example of which is Carbon Mapper (https://www.planet.com/carbon-mapper/), a nonprofit organization that is dedicated to collecting carbon emissions data utilizing satellite imagery. Carbon Mapper is in the process of deploying a hyperspectral satellite constellation with the ability to pinpoint, quantify, and track point-source methane and CO_2 emissions. Once complete, it should allow a hitherto unprecedented level of data access to GHG emissions data around the world.

7.5   CLIMATE RISK IN INVESTMENT PRACTICE

Having now taken a rapid view of climate risk methodologies and types, the question arises on how to actually utilize this vast amount of data and information for investment purposes.

Besides the creation of novel approaches, which are emerging with increasing frequency, there are a series of ready-made products on the market that allow the ESG practitioner to leverage climate risk concepts and ideas without the need to build indices or analytics from scratch. The more predominant of these are climate change indexes, which are available in different types and graduations from most major providers. Most of these are constructed by adjusting the weights in the parent index to reflect a judgmental score of "greenness" of individual companies. The new weights w_i in the index are therefore defined by:

$$w_i = \frac{s_i w_i^{parent}}{\sum_j s_j w_j^{parent}}$$

LOW CARBON TRANSITION SCORE	LOW CARBON TRANSITION CATEGORY		LOW CARBON TRANSITION RISK / OPPORTUNITY	
Score = 0	**ASSET STRANDING**		Potential to experience "stranding" of physical / natural assets due to regulatory, market, or technological forces arising from low carbon transition.	Coal mining & coal based power generation; Oil sands exploration/production
	TRANSITION	PRODUCT	Reduced demand for carbon-intensive products and services. Leaders and laggards are defined by the ability to shift product portfolio to low-carbon products.	Oil & gas exploration & production; Petrol/diesel based automobile manufacturers, thermal power plant turbine manufacturers etc.
		OPERATIONAL	Increased operational and/or capital cost due to carbon taxes and/or investment in carbon emission mitigation measures leading to lower profitability of the companies.	Fossil fuel based power generation, cement, steel etc.
	NEUTRAL		Limited exposure to low carbon transition carbon risk. Though companies in this category could have exposure to physical risk and/or indirect exposure to low carbon transition risk via lending, investment etc.	Consumer staples, healthcare, etc.
Score = 10	**SOLUTIONS**		Potential to benefit through the growth of low-carbon products and services.	Renewable electricity, electric vehicles, solar cell manufacturers etc.

FIGURE 7.22   Example: "Low carbon transition score" definition used by MSCI.

where

s_i = relevant score

w_i^{parent} = original weight of security i

The exact way in which the score is defined varies between indexes and index providers, but in general terms it is expected to reflect GHG emissions intensity, asset stranding due to climate change, relative "greenness" of revenue, and other environmental features, as discussed earlier in this chapter.

It is also important to factor how weights are largely based on current GHG emissions intensity and similar current measurements rather than on the market perception of the extent to which a particular security is exposed to climate transition risks. We come back to this distinction in later parts of the text.

Figure 7.22 provides an example of how MSCI calculates the carbon transition scores used in its climate change indexes.

It is interesting to note how some of the available indices also determine relative weights by considering projected impact of future carbon prices (under an ETS) on index constituents' revenues (usually under the assumption of unchanged GHG emission intensity). An example of this is provided by the climate change indexes published by S&P, as shown in Figure 7.23, which includes both types.

Green Risk Factor. We have previously discussed risk factor investing as a natural extension of CAP-M theory. If we assume that an environmental score is available for every constituent security, we can then repeat the Fama-French procedure to construct a "brown minus green" BMG risk factor.

We split the constituents into three subportfolios—brown, green, and neutral—and define the BMG risk factor return (R_t^{BMG}) as return of the brown portfolio (R_t^B) less the return of the green portfolio (R_t^G):

$$R_t^{BMG} = R_t^B - R_t^G$$

where both portfolios are value-weighted by market capitalization.

Overview of S&P DJI's Climate Indices

CATEGORY	S&P FOSSIL FUEL FREE INDICES	S&P CARBON EFFICIENT INDICES	S&P CARBON PRICE RISK 2030 ADJUSTED INDICES	S&P PACT™ INDICES
Objective	Exclude companies with embedded carbon reserves	Reduce index carbon intensities within industries	Reduce risk from companies exposed to carbon pricing	Align with a 1.5°C scenario
Carbon Data Used	Fossil fuel reserves	Carbon efficiency (carbon-to-revenue footprint)	Carbon price risk premium	Multiple datasets, including transition data and physical risk data
Methodology	Divest from any company with fossil fuel reserves	Tilt toward low-carbon-emission stocks using the S&P Global Carbon Standard	Reweight companies based on their current emissions and the potential impact of 2030 carbon prices	Optimized to meet multiple climate objectives and minimize active share
Companies Excluded?	Yes	Yes	No	Yes

Source: S&P Dow Jones Indices LLC. Table is provided for illustrative purposes.

FIGURE 7.23   S&P climate indexes overview.

BMG is now our new risk factor based on the environmental score, as can be seen visually in Figure 7.24.

Scoring Approach. In order to compose the carbon risk factor, we need to have an established methodology to calculate the underlying environmental score. While there are multiple options, we choose to highlight the one proposed by Görgen et al.[16] The starting dataset is composed of 55 carbon risk proxy variables from sources such as Carbon Disclosure Project and sustainalytics. Each of the 55 variables is transformed into a binary 0/1 based on whether the value is above or below the sample median; the variables are then grouped into three categories that may affect the constituent security's value differently:

- *Value chain* (V) reflects current GHG emissions.
- *Public perception* (P) reflects external environmental image of the firm: ratings, controversies, disclosure of environmental information, etc.
- *Nonadaptability* (A) reflects potential future emissions determined by emission reduction targets and environmental R&D spending.

Variables are averaged within each category, and the final score is defined as follows:

$$S = \left(\frac{2}{3} + \frac{A}{3}\right)(0.7V + 0.3P)$$

[16] Maximilian Görgen, Andrew Jacob, Martin Nerlinger, Ryan Riordan, Martin Rohleder, and Marco Wilkens, "Carbon Risk," August 10, 2020). Available at SSRN: https://ssrn.com/abstract=2930897

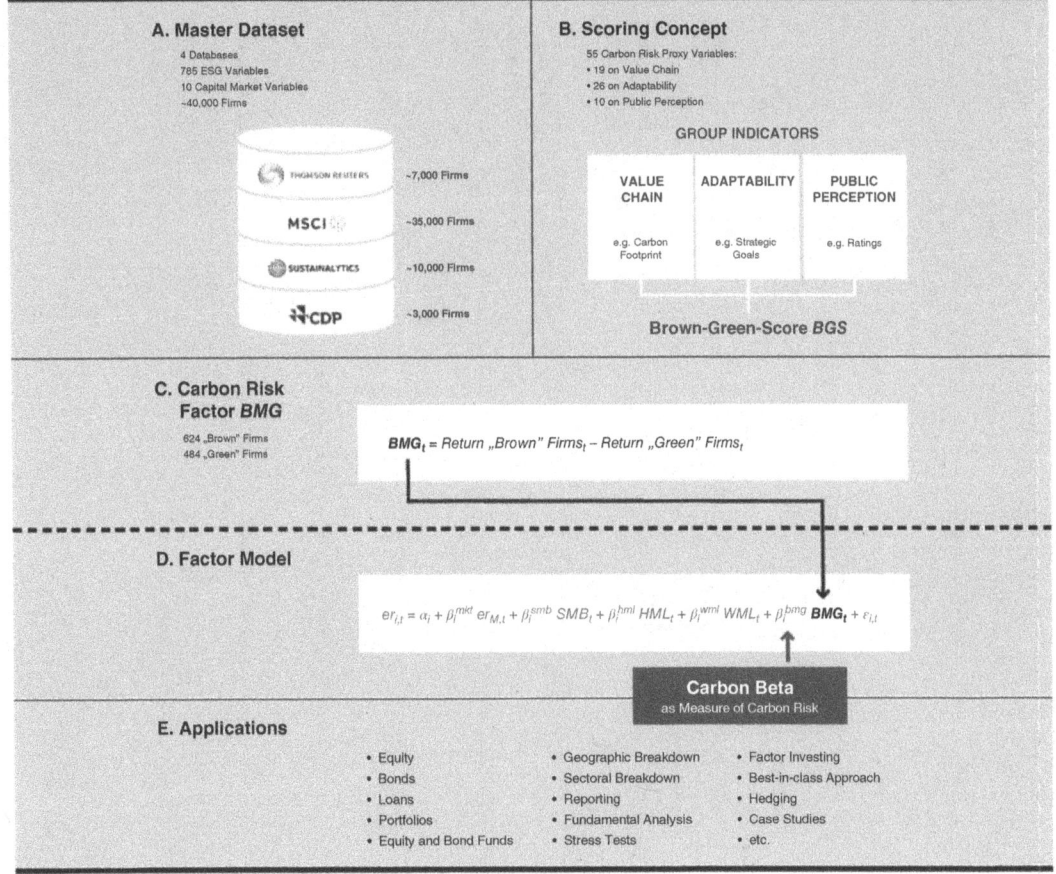

FIGURE 7.24   CARIMA model.
Source: Julia Ann Blinger and Chiara Colesanti Senni, "Taming the Green Swan: How to Improve Climate-Related Financial Risk Assesments," *Economic Working Paper Series* 20 (340) (July 2020), https://www.researchgate.net/publication/344269619_Taming_the_Green_Swan_How_to_improve_climate-related_financial_risk_assessments

The risk factor calculated in this fashion may be further subjected to the same types of analysis as risk factor series derived in other ways. As discussed in Chapter 2, a plethora of risk factors may be defined in a similar manner, and many of them are proven to contain information that is valuable to the researcher.

Climate Risk in Context. Chapter 7 provided a general overview of climate risk, arguably the most important and most consequential among E, S, and G "flavors." We started with a general overview of the current scientific perspectives on climate change, followed by a discussion of accelerating regulatory response to climate change in different jurisdictions and different approaches to modeling climate change in conjunction with its economics. We attempted to give particular emphasis to modern regulatory and governmental constructs created to address climate change, such as the concept of carbon pricing and its varying existing and proposed implementations around the globe. We concluded with a brief description of the forms in which climate risk had entered the investment universe and the specific instruments available to investors that quantify climate risks.

In the next chapter, we shift our focus to regulation of banks (the "sell side") and look more closely at stress testing – one of the main tools of financial risk management – and how banks and banking regulators use it to manage climate risks in banks' portfolios.

CHAPTER 8

Stress Testing for Banks

8.1 STRESS TESTING AS A RISK MANAGEMENT TOOL

We define *stress testing* as exercises of forward-looking assessment of the potential impact of various adverse events and circumstances on a banking organization. Banks are required to develop and implement effective stress testing frameworks as part of their broader risk management and governance processes.

Stress testing is an important approach to the quantification of risks the banking institution faces, alongside (notional) exposure measurement and VaR-like (value at risk) metrics that estimate loss as a distribution quantile. Unlike VaR, stress testing focuses on estimating loss outcomes (for a particular portfolio/product/business segment or for the entire bank as a whole) under a particular discrete scenario, describing a particular event or a macroeconomic or market outcome. A few simple but typical examples are:

- Estimate the profit and loss (P&L) impact on the bank's trading business if the oil prices fall or rise by 50%.
- Estimate the total change in the bank's capital if Italy leaves the Eurozone.
- Estimate the impact on the bank's liquidity if China experiences a severe macroeconomic recession.

A stress testing exercise is generally based on a specific scenario (e.g., "oil prices fall 50%" or "Italy leaves the Eurozone" used above), and its result is an estimate of impact to P&L, capital, or liquidity.

Impact on P&L is evaluated by the income statement, capital impact by the balance sheet statement, and liquidity impact using ratios (e.g., the ratio of high-quality liquid assets on the balance sheet to cash outflows over a set period).

Regulatory Guidance on Stress Testing

In the United States, the main regulatory document governing stress testing of financial institutions is Letter SR 12-7, "Guidance on Stress Testing for Banking Organizations with Total Consolidated

Assets of More Than $10 Billion" jointly issued by the Federal Reserve and the Office of the Comptroller of the Currency.[1] This document outlines principles that banks' stress testing programs should follow:

- *Principle 1.* A banking organization's stress testing framework should include activities and exercises that are tailored to, and sufficiently capture, the banking organization's exposures, activities, and risks.
- *Principle 2.* An effective stress testing framework employs multiple conceptually sound stress testing activities and approaches.
- *Principle 3.* An effective stress testing framework is forward-looking and flexible.
- *Principle 4.* Stress test results should be clear, actionable, well supported, and inform decision-making.
- *Principle 5.* An organization's stress testing framework should include strong governance and effective internal controls.

Similar guidance has been issued by regulators in other jurisdictions (e.g., ECB, PRA, and others). Many of these are, in turn, based on the Basel Committee's guidance: https://www.bis.org/bcbs/publ/d450.htm.

Top-Down vs. Bottom-Up Stress Testing. As the name suggests, there are two general approaches to assessing the impact of a particular scenario. In a top-down approach, the scenario narrative (starting point of the scenario process) is translated into projections for high-level macroeconomic and market variables. For instance, GDP, unemployment, and inflation rates are projected over a number of subsequent quarters; losses under this scenario are then estimated at a portfolio level, using, for example, historical regression relationships between the credit portfolio's default losses and macroeconomic variables such as the GDP of the country of risk/domicile. Alternatively, the impact of the narrative may be evaluated individually for every obligor in the portfolio, based on knowledge of each obligor company's business and idiosyncratic factors. These individual assessments aggregated across all obligors provide a portfolio credit loss estimate based on a bottom-up approach.

Most of the discussion here (unless specifically noted as such) applies to top-down stress testing.

Stress-Testing Process. A stress-testing exercise generally is composed of several distinct process stages illustrated in Figure 8.1. Each stage of the process represents a distinct activity critical to the end-to-end process.

Stress Scenarios. Stress scenarios are processes that banks have for designing scenarios for enterprise-wide analytics reflective of their unique business activities and associated vulnerabilities. Each bank develops a suite of specific scenarios that capture its material risks and vulnerabilities under a variety of stressful circumstances. The regulators expect these scenarios to be incorporated into the overall capital planning processes.

We define *stress scenario* as a combination of a (optional) narrative and a vector of shocks for relevant market and/or macroeconomic variables.

The basic approach to scenario design looks, in general terms, like this:

- *Choose the primary variables* to stress, covering both macroeconomic/market variables: GDP, interest rates, and idiosyncratic risks.
- *Design and expand the scenario*: Generate shocks for the primary variables. Secondary variable shocks are then determined as conditional expectations on the primary ones.
- Finally, *compute losses* (and capital impact, etc. as appropriate) under the scenario.

---

[1] Board of Governors of the Federal Reserve System, Federal Deposit Insurance Corporation, and the Office of the Comptroller of the Currency, "Guidance on Stress Testing for Banking Organizations with Total Consolidated Assets of More Than $10 Billion," SR Letter-17 Letter Attachment, May 14, 2012, https://www.federalreserve.gov/supervisionreg/srletters/sr1207a1.pdf

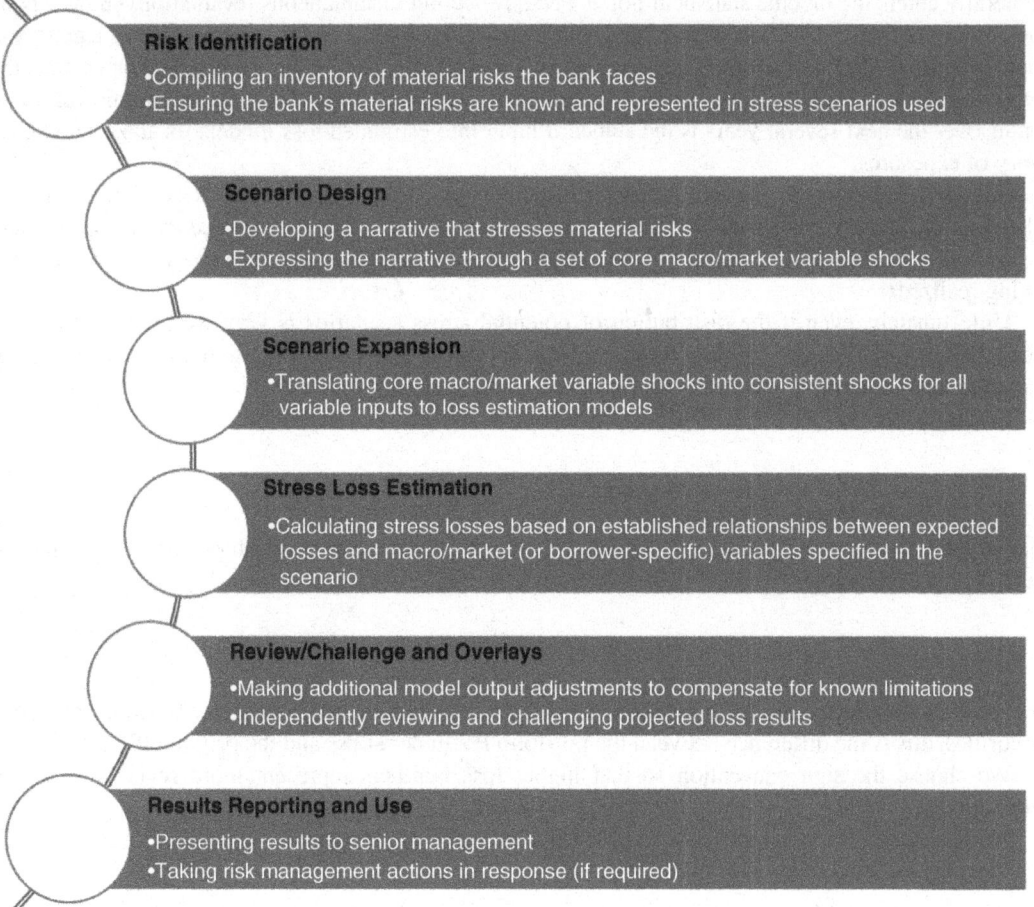

Risk Identification
• Compiling an inventory of material risks the bank faces
• Ensuring the bank's material risks are known and represented in stress scenarios used

Scenario Design
• Developing a narrative that stresses material risks
• Expressing the narrative through a set of core macro/market variable shocks

Scenario Expansion
• Translating core macro/market variable shocks into consistent shocks for all variable inputs to loss estimation models

Stress Loss Estimation
• Calculating stress losses based on established relationships between expected losses and macro/market (or borrower-specific) variables specified in the scenario

Review/Challenge and Overlays
• Making additional model output adjustments to compensate for known limitations
• Independently reviewing and challenging projected loss results

Results Reporting and Use
• Presenting results to senior management
• Taking risk management actions in response (if required)

FIGURE 8.1   Generalized stress-testing process.

The Federal Reserve Board provides a level of brief guidance on scenario design in the context of regulatory capital adequacy tests (Comprehensive Capital Analysis and Review [CCAR]/Dodd-Frank Act Stress Tests [DFAST] stress test), as follows:

The set of variables that a [bank] includes in its stress scenario should be sufficient to address all material risks arising from its exposures and business activities. A business line could face significant stress from multiple sources, requiring more than one risk factor or macroeconomic variable. The scenario should generally contain the relevant variables to facilitate pro forma financial projections that capture the impact of changing conditions and environments. [Banks] should have a consistent process for determining the final set of variables and provide this rationale as part of the scenario narrative.

It is important, for the purpose of stress scenario design, to distinguish the balance sheet exposures carried at *fair value* from those carried at *historical cost*. The former category is sensitive to market pricing and will respond instantaneously to market shocks, which usually occur very rapidly (over the course of days or even intraday). The appropriate form of stress scenarios for these is therefore a vector of essentially instantaneous shocks to relevant market quantities (prices, yields, credit spreads, etc.). On balance, other risk exposures are not held at fair value and are therefore immune (with some exceptions, such as "other than temporary impairment," etc.) to market sell-offs. The impact of those risk exposures generally enters the income statement not as P&L, reflecting instantaneous revaluation, but as a combination of default losses (net of recovery) and increase in credit reserves. Losses for this category of risk exposures (held at historical cost) are usually modeled based on future projections of (mostly) macroeconomic variables. Thus, a set of (usually quarterly) projections of macroeconomic variables' paths over the next several years is the standard input into estimated loss models for the second category of exposures.

Scenario Likelihood. We will focus on instantaneous stress scenarios (vectors of instantaneous shocks) first, although the discussion here is readily extensible to quarterly macroeconomic projections.

Scenario likelihood is defined as the probability of a given stress scenario (or a worse one) being realized.

Unfortunately, even if the distribution of potential stress scenarios is very well behaved (e.g., if scenarios are multivariate normal), translating the definition above into precise mathematical terms is far from straightforward. We start with the definition of scenario severity.

Let us denote

$$\vec{s} = (s_1, \ldots, s_N)$$

our stress scenario vector, where N is the number of risk factors (market variables) that our portfolio is sensitive to, and denote

$$F(\vec{s})$$

a scalar function that converts the scenario vector into a loss for our portfolio. (For a portfolio of market securities, this is the difference between the portfolio PV under stress and the original PV value.)

We choose the sign convention so that higher loss numbers represent more severe loss to the portfolio.

Next, assume $\vec{s}$ is a random vector drawn from the space of all possible vector shock values.

Then the joint distribution of

$$\vec{s} = (s_1, \ldots, s_N)$$

implies a particular distribution of $F(\vec{s})$.

We define *scenario severity* of a particular scenario vector $\vec{s}^*$ as the value of the inverse cumulative distribution (quantile) function of the loss distribution that corresponds to the $F(\vec{s}^*)$ argument.

Now assume that the multivariate distribution of scenarios has a continuous probability density function $p(\vec{s})$ and we can further define $p^* = p(\vec{s}^*)$.

The equation

$$p(\vec{s}) = p^*$$

defines a particular surface in the space of all plausible stress scenarios.

If the distribution of scenarios is reasonably well behaved, then the so-defined surface will separate the stress scenario space into an "inside" domain containing the origin and the "outside" one.

The *scenario likelihood* of scenario $\vec{s}^*$ can then be defined as the probability of a scenario vector being in the "outside" domain.

For example, if $\vec{s}$ follows multivariate normal distribution, then the surface described above is an ellipsoid centered at the origin, and the likelihood is defined as the probability of $\vec{s}$ being realized outside of the ellipsoid.

With more realistic empirical distributions, this surface is no longer a true ellipsoid, but the likelihood can be calculated the same way by integrating the PDF function outside the surface.

Unfortunately, even for two variables under the bivariate normal distribution assumption, our interpretation of scenario likelihood may lead to counterintuitive results. For example, certain scenarios are assigned lower likelihood due to being outside the ellipsoid, even though shocks to both variables are smaller than those for some scenarios on the ellipsoid. This feature suggests the need for a different likelihood definition, but known alternative definitions have not proven more robust or more intuitive at this point.

Mahalanobis Norm. Having discussed the geometric definition, we now introduce the closely related concept of *Mahalanobis norm*, which is useful in comparing the likelihood of two scenarios.

The Mahalanobis norm of scenario $\vec{s}$ is defined as

$$\sqrt{\vec{s}^T \Omega^{-1} \vec{s}}$$

One may verify that it satisfies all the properties of a geometric norm (distance from origin). A scenario with a higher Mahalanobis norm compared to another scenario is the less likely one.

It is easy to see that, if the scenarios are normally distributed, the Mahalanobis norm is proportional to the log-likelihood of the normal distribution $\sqrt{-2 \ln p}$.

The squared Mahalanobis norm follows the chi-squared distribution with n degrees of freedom, where n is the number of dimensions of the normal distribution.

Norm definitions extending the concept of Mahalanobis norm to more general distributions have also been proposed. For instance, one may first "normalize" all one-dimensional variables before computing the Mahalanobis norm of the transformed variables. Here, the transformation applied to each is

$$f(s) = N^{-1}\left(CDF(s)\right)$$

where CDF is the cumulative distribution function of the relevant one-dimensional variable, which may be determined empirically; this transformation converts a variable of any (known) distribution into an equivalent normally distributed one. (This generalization is related to the concept of Gaussian copula.)

Stress Loss and Capital Impact. The impact on the bank's income (including other comprehensive income) is typically modeled separately item by item on the income statement. Different items may be sensitive to either future macroeconomic variables' projection paths or to instantaneous market shocks (or both).

The ultimate objective of the stress test is to assess the resulting net impact to either the bank's earnings (Net income/P&L) or its capital (impact by the retained portion of earnings, other comprehensive income, and the bank's capital actions such as dividend distribution, share buybacks, etc.). If the stress test is used to assess capital adequacy (rather than just the Earnings/Stress loss impact), the metrics of ultimate interest are capital and leverage ratios. These ratios usually have prescribed regulatory minimums and are therefore a primary regulatory tool that limits banks' risk-taking. The most common/relevant/popular ratios are:

- CET1 capital ratio = Common equity Tier 1/Risk-weighted assets (RWA) ≥ 4.5%
- Tier 1 capital ratio = Tier 1 capital/Risk-weighted assets (RWA) ≥ 6%
- Leverage ratio = Tier 1 capital/Average total consolidated assets ≥ 4%

Typically, there are established explicit internal limits on stress losses that a given portfolio may sustain under a stress scenario of certain likelihood, to allow for prudent internal management of risk. The levels for stress loss limits are to be established consistently with the businesses' overall risk appetite.

TABLE 8.1   Impact on a stylized bank's income statement.

Income statement item	Approach / Comments
Pre-provision net revenue (PPNR)	Forecasting PPNR under stress is quite difficult and requires making material assumptions regarding future exposures and business volume growth. Macroeconomic variable projections are usually required as input, but the link between macroeconomy and PPNR is understandably not strong.
+ Net interest income (income less expense)	
+ Total noninterest income	
+ Trading securities P&L	Aside from market-making business's PPNR projection for the period, an instantaneous P&L from securities price shock is usually assessed. This P&L impact assumes no change to current exposures and requires instantaneous market risk factor shocks as input. Also includes changes in credit valuation adjustment for the trading book and other similar categories.
+ Investments income	Similar to trading securities, certain long-term investments (large strategic equity positions or alternative investments) are carried at fair value and therefore experience an instantaneous price shock. Similar immediate impact is assessed on fair-value loans and held-for-distribution securities (newly issued loans and bonds).
+ Commissions and fees earned	
+ Other operating income	
– Provision for loan losses	Includes provisions for period default losses net of recovery, as well as changes in future lending reserves. Under GAAP, loan reserves are estimated using the current expected credit loss (CECL) approach, where reserves held are calculated as a function of future macroeconomic variable projection paths.
– Other operating expenses	Includes operational risk losses (due to operational errors and/or fraud), legal penalties, and other miscellaneous categories of losses. These may be sensitive to macroeconomic projections or sometimes not dependent on either macroeconomic projections or instantaneous market shocks. Most operating expenses for a bank are related to IT costs and employee compensation; these categories tend to be less volatile than others.
Pretax income	
– Income tax expense	Taxes are difficult to forecast reliably; they are generally not directly sensitive to either type of scenarios (macroeconomic or instantaneous market shocks).
Net income	
+ Other OCI	
+ Other comprehensive income (OCI)	OCI is sensitive primarily to market variables, and specifically to their projections over time, as opposed to instantaneous shocks.
+ Unrealized gains/losses on debt securities and hedges	Banks tend to hold large portfolios of (primarily) interest rate securities to actively manage their balance sheet mismatch between their lending (assets) and deposits and other sources of funding (liabilities). These securities are held on the balance sheet at their fair value, but market repricing of these securities does not contribute directly to the bank's P&L; rather, their repricing is reflected in Other Comprehensive Income (below the line).
+ Foreign currency translation adjustment	Global banks hold large amounts of capital in foreign subsidiaries, denominated in foreign currencies. Banks may hedge all or part of the resulting FX exposure.

8.2   MACROECONOMIC STRESS SCENARIOS FOR CLIMATE RISK

NGFS Climate Scenarios. An important authoritative source of scenarios for the financial industry (and beyond) is the Network for Greening the Financial System (NGFS). The NGFS has developed a common set of scenarios designed to act as a foundation for analysis across many institutions, creating much needed consistency and comparability of results.

Financial regulators, as well as banks, use these NGFS scenarios to better understand the risks to the financial system, economies, and the banks' own business and balance sheets. NGFS scenarios are summarized in the NGFS Climate Scenarios for Central Banks and Supervisors.[2] We encourage the reader to study this excellent presentation in its totality.

The NGFS scenarios describe multiple alternative evolution paths for climate change and climate policy in order to provide a common reference framework. The NGFS's approach to scenario development is outlined in Table 8.2.

The NGFS scenarios demonstrate a range of potential lower-risk and higher-risk outcomes. It is useful to classify the six NGFS scenarios along two dimensions, as illustrated by Figure 8.2. Furthermore:

- *Orderly* scenarios assume climate policies are introduced early and become gradually more stringent. Both physical and transition risks are relatively subdued.

- *Disorderly* scenarios explore higher transition risk due to policies being delayed or divergent across countries and sectors. For example, carbon prices increase abruptly after a period of delay.

- *Hothouse world* scenarios assume that some climate policies are implemented in some jurisdictions, but globally, efforts are insufficient to halt significant global warming. The scenarios result in severe physical risk including irreversible impacts like sea-level rise.

Top-level climate change and carbon pricing assumptions across six scenarios differ as follows (see also Figure 8.3 for temperature and carbon price paths under different scenarios).

Orderly scenarios:

- *Net Zero 2050* limits global warming to 1.5°C through stringent climate policies and innovation, reaching global net zero CO_2 emissions around 2050. Some jurisdictions such as the US, EU, and Japan reach net zero for all GHGs.

- *Below 2°C* gradually increases the stringency of climate policies, giving a 67% chance of limiting global warming to below 2°C.

TABLE 8.2   Characteristics of NGFS scenario approach.

Comparison	Economic impacts
External research partner	National Institute of Economic and Social Research (NIESR)
Models	National Institute Global Econometric Model (NiGEM) v1.21 integrated assessment models (IAMs) (only GDP provided as an output in the database)
Inputs	Carbon prices, use of energy services, primary energy mix, physical risk damage functions
Key assumptions and uncertainties	Econometric relationships between variables hold; rational expectations and perfect foresight
Outputs	GDP (and components), unemployment, inflation, productivity, personal disposable income, house prices, interest rates, exchange rates, equity prices, etc.
Time horizon	Annual steps, up to 2050 (NiGEM)

Source: Adapted from NGFS 2021

---

[2] Network for Greening the Financial System, "NGFS Climate Scenarios for Central Banks and Supervisors" (June 2021), https://www.ngfs.net/sites/default/files/medias/documents/ngfs_climate_scenarios_phase2_june2021.pdf

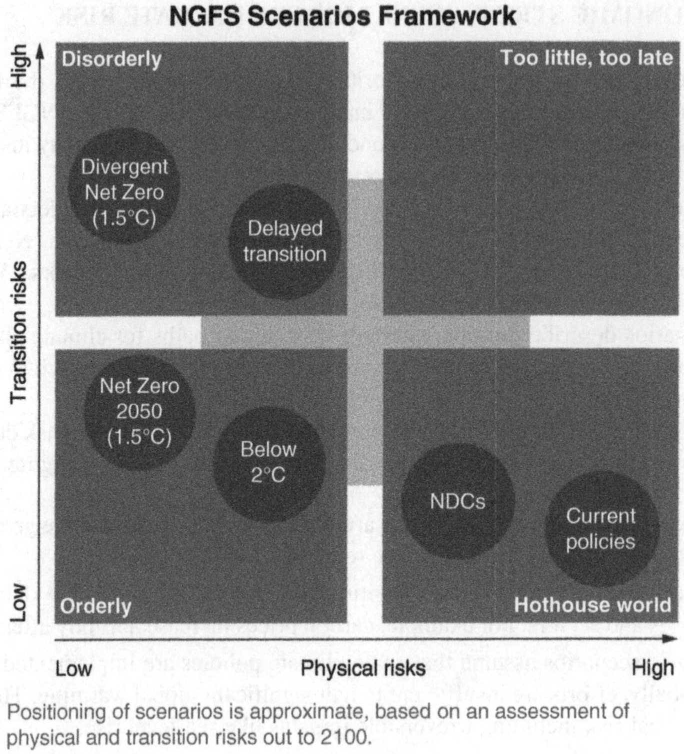

Positioning of scenarios is approximate, based on an assessment of
physical and transition risks out to 2100.

FIGURE 8.2   NGFS scenarios framework.
Source: NGFS 2021 / NGFS

Disorderly scenarios:

- *Divergent Net Zero (NZ)* reaches net zero around 2050 but with higher costs due to divergent policies introduced across sectors leading to a quicker phase-out of oil use.
- *Delayed transition* assumes annual emissions do not decrease until 2030. Strong policies are put in effect at that point to limit warming to below 2°C. CO_2 removal is limited.

Hothouse world scenarios:

- *Nationally determined contributions (NDC) scenario* includes all currently pledged policies even if not yet implemented.
- *Current policies* scenario assumes that only currently implemented policies are preserved, leading to maximum physical risks.

Nonfinancial assumptions made by scenarios are outlined side by side in Figure 8.4 (intensity of grey in the table).

There is a variety of transmission channels, through which climate change propagates through the economy and financial system and manifests in financial risks, as seen in Figure 8.5.

The NGFS scenarios contain projections for GDP, inflation, and unemployment, as well as the evolution of interest rates, commodity prices, and others.

These scenarios are designed to describe vastly different outcomes. Even considering this variability of outcomes, significant uncertainty remains in the future projections, due to the intrinsic uncertainties of the models and the known and unknown unknowns involved in the climate change phenomenon.

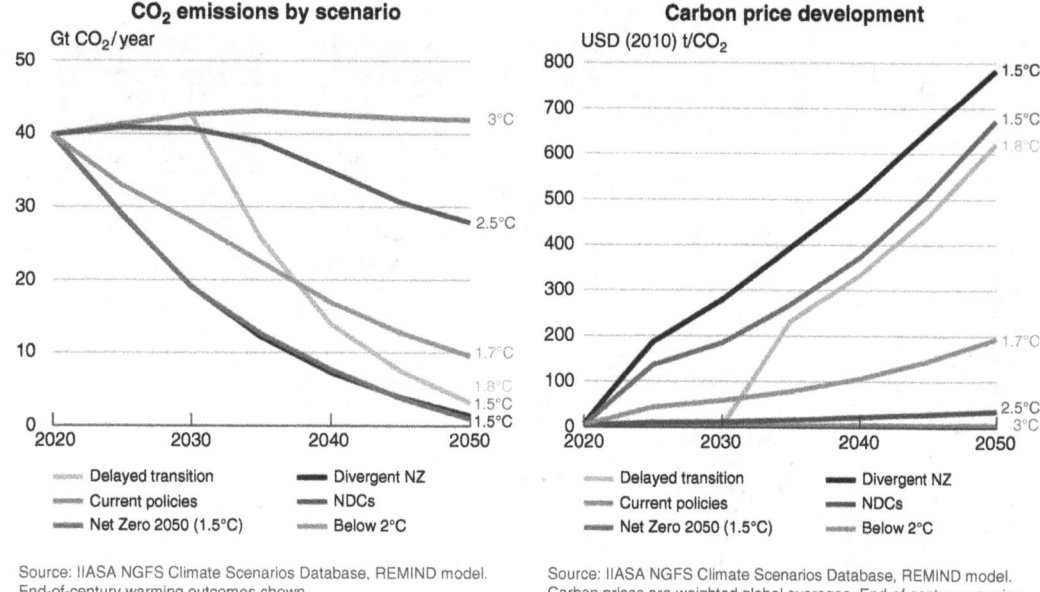

FIGURE 8.3 Temperature and carbon price paths under different scenarios.
Source: NGFS 2021 / NGFS

Category	Scenario	Physical risk	Transition risk			
		Policy ambition	Policy reaction	Technology change	Carbon dioxide removal	Regional policy variation
Orderly	Net Zero 2050	1.5°C	Immediate and smooth	Fast change	Medium use	Medium variation
	Below 2°C	1.7°C	Immediate and smooth	Moderate change	Medium use	Low variation
Disorderly	Divergent Net Zero	1.5°C	Immediate but divergent	Fast change	Low use	Medium variation
	Delayed transition	1.8°C	Delayed	Slow/Fast change	Low use	High variation
Hothouse World	Nationally Determined Contributions (NDCs)	~2.5°C	NDCs	Slow change	Low use	Low variation
	Current policies	3°C+	None – current policies	Slow change	Low use	Low variation

FIGURE 8.4 Physical and transition risks in orderly, disorderly, and hothouse world scenarios.
Source: NGFS 2021 / NGFS

It is worth mentioning that there is also significant variability and uncertainty in macroeconomic paths among different geographies.

World GDP impacts from transition risk are slightly positive in Net Zero 2050 as negative impacts on demand from higher carbon prices and energy costs are more than offset by the recycling of carbon revenues into government investment and lower employment taxes. GDP impacts are negative in the disorderly scenarios, as the speed of the transition, combined with investment uncertainty, affects consumption and investment. GDP losses from physical risks scale with the change in temperatures in the scenario. In the orderly scenarios, physical risks dominate (see Figure 8.6).

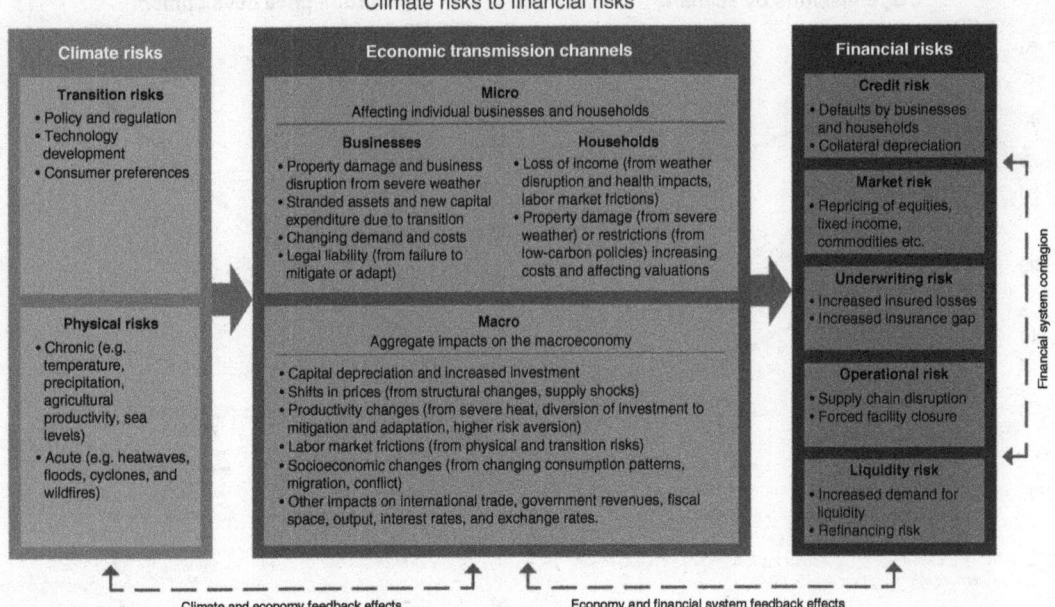

FIGURE 8.5   Transmission channels: Climate risks to financial risks.
Source: NGFS 2021 / NGFS

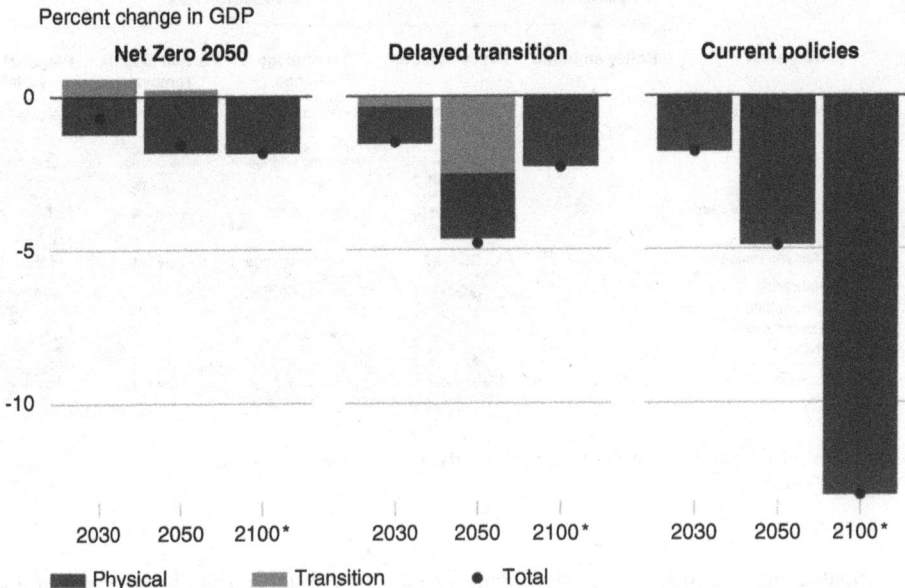

*Economic impacts are modeled out to 2050. To obtain an estimate of impacts in 2100, we took the estimate of chronic physical risk impacts based on the damage function, extrapolated acute physical risk increase (based on the period 2022-2050) up to 2100, and assumed no transition risk impacts at this point (ie. the GDP loss is solely due to physical risk).

Source: IIASA NGFS Climate Scenarios Database, NiGEM based on REMIND. IAM data and damage estimates from Kalkuhl & Wenz (2020).

FIGURE 8.6   GDP impacts relative to prior trend.
Source: NGFS 2021 / NGFS

Note that there is significant uncertainty remaining around macroeconomic projections under all proposed scenarios. It is important to note that some academic research suggests economic outcomes much more severe than those represented in the NGFS scenarios (see Figure 8.7).

A key driver of transition risk is the future pathway of fossil fuel prices and consumption volumes, with imminent spillover effects on the broader economy. Evidently, significant uncertainty remains around commodity path projections (Figure 8.8).

Bank of England Climate Biennial Exploratory Scenario Exercise. The Bank of England (BoE) conducts Biennial Exploratory Scenario (BES) exercises to stress-test financial institutions against a wider range of adverse conditions than those used in its standard capitalization tests. The 2021 BES focused on climate change–induced scenarios. It is also likely that BoE will incorporate climate stress testing into its general stress testing requirements for its supervised financial institutions going forward.

Climate BES 2021 (CBES) was intended by BoE to explore vulnerability of current business models to climate change. Participating banks measure the impact of the scenarios on their 2020 year-end balance sheets, which represents a proxy for their current business models. For banks, the CBES focuses on the credit risk in the banking book, with an emphasis on detailed analysis of risks to large corporate counterparties. For insurers, the CBES focuses on changes in invested assets and insurance liabilities. The CBES also explores how firms intend to adapt their business models over time, considering climate changes. The exercise also covers the management actions participants would anticipate taking in the published scenarios as well as participants' present and future planned approaches to managing climate risk.

Estimates of GDP losses from rising temperatures in the academic literature

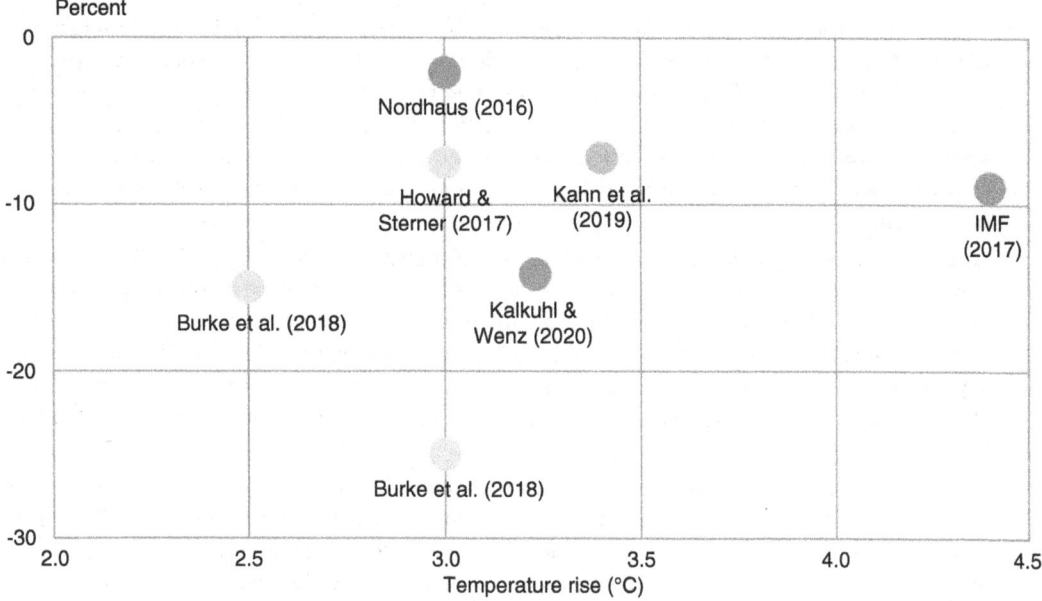

Source: As shown. Shade of marker reflects temperature baseline used in the underlying study. Burke, Howard, & Sterner (lightest shade) measure temperature rise relative to pre-industrial levels. Kahn (medium shade) uses a baseline of 1960–2014. Nordhaus, IMF, and Kalkuhl & Wenz (darkest shade) use a near-term baseline (ranging from 2005–present day).

FIGURE 8.7 Estimates of GDP losses from rising temperatures in the academic literature.
Source: NGFS 2021 / NGFS

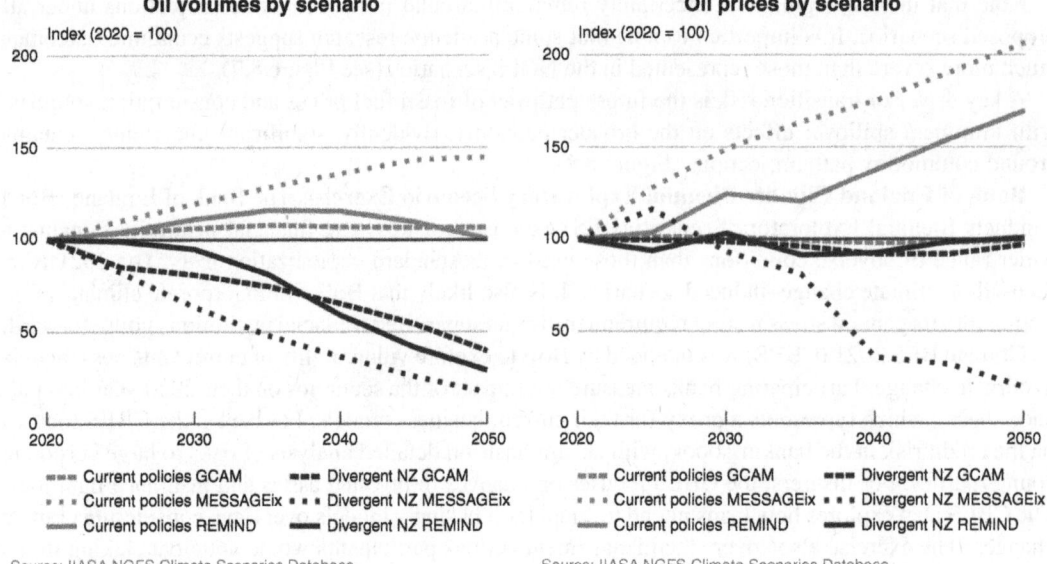

FIGURE 8.8 Oil volumes and oil prices by scenario.
Source: NGFS 2021 / NGFS

CBES considers three scenarios:

- *Early action.* The transition to a net zero emissions economy starts in 2021, so carbon taxes and other policies intensify gradually over the scenario horizon. Global CO_2 emissions are reduced to net zero by around 2050. Global warming is limited to 1.8°C by the end of the scenario. Some sectors are more adversely affected by the transition than others. The overall impact on GDP growth is muted, particularly in the latter half of the scenario once a significant portion of the required transition has occurred and the productivity benefits of green technology begin to be realized.

- *Late action.* The implementation of policy to drive transition is delayed until 2031 and is then significantly more abrupt. Global warming is also limited to 1.8°C by the end of the scenario. The more compressed nature of the transition results in material short-term macroeconomic disruption, particularly for carbon-intensive sectors. GDP contracts sharply globally. The rapid sectoral adjustment associated with the sharp fall in GDP reduces employment and results in stranded assets, with further consequences for demand and spending. Risk premia rise across multiple assets.

- *No additional action.* The no-action scenario primarily explores physical risks from climate change. No new climate policies are introduced beyond those already implemented. Global temperature levels increase by 3.3°C by the end of the scenario. This leads to material change in the sea level and a rise in the frequency and severity of severe weather events such as heatwaves, droughts, wildfires, tropical cyclones, and flooding. Global GDP growth is permanently lower and macroeconomic uncertainty increases.

Figure 8.9 provides an at-a-glance risk comparison between early, late, and no additional action scenarios. These scenarios are are broadly consistent with the NGFS ones, as can be seen from the mapping table in Figure 8.10.

These scenarios are broadly consistent with the NGFS ones, as can be seen from the mapping table in Figure 8.10.

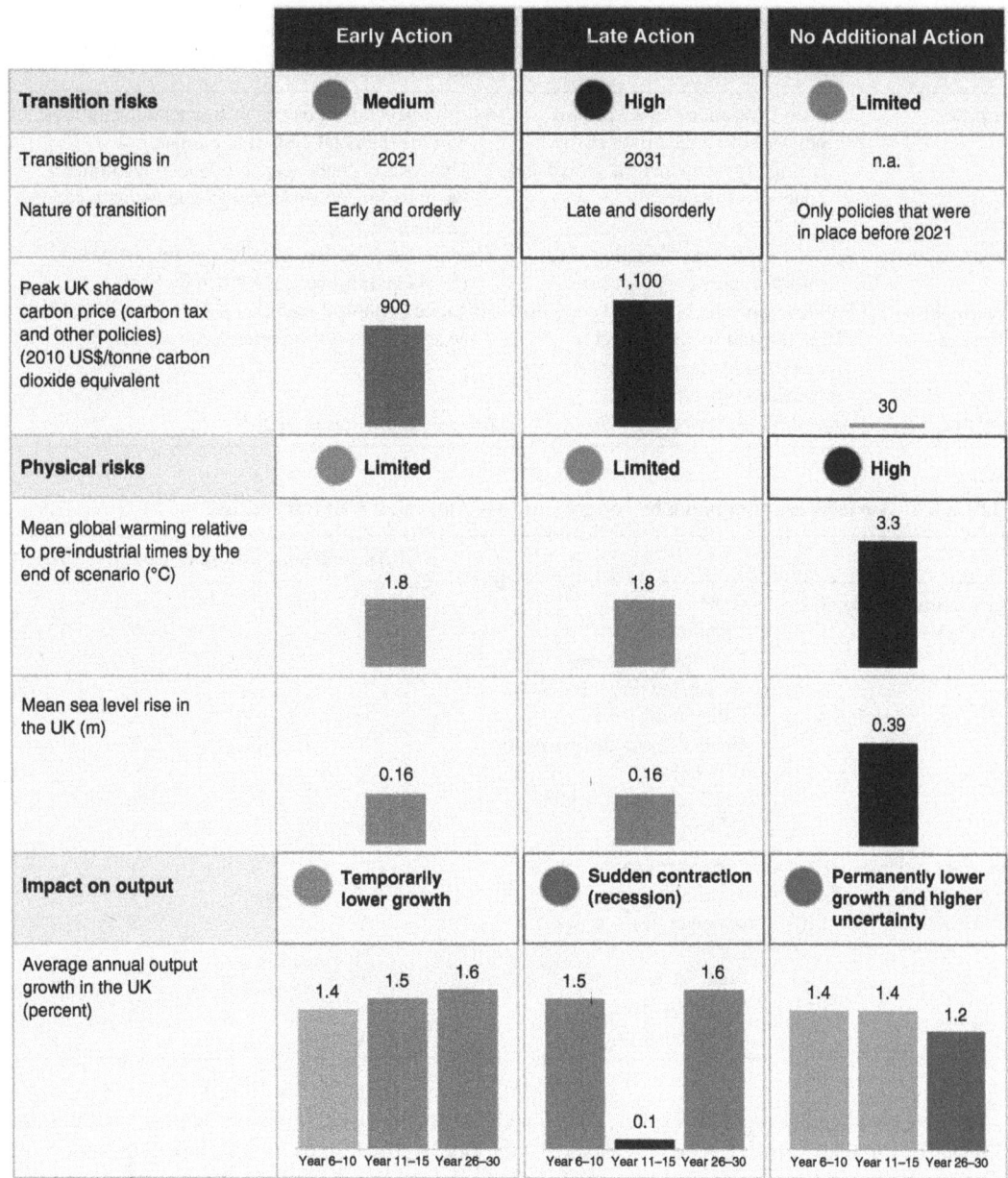

FIGURE 8.9   CBES risk comparison with early, late, and no additional action.
Source: https://www.bankofengland.co.uk

CBES scenario	NGFS scenario	NGFS Integrated Assessment Model driving physical risk assumptions	NGFS Integrated Assessment Model driving transition risk assumptions
Early Action	Net Zero 2050	GCAM 5.3 – 50th percentile (based on Disorderly transition)	REMIND-MAgPIE 2.1–4.2
Late Action	Disorderly transition		
No Additional Action	Current policies	GCAM 5.3 – 90th percentile	

FIGURE 8.10   NGFS risk comparison with early, late, and no additional action.
Source: https://www.bankofengland.co.uk

TABLE 8.3   High-level comparison between NGFS and BoE CBES scenarios.

	NGFS scenarios	Bank of England CBES
Purpose	Provide a common framework for analysis of climate risks to the financial system and the global and country economies.	Assess financial exposures of financial institutions and the financial system to climate risk. Understand challenges to financial institutions' business models and strategy and assess potential changes in strategy.
Target audience	As basis for financial regulators to inform supervisory exercises.	Exercise for large UK-based financial institutions (banks and insurers) governed by BoE.
Geographic scope	Variables specified for ~100 countries, but a much smaller subset of macroeconomic or financial variables types than BoE.	Financial variables' paths for US, EU and UK. Macroeconomic variables focus on G10.
Horizon	Annual projections until 2050.	Annual projections until 2050.

TABLE 8.4   Variable representation by category in NGFS and BoE CBES scenarios.

		NGFS scenarios	Bank of England CBES
Macroeconomic variables	GDP	Y	Y
	Inflation (CPI)	Y	Y
	Unemployment rate	Y	Y
	Real Estate Price Index	Y	Y
	Policy rate	No	Y
	Gross value added by sector	Y	Y
	Population	Y	No
	GHG emissions volume	Y	No
	Carbon price	Y	Y
Financial variables	Credit spreads	No	Y
	Sovereign yields	Y	Y
	Interest rates	Y	Y
	FX	No	Y
	Equity prices	Y	Y
	Volatility index	No	Y
	Commodity prices	Y	Y

The BoE additionally provides explicit annual paths until 2050 for 97 macroeconomic variables and 57 financial variables, which can be downloaded at the BoE website: https://www.bankofengland.co.uk/stress-testing/2021/key-elements-2021-biennial-exploratory-scenario-financial-risks-climate-change.

Scenario Sources Comparison. We compare, briefly, the NGFS and BoE CBES scenarios in Table 8.3. Overall and unsurprisingly, the BoE scenarios focus more on financial projections and are more specific to the financial industry in terms of their objective and construction. These BoE scenarios may be viewed as a more specific/granular adaptation of the broader NGFS framework to financial institutions' stress testing.

While the NGFS geographic coverage is much more granular, the variable coverage is significantly larger in BoE scenarios, as shown in Table 8.4.

8.3   CLIMATE LOSS MODELING

As discussed in section 8.1, there is a wide range of approaches to estimating potential losses under a given scenario. The way expected losses are calculated for a particular scenario depends on whether we focus on instantaneous losses due to repricing of price-sensitive exposures or on credit losses in future periods and relevant credit reserving.

Credit-reserving models are generally outside the scope of this text; however, even for instantaneous shocks where loss estimation is reduced to repricing of exposures, a significant body of work is needed to convert our starting point of a scenario narrative into the ultimate loss estimate. This work is mainly on prescribing appropriate shocks for different traded instruments.

Calibration of Shocks. We start designing our scenario by assuming a generic inflationary risk-off scenario (policy interest rates rise, while risky assets depreciate across asset classes) calibrated to a specific likelihood. (See the section on likelihood and Mahalanobis norm for a likelihood calibration discussion.) We will use this risk-off scenario as a general baseline.

Scenario design is, by definition, a largely judgmental process. Adjusting a generic adverse scenario is, obviously, not the only available approach; the alternative where stress scenarios are designed and calibrated "from scratch" is equally viable.

We will now introduce further adjustments to our generic scenario.

Impact Differentiation by Industry. The first critical step in determining the ultimate impact of carbon tax on market prices is the estimation of tax impact on the corporates' income statements. We estimate gross margin impact of carbon tax by following a sequence of calculations:

- *Retrieve historical data on Scope I emissions by industry.* These can be sourced from EXIOBASE, a public database of global ecological data.[3]
- *Retrieve GDP by industry data.* These are available from numerous sources (e.g., compiled by Bloomberg). One may need to map industry classifications, though, since government agencies such as the Bureau of Economic Analysis (BEA) use a somewhat different industry taxonomy from, say, Global Industry Classification Standard (GICS).
- *Estimate next-year emissions by industry.* Assuming unchanged (in the near term) emissions' intensity per \$1 of GDP by industry, we therefore assume that emissions by industry grow at the same rate as real GDP of each industry. We can use BEA growth forecasts or another source for GDP projections. Similarly, we apply the same GDP by industry projections to generate dollar GDP estimates.
- *Estimate lost revenue.* The dollar loss by industry (gross margin impact) is a product of three factors:

  1. Estimated next-year emissions by industry (measured in tons of CO_2 emissions, CO_2e).
  2. Carbon tax (in dollars per ton of CO_2e).
  3. Pass-through ratio: 100% if none of the tax is passed through to the consumer and therefore the tax is fully absorbed by the producer, 0% if the tax is fully passed through and therefore the producer's gross margin is unaffected, or an estimated ratio value in between.

     Once we have estimated dollar impact, we convert it to relative (percentage) impact to earnings by dividing the amount by the GDP amount by industry.

Next, we must convert estimated earnings impact for each industry into a change estimate for market prices.

A somewhat optimistic calculation assumes that equities' P/E is not impacted by the carbon tax introduction: By definition, stock price is decomposed into a product of estimated earnings and P/E ratio. If the P/E ratio is indeed unaffected by the tax (alternatively, valuation assumptions about earnings growth and discount rate do not change), the equity price impact in percentage points equals the percentage impact to earnings.

It is probable (as it is the stated goal of the carbon tax!) that the introduction of the tax will signal that profound changes to the industry's strategy/business model are required. This likely means that,

---

[3] "EXIOBASE 3," March 8, 2021, https://zenodo.org/record/4588235#.YvF0Wy-B1cB. For background information on EXIOBASE, please refer to Arnold Tukker, Richard Wood, and Stefan Giljum, "Relevance of Global Multi Regional Input Output Databases for Global Environmental Policy: Experiences with EXIOBASE 3," *Journal of Industrial Ecology* 22(3) (April 2018) 477–484, https://onlinelibrary.wiley.com/toc/15309290/2018/22/3

until the industry adapts to the new strategic environment, which is time-consuming and costly, it should be worth less for the same amount of dollar earnings than before the tax introduction (i.e., its P/E ratio is expected to decrease, more significantly for more polluting industries).

We also expect it to be likely that an assumption of unchanged P/E ratio will therefore underestimate the total shock. Additionally, we must also expand the equity price shocks determined in this way to include shocks to other asset classes, particularly credit.

Deriving consistent credit spread shocks is far from trivial; a more sophisticated derivation would rely on a family of capital structure models including the Merton model, which established a relationship between a corporate entity's equity and debt prices and equity volatility.

A discussion of capital structure models, however, is beyond the scope of this text, and we shall leave it to our readers to research on their own, if so inclined.

A much simpler and more practical alternative is to observe how a corporate entity's equity and debt prices historically reacted to adverse scenarios.

The relationship between equity and debt prices changes with rating and industry. This is primarily due to different levels of leverage typical for each category; for example, lower-rated companies tend to have higher leverage, and therefore their debt prices react to an adverse macro shock more strongly relative to their equity.

In practice, we bucket our corporate portfolio by rating and industry and observe the ratios between equity and debt price shocks in an adverse past episode (e.g., 2008 Global Financial Crisis) separately for each bucket.

Chapter 7 discusses a sovereign climate risk model that assesses sovereigns based on their exposure to climate risks. The actual magnitude of a credit spread shock sovereign debt will experience under the scenario is a function of two components:

1. Exposure to climate risks assessed by the sovereign climate risk model or an alternative model with the same purpose
2. The ability of a sovereign to withstand this adverse impact, which can be roughly proxied by its current credit rating

A few other important considerations remain, especially those regarding credit indexes and structured credit and physical risks, including risks to real estate:

- *Credit portfolio products.* We have so far focused on deriving shocks to individual corporate and sovereign obligors. The shock to credit indexes (which are widely used for hedging spread risk and therefore typically constitute a large portion of a bank's portfolio) must be assigned consistently with the shocks to individual index constituents. Similarly, structured credit instruments (e.g., collateralized loan obligations) will experience a market stress that is driven, at least in part, by the stresses to the instruments in the underlying collateral portfolio.

- *Balance sheet and earnings impact beyond carbon tax.* Corporates in many industries may be materially affected in ways other than the carbon tax introduction already discussed. For example, the insurance industry may experience a severe hit to its earnings because insurance payout liabilities will increase drastically as the physical risk increases (more frequent flooding, hurricanes, wildfires, etc.). Real estate valuation will also be severely affected; companies with major real estate holdings may experience significant write-downs due to impairment. Similarly, the energy industry will be heavily exposed to the risk in "stranded assets"; energy reserves on companies' balance sheets will need to be written down.

The following section briefly demonstrates how to apply these concepts in practice.

8.4 CLIMATE STRESS TESTING EXERCISE

We conclude with a realistic do-it-yourself stress testing exercise. The reader is encouraged to follow the instructions below to perform a stress testing exercise given a particular scenario narrative focused on climate risk. Please apply this scenario to a stylized model of a bank. It may be helpful to use 10-K filings of an existing bank of your choosing when performing the exercise.

Scenario Narrative. The scenario we consider focuses on the transition risks; its assumptions are close to those under the Bank of England CBES "early action" scenario. In order to achieve "Net Zero 2050," governments of the US, UK, and EU agree to immediately introduce a common carbon tax of $100 per ton of CO_2 emissions, increasing at a rate of $50 per ton of CO_2e over the next five years and at a rate of $30 per ton of CO_2e thereafter.

The governments are expected to use the tax proceeds to – at least partially – alleviate the negative shock to the economy. This will be done via three channels:

1. *Subsidies to consumers and small businesses*, coupled with tax breaks and incentives promoting energy efficiency and low-carbon-emission technologies.

2. *Incentives for businesses* to convert production and adopt low-emission technologies instead. Carbon cap-and-trade system, where free carbon credits are gradually phased out over the next several years.

3. *Large government-led infrastructure projects* to facilitate the economy's transition to zero-emission technologies (e.g., modernization of the electricity distribution grid, electric vehicle charging stations grid, etc.).

We conservatively assume that the new carbon taxes are fully internalized by corporate earnings except for the utilities industry. Utilities are assumed to fully pass the new tax onto consumers, resulting in an inflation spike.

Commodity prices rise universally. The inability to adjust consumer behavior and adopt new technologies in the near term and a sharp rise in energy costs leads to significantly higher fuel prices. Industrial metals also appreciate due to increased demand from technology retrofitting needs.

Policy responses are notoriously difficult to predict given the lack of historical consistency. Higher commodity prices affect product prices downstream, leading to a rise in inflation. The assumption we are making is that, to combat inflation concerns that will be considered more relevant than the fear of initiating a recession, the central banks will raise interest rates in a coordinated manner.

Finally, drag from the new tax on the current fossil fuel–dependent economy before its future adaptation, resulting recession fears, and a surprise drop in future earnings and therefore attractiveness of large segments of the corporate sector result in a general risk-off environment. Risk premia rise across all asset classes: Credit spreads widen, volatility in all markets increases, and equity prices fall.

Market Scenario Design Steps. We will focus on stress testing the trading book here, although the steps below may be expanded to include banking book stress testing, as well as risk types beyond market risk. The background behind these steps has been explained in Section 8.3. Please follow the scenario design steps below for this exercise:

- *General risk-off scenario*. Define a generic scenario where, consistent with the narrative above, credit spreads rise uniformly, short interest rates rise, and energy prices increase. Preserving correlations between these three risk factors, calibrate the shock magnitude so that the scenario defined by a three-dimensional vector of shocks has a likelihood of 1-in-50 years. Use the Mahalanobis norm of the three-dimensional scenario vector to establish scenario likelihood.

- *Impact of carbon tax on corporate earnings*. Estimate the tax impact on companies' earnings using the approach described in Section 8.3. Use publicly available statistics data as necessary.

- *Corporate equity prices*. Choose an approach for translating earnings' impact estimates into impact on equity prices.
- *Corporate credit spreads*. Choose an approach for translating earnings' estimates into impact on debt prices changes (either directly from financial statements' impact or derived from equity price shock).
- *Sovereign credit*. Using publicly available data, estimate the relative vulnerability of relevant sovereigns and their respective credit spread shocks.
- *Structured credit and credit index impact*. From the credit spread shocks derived in the two previous steps, consistently estimate the shocks to major credit indexes (and structured credit positions, if relevant).
- *Additional impact on insurance industry*. The insurance industry is especially vulnerable to the physical risks involved in this scenario and is expected to experience adverse impact beyond that stemming from the imposition of carbon tax. Estimate the increase in insurance payout costs based on available data regarding industry exposure.
- *Additional impact on real estate*. Assess which direct or derivative real estate exposures (whether commercial and residential) are affected and quantify the effect on pricing.
- *Additional impact of stranded assets on the energy industry*. Similarly, estimate the impact on proven reserves on the energy industry's balance sheets and devise an approach to estimate incremental pricing changes of relevant write-downs.

Stress Loss Estimation. For our illustrative exercise, let us assume that the bank's hypothetical trading book has the following risk allocation:

- $5 mm equity delta (sensitivity to 1% increase in equity prices)
- $2 mm vega (sensitivity to 1 point increase in equity volatility)
- $20 mm interest rates DV01
- $10 mm sovereign CR01 (30% Italy, 30% Mexico, 40% developing EMEA)
- $15 mm corporate CR01 (industry mix mirrors industries' contributions to the US GDP)
- $1 mm delta to oil
- $1 mm delta to commercial real estate

To conclude the exercise, try to estimate the stress loss the portfolio above would experience under the scenario described.

8.5 CONCLUDING NOTES

As we come to the end of this book, it is a good opportunity to take stock of what topics we covered and the key takeaways.

Primarily, we have highlighted the underlying fundamentals upon which the pillars of ESG finance rest. In the environmental dimension, this has taken the form of a review of the science behind climate change and the impacts that it will have on the environment and human activities, as shown in Chapter 7. The social and governance dimensions, on the other hand, were brought into focus in Chapter 1.

After setting the basis for the topics that ESG finance engages in, we shifted our focus to what data, tools, methodologies, and practical coding examples are required for the practitioner of quantitative ESG finance to excel in the field.

While it has not been possible to cover every possible aspect and technique of interest, we tried to ensure that the major areas and topics of relevance were covered.

These topics included data (text data, in Chapter 5, and alternative data, inclusive of satellite data, in Chapter 4), modeling techniques (ABMs in Chapter 6, factor investing and smart beta in Chapter 2, and stress testing in Chapter 8) and an overview of ESG ratings (Chapter 3).

Wherever possible, without sacrificing conciseness and readability, we provided references and citations for further reading by our audience.

Overall, we hope this is a useful set of tools and techniques, coupled with a solid understanding of the basic principles behind quantitative ESG finance, which will be used as a reference in everyday work by model developers, model validators, investors, and innovators in the ESG space.

Index

A

ABM-Economica population model, 140, *142*
Accern, 82
Actions. *See* Properties, Actions, Rules, Time, Environment
Acute risk, 177
Aerial imagery (alternative data type), 77
Aerial surveillance (alternative data type), 53
Agent-based modeling, 4, 129, 131f
Agent-based models (ABMs), 4, 138–141
  academic/regulatory publications review, 154–156
  COVID spread, modeling, 157e–163e
  elements, combination, 133
  ESG field usage, 132
  framework, 134f
  generalized ABM, context component, 135f
  operating principles, 136
  overview, 133–135
  results, 144f
  sensitivity analysis, 140
  shared characteristics, 133–134
  structure, 133
  usage/applicability, 131–132, 139–140
Alphabetic tokens, 111e
Alpha, definition, 40–41
Alternative data, 3, 53–54, 75–81
  clearinghouse, 77
  types, 53, 76–77
Alternative equity indices, stock selection/weighting decisions, 47t
Alternative scoring technique, 61–69
Alternative text data, 3–4, 105
American sports documents, word content classification, 119f, 121f
Animal welfare, 8
Application Process Interface (API), implementation, 98
Arabesque, 75, 82
Arbitrage Pricing Theory, 48
Asia-Pacific (APAC) countries, ESG adoption (lag), 5

Asset-backed securities (ABS), impact, 34
Assets under management (AUMs), 5
Atmosphere Global Climate Models (AGCMs), 193
Atmosphere with the ocean Global Climate Models (AOGCMs), 193
Atmospheric carbon dioxide
  concentration, 172
  historical records, 168
  human activities, impact, 172, 174–175
  partial pressure, reconstruction, 171

B

Babbage, Charles, 81
Bag-of-words, 114, 114t
Balance sheet/earnings impact, carbon tax (relationship), 222
Ball, John, 171–172
Bank of England (BoE) CBES scenarios, comparison/ variable representation, 220t
Banks
  income statement, impact, 212t
  stress testing, 4, 207
Berkley Earth project, 165
Beta, definition, 40–41
Bidirectional Encoder Representations from Transformers (BERT), 107
Biodiversity loss, halt (SDG goal), 28
Bloomberg data variables, usage, 71e
Boom-and-bust population cycles, 145f
Boostrap aggregating (bagging), 69–70
Box models (climate model), 192
"Brown minus green" BMG risk factor, 203
Brute-force Sharpe ratio optimization, 44e

C

Cap-and-trade, 199
Capital Asset Pricing Model (CAPM), 41, 48
Capital ratio, 211
Carbon cycle, 168–171, 168f

Carbon dioxide, 175–181. *See also* Atmospheric
       carbon dioxide
   atmospheric concentration, correlation, 167
   global carbon dioxide concentrations, 173f
   global temperature, relationship, 175–181
   monthly mean carbon dioxide concentration, 173f
   records, compilation, 167f
   release, 174
   scenarios, projection, 181
Carbon Disclosure Project (CDP), 200, 204
Carbon Mapper, usage, 202
Carbon pricing/prices, 199–202, 200f, 201f
Carbon reservoirs, 170–171
Carbon risk, 180, 199–203
   measurement, 199–202
   scoring approach, 204–205
Carbon taxes, ETS (relationship), 199
CARIMA model, 205f
Chi-square, application, 64
Chronic risk, 177
Cities/human settlements, inclusiveness/safety (SDG
       goal), 27–28
Clarity AI, 82
Classification and regression tree (CART), 63
Clay Minerals Ratio, 90–91, 91f
Climate Action Tracker, 187
Climate Bonds market, Climate Bonds Initiative representa-
       tion, 34–35
Climate change, 8
   mitigation scenarios, 184
   projections, 183–184
   regulatory response, 185–191
   scenarios, power production changes, 185f
Climate change modeling, 130, 191–198
   macroeconomic/physical constraints, 194–196
Climate loss model, 220–222
Climate models, types, 192–193
Climate risk, 1
   combatting, international programs (examples), 187t
   investmente practice, 202–205
   macroeconomic stress scenarios, 213–220
   macro perspective, 4, 165
   regulation, financial regulators (involvement), 188t–189t
   TCFD report, 179t–180t
   types, 177–180
Climate scenarios, SENSES toolkit (usage), 183–184
Climate stress testing, exercise, 223–224
Coal Mine Tracker (GEM), 202f
Cobb-Douglas production function, 194
Color map *(cmap)* argument, 94e
Commercially available indexes, 47
Computable general equilibrium (CGE), 130
Conference of Parties (COP), 186
Conservative Minus Aggressive (CMA), 49, 52e, 53e
Consumer protection, 8
Consumption/production patterns, sustainability
       (SDG goal), 28
Copernicus Open Access Hub (online service), 98
Corporate ESG reports, 108, 109e–113e
Corporate governance, concerns, 9
Cost complexity pruning, 68, 69

Covariance matrix, 44e
COVID, 157e–163e
Credit card data (alternative data type), 53, 76–77
Credit portfolio products, 222
Credit spread shock sovereign debt, components, 222

D
Data, 77–79, 81. *See also* Alternative data
   Cambrian explosion, 76f
   handling, 100e
   mining, decision trees (usage), 62
   overfitting, 67
   sources, 78t–79t, 81t
Datarade, 75, 77, 82
Decision tree, 61f, 62–66
   class, *plot-tree* method, 73
   confusion matrix, example, 66f
   pruning, concept/application, 67–69
Deep learning, usage, 103
Desertification, combatting (SDG goal), 28
Digital Elevation Model (DEM), 85
Direct environmental drivers, 180
Diversification ratio, 43e
Document frequency (DF), 115
Dow-Jones Industrial Average Index (DJIA) (index
       methodology), 40
Driver variables, 71e
Dynamic Integrated Model of Climate and Economy (DICE)
       model, 194, 196f
Dynamic stochastic general equilibrium (DSGE),
       129, 130

E
Earthdata, 86
EarthPy, usage, 92e–98e
Earth-system Models of Intermediate Complexity (EMICs)
       (climate model), 192
Economic growth, promotion (SDG goal), 27
economic man assumptions, 130
EDGAR database, 109e
Education, ensuring (SDG goal), 26
Emerging population dynamics
   ABM results, 144f
   boom-and-bust population cycles, 145f
   calories requirements, addition, 143–145
   calorie stashing capability, addition, 145–148
   case study, 140–153
   family distribution, 152f
   family members/per-capita assets, 152f
   income stratification, 153f
   inheritance, simulation, 151f
   Logistic Growth curves, 148, 148f
   model, 149–151, 149f, 150f
   parental care, simulations, 149f, 150f
   population age distribution, cyclical waves, 147f
Employee retention, 9
Energy access, ensuring (SDG goal), 27
Energy data, 80
Environmental concerns, 7–8
Environmental data, 79–80

Environmental, social and corporate governance (ESG)
    ABMs, usage, 132
    applications, 75–81
    attributes, 77
    claims, 21
    data, 80–83
    debt issuance forecast, 7f
    evaluation ranking, generation, 58
    finance, 1– 5, 9–10, 129
    global ESG AUMs, projection, 6f
    international organizations/associations (context), 11t
    investment performance, 21–23
    online data, retrieval, 13e–20e
    profile (building), metrics (usage), 58–60
    quarterly ratings data, 24e
    reports, 116e–118e, 125e
    risk factors, 22, 54
    scenario, PARTE framework (application), 136–138
    scores, usage, 20–23
    strategies, 11
Environmental, social and corporate governance (ESG) ratings, 55
    historical performance analysis, contrast, 23e–25e
    materiality/value chain, 58
    methodologies, 57–61
    metrics, 58
    performance, 18e–20e
    providers, 55–56
    purpose, 55
    replication, ESG data basis, 71e–74e
    samples, exploratory analysis, 56e–57e
Environment-related drivers, 180–181
EPICA Dome C temperature anomaly, 167f
Equal risk contribution portfolio, 43
Equal-weighted index, 40
Equity risk factor, 21
European 3Q sustainable funds launch per theme, 6f
Europe, the Middle East and Africa (EMEA), ESG market, 2, 5
Executive compensation, 9
Exponential curves, examples, 143f
Exponential decay curve, example, 143f
Exponential growth curves, 147
Exponential population growth (equation), 143f

F

Factor indices (MSCI family), 49t
Factor investing, 3, 39
False labeling/endorsement, impact, 12
Fama-French factors, 49–50
Fama-French risk factors, 51e
Fama-MacBeth regressions, 50, 51e, 52e
FAMILIES variables, 151
Family distribution, 152f
Ferrous Minerals Ratio, 91, 92f
Financial media news, 106f
Fixed income performance, 23
Food production, global greenhouse gas emissions (relationship), 176t, 177t

Food security, achievement (SDG goal), 26
Forests, management (SDG goal), 28
Friedman, Milton, 9

G

Gender equality, achievement (SDG goal), 26
Generalized ABM, context component, 135f
Generally Accepted Accounting Principles (GAAP), 105
Geographic dimension, introduction, 22
Geospatial data, 80
Getting Started with Natural Language Processing (Kochmar), 106
Gini impurity, 64–65
Global carbon dioxide concentrations, 173f
Global Change Data Lab data, 167
Global Climate Models (General Circulation Models) (GCMs) (climate model), 193
Global cooling/warming/neutral categories, evidence prediction/implication/providing (papers), 166f
Global Equity Model (Barra), 53
Global greenhouse gas (GHG) emissions, 174f–175f, 176t–177t, 178, 193
Global greenhouse gas (GHG) liabilities, 181
Global Minimum Variance index, optimization problem, 43
Global Sustainable Investment Alliance (GSIA), 11, 11t
Global temperature, carbon dioxide levels (relationship), 175–181
Goldbaum, 82
"Goodness" function, measure, 65
Governance profile, 59–60
Green Bond Principles (GBP), 31–32
Green bonds, 31–33, 36t
green risk factor, 203–204
Greenscamming, 13, 30
Green, social, and sustainable (GSS) volumes, 34f
Greenwashing, occurrence, 11–12

H

Herfindahl-Hirschman index, 43e
Hidden trade-offs, impact, 11
High Minus Low (HML), 50, 52e
Historical data unavailability, 20
Historical performance, observations, 22
Human population, growth, 143f
Human rights, 8
Hunger, cessation (SDG goal), 26

I

Impact differentiation, 221
Income inequality, reduction (SDG goal), 27
Income stratification, 153f
Index, 39
    commercially available indexes, 47
    construction, 39–40
Indexica, 54
Industrialization, promotion (SDG goal), 27
Information gain function, 65
Infrastructure, building (SDG goal), 27
Inheritance, 150–151, 151f

Innovation, fostering (SDG goal), 27
Integrated Assessment Models (IAMs), 193–194
Integrated water resource management (IWRM), implementation (SDG goal), 27
Intensity-based indexes, 86
International Capital Market Association (ICMA) green bonds, core components, 31–32
International Financial Reporting Standard (IRFS), Standard 9, 105
International organizations/associations (ESG context), 11t
Investment, active return (measure), 30
ISS ESG, 82

J
JSON string, generation, 99e

K
K-means algorithm, usage, 126–127
K-Means Clustering, 126

L
Land, average temperatures, 166f
Land-based meteorological stations, average temperature, 165
Land degradation, halt/reversal (SDG goal), 28
Landsat Enhanced Thematic Mapper+ (ETM+), 85
Landsat images, 85
Landsat Thematic Mapper (TM), 85
Latent Dirichlet Allocation (LDA), 118–122, 122e, 123e, 127
Learning opportunities, promotion (SDG goal), 26
Lemmas, usage, 122e
Lemmatization, 107–108
Liability risks, 180
Litigation drivers, 181
Litigation risk, 178
Logistic Growth curves, 148, 148f
Long-term preparedness assessment, 58, 60–61
Look-ahead bias, ESG scores (usage), 20
"Low carbon transition score" (MSCI usage), 203f
Lowercase, standardization, 107
Low-volatility indexes, 41, 41e–43e, 47
LuxFLAG (third-party label), 30–31

M
Machine learning, 72e
  decision trees, usage, 62
Mahalanobis norm, 211
Management structure, 9
Market cap-weighted index, 40
Market portfolio return, 41
Market risk, 178
Market scenario design steps, 223–224
Massively multiplayer online role-playing games (MMORPG), 133
matplotlib, usage, 116e
McKinney, Wes, 41e
Milankovitch cycles, 172
Minimum/maximum frequency threshold setting/filtering, 107

Miotech, 83
Modified Normalized Difference Water Index (MNDWI), 88–89, 90f
MODIS, 85
Monthly mean carbon dioxide concentration, 173f
Moore's law, 138, 139f
Morgan Stanley Capital International (MSCI), 48, 55, 56e
  ESG regulation, 10f
Morningstar, investment research/services, 56
Mortality rates, 141
Mortgage-backed securities (MBS), impact, 34
Most diversified portfolio, concept, 43e
Multispectral Scanning System (MSS), 85

N
Natality rates, 141
Natural language processing (NLP), 4, 105–108
  analysis, pre-processing (steps), 108f
  body of knowledge, 127
  LDA function, 119
  text preparation, 107
Natural Language Processing and Computational Linguistics (Kurdi), 106
n-dimensional vector, 114
Network for Greening the Financial System (NGFS), 7, 11t
  comparison/variable representation, 220t
Nigerian coastline, heat stress/socioeconomic dataset mapping, 198f
Night Light Index, 83, *83f*
Node-splitting functions, 65
Normalized Difference Moisture Index (NDMI), 89–90, 90f, 96e
Normalized Difference Snow Index (NDSI), 97e
Normalized Difference Vegetation Index (NDVI), 86–88, 87f, 96e
Normalized Difference Water Index (NDWI), 88–89, 97e
Nutrition, improvement (SDG goal), 26

O
One Planet Summit, 11t
Online satellite data, access, 98e–103e
Optimization-based IAM, workflow (example), 193f
Optimization-driven indexes, 43e
Option-adjusted spreads (OAS), analysis, 34
Ordinary Differential Equations, usage, 140
Ordinary Least Squares (OLS) regression formula, 52e
Outlier topics, 126–127
OWL Analytics, 75, 82

P
pandas.crosstab (utility), 124e
pandas-datareader package, usage, 41e, 50e
Parental care, simulations, 149f, 150f
Paris Agreement, alignment, 186f
Partial pressure of ancient atmospheric carbon dioxide (pCO_2), measurement, 171
Performance analysis, weaknesses, 20
Phi function, 65
Physical risks, 8, 176–181

plot_tree method, 73
Policy/regulatory drivers, 181
Policy risk, 178
Political data, 80
Population age distribution, cyclical waves, 147f
Population model ABM, buildup, 140
Portfolio index weighting, application, 20
Poverty, cessation (SDG goal), 26
Preparedness opinion metrics, 58
Preparedness scores, 58
Price-weighted index, 40
Principles for Responsible Investment (PRI), 10
Proba-V, 86
Proceeds, management/usage, 31, 32, 35, 37
Productive employement, promotion (SDG goal), 27
Project evaluation/selection, processing, 31–32, 35
Properties, Actions, Rules, Time, Environment (PARTE), 134–141, 144–150
    framework, application, 136–138, 157
    setup, 136
Python (scripting language), 2, 72
    ML libraries, 107
    NLP library, 111e
Python for Data Analysis (McKinney), 41e

Q

Quantitative methods, 2–3
Question/goal, definition (clarity), 139

R

Radiative-convective models (climate model), 192
Random forest, 69–70
Random normal distribution, usage, 159e
RasterIO, usage, 92
read_html function, 50e
Real-time signals, 81
Red Green Blue (RGB)
    image, visualization, 101e
    intensities, multiplication, 94
    visible array, saving, 102e
"Reduction in entropy" function, 65
Refinitiv, 54
Regression trees, 66–67
    alternative scoring technique, 61–69
    usage, 67f
Reporting, importance, 32, 37
Reputation risk, 179
Residual sum of squares (RSS), decrease, 67–68
Risk factor (RF), 1, 48–50
    analysis, 18e
    beta, 30
    deep learning, 53
    family, 39
    indexes, approaches, 3
    universe, expansion, 53–54
    zoo, 53
Risk premia series, estimation, 50e–53e
Robust Minus Weak (RMW), 49, 52e
R (scripting language), usage, 2

S

Satellites (alternative data type), 53, 77
    data processing, 83–91
    imagery processing, methodologies/indices, 84–86
    images (processing), EarthPy (usage), 92e–98e
Scenario narrative, 223
Security Market Line (SML) equation, extension, 48
Self-reported data, 81
Sendair Framework for Disaster Risk Reduction (SDG goal), 27–28
Sense Folio, 82
SENSES toolkit, usage, 183–184
Sensitivity analysis, 140
Sentiment (alternative data type), 53, 76
Sentinel, 85t
    bands, 85t, 89, 93e
    data, 87, 98
    images, 84
Shared socioeconomic pathways (SSPs), 181, 182f, 182t–183t, 184f
Sharpe ratio maximization, 43e
Shocks, calibration, 221
Shortwave infrared (SWIR) bands, 90–91
Short words, exclusion, 107
Sin stocks, 8
Small Minus Big (SMB), 49, 53
Smart beta, 3, 39–41, 47
Social/behavioral drivers, 181
Social bonds, 31, 34–38
Social Bonds Principles (SBP), 34, 35, 37
Social concerns, 8
Socially responsible investing (SRI), 1, 7, 33f
Social profile, 59
Social risk factors, 22
Soil Adjusted Vegetation Index (SAVI), 87–88, 88f
Solow, Robert, 129, 130
Sorted portfolio approach, 22
Sovereign climate risk model, 198–199, 198f
SpaceKnow Africa Night Light Index, 83, *83f*
SpaCy (Python NLP library), 111e, 112e
spaCy, usage, 108
Spherical Cow critique, 129
Standard & Poor's (S&P) climate indexes, 204
Standard & Poor's (S&P) constituents
    function, 110e
    historical performance analysis, contrast, 23e–25e
    stocks, 109e
Standard & Poor's (S&P) Global Ratings, 56
Standard & Poor's (S&P) stocks, universe, 117e
Stock selection, 47e
Stop words, removal, 107
Stranded assets, 8, 180
Stress loss, capital impact, 211
Stress loss estimation, 224
Stress testing, risk management tool, 4, 207–211
Substance/third-party review, absence (impact), 11
Sullivan Code of Conduct, 9
Sullivan, Leon, 9

Sustainability, 7–8, 25–38
  bonds, 31
  table, yfinance internal population method, 15e–16e
Sustainable development, 28, 29
Sustainable Development Goals (SDGs) (Global Goals),
        25–29, 25f
  country profile (Russian Federation), 30f
  E/S/G category, grouping, 29f
  targets/achievement means, 26–29
Sustainable Development Report (SDR), 29
Sustainable finance, 25–38
Sustainable investing, core approaches, 12t
Sustainalytics, 82
Systematic factors, 48t

T
Talent diversity, 8
Task Force on Climate-Related Financial Disclosures
        (TCFD) report/recommendations,
        60,179t–180t, 190–191
Technology risk, 178
Term frequency (TF), 114, 116e
  metric, 115
  vectorizer, 122e
Term frequency-inverse document frequency (TF-IDF),
        115, 116e, 118, 118e
Terrestrial ecosystems, sustainability
        (SDG goal), 28
Third-party statistics, 81
TIFF file, saving, 103e
Tokenization, 107
Top-down induction of decision trees (TDIT), 63
Topic modeling, 114–115
Total output *(Q)*, Cobb-Douglas production function
        definition, 194
Total portfolio volatility, 43e
Transistors, number (doubling), 139f
Transition risks, 176–181
Transport/logistics data, 80
Tree-building algorithm, 64
Tree pruning, concept/application, 67–69
Trucost, 200
Truvalue Labs, 75, 82

U
Unconstrained investment strategy, 21
United Nations Framework Convention on Climate Change
        (UNFCC), 186
United Nations General Assembly (UN-GA), SDG goals, 25
"Use of Money" (Wesley), 9
US green bond market, evolution, 35f

V
Vagueness/misleading claims, impact, 12
Value chain, 58
Variable importance (determination), random forests (usage), 70
Variance, reduction, 65
Visible Atmospherically Resistant Index (VARI), 88, 89f, 97f
Visible light view, NDVI (contrast), 87f

W
Water/sanitation, ensuring (SDG goal), 26–27
Weakest link pruning, 68
Wealth, stratification (appearance), 147
Web scraping, 16e–18e, 53, 76
Weighted average volatility, 43e
Weighting decisions, 47t
Weights, difference (systematic approach), 45t–46t
Well-being, promotion (SDG goal), 26
Well-known text (WKT), 98, 99e, 103e
Wesley, John, 9
What if? analysis, 136
WIREs review, 132
Women/girls, empowerment (SDG goal), 26
WordCloud, usage, 116e–117e
Word content classification, 119f
World Bank Climate Change Knowledge Portal (CCKP), 187

Y
yfinance package, 13e–16e

Z
Zero-dimensional (0d) models (climate model), 192
Zero-length report strings, usage, 110e
Zions Bancorp, PDF report, 112e